Cities such as New York, Tokyo, and London are the centres of transnational corporate headquarters, of international finance, transnational institutions, and telecommunications. They are the dominant loci in the contemporary world economy, and the influence of a relatively small number of cities within world affairs has been a feature of the shift from an international to a more global economy which has taken place during the 1970s and 1980s. This book brings together the leading researchers in the field to write seventeen original essays which cover both the theoretical and practical issues involved. They examine the nature of world cities, and their demands as special places in need of specific urban policies; the relationship between world cities within global networks of economic flows; and the relationship between world city research and world-systems analysis and other theoretical frameworks.

World cities in a world-system

World cities in a world-system

edited by

Paul L. Knox and Peter J. Taylor

 CAMBRIDGE
UNIVERSITY PRESS

Published by the Press Syndicate of the University of Cambridge
The Pitt Building, Trumpington Street, Cambridge CB2 1RP
40 West 20th Street, New York, NY 10011–4211, USA
10 Stamford Road, Oakleigh, Melbourne 3166, Australia

First published 1995

Printed in Great Britain at the University Press, Cambridge

A catalogue record for this book is available from the British Library

Library of Congress cataloguing in publication data

World cities in a world-system / edited by Paul L. Knox and Peter J.
  Taylor.
      p.   cm.
    ISBN 0 521 48165 1 (hardback). – ISBN 0 521 48470 7 (pbk.)
    1. Metropolitan areas.   2. International economic relations.
  I. Knox, Paul L.   II. Taylor, Peter J.
  HT330.M37 1995
  307.76′4 – dc20   94–32444   CIP

ISBN 0 521 48165 1 hardback
ISBN 0 521 48470 7 paperback

CE

Contents

Contributors

JANET LIPPMAN ABU-LUGHOD New School for Social Research, New York

ROBERT A. BEAUREGARD School of Planning and International Affairs, University of Pittsburgh

JOHN FRIEDMANN Department of Urban and Regional Planning, University of California, Los Angeles

RAMÓN GROSFOGUEL Fernand Braudel Center, Binghamton University

DAVID J. KEELING Department of Geography, Western Kentucky University

ROGER KEIL Department of Urban and Regional Planning, University of California, Los Angeles

ANTHONY D. KING Department of Sociology and Department of Art History, Binghamton University

ANDREW KIRBY Department of Geography, University of Arizona

PAUL L. KNOX Department of Urban Affairs and Planning, Virginia Polytechnic Institute and State University

DONALD LYONS Department of Geography, University of North Texas

SALLIE MARSTON Department of Geography, University of Arizona

SCOTT SALMON Department of Geography, Miami University, Ohio

SASKIA SASSEN Department of Urban Planning, Columbia University

DAVID SIMON Centre for Developing Areas Research, Department of Geography, Royal Holloway, University of London

KENNETH SEASHOLES Department of Geography, University of Arizona

DAVID A. SMITH Department of Sociology, University of California, Irvine

MICHAEL PETER SMITH Department of Applied Behavioral Sciences, University of California, Davis

PETER J. TAYLOR Department of Geography, University of Newcastle Upon Tyne

MICHAEL TIMBERLAKE Department of Sociology, Anthropology and Social Work, Kansas State University

GRAHAM TODD Department of Political Science, York University, Ontario

PETER M. WARD Department of Sociology and the Lyndon Baines Johnson School of Public Affairs, University of Texas at Austin

Preface

This book is an outcome of a conference that we organized in 1993 on World Cities in a World-System. Held at the Center for Innovative Technology, adjacent to Dulles International Airport, near Washington DC, the conference brought together a group of speakers and an audience with a very broad range of perspectives on world cities. We were very pleased with the outcome. The phenomenon of world-city formation has raised a number of important theoretical issues and practical questions that all benefit from a wide-ranging, cross-disciplinary dialogue. This volume is based on a selection of the papers that were presented at the conference. Both the conference and this volume are the result of the contributions of many individuals. We would particularly like to thank John Friedmann for his organizational help and his gracious consent to our use of his work as both a focus and a foil. Ian Watson provided invaluable contributions both as a research assistant and conference organizer. The College of Architecture and Urban Studies and the Department of Urban Affairs and Planning at Virginia Polytechnic Institute and State University provided financial support.

PAUL KNOX
PETER TAYLOR

Part 1

Introduction: world city, hypothesis and context

1   World cities in a world-system

Paul L. Knox

Evidence of the globalization of the world economy is everywhere, from supermarket shelves to clothes tags. Similarly, the dominance of a relatively small number of cities within world affairs is continually scrolled through newcasts, business reports, and popular media. At face value, there is nothing very special in this: it is widely accepted as part of the conventional wisdom about the state of the world today. Closer scrutiny, however, reveals both the globalization of the economy and its associated patterns of urbanization to involve much more than meets the eye in the supermarket or on the television news. Both rest on a complex web of interdependent and quite stealthy processes that are, collectively, of fundamental importance to the political economy of contemporary societies. In this book, the nature of world cities and their relationships with one another and with the world economy are examined within various conceptual frameworks and analysed at several spatial scales. This chapter introduces the major themes of the book, setting them within the context of different perspectives on globalization and on world cities.

Perspectives on globalization

During the 1970s and 1980s there was an important shift from an international to a more global economy. In the international economy goods and services are traded across national boundaries by individuals and firms from different countries, and the trade is closely regulated by sovereign nation-states. In the global economy goods and services are produced and marketed by an oligopolistic web of global corporate networks whose operations span national boundaries but are only loosely regulated by nation-states. Just how important the shift has been, and how it should be interpreted and understood in theoretical terms, are still very much contested issues. Certainly, the globalization of the world-system must be recognized as having roots that go back well over a century. Robertson (1990) argues that the nineteenth-century idea of

3

the homogeneous unitary nation-state was in fact part and parcel of the initial transition toward a global infrastructure (international agencies and institutions, global forms of communication, the acceptance of unified global time, the development of global competitions and prizes, the development of standard notions of citizenship and human rights) that constituted the key precondition for the recent acceleration of economic globalization.

Any uncertainty over the recent acceleration of globalization must be attributed in part to its stealthiness. It was – and still is – easy to read the *internationalization* of the economy from trade figures or from consumer goods. The American purchaser of a replica soccer jersey for the Irish national team, for example, can see at once that it was made in China and that it features the name of a German automobile manufacturer (Opel) as a sponsor to the team. As a soccer fan, he or she may know that the manufacturer of the jersey (Adidas), a German firm, is now French-owned; it is much less likely that he or she will happen to know that the team sponsor, Opel, is a subsidiary of (American) General Motors (GM). The *globalization* of the economy is less easily read. Trade figures are infrequently reported in terms of flows between or within corporations, while the global elements in many products are invisible. Take, for example, an ostensibly American car such as the Pontiac Le Mans. Of the sticker price of $20,000, only $7,600 goes to Americans (workers and management in Detroit, lawyers and bankers in New York, lobbyists in Washington, and GM shareholders all over the country). Of the rest, 48 per cent goes to South Korea for labour and assembly, 28 per cent to Japan for advanced components such as engines and electronics, 12 per cent to Germany for styling and design engineering, 7 per cent to Taiwan and Singapore for small components, 4 per cent to the United Kingdom for marketing, and about 1 per cent to Barbados or Ireland for data processing (Reich 1991).

The automobile industry, along with the pharmaceutical industry and the steel industry, has in fact been in the vanguard of economic globalization, with a history of transnational joint ventures, personnel exchanges, cross-licensing research, production partnerships, and shared ownership that goes back several decades. Through such arrangements, for example, Chrysler is linked to Mitsubishi, Samsung, Fiat, and Volkswagen; GM to Toyota, Isuzu, and Suzuki; Ford to Mazda, Jaguar, and BMW; Nissan to Volkswagen and Daewoo; Mitsubishi to Hyundai; Renault to Volvo. In the past fifteen to twenty years, transnational corporations with strategic links and alliances have come to dominate many other industries, especially those associated with the high-technology spearhead for the next Kondratiev cycle.

(Thus, for example, strategic alliances link Motorola to Nippon Electric Company and, in turn, to Hitachi; Nippon Telephone and Telegraph is linked to IBM as well as to Mitsui and Hitachi; Sony to RCA; Ericsson (Sweden) to Honeywell and Sperry; Ricoh to Rockwell; Siemens to Intel; Fujisu to Texas Instruments (Petrella 1991).) Meanwhile, the most innovative companies have moved away from the massive, vertically integrated, Fordist organizational principles of the first-generation transnationals, 'downsizing' to exploit economies of scope within network corporations. These are the corporations that have been most successful in exploiting the Japanese *kanban* strategy of flexible production systems, with telematics (advanced combinations of telecommunications and computing technologies) underpinning a new (and much more variable) geometry of international economic activity and a new social division of labour (Castells 1989; Sayer and Walker 1992).

In tandem with the globalization of industry, part cause and part effect, has been the globalization of finance. Following Thrift (1989), we can recognize three main components of the globalization of finance: (1) the growth of the Eurodollar market and the consequent growth in trading in exchange rates of domestic currencies; (2) the emergence of transnational banks and investment companies, the development of a global venture-capital industry, and the advent of 24-hour global trading in capital and securities markets; and (3) increasing interest by national governments, encouraged by transnational organizations such as the World Bank, the IMF, and the OECD, in attracting foreign investment. The globalization of finance has been an important enabling factor in the globalization of industry, facilitating transnational corporations' need for access to enormous amounts of capital for mergers, acquisitions, and operational restructuring (Versluyen 1981). It has brought about a shift from banks' traditional role of supporting trade between nations and firms to one of supporting the expansion of the manufacturing capacity of large corporations, and of partnerships between states, international financial institutions, and private capital (Sachar, 1990). At the same time it can be argued that some key aspects of the globalization of finance were a result of the special needs of transnational manufacturing corporations in their drive for global production and marketing capacity (Parboni 1981). Anthony Sampson argues that 'The global money that has emerged in the last two decades has baffled most people. It has no visible home; out of the auditors' sight, this global money slips between tax havens, treasuries, and investigators; and it is not accountable to any nation or government' (1991: 64). Accelerated by telematics (Moss 1987) and cut loose by government deregulation, the mobility of capital and fluidity of capitalist relations of production have brought an entirely new dimension to the world economy, with the Japanese, in particular, becoming expert at the science of *zai-tech* (financial engineering) and the art of flexible specialization (Kenny and Florida 1988).

This new mega-cephalic corporate and financial dimension has, in turn, driven another important dimension of globalization: a series of cultural flows that has come to underpin the contemporary world-system. Appadurai (1990) suggests that there are five different dimensions to such flows: 'ethnoscapes' (produced by flows of business personnel, guestworkers, tourists, immigrants, refugees, etc.); 'technoscapes' (flows of machinery, technology, and software produced by transnational corporations and government agencies); 'finanscapes' (flows of capital, currency, and securities); 'mediascapes' (flows of images and information through print media, television, and film); and 'ideoscapes' (flows of ideological constructs, mostly derived from Western world-views: e.g. democracy, sovereignty, representation, welfare rights, etc.). To these I would add a sixth: 'commodityscapes', produced by flows of material culture that encompass everything from architecture and interior design through to clothes and jewellery.

The Hanseatic dimension and triadic techno-nationalism in the world economy

This, of course, is where world cities come in. World cities are centres of transnational corporate headquarters, of their business services, of international finance, of transnational institutions, and of telecommunications and information processing. They are basing points and control centres for the interdependent skein of financial and cultural flows which, together, support and sustain the globalization of industry. 'The new world order taking shape is not the one imagined by the obsolete statesmen of the cold war era. Rather than an order of nation-states weighing in one a new global balance of power, an archipelago of technologically highly developed city-regions – or mass-consumer *technopoles* – is evolving' (Petrella 1991: 59). This archipelago is likened by Petrella to the Hanseatic League of thirteenth-century to fifteenth-century Europe, when trade within and between the Rhineland and the Baltic was organized and controlled by autonomous cities.

The importance of the contemporary archipelago of world cities within the world economy has been intensified by the strategic policies of restructured transnational corporations. The basic idea is to achieve commercial supremacy by focusing on the seven or eight hundred million consumers in the triad of core economies within the world-system (i.e. Europe, the United States of America, and Japan) who are able to sustain materialistic lifestyles. This is what Sony's Akio Morita means when he uses the term 'global localization'; Kenichi Ohmae, a management strategist, calls it a 'global insider' strategy. Seen in a broader perspective, it forms the logical framework for the tactical flexibility of transnational corporations. It is this flexibility, of course, that underpins the *new regime of accumulation* – neo-Fordism – that has rewritten the economic geography not only of core countries but also of semi-peripheral and some peripheral countries. In these new economic landscapes the archipelago of world cities not only represents the most important 'theatres of accumulation', but also constitutes the locus of key managerial, financial, research and development, business service, and information processing and interpreting functions.

The triadic strategy and flexible tactics of transnational corporations have been bolstered by the national governments of core countries, which have vigorously pursued policies aimed at financial deregulation, (selective) trade reforms, less restrictive labour markets, and heavy subsidies for telematics and for science and technology with commercial potential. Riccardo Petrella calls it 'triadic techno-nationalism'; a broader perspective allows us to see it as part of the new *mode of regulation* associated with neo-Fordism (Hirst and Zeitlin 1992; Itoh 1992; Jessop 1992). The chief beneficiaries, in spatial terms, have been the world cities of the core economies, the 'mass-consumer technopoles' that have become pre-eminent centres of commercial innovation and corporate control, undisputed centres of taste-making, crucibles of consumer sensibility, and seedbeds of material culture.

It follows from all of this that world cities and the world-system must be problematized together, as John Friedmann and Goetz Wolff (1982) argued more than a decade ago (see also Friedmann 1986 and Rodriguez and Feagin 1986).

Perspectives on world cities

Recognizing world cities as control points, as powerful centres of economic and cultural authority within the contemporary world-system, begs the important question of what we mean by 'power' and 'control'. Without reifying cities themselves as actors, we can readily see that the distinctiveness of world cities is in their nexus of decision-making and interaction relating to economic, cultural, and political information. Their significance within a world economy that has been dramatically decentralized through the globalization of industry (the 'new international division of labour') and the advent of telematics lies in their role as centres of *authority*, as places that are able to generate and disseminate discourses and collective beliefs, that are able to develop, test, and track innovations, and that offer 'sociable' settings for the gathering of high-level information (economic, political, cultural) and for establishing coalitions and monitoring implicit contracts: 'Thus the world economy may have become more decentralized, but it is not necessarily becoming *decentred*' (Amin and Thrift 1992: 576). In chapter 2 John Friedmann examines the 'theoretical object' of world cities, elaborating the conceptual issues involved in pursuing the rather elusive notion of world cities, and arguing that the world city paradigm allows us to make visible some of these important dimensions of the meta-narrative of capital. In chapter 3 Peter Taylor reviews the changing role of world cities in relation to the evolving world-system. In chapter 4 Saskia Sassen shows how the concentration and specialization of financial and service functions within the contemporary global urban system has fostered localized economic cores so potent that they have generated entirely new production complexes.

The multidimensional nature of world cities as distinctive settings and centres of authority begs another question: that of the homogeneity of world cities as a class of metropolitan areas. It is clear that New York, London, and Tokyo stand in a league of their own, even though the discourse on world cities generally admits a dozen or more additional cases. It is also clear that there are some significant differences between New York, London and Tokyo, not just as metropolitan areas but also as world cities. Tokyo's status is based very largely on the economic dimensions of world city-ness, with little of the cultural diversity or dynamism of London and New York, and nothing comparable to their legacies of political and military hegemony. Tokyo's economic control functions, moreover, derive more from neo-Fordism and flexible specialization than from the (late) Fordist regime of accumulation that established the foundation for the world city-ness of London and New York (Cybriwsky 1991; Fujita 1991; Machimura 1992; Miyamoto 1993). London and New York, meanwhile, are differentiated from one another in terms of governance and politics: London is a capital city with an imperial past, a city of migrants that is driven by class politics; New York is a city of immigrants, driven by ethnic politics (Fainstein, Gordon, and Harloe 1992; Sassen 1991, 1994; Shefter 1993). As Robert Beauregard points out in chapter 13 (and as Peter Rimmer (1986) recognized), world cities must be seen as differentiated not only through the different relationships that each develops with respect to its role as regional interface between core, semi-periphery, and periphery, but also through their internal mediation of macro-level economic, cultural, and political processes by way of the contingent conditions of local socio-economic and political structures – and, indeed, through the physical structure of metropolitan areas. In chapter 10 Janet Lippman Abu-Lughod shows how the reactions and fates of two American world cities – New York and Chicago – have been contingent not only on world-system forces over time, but also on the specificities of their individual historical trajectories, their strategic locations within the US and world urban systems, and their respective demographic composition.

Although Friedmann's heuristic hypothesis of a hierarchy of world cities with distinctive and convergent characteristics has strong appeal, the very nature of the contemporary world-system (with the flexibility of corporations within global networks and the warpage of new telecommunications media constantly revising the role of 'lower-order' world cities) means that a hierarchical classification of world cities is less and less satisfactory. This is particularly true if world cities are to be theorized in terms of their relation to world-system processes. Cities' hierarchical positions (especially 'secondary' world cities in the triadic core and the regionally dominant world cities in semi-peripheral and peripheral areas) may be reversed according to the kind of functions considered: corporate management versus transnational NGOs (non-governmental organizations) versus cultural leadership. Take Milan, for example: strong at the global scale in terms of cultural leadership, strong in Mediterranean Europe in terms of finance, but relatively dependent in terms of corporate control and information processing activities.

It may be more useful, therefore, to think in terms of functional classifications. Figure 1.1 shows every city with at least one headquarters office of a Fortune Global 500 company *and* with at least one head-quarters office of an international non-governmental organization (NGO) or inter-governmental agency (IGO). The primacy of each city is also shown, as a crude indication of its cultural dominance. Such classifications do allow the *nature* of metropolitan dominance within the world-system to be pursued. Note, for example, the way that figure 1.1 brings out the very different characters of London, New York, and Tokyo as world cities. It must be recognized, though, that this sort of approach opens up the issue of how we might justify specific functional criteria (such as those used illustratively in figure 1.1). This is an issue addressed in chapter 8 by David Simon, who argues that world cities, as defined by Friedmann and others, should be seen as a subset of a larger group of major cities with significant supranational roles. David Smith and Michael Timberlake, on the other hand, point to the methodological logic of network analysis as a means of mapping the structural relationships and clarifying the functional interdependencies of world cities (chapter 5).

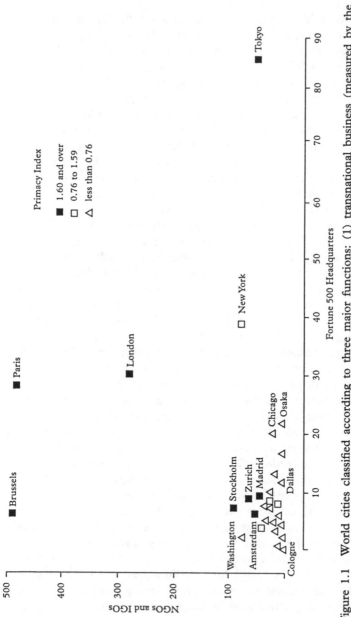

Figure 1.1 World cities classified according to three major functions: (1) transnational business (measured by the number of global Fortune 500 headquarters located in each metropolitan area, 1993); (2) international affairs (measured by the number of NGOs and IGOs located in each metropolitan area, 1993); and (3) cultural centrality (national urban primacy: the ratio of the city's population to that of the largest, or next largest, city, 1992). Included on the figure but not identified: Atlanta, Düsseldorf, Frankfurt, Hamburg, Hartford (CT), Houston, Los Angeles, Milan, Montreal, Munich, Nagoya, Philadelphia, Rome, San Francisco, and Toronto.

The social construction of world cities

Problematizing world cities in this way (in terms of different but interrelated functions relative to core, semi-periphery and periphery) inevitably raises the question of *scale*: at what level of resolution can we best identify and/or theorize the functional dynamics of world cities? Here we are confronted with a knotty problematic of its own. Although geographers have long wrestled with the issue of scale, we do not have any coherent, critically thought-out language for different scales that could be deployed in examining the ways in which world cities are constructed and sustained. For world cities, like any other place, *are* socially constructed, and at different scales. 'The making of place implies the production of scale in as far as places are made different from each other; scale is the criterion of difference not so much between places as between different *kinds* of places' (Smith 1993: 99). As Neil Smith goes on to point out, geographic scale is hierarchically produced as part of the social and cultural, economic and political landscapes of contemporary capitalism and patriarchy. At the same time, 'The construction of scale is not simply a spatial solidification or materialization of contested social forces and processes; the corollary also holds. Scale is an active progenitor of specific social processes. In a literal as well as a metaphorical way, space *contains* social activity and at the same time provides an already partitioned geography within which social activity *takes place*' (Smith 1993: 101).

A conventional sequence of scales might be: body, home, community, urban, region, nation, world-region, global. World-systems theorists would add (not merely add, perhaps, but emphasize) core–periphery. World cities cut across several of these, from the urban through regional, national, and core–periphery scales to the global. We can locate world city-ness, in other words, at several different scales: from the global urban system to the relatively small social worlds that constitute the milieux of what Tom Wolfe (1987) called the 'masters of the universe': the key 'players' in transnational business and finance. In terms of theorizing world cities, we can recognize at least four pertinent scales:

1 *The global urban system.* Though the literature on urban systems remains dominated by descriptions and analyses of nationally bounded urban systems (see, for example, Bourne et al. 1989; Van der Woude 1990), we are beginning to understand more about the global urban system: not just through hierarchical classifications (see, for example, Brown 1991) but also through analyses of the networks and interdependencies through which the global urban system is constructed (see, for example, Smith and Timberlake in chapter 5).

2 *The regional interface* between world cities and nation-states or groups of nation-states that constitute core, semi-peripheral, or peripheral regions. It is at this scale that we can see how world city, world-system processes are challenging the nature of the boundaries and borders of conventional perspectives on place and scale, producing changes that are at once both liberating and intrusive (Mlinar 1992). In chapter 9, for example, Ramón Grosfoguel analyses the historical–structural developments that explain the emergence of Miami as a world city, arguing that the logical of capitalist accumulation within the world-system has not been the only determinant of world city formation: in Miami's case, geopolitical security and geopolitical symbolism have contributed significantly to world city status.

3 *The placelessness of world cities*, a dimension of world cities that can only be scaled in the metric of 'cyberspace' (Benedikt 1992). The space of information flows that Castells (1989) takes to constitute a new 'mode of development' is increasingly rendering traditional, discrete metropolitan areas into discontinuous city spaces of financial, economic, cultural, and intellectual communities. And, though world cities contribute the bulk of these spaces, they extend throughout the geographic realm of the triadic core of the world-system, lending world city-ness to many locales. In chapter 6 Donald Lyons and Scott Salmon present evidence that the globalization of the world economy is redefining the linkages within the US urban system and, in the process, expanding the global control potential of some cities further down the urban hierarchy.

4 *The metropolitan scale*, within which labour markets, social networks, and the built environment are structured and restructured in order to accommodate world city functions, along with other, traditional, metropolitan functions (Douglass 1993; Sassen 1991).

At the same time, we must recognize the interdependence between scales that is an important dimension of the world city phenomenon. This is emphasized by Peter Taylor (chapter 3), who describes the changing nature of the mutuality between the compartmentalized territorial organization of nation-states and the functional pattern of points and flows between major cities within the evolving world-system.

Global metropolitanism and the fast world

As stressed in much of the literature, world cities are very much a product of the enabling technology of telematics. They are also, as the same literature also emphasizes, the enabling structure for an emergent 'informational economy'. Yet we are still a long way from William

Gibson's depiction (1984, 1987) of a dystopian information society whose governing economy is transnational and cyberspatial, whose cities are populated by technology-dependent individuals. From a world-system perspective we can view world cities as tending to undermine the narratives and myths that have sustained the construction of nations from states and vice versa. The other side of this coin is that world cities, as proscenia for materialistic, cosmopolitan lifestyles, as crucibles of new narratives, and as carriers of new myths, can be seen as being central to the construction of new, transnational sensibilities. These sensibilities, together with the cultural flows that sustain them, are seen by some as adding up to a global culture (Featherstone 1990, 1993). A key issue here, of course, is *where* such a culture is located, both geographically and socially. Another important issue concerns whether or not the development of a global culture necessarily entails a weakening of the sovereignty of nation-states (Arnason 1990; Mlinar 1992). Samuel Huntington (1993) has suggested that world politics is entering a new phase, in which the fundamental sources of conflict will not be ideological or economic, but cultural. This points to yet another important issue: the place of culture in world-systems theory (Bergesen 1990; Boyne 1990; Wallerstein 1990). Several of the chapters in this book explore the political and cultural dimensions of global metropolitanism. Anthony King (chapter 12) treats world cities as cultural spaces with significance for the construction of new cultural and political identities. Michael Smith (chapter 14) develops this approach through a portrayal of the globalization of grassroots politics of transnational migrants, exiles, and refugees. Graham Todd provides a rather different perspective through a portrayal of the social spaces of globalization that have been generated through service-sector growth (chapter 11). Andrew Kirby, Sallie Marston, and Kenneth Seasholes point out in chapter 15 that grassroots movements from a variety of social strata have begun to respond to global processes of political and economic restructuring by channelling their energy into 'municipal foreign policy', a transnational politics that transcends the formal realities of international affairs.

Such issues require us to consider carefully the nature of global metropolitanism. On the one hand, as John Friedmann points out in chapter 2, there is a dimension of global metropolitanism that is rooted in the explosively growing transnational capitalist class, the new bourgeoisie and new *petite bourgeoisie* who define themselves through globally oriented, populist value systems and through possession of high-end consumer goods: clothes by Hugo Boss and Issey Miyake, wheels by BMW and Jaguar, watches by Cartier, kitchen gadgets by

Braun and Krups, sound system by Bang & Olufsen; a condo in Grand Cayman in January, a cottage in Provence in June, Beaujolais Nouveau in November (Bourdieu 1984, 1993; Hannerz 1992; Sklair 1991).

There is another dimension of global metropolitanism that is more widely accessible. A product of satellite communications networks, high bandwidth cable and radio-frequency systems and, above all, of global markets in television (especially music television) and advertising, this is the dimension of the permanently ephemeral and the immediately accessible. The lingua franca of this global metropolitanism is the patois of American television soap operas and comedy series; its dress code and world-view are taken from MTV and the sports pages; its politics is from the cyberpunk *Mondo 2000*, and its lifestyle is defined by promotional 'spots' for Budweiser, Coca-Cola, Levis, and Nike (Twitchell 1992).

These two dimensions of global metropolitanism are, of course, intertwined in a dialectic of their own. The more global pop culture draws from the hedonistic materialism of the transnational élite, the more the latter is driven toward creative distinctiveness in its attitudes and material ensembles. The more self-consciously stylish the new bourgeoisie, the more tongue-in-*chic* the wannabees and the cyberpunks. Meanwhile, both dimensions are also part of a large dialectic: between modernity and postmodernity. At face value global metropolitanism may seem to be a straightforward expression of modernity, a (somewhat debased) meta-culture of Eurocentric universalism that draws on the meta-narrative of Western capitalism and the Enlightenment project. Yet the hedonism, cosmopolitanism, ephermeralism, and populism of metrocentric global cultures are distinctively postmodern. There is clearly a good deal of grist here for the mill of critical social theory that is concerned with modernity and postmodernity. In particular, and from a world-systems perspective, there are debates to be pursued in terms of the relationships between modernity/postmodernity and post-colonialism. From a world cities perspective there are debates to be pursued in terms of the relationships between modernity/postmodernity and ways of life in world city milieux.

The fast world, cyburbs and cyberia

Yet, intriguing and significant as global metropolitanism may be, we should not lose sight of the fact that we are talking here about phenomena that directly affect only a fraction of the world's population. Another defining characteristic of global metropolitanism is that it represents a 'fast world' (the triadic core and its archipelago of world cities) that is becoming decoupled from the 'slow world' (the periphery). Economic polarization and dependent development have been compounded by the effects of transport infrastructure (as David Keeling shows in chapter 7) and of the time–space compression introduced by the telematics that now undergird the fast world. As Alvin and Heidi Toffler observe, the old adage 'time is money' is becoming obsolete: 'In the new accelerated system of wealth creation, it is being superseded by a new hidden law of economics in which time is no longer just money. Now each unit of saved time is actually worth more money than the last unit. The faster economic processes work, the more wealth is created in the same period with the same or even fewer resources' (Toffler and Toffler 1991: 56). This presages a phase of world development in which the mega-cities of the periphery will fare no better than the catatonic agrarian societies that have fuelled their (demographic) growth, and in which both will lapse decisively and irretrievably into a 'slow' economic time zone.

Much the same kind of scenario can be envisaged within the fast world, since it is clear that the decoupling of fast and slow is being reproduced internally, and seems set to continue. Just as we can see the world city-ness of regional metropoli, so we can see the Third World-ness of world cities. We do not yet have the linguistic or conceptual apparatus with which to deal with such phenomena, however. New worlds require new words and new ways of thinking. Thus Richard Ingersoll, for example, envisages a rearticulation of class structure within the metropoli of the fast world, with 'infocrats' at the top controlling the production of electronic information. Below them will be various grades of 'cyberproletariats', who will depend on telematics in their work. Finally, at the bottom will be a growing underclass, the 'lumpentrash': 'those who literally do not, and probably will never, compute' (Ingersoll 1993: 5). We might, then, envisage infocrats inhabiting the spaces of global metropolitanism, with the cyberproletariat in cyburbia and the lumpentrash in the cyberia of inner-city ghettos and ageing industrial suburbs. The socio-spatial polarization and restructuring of world cities is already a topic of extensive analysis (see, for example, Fainstein, Gordon, and Harloe 1992; Fujita 1991; Machimura 1992; Mollenkopf and Castells 1991; Pryke 1991; Sassen 1991, 1994). What has been less closely examined, however, is what this polarization means in terms of ecological degradation, the local politics of policy-making, and the whole question of managing and administering highly polarized world cities. As we have seen world cities must be theorized at several different scales. In chapter 16 Roger Keil's discussion of the environmental problematic in world cities shows very clearly how ecological degradation must be understood not only in terms of a fragmented and polarized local polity but also in terms of the changing regulatory mechanisms and socio-cultural sensibilities at both national and global scales. Peter Ward (chapter 17) describes the administration and governance of world cities as the 'missing link' of the world city research paradigm, arguing that a focus on political–administrative structures allows the 'voice' of each city to come to the fore, exposing the power relations within it.

The way forward

We have, then, come a long way since John Friedmann wrote his seminal paper on the world cities hypothesis (reproduced in the appendix to this volume). Meanwhile, the world itself has changed significantly, both in terms of the dynamics of the world-system and in terms of the role of world cities within it. In this context, making intellectual headway requires that we are attentive to three broad dimensions of research and debate. The first concerns the need to clarify, extend, and update the overall conceptual and theoretical frameworks we use. The second concerns the need to extend our discussion of world cities within the context of regional, national, and global urban systems. The third concerns the need to examine the dialectics of globalization and localization, particularly in terms of the relationships between world city status and the political economy of urbanization. These three key themes are reflected in the organization of this volume into three parts.

The three chapters that comprise the remainder of part 1 address the question of how to define the theoretical object(s) of world city research. This involves several key issues, including:

- the conceptual and theoretical relationship of world cities to other metropolitan areas, especially the 'mega-cities' of the underdeveloped periphery;
- the relationship of world city research to the broader framework of world-systems theory and to other broad theoretical frameworks;
- the extent to which there has in fact been a significant discontinuity in the attributes and functions of contemporary world cities when seen in their *longue durée* context; and
- the role of place within the contemporary world-system, particularly with regard to the centralization and dispersal of different economic activities.

In part 2 we turn to the examination of world cities as key components of regional, national, and global urban systems. The issues here are more empirical in nature. They include:

- the nature of the networks of structural relationships and functional linkages that tie places together within the contemporary world-system;
- the degree to which clear hierarchies of world cities exist, and the extent to which these hierarchies may vary according to particular world city functions (such as corporate headquarters, financial services, and international agencies);
- the degree to which the increased globalization of the world economy is in fact channelled through the basing points of world cities; and
- the extent to which cities' participation in global systems can in fact be attributed to the imperatives of capital accumulation – rather than, for example, geopolitical imperatives or the strategic imperatives of a specific metropolitan political economy.

This last issue brings our attention to a different geographic scale, and to the relationships between world city status and the political economy of urbanization, which provides the overall theme for part 3 of this volume. The issues here are both empirical and theoretical. They include:

- the significance of world cities as sites for the construction of new cultural and political identities, and for new processes of political and cultural transformation;
- the relationship of the global to the local, particularly with respect to the dynamics of modernity and postmodernity, and to questions of identity, representation, and cultural change;
- the distinctiveness of the problems experienced by world cities – particularly with regard to governance, social polarization, and environmental degradation – and the need for equally distinctive policy responses.

Our ability to address these problems effectively will depend in large measure on our ability to understand the whole phenomenon of world cities within the broader context of the evolving world-system. The contributions to this volume are offered in the spirit of developing this understanding.

REFERENCES

Amin, A. and Thrift, N. 1992. 'Neo-Marshallian nodes in global networks'. *International Journal of Urban and Regional Research*, 16(4): 571–87.
Appadurai, A. 1990. 'Disjuncture and difference in the global cultural economy'. In *Global Culture: Nationalism, Globalization, and Modernity*, ed. M. Featherstone, pp. 295–310. Newbury Park CA: Sage.
Arnason, J. P. 1990. 'Nationalism, globalization, and modernity'. In *Global*

Culture: Nationalism. Globalization, and Modernity, ed. M. Featherstone, pp. 207–36. Newbury Park CA: Sage.

Benedikt, M. 1992. *Cyberspace First Steps*. Cambridge MA: MIT Press.

Bergesen, A. 1990. 'Turning world-system theory on its head'. In *Global Culture: Nationalism. Globalization, and Modernity*, ed. M. Featherstone, pp. 67–82. Newbury Park CA: Sage.

Bourdieu, P. 1984. *Distinction: A Social Critique of the Judgement of Taste*. London: Routledge and Kegan Paul.

1992. *The Field of Cultural Production*. New York: Columbia University Press.

Bourne, L., Sinclair, R., Ferrer, M., and d'Entremont A. (eds.). 1989. *The Changing Geography of Urban Systems*. Navarra, Spain: Department of Human Geography, Universidad de Navarra.

Boyne, R. 1990. 'Culture and the world-system'. In *Global Culture: Nationalism. Globalization, and Modernity*, ed. M. Featherstone, pp. 57–62. Newbury Park CA: Sage.

Brown, R. H. 1991. *The Global-Economy Urban Hierarchy*. Phoenix: Bronze Age Publishers.

Castells, M. 1989. *The Informational City: Information Technology, Economic Restructuring and the Urban–Regional Process*. Oxford: Basil Blackwell.

Cybriwsky, R. 1991. *Tokyo. The Changing Profile of an Urban Giant*. World Cities Series, ed. R. J. Johnston and P. L. Knox. London: Belhaven.

Douglass, M. 1993. 'The "new" Tokyo story. Restructuring space and the struggle for place in a world city'. In *Japanese Cities in the World Economy*, ed. K. Fujita and R. C. Hill, pp. 83–119. Philadelphia: Temple University Press.

Fainstein, S., Gordon, I., and Harloe, M. (eds.). 1992. *Divided Cities. New York and London in the Contemporary World*. Oxford: Basil Blackwell.

Featherstone, M. (ed.). 1990. *Global Culture: Nationalism, Globalization and Modernity*. Newbury Park, CA: Sage.

1993. 'Global and local cultures'. In *Mapping the Futures. Local Cultures, Global Change*, ed. J. Bird et al., pp. 169–87. London: Routledge and Kegan Paul.

Friedmann, John. 1986. 'The world city hypothesis'. *Development and Change*, 17 (1): 69–84. (Reproduced as appendix in this volume.)

Friedmann, John and Wolff, Goetz. 1982. 'World city formation. An agenda for research and action'. *International Journal of Urban and Regional Research*, 6 (3): 309–44.

Fujita, K. 1991. 'A world city and flexible specialization: restructuring the Tokyo metropolis'. *International Journal of Urban and Regional Research*, 15: 269–84.

Gibson, W. 1984. *Neuromancer*. New York: Ace Books.

1987. *Count Zero*. New York: Ace Books.

Hannerz, U. 1992. *Cultural Complexity. Studies in the Social Organization of Meaning*. New York: Columbia University Press.

Hirst, P. and Zeitlin, J. 1992. 'Flexible specialization versus post-Fordism'. In *Pathways to Industrialization and Regional Development*, ed. M. Storper and A. J. Scott, pp. 70–115. London: Routledge and Kegan Paul.

Huntington, S. P. 1993. 'The clash of civilizations?' *Foreign Affairs*, 72: 22–49.

Ingersoll, R. 1993. 'Computers "R" us'. *Design Book Review*, 27: 5.

Itoh, M. 1992. 'The Japanese model of post-Fordism'. In *Pathways to Industrialization and Regional Development*, ed. M. Storper and A. J. Scott, pp. 116–34. London: Routledge and Kegan Paul.

Jessop, R. 1992. 'Post-Fordism and flexible specialization. Incommensurable, contradictory, or just plain different perspectives?' In *Regional Development and Contemporary Industrial Response*, ed. E. Ernste and V. Meier, pp. 25–43.

Kenny, M. and Florida, R. 1988. 'Beyond mass production: production and the labor process in Japan'. *Politics and Society*, 16: 121–50.

Machimura, T. 1992. 'The urban restructuring process in Tokyo in the 1980s: transforming Tokyo into a world city'. *International Journal of Urban and Regional Research*, 16(1): 114–28.

Miyamoto, K. 1993. 'Japan's world cities'. In *Japanese Cities in the World Economy*, ed. K. Fujita and R. C. Hill, pp. 533–82. Philadelphia: Temple University Press.

Mlinar, Z. 1992. *Globalization and Territorial Identities*. Aldershot: Avebury Press.

Mollenkopf, J. and Castells, M. (eds.). 1991. *Dual City: Restructuring New York*. New York: Russell Sage Foundation.

Moss, M. 1987. 'Telecommunications, world cities, and urban policy'. *Urban Studies*, 21: 524–46.

Parboni, R. 1981. *The Dollar and its Rivals*. London: Verso.

Petrella, R. 1991. 'World city-states of the future'. *New Perspectives Quarterly*, 8: 59–64.

Pryke, M. 1991. 'An international city going global: spatial change in the City of London'. *Environment & Planning D: Society and Space*, 9: 197–222.

Reich, R. 1991. 'Brainpower, bridges, and the nomadic corporation'. *New Perspectives Quarterly*, 8: 67–71.

Rimmer, Peter J. 1986. 'Japan's world cities: Tokyo, Osaka, Nagoya, or Tokaido megalopolis?' *Development and Change*, 17(1): 121–58.

Robertson, R. 1990. 'Mapping the global condition: globalization as the central construct'. In *Global Culture: Nationalism. Globalization, and Modernity*, ed. M. Featherstone, pp. 15–30. Newbury Park CA: Sage.

Rodriguez, N. P. and Feagin, J. R. 1986. 'Urban specialization in the world system'. *Urban Affairs Quarterly*, 22: 187–220.

Sachar, A. 1990. 'The global economy and world cities'. In *The World Economy and the Spatial Organization of Power*, ed. A. Sachar and S. Öberg, pp. 149–60. Aldershot: Avebury.

Sampson, A. 1991. 'Global money'. *New Perspectives Quarterly*, 8: 67–71.

Sassen, S. 1991. *The Global City: New York, London, Tokyo*. Princeton NJ: Princeton University Press.

  1994. *Cities in a World Economy*. Thousand Oaks CA: Pine Forge/Sage.

Sayer, A. and Walker, R. 1992. *The New Social Economy*. Oxford: Basil Blackwell.

Shefter, M. (ed.). 1993. *Capital of the American Century. The National and International Influence of New York City*. New York: Russell Sage Foundation.

Sklair, L. 1991. *Sociology of the Global System: Social Change in Global Perspective*. Baltimore: Johns Hopkins University Press.

Smith, N. 1993. 'Homeless/global: scaling places'. In *Mapping the Futures. Local Cultures, Global Change*, ed. J. Bird et al., pp. 87–119. London: Routledge and Kegan Paul.

Thrift, N. 1989. 'The geography of international economic disorder'. In *A World in Crisis?* 2nd edn. ed. R. J. Johnston and P. J. Taylor, pp. 16–78. Oxford: Basil Blackwell.

Toffler, A. and Toffler, H. 1991. 'Economic time zones: fast versus slow'. *New Perspectives Quarterly*, 8: 56–8.

Twitchell, J. B. 1992. *Carnival Culture: The Trashing of Taste in America*. New York: Columbia University Press.

Van der Woude, A., de Vries, J., and Hayami, A. 1990. *Urbanization in History. A Process of Dynamic Interaction*. Oxford: Clarendon Press.

Versluyen, E. 1981. *The Political Economy of International Finance*. Aldershot: Gower.

Wallerstein, I. 1990. 'Culture as the ideological battleground of the modern world-system'. In *Global Culture: Nationalism, Globalization, and Modernity*, ed. M. Featherstone, pp. 31–56. Newbury Park CA: Sage.

Wolfe, T. 1987. *Bonfire of the Vanities*. New York: Farrar, Straus, Giroux.

2 Where we stand: a decade of world city research

John Friedmann

As an interlocking system of production and markets, the global economy is a discovery of the 1970s (Barnet and Müller 1974). At the time there was a good deal of controversy over the so-called 'new international division of labour' (Fröbel et al. 1980) and a centuries-old 'world system' (Wallerstein 1974). Research paradigms were being born.

The significance of these theoretical developments for the study of urbanization was not recognized until the early 1980s (Cohen 1981; Friedmann and Wolff 1982). Ten years have passed since then, and this chapter is an attempt to survey what we have learned and to assess where we stand in the study of world cities. I begin with a discussion of some conceptual issues: what is the 'theoretical object' of world cities research? How shall we define the elusive notion of world city? I then launch into an extended review of the literature, including theoretical developments in the 1980s and empirical studies in the early 1990s. The third section takes a closer look at the notion of a structured hierarchy of world cities and argues the need to remain ever alert to economic and political changes that may lead to the rise and fall of world cities that are linked to each other in 'antagonistic co-operation'. Next, I turn to consider that remnant – a majority of the world's population – that for all practical purposes is excluded from the capitalist 'space of accumulation' and consequently also from world city analysis. I argue that our understanding of the urban dynamic remains incomplete unless we consider both the internal and external proletariats of world cities. A brief coda concludes my discussion.

Conceptual issues

A certain ambiguity attaches to the world city hypothesis as originally formulated (Friedmann 1986). Is it a heuristic, a way of asking questions about cities in general, or a statement about a class of particular cities – world cities – set apart from other urban agglomerations by specifiable

21

characteristics? Judging from a review of the relevant literature – in the next section of my chapter – the answer apparently is that it is both. We have found the hypothesis useful in the story of cities, whatever their claims to world city status may be; we have also zeroed in on a class of cities which, without being too precise about their specific role in the global economy, we choose to call global or world cities.

How are we to define this class? Please note that we are talking here about cities as spatially organized socio-economic systems; we are talking about *places* and *sites* rather than *actors*. With this proviso, I shall now proceed in a series of discrete steps to define, rigorously I hope, the class of cities that is the object of our study. And I will do so by positing a series of 'agreements' about what I take to be our theoretical object.

First, we have to agree that cities articulate larger regional, national, and international economies. That is to say, cities serve as *centres* through which flow money, workers, information, commodities, and other economically relevant variables. As centres they extend their influence into a surrounding 'field' or region whose economic relations they 'articulate' into the global economy or *space of global accumulation*. Amin and Thrift have stated recently why, in their view, urban centres are still required for a decentred economy. Spatial concentration, they argue, solves certain problems of corporate management, including *representation* (how to think and talk about the global system), *social interaction* (gathering information, tapping into particular capitalist structures, making agreements, forming coalitions, cementing relations of trust), and *innovation* (incubating product innovations, marketing new products, experimenting with financial innovations, and gaining access to representation and interactive networks) (Amin and Thrift 1992: 576).

Second, we have to agree that there is such a thing as a *space of global accumulation*, that is, a set of national and regional economies that serves the purposes of capital accumulation on a 'world-wide' scale. This space includes areas of primary production (e.g. rainforests and minerals in the Amazon Basin), specific production sites (localizations of production), and, of course, spatial concentrations of consumers.

In one sense this global space is co-terminous with planet Earth: from the Arctic to the Antarctic, from the Atlantic to the Pacific, there is no place that is not actually or potentially of use in the process of capital accumulation. But in another and more relevant sense the space of global accumulation is much more restricted. Large parts of the world's population are not incorporated into this space or, if they are, make only a marginal contribution as either direct producers or consumers. I shall come to speak of this in a moment. For now it will be sufficient to say that the space of global accumulation, defined by a set of interdependent regional and national economies, encompasses only a fraction of the earth's surface and an even smaller fraction of its population. It is this more restricted set of space economies precisely that is the space being articulated, or organized, through the network of world cities.

Third, we have to agree that world cities are large, urbanized regions that are defined by dense patterns of interaction rather than by political–administrative boundaries. Deyan Sudjik (1992) calls the largest of them 'hundred-mile' cities; typically they have populations of between one and twenty million or more.

Fourth, we have to agree that these regional cities – the commanding nodes of the global system – can be arranged into a *hierarchy of spatial articulations*, roughly in accord with the economic power they command. At the top we find the cities that are the subject of Saskia Sassen's researches: the command and control centres of the global economy, New York, London, and Tokyo (Sassen 1991). After that, the going becomes more contentious because we lack unambiguous criteria for assigning particular cities to a specific place in the global system. There are cities that articulate large national economies into the system, such as Paris, Madrid, and São Paulo; others have a commanding multi-national role, such as Singapore and Miami; and still others, such as Chicago and Hong Kong, articulate important subnational (regional) economies (see table 2.1).

But establishing such a hierarchy once and for all may, in any event, be a futile undertaking. The world economy is too volatile to allow us to fix a stable hierarchy for any but relatively short stretches of time. Assigning hierarchical rank may therefore be a less compelling exercise than recognizing the existence of differences in rank without further specification and, based on this rough notion, investigating the articulations of particular world cities with each other.

Hierarchical relations are essentially relations of power, and competition for place is always severe among cities. Not only are world cities constantly engaged in an equilibrating act to adjust their economies to the processes of 'creative destruction' that are endemic to industrial capitalism, they are themselves driven by relentless competition, struggling to capture ever more command and control functions that comprise their very essence. Competitive *angst* is built into world city politics.

Fifth, and last, we have to agree that the *dominant culture* of world cities is cosmopolitan, as defined by its controlling social strata whom Leslie Sklair (1991) calls the transnational capitalist class. The lingua franca of this class is English, and its class style of consumption is the

24   *John Friedmann*

Table 2.1 *Spatial articulations: 30 world cities*

1   **Global financial articulations**
    #   London* A (also national articulation)
    #   New York A
    #   Tokyo* A (also multinational articulation: SE Asia)

2   **Multinational articulations**
    #   Miami C (Caribbean, Latin America)
    #   Los Angeles A (Pacific Rim)
    #   Frankfurt C (western Europe)
    #   Amsterdam C or Randstad B
        Singapore* C (SE Asia)

3   **Important national articulations (1989 GDP>$200 billion)**
    #   Paris* B
    #   Zurich C
        Madrid* C
        Mexico City* A
        São Paulo A
        Seoul* A
    #   Sydney B

4   **Subnational/regional articulations**
        Osaka-Kobe (Kansai region) B
    #   San Francisco C
    #   Seattle C
    #   Houston C
    #   Chicago B
    #   Boston C
    #   Vancouver C
    #   Toronto C
        Montreal C
        Hong Kong (Pearl river delta) B
    #   Milano C
        Lyon C
        Barcelona C
    #   Munich C
    #   Düsseldorf–Cologne–Essen–Dortmund (Rhine–Ruhr region) B

Population (1980s):
A   10–20 million
B   5–10 million
C   1–5 million
*   national capital
#   major immigration target

For European cities, I have benefited greatly from Klaus R. Kunzmann and Michael Wegener, *The Pattern of Urbanization in Western Europe 1960–1990.*

envy of virtually all subaltern classes. The culture of the transnational capitalist class leads its members to be clairvoyant in some regards, but also to be self-deceptive and even blind in others. Typically, they confuse their own class interest – which is the smooth, uninterrupted functioning of the global system of accumulation – with national or local territorial interest, as in the notorious words of Charles Wilson: 'What is good for General Motors is good for the United States.' And sooner or later this misperception leads to an endemic conflict with subaltern classes whose interests are typically more territorial and local. Different authors have called attention to this basic contradiction within advanced capitalism; I have called it the contradiction between 'life space and economic space' (Friedmann 1988).

A growing social schizophrenia has resulted between, on the one hand, regional societies and local institutions and, on the other hand, the rules and operations of the economic system at the international level. The more the economy becomes interdependent on the global scale, the less can regional and local governments, as they exist today, act upon the basic mechanisms that condition the daily existence of their citizens. The traditional structures of social and political control over development, work, and distribution have been subverted by the placeless logic of an internationalized economy enacted by means of information flows among powerful actors beyond the sphere of state regulations (Castells 1989: 347).

Let me now sum up the five agreements that, together, constitute a definition of our 'theoretical object'. I have called them agreements, because we are dealing here with a conceptualization that is the starting point of an emerging research paradigm. Without this substantial agreement we may have to part company. It is not a question of being right or wrong, but of how we want to look at the world, and for what purpose.

1 World cities articulate regional, national, and international economies into a global economy. They serve as the organizing nodes of a global economic system.

2 A space of global capital accumulation exists, but it is smaller than the world as a whole. Major world regions and their populations are, at present, virtually excluded from this space, living in a permanent subsistence economy.

3 World cities are large urbanized spaces of intense economic and social interaction.

4 World cities can be arranged hierarchically, roughly in accord with the economic power they command. They are cities through which regional, national, and international economies are articulated with

the global capitalist system of accumulation. A city's ability to attract global investments ultimately determines its rank in the order of world cities. However, its fortunes in this regard, as well as its ability to absorb external shocks from technological innovations and political change, are variable. Cities may rise into the rank of world cities, they may drop from the order, and they may rise or fall in rank.

5 The controlling world city strata constitute a social class that has been called the transnational capitalist class. Its interests are the smooth functioning of the global system of accumulation; its culture is cosmopolitan; and its ideology is consumerist. Its presence gives rise to often severe conflict between itself and subaltern classes who have more locally defined territorial interests and whose rise into the transnational class is blocked.

Recent research

I want to turn now to some recent studies that have used the emerging world city paradigm for their subject matter. I will do so in three steps. First, I would like to tell the backstory to the emerging paradigm: what are the theoretical debates that underlie world city research? Second, I will review two large-scale, comparative studies of world cities at the very apex of the global hierarchy. And third, I will take a brief look at some specific city studies.

Backstory

At the outset, I would like to insist that what we are studying here is a historically unprecedented phenomenon and not merely a continuation of what, in one form or another, has been around for a very long time (Chase-Dunn 1985). In the next chapter Taylor discusses world cities in the *longue durée* of history, and this is a proper area of study. But history is not a continuous, unbroken narrative. There are 'befores' and 'afters' as well as radical breaks and new beginnings. I shall therefore follow Amin and Thrift (1992) when they write that between the 1970s and 1980s there occurred an important shift, 'a move from an international to a global economy'.[1] They describe this new economy in terms of four characteristics: the functioning of industries on a world scale through the medium of global corporate networks; an increase in oligopolistic, progressively centralized power; an ongoing process of corporate decentralization through new forms of subcontracting, joint ventures, and other forms of networked organization and strategic alliances; and finally, a new, more volatile balance of power between nation-states and corporations, resulting in the increasing prominence of cross-national issue coalitions 'uniting fragments of the state, fragments of particular industries, and even fragments of particular firms in a worldwide network' (Amin and Thrift 1992: 574–5, citing Moran 1991). One can debate the particulars of this formulation and still conclude that the capitalist economy today is organized in ways that are dramatically different to those that existed right up to the 1960s, and that we are in the midst of a major *transition* in the regulationist regime of advanced industrial capitalism.

An ongoing controversy about the precise nature of this new world economic order is found in the literature on Fordism, a term originally coined by Antonio Gramsci but given currency by Alain Lipietz and his followers in the French 'regulationist' school (Lipietz 1989). In Lipietz's formulation the Fordist regime of accumulation was based, in the final instance, on the idea of mass production, mass consumption, and a Keynesian system of state regulation. A controversy has sprung up on precisely the question of whether we are now moving into a new regime of post-Fordist, flexible accumulation or are merely in an unnamed 'restructuring phase' of capitalism (Lovering 1990; Sayer 1989; Soja 1989; Storper and Walker 1989). Since we are only a little way into this new 'post'-era (post-Fordist, post-modern, post-communist, etc.), it is probably futile for the present to search for a definitive answer to this question. But all participants in the debate seem agreed that we are facing a new economic landscape along with a new alignment of class forces within the continuing evolution of the capitalist mode of production.

Building on the path-breaking work of Piore and Sabel (1984) among others, Michael Storper and Richard Walker (1989) forge new ground in the geography of flexible accumulation. Theirs is a Schumpeterian vision of capitalism, where periods of rising waves of technological and product innovation are followed by declines of older and rapidly obsolescing industries in a never-ending and competitively driven process of 'creative destruction'. In its specificity, their work goes beyond Lipietz, however, with their emphasis on new technologies and forms of capitalist organization (i.e. 'flexibility'). Mass consumption plays a secondary role in their account, to the primacy of gains in productivity and the extraction of surplus value (Storper and Walker 1989: 202–5). Consequently they focus on production ensembles (above all, in manufacturing) and on a geography of production sites that is in many ways reminiscent of François Perroux's *pôles de croissance* and Walter Isard's production complexes of some forty years ago.

Manuel Castells' book, *The Informational City*, was published in the same year as Storper and Walker (1989) and draws on some of the same literature. In this essentially synthetic work Castells tries – unconvincingly in my view – to define an 'informational mode of development'. Nevertheless, the book is important in a number of ways. Like so many contemporary economic sociologists and geographers, Castells is trans-fixed by 'high-tech', the ensemble of advanced, information-based technologies for which the microchip may stand as symbol. These technologies, argues Castells, have created a deterritorialized 'space of flows' which overcomes terrestrial barriers by creating instantaneous access to a network of strategic stations located around the world. One may wish to illustrate this with reference to the communication links that manage global air traffic or the financial dealings of world capital markets. Access to this space, and control over its principal nodes, have become critical for the players in the game of capital accumulation. By the same token, those who lack access to this networked space are disempowered and, to varying degrees, dependent on whatever crumbs of information power holders may be willing to share. Inherent in this formulation is a dualism of incorporation/exclusion which foreshadows some of the facets of world city research on which I will comment below.

The final background to which I would like to draw attention is Leslie Sklair's *Sociology of the Global System* (1991). Although Sklair is not a member of the 'invisible college' of world city researchers, his study is nevertheless pertinent. His focus is the so-called transnational capitalist class. 'The theory of the global system developed in this book,' he writes, 'proposes that the primary agent in the political sphere is a still-evolving *transnational capitalist class*. The institutions of the *culture-ideology of consumerism*, as expressed through the trans-national mass media, are the primary agents in the cultural-ideological sphere' (Sklair 1991: 53, original emphasis). Sklair thus draws our attention to the social and political actors who have created the new global economic order and who will have to maintain ('reproduce') it. He also reminds us of the importance of ideology in undergirding the hegemony of global capitalism and its 'space of flows'. I shall return to this point later.

Major comparative studies

Now I want to comment on two exceptional, very different, recently published books on world cities: Saskia Sassen's *Global City*, an exemplary and highly imaginative work of political economy (1991) and Deyan Sudjik's iconoclastic essays in *The 100 Mile City* (1992) which bypasses academic debates (with a bonus to the reader: no jargon!) to present us with a close-up view of how the 'global city' has come about. Its object is the built environment.

Since Manuel Castells' influential work on the politics of cities (1983) which, he claimed, revolves around issues of collective consumption, scholars have treated urban phenomena primarily from the perspective of social reproduction. For their part, neo-classical economists, to the extent that they treated them at all, subsumed much of what we know about cities under vaguely defined (and rarely specified) agglomeration economies. Labour economists focused additionally on the functioning of urban labour markets. Explicitly rejecting these approaches, Sassen favours a paradigm that emphasizes the *production of financial and producer services*, not as a residual category subsumed under an estimated employment multiplier with manufacturing at the base, but as a productive activity in its own right. What these services produce, she argues, is 'control capability' over a geographically dispersed set of global production sites and service outlets. Geographical decentralization requires centralization of command structures and, for the global economy as a whole, control capability has come to be centred, among others, in the three metropolitan areas of New York, London, and Tokyo. Sassen approaches global cities as sites for the production of producer services and as financial market-places for the buying and selling of securities.

This proves to be an exceedingly useful point of departure. Blessed with what C. Wright Mills called sociological imagination, a quality rare in any social science discipline, Sassen draws out of her researches a series of fascinating hypotheses, speculations, intuitions, and questions that will do much to inform our work in the years ahead. Let me give a few examples taken from her masterful summation.

Looking at the local consequences of the globalization of economic activity, she asks whether a new *urban regime* is in the making:

By focusing on production processes in the new industrial complex, the analysis makes it possible to see in relation to one another the full range of jobs, firms, and households involved in each city, from the top to the bottom, from those that are quintessentially postindustrial to those that look as though they belong to an earlier industrial era but are necessary to the operation of the new industrial complex. In this perspective, such developments as the growth of an informal economy and the casualization of the labor market ... emerge not as anomalous or exogenous to these advanced urban economies but are in fact part of them. A new class alignment is being shaped, and global cities have emerged as one of the main arenas for this development: They contain both the most vigorous economic sectors and the sharpest income polarization. (Sassen 1991: 337)

And in another place:

Yes, manufacturing matters, but from the perspective of finance and producer services, it does not have to be national ... One of the key points developed in this book is that much of the new growth rests on the decline of what were once significant sectors of the national economy, notably key branches of manufacturing that were the leading force in the national economy and promoted the formation and expansion of a strong middle class. (328)

And on urban form:

Arguably, a new phase of innovation in telecommunications technology might make the current infrastructure obsolete and lead to the equivalent of the earlier 'suburbanization' of large-scale manufacturing that resulted from the obsolescence of the physical structures that housed manufacturing in large cities. At that point we could, conceivably, enter a whole new phase in the development of the urban economic system. (330)

Or on the global market for capitals and services:

growth in the new industrial complex is based less on the expansion of final consumption by a growing middle class [as under Fordism] than on exports to the international market and on intermediate consumption by other firms and governments or, more generally, consumption by organizations rather than individuals. The key, though not necessarily the largest, markets are not the consumer markets but the global markets for capital and services. These are the markets that shape society and economy. (333)

By far the most fascinating, because least familiar, global city discussed by Sassen is Tokyo. Only seven years ago, Peter Rimmer expressed surprise at his discovery that 'the parallels between Tokyo and Los Angeles [as putative world cities] were greater than imagined' (Rimmer 1986: 152). Now Japanese scholars have begun their own investigations into urban restructuring. A recent article by Takashi Machimura carries the telling subtitle 'Transforming Tokyo into a world city' (Machimura 1992). Machimura pauses on the horns of a dilemma: is Tokyo to be merely 'a giant growth machine solely for the processing of global capital and information? At present, much is uncertain' (192). Implied in this question is the fate of Tokyo as the capital of Japan, an island nation which, like the United Kingdom, has a strong sense of its own identity.

Like other writers, Sassen poses a similar question when she defines her set of global cities as a 'new type of city', though she is careful to moderate this abstract conception by insisting that each city is also a specific place, with its own history and way of life. What I should like to add to this is that it may be helpful to distinguish global cities that are national capitals (Paris, Madrid, London, and Tokyo *inter alia*) and those, such as Frankfurt, New York, Toronto, Los Angeles, São Paulo, and Osaka, that are not. Of necessity, capital cities are Janus-faced and thus less likely than other cities to become 'giant growth machines' to the exclusion of national/local considerations. Where capital cities are concerned national governments may impose their own will on the city.

A second point to remember in the comparative study of global cities (or world cities: I will, henceforth, use the two designations interchangeably) is that countries have very different policies with regard to foreign immigration, and this has major consequences for world city formation. Tokyo's case is notorious, and although Sassen discovers an 'underclass' of foreign workers there, their numbers are (still?) relatively insignificant. More than 95 per cent of Tokyo's resident population remains Japanese. This is obviously not the case with New York or London nor, increasingly, with cities on the European continent.

Among cities (and states) with very strict immigration controls is Singapore. Faced with rising land values, an increasingly affluent labour force, and a view of itself as a budding 'world city', Singapore opted to peacefully colonize adjacent regions in Malaysia and Indonesia, thus constituting what some like to call an economic triangle (Parsonage 1992). The story is too complicated for retelling here. Suffice it to say that this policy reserves to Singapore high-wage jobs in the dominant financial and producer services while creating labour-intensive activities in manufacturing and tourism in the outlying peripheral regions of Johor and Riau. Significantly, in his account of the growth triangle, James Parsonage signals the importance of ethnic relations in Signapore's expansionary politics. 'Ethnicity continues to be a salient political factor in all three states,' he writes. 'Any notion of Southeast Asia's "coming of age" will be conditional upon the demands of capital accumulation in a changing global economy to continue to transform social and political structures which have been rooted in antagonistic ethnic consciousness' (Parsonage 1992: 317). These remarks echo the gathering thunder of racial–ethnic–religious animosities of world cities in Western Europe and North America, especially in the USA, with their large immigrant quotas from diverse regions on their respective peripheries.

My third and final comment on Sassen's excellent book relates to her chosen focus on producer and financial services. I would agree with her that these services are essential to the management of the global production complex. But I would also argue that we must consider, as a separate category, the cultural services that are crucial for ensuring the hegemony of transnational capitalism through what Leslie Sklair calls its culture-ideology of *consumerism* (Sklair 1991): major news services, television, the motion picture industry, major newspapers, publishing, communications consultants, and advertising agencies. It is their under-standing of the world that we feed off, that shape our ideas and our responses to political situations. Professionals in these industries are every bit as important as bankers, accountants, realtors, and insurance agents. They are increasingly networked internationally, employ tens of thousands of workers across the entire spectrum of jobs, from newspaper delivery boys and movie 'gophers' to the moguls of recording and TV studios, and they are concentrated in global cities. Their task is to create and reproduce a popular consensus around transnational interests. As instruments of hegemony they do not always play by the rules, but their role in creating a positive image of global capitalist accumulation is critical.

I now pause briefly to consider Sudjik's *The 100 Mile City*. This book, stunningly illustrated with black-and-white photographs by Phil Sayer, is in a class by itself. Leonie Sandercock compares Sudjik's writing to Lewis Mumford, Jane Jacobs, Marshall Berman, and Mike Davis, all of them, of course, largely from outside the academy:

His central argument is the by now familiar view that the world cities are inextricably linked as a single system, one which demands sharper competition between them. And it is property developers, not planners or architects, who are primarily responsible for the shape and appearance of today's cities. Large-scale speculative developments – offices, shopping centers, hotels, and luxury housing – shape the fabric of the city. Developers ... choose the architect and set the budget. Architecture becomes little more than cosmetic, and public planners are under instruction from beleaguered city governments to 'facilitate' development. (Sandercock 1992: 3)

What is nevertheless new, is Sudjik's complete immersion in the city-building processes of the global city. Unsentimentally, he embraces change as inevitable. Like Rayner Banham's paean to the 'four ecologies' of Los Angeles (Banham 1974), Sudjik's is an eye-opening new reading of the physical form of the five cities he has studied: Paris, London, New York, Los Angeles, and Tokyo. His sharpest criticism falls on those who would be blind to the values of the cosmopolitan culture of world cities, especially the idolaters of territorially based communities. Although his book falls outside our theoretical domain, Sudjik succeeds in describing the new regional city in ways that will be instantly familiar to Sassen and the rest of our 'invisible college'.

Specific city studies

Of the single city studies, the volume recently edited by John Mollenkopf and Manuel Castells is by far the most impressive (Mollenkopf and

Castells 1991). *Dual City: Restructuring New York* explores some of New York's characteristics as a global city, including its information economy, the public sector, the new dominant social strata, social (dis)organization, political inequality, the informal economy, and even a bow in the direction of comparative studies with Los Angeles and London. The editors' conclusion takes up the theme of socio-economic polarization, already raised by Friedmann and Wolff in 1982 and taken up again in Sassen (1992). Although they begin their chapter with a quotation from Plato's *Republic* about the 'two cities of the rich and the poor', they clearly want to say something that goes beyond this ancient dualism. New York society, they say, is dominated by two opposing forces:

(a) The upper professionals of the corporate sector form an organizational nucleus for the wider social stratum of managers and professionals. They constitute a coherent social network whose interests are directly linked to the development of New York's corporate economy.
(b) The remaining social strata occupy increasingly diverse positions and have plural interests and values. Neighborhood life thus becomes increasingly diverse and fragmented, hindering alliances among these groups.
   As a result, the tendency toward cultural, economic, and political polarization in New York takes the form of a contrast between a comparatively cohesive core of professionals in the advanced corporate services and a disorganized periphery fragmented by race, ethnicity, gender, occupational and industrial location, and the spaces they occupy. (Mollenkopf and Castells 1991: 402)

They then go on to deconstruct the formulation of a polarized society by stressing the diversity among the second, subaltern group, arguing that within each category there are further social 'cleavages'. In this way polarization is made almost to disappear into a celebration of post-modern 'difference'.

To stress social disorganization as a *source* of subalternity is misleading. Theoretically more consequential would be the relative access of subaltern groups to the information flows of the global economy. In his earlier study (1989) Castells had stressed this lack of access as a structural source of disempowerment. It is surprising not to see his argument restated, perhaps in more elaborate form, in *Dual City*.

London has produced two books that avail themselves of the world city paradigm. One, by Nigel Thrift and A. L. Leyshon, *Making Money: The City of London and Social Power in Britain* (forthcoming) was not available at the time of writing. The other is Anthony King's *Global Cities: Post-Imperialism and the Internationalization of London* (1990). King is particularly interested in the physical city, a concern he shares with Sudjik. But unlike the latter, he is deeply concerned with history.

He sees London's present-day status as global clearing-house as a continuation of her imperial role in earlier centuries. In the first part of this chapter I was at pains to argue that the global economy we live in has a new and unprecedented structure, that we are *in transition* from one type of economy to another. King acknowledges this change, understood by him as a change in the spatial division of labour. But he emphasizes continuities:

> whilst there is a massive change between the old and the new mode of production [*sic*], there are also continuities in the localities where they take place. The identity of these localities and the built environment that helps to create it, are instrumental in explaining why such continuities persist. (King 1990: 68)

It is a point worth pondering, both methodologically and in terms of world city theorizing. Theory soars into abstract regions where fine differences scaled to an earthly terrain tend to become invisible. If we neglect the other face of world cities – their rootedness in a politically organized 'life space', with its own history, institutions, culture, and politics (the difference between Paris and London, for example) – much of what we observe will remain unintelligible.

King sums up his own impressions of London in the era of Margaret Thatcher, and of world cities more generally, by observing that the city has become increasingly 'unhooked from the state where it exists, its future decided by fortunes over which it has little control' (King 1990: 145–6). The Docklands scheme – Europe's largest real-estate venture during the 1980s – is placed in evidence of this claim. Meanwhile, with the demise of Olympia and York, its largest developers, the Docklands have fallen on very hard times. During the Thatcher era it was called the 'flagship' of the government's urban policy. King might have pointed out that during the Thatcher era national interest was perceived to be largely coincident with the interests of the transnational capitalist class, and no inherent conflict between the two was claimed to exist.

Finally, I want to draw attention to a volume of *Comparative Urban and Community Research* edited by Michael Smith (1992) which contains several world city essays, most notably by Roger Keil and Peter Lieser on Frankfurt and a comparative piece on Amsterdam and Los Angeles by Edward Soja (Keil and Lieser 1992; Soja 1992). Soja's piece is an excellent demonstration of how differences in scale can influence comparisons. Central Amsterdam would seem to have little in common with Los Angeles, but as soon as our eyes are raised to the level of the regional city, some startling similarities emerge. Soja remains agnostic on the question of a new post-Fordist regime of accumulation; he is more comfortable with the vaguer, more pragmatic notion of 'restructuring'. Applying this notion to both Dutch and southern Californian regions, centred in Amsterdam and Los Angeles respectively, he finds both world cities undergoing very similar processes of economic, social, and spatial change.

Keil and Lieser, on the other hand, focusing on the municipality of Frankfurt as the core of their world city region, report on a new policy of urban regulation, which has helped to shape the globalization processes of that city. They make use of Lipietz's Fordist and post-Fordist terminology, and find that his 'mode of regulation' concept is useful as a key to the meaning of politics in this premier German global city. Their conclusions are worth pondering:

First, integration of the local, national, and global levels of analysis is a precondition for an understanding of current processes of world-city formation here. For this reason, more research using this integrative method needs to be done at other places in order to overcome the methodological dilemma of the world-city hypothesis.

Second, even though the conservative Wallman regime helped propel the city into the global age, the mode of political regulation that the conservative regime represented is by no means the only possible one. Both modest and radical reform might be able to modify the 'inevitability' of growth, economic development, racism and selective exclusion, local powerlessness, and the fetishism of the urban image. Their success will depend partly on the social and political mobilization of their clientele in the civil society of the city ...

Third, the analysis showed that any given system of local regulation, any structured coherence, is indeed only a temporary arrangement suffering from a chronic instability. Its spatial borders, its class structure, and its economic base are constantly being redefined. (Keil and Lieser 1992: 59–60)

In conclusion, when we look back at this review of the literature, it becomes clear that we stand on a threshold in our researches. The works under review have opened up a vast research terrain. Many more partial studies than those reviewed here become intelligible only within the world city paradigm (see, for example, the story of Singapore's economic triangle (Parsonage 1992), Sharon Zukin's account of restaurants in New York City (Zukin 1992), and Allan Heskin's study of the route 2 housing co-operative (Heskin 1991)). At the same time, we must remember that the dynamism of the political economy of capital is so great that no single paradigm is likely to remain intact for more than a couple of decades at most. The world city hypothesis has proved useful as a theoretical framework, but the real city is swiftly changing into something else, and eternal vigilance over ongoing change processes is the price of our knowledge.

The changing order of world cities

A few years ago, I was invited by the government of Singapore to speak on world cities. In private conversations with senior government officials it became clear to me what the government really wanted. Singapore was embarking on 'the next lap' (Government of Singapore 1991), and officials hoped to hear from me how their city state might rise to the rank of a 'world city'. The golden phrase had become a badge of status, just as 'growth poles' had been in an earlier incarnation. There was little I could say that the government did not already know. But to me this question pointed to an ongoing competitive struggle for position in the global network of capitalist cities and the inherent instability of this system. I want to illustrate this volatility by examining briefly some of the cities that I included in my earlier list of world cities (Friedmann 1986) as well as some cities I did not include.

Singapore

Singapore's strategy to create a growth 'triangle' with itself as controlling centre has already been mentioned. An energetic policy of maintaining its leading position within South-east Asia is also bearing fruit, despite the rapid growth of the Malaysian and Thai economies within recent years, especially around Bangkok, largely as a result of Japanese investments. Singapore can therefore be said to be consolidating its position as South-east Asia's 'control centre'. The importance of the country's ethnic policies has also been remarked upon. It is likely to remain a crucial factor for its continued role in the region.

Hong Kong

There remains a good deal of uncertainty about Hong Kong's future after the colony rejoins the People's Republic of China in 1997. Local capitalists are spreading their risks. But the economy of this world city enclave continues to boom and is becoming increasingly consolidated with the burgeoning industrial economy of the Pearl river delta, including Guangzhou and Shenzhen (Chung-Tong Wu 1993). The capitalist foothold in China is being widened and, without political disaster, the Hong Kong economy is likely to remain an important and increasingly strategic outpost of global capitalism, articulating much of the south China economy with the rest of the world.

Shanghai

Until quite recently Shanghai has remained in the backwater of Chinese economic reformism. Its heavy industries are mostly obsolete by world standards and cannot at present compete on the international market. On the other hand Shanghai is China's most important industrial city and, in recognition of this, has been assigned provincial status. It is now trying to lift itself into the twenty-first century through bold plans for Pudong (east Shanghai) on the right bank of the Huang-po river. With the assistance of the World Bank and Asian Development Bank, basic infrastructure is being installed to link the old with the new city and to build, on the right bank, a series of internationally oriented urban districts: port, airport, financial and business district, technology park, research institutions, university, free trade zone, export production zone, and so forth. The plan is long-term and is being implemented now. If it succeeds in its hopes and expectations it may draw some international attention away from the dynamic Pearl river delta and open the Yangtze Basin to the same sort of capitalist penetration that south China is already experiencing (Friedmann 1991).

Seoul

The South Korean capital appears to be losing some of its appeal to outside, especially Japanese, capital. There are several reasons for this, including rising labour costs and a complex bureaucracy. Although South Korea's economy is doing well it remains cut off from North Korea and so provides no access to markets other than its own. Korean capital is outward-bound, and its markets are increasingly abroad, especially on the west coast of the United States. But Seoul is not so much a world city, rather it is the capital city of South Korea. If the two Koreas should ever reunite this picture may change, especially if north China markets can be accessed from Seoul.

Osaka

Osaka, the central city of the Kansai region of Japan that also includes Kobe and Kyoto, was not on my original list of world cities, partly because the principal control functions of the Japanese economy appeared to be concentrated in Tokyo. But the economic weight of Osaka is considerable, and the negative externalities of further concentration in Tokyo are becoming apparent. Osaka now has a 24-hour international airport on reclaimed land in the bay as well as important new developments in knowledge-industries. The Japanese are imagining a *linear* city extending through Nagoya into Tokyo along the old *shinkansen* line, but centres will still be needed. Further advances in communication technology, a technology in which the Japanese are world leaders, may well turn the Osaka–Kobe region into an important international control centre, second only to Tokyo.

Vancouver and Seattle

I group these two cities together though neither was on my 1986 list. It has become clear, however, that both are playing important roles in articulating their respective regions with the rapidly growing Pacific Rim economy in Asia. Both cities, especially Vancouver, have received large numbers of Asian, primarily Chinese, immigrants, many of them well-to-do, while Hong Kong as well as Japanese money is pouring in and transforming their respective skylines. With the North American Free Trade Agreement (NAFTA) the two regional economic capitals may develop certain complementarities. Their separate identities will no doubt remain, but from an economic point of view Seattle and Vancouver might well be viewed as a single economic region in the making. The cities are little more than 200 km. apart and, disregarding national boundaries, their respective commuting sheds could easily be made to overlap.

Mexico City

With the NAFTA treaty ratified Mexico City will be officially integrated with the North American economy even as it remains the nation's capital. Both conceptually and politically this will be a major step. On the other hand, Mexico City's future as a world city is far from clear. The Mexican state is undergoing a major restructuring and many state enterprises are being privatized. Environmental conditions in Mexico City continue to deteriorate, while regional cities – Guadalajara, Monterrey, Tijuana – are experiencing hyper-rapid growth. The nearness of US cities such as Houston, Los Angeles, and San Diego to Mexican production sites suggests the distinct possibility that certain control functions will remain in the USA (Los Angeles, Houston) rather than relocate to Mexico City.

Rio de Janeiro and Buenos Aires

Both cities have lost significant potential as world cities within the last few years, leaving São Paulo as the principal centre on the east coast of

South America. Rio was never able to capture the leading headquarter and financial institutions that it would have needed to maintain a leading role in Brazilian economic life, and Buenos Aires' economy – largely identical with that of Argentina – has been beset by numerous problems. I would argue therefore that both cities should no longer be listed among even the third rank of world cities. São Paulo, of course, continues to play its role as principal 'articulator' of Brazil's economy within the global system.

Johannesburg

In my original formulation Johannesburg was the only world city in Africa. But this was before the international boycott of South Africa and prior to the current political struggle of the black majority for political control of the country. This struggle is likely to continue and to create large uncertainties, which will make it difficult for Johannesburg to recapture its world city position.

Frankfurt

There is a currently ongoing inter-city competition to become Europe's financial centre. At issue is the European Central Bank, and the contenders are London, Paris, Luxembourg, Frankfurt, and Berlin. Berlin, of course, has become a contender because of the reunification of the two Germanies. Along with foreign capital West German investments are being made in Berlin on a very large scale, as that city readies itself to become the political capital of Europe's largest economic power. Whether Berlin becomes something more than a national capital (in an era of declining state powers) remains to be seen. Much will depend, one would think, on what happens in Russia and Poland. If these East European countries succeed in mounting a vigorous capitalist economy in the next twenty years we can expect Berlin to become an important control centre, along with, perhaps, St Petersburg and Moscow. In the meantime Frankfurt's economic future hinges heavily on its international financial role at the crossroads of Western Europe.

Düsseldorf and Munich

Neither city appeared on my 1986 list. Düsseldorf, of course, is the most important city immediately adjacent to the Ruhr area, a region of declining coal, iron, and steel, and it is attempting to restructure itself.

Given its considerable human capital, its efforts may well succeed and, within ten to twenty years, Düsseldorf may become a major world city. Munich, meanwhile, has become the focal point for Germany's 'high-tech' industry, the equivalent of the US 'sunshine belt'. Whether it can turn this industrial into a finance/producer service advantage on the model suggested by Saskia Sassen remains to be seen.[2]

Vienna

The Austrian capital played an important 'neutral' role during the Cold War era, and it flourished accordingly. Whether it can retain a global role, given the redrawn political map of Eastern Europe, is questionable. Vienna does occupy a strategic 'gateway' position relative to the countries that were formerly parts of the Habsburg Empire. Budapest, for example, is subordinated to Vienna economically, and the new capital city of Slovakia, Bratislava, is even more so. But Czechoslovakia has split into two, while the former Yugoslav republics are engaged in a civil war whose ultimate end is not foreseeable. Vienna's 'natural' hinterland to the east has suddenly become exceedingly weak economically, and the city has nothing to 'articulate' except for its own small industrial economy. Its future as a significant world city is in doubt.

Rotterdam and Amsterdam

In 1986 I listed Rotterdam as a world city, thinking of it as the largest industrial and port city in Holland. But the financial and service capital of Holland is Amsterdam, and if that city is seen as lying at the centre of an urban region, as Soja argues that it should (Soja 1992), then clearly the centre of gravity should shift to Amsterdam.[3]

The thumbnail sketches above are drawn from newspaper accounts and sporadic readings over the last few years and do not reflect original research. But they do suggest that the network of world cities is continuously under tension, and that the order of world cities, even in a short interval of six or seven years, can undergo significant changes. Again I need to stress that we do not have clear-cut, agreed criteria that would allow us to validate world city claims unambiguously for any but the very top cities in the hierarchy. This is a critical gap in our knowledge. Still, as my review of probable candidates for world city status suggests, changes are constantly underway. In fifty years' time, the map of world city networks will look very different from the one I drew in the mid-1980s.

Techno-apartheid for a global underclass?

The reverse side of the global space of accumulation and its homologous 'space of flows' (Castells) are the fragmented life-spaces inhabited by people who are excluded from it. The subheading above captioned originally an Op-Ed piece in the *Los Angeles Times* written by Riccardo Petrella, a Eurocrat working on technological forecasting. He describes the network of world cities as 'a high-tech archipelago of affluent, hyper-developed city regions ... amid a sea of impoverished humanity.... Imagine [he continues] how such an order would redraw the world map: on one side we would see a dynamic, tightly linked archipelago of technopoles constituting less than one-eighth of the world's population; on the other would be a vast, disconnected and disintegrated wasteland that is home to seven out of every eight inhabitants on Earth' (Petrella 1992). This excluded seven-eighths is the Achilles' heel of global capitalism. Perhaps Bosnia and Somalia are the precursors of what the future has in store for us.[4]

This stark, admittedly dualistic, view runs counter to both the playful ironics of post-modern philosophies and neo-Marxist insistence that capitalism and, perforce, exploitation are now found everywhere, that there are no excluded parts of the global economy. But against these views I would maintain that the drama of exclusion is both real and brutal, and that the ubiquitous capitalist economy is present only in an abstract, formal sense. With some amendments, the world map is, in fact, the way Petrella has drawn it: a core space articulated by a small number of regional control centres and a fragmented marginalized periphery. If Bosnia and Somalia represent the ultimate collapse of social order and thus extreme instances of the consequences of exclusion, with all their horror and war-lords and crimes against humanity, Brazil with its 1,000 per cent inflation and Peru's civil war with drug-lords and Shining Path guerrillas are perhaps closer to home: they are part of our very own West.

São Paulo and the affluent metropolitan classes of Brazil do not require the country's disempowered poor as either producers or consumers. In that sense, I would argue, more than 50 per cent of Brazil's population is economically irrelevant and, at worst, constitutes a drain on the economy (welfare, police, prisons). Still, civil order is being preserved in Brazil. This is not Peru's story, however. Lacking a São Paulo, that country of 22 million has been excluded wholesale from the global space of accumulation and, at the time of writing, appears to be heading down the road of Somalia or Kampuchea.

The fragmented periphery – only nominally integrated with the space of accumulation – is of course the source of large-scale labour migrations to the powerful control centres of the world economy: West Africans in Paris; *Volksdeutsche*, Poles, and Turks in Berlin, Frankfurt, Düsseldorf, and Munich; Pakistanis, West Africans, and Jamaicans in London; Puerto Ricans in New York; Haitians, Cubans, and Central Americans in Miami; Mexicans, Salvadoreans, Filipinos, Armenians, Thais, and Vietnamese in Los Angeles. In Brazil, immigrants to São Paulo have come from the national periphery, and this is true for Mexico City as well. Tokyo's story is different. Here the national government severely restricts immigration and has opted instead for a massive capital export strategy, directed initially at Korea, then shifting its focus to South-east Asian core regions, and now hoping to crack open the doors to China and Siberia. With this strategy Tokyo seeks primarily offshore, low-cost production sites and potential markets for Japanese companies, as well as access to raw materials. But, intended or not, helping to raise income at strategic locations on the Pacific Rim will also, one suspects, contribute to reducing pressures for out-migration that would have Tokyo and Osaka as its targets. Essentially the Japanese government is pursuing an implicit 1960s growth-pole policy on an international scale (Friedmann 1966). Even so, Saskia Sassen paints a dramatic picture of Tokyo's invisible foreign workers in an early morning shape-up in one of Tokyo's seedier inner-city wards (Sassen 1992: 297–9). Tokyo needs cheap workers ready to take on dirty, unpleasant jobs that most Japanese are no longer prepared to accept. What is now only a trickle of immigrants may some day turn into an unstoppable river. But it has not happened yet.

So I do not think that we can focus only on the global cities and the space of global accumulation that they articulate. We must understand global cities in relation to their respective peripheries, to both their external and internal proletariat. This stretches our research agenda wide, perhaps too wide. It opens up questions of international labour flows and investment, a study pioneered within the world city paradigm by Saskia Sassen (1988). It leads us to look at the range of activities lumped together under the generic heading of informal economy (Portes et al. 1989). It encourages micro-studies of immigrant populations and the remittances they send home. It asks questions about alternatives to the global model of growth unlimited for one-third to a half of the world's population (Friedmann 1992). And it raises questions about the possible limits to growth, not only in the ecological sense so popular today, but also in a political sense. If the global periphery becomes destabilized, or if migrant labourers arrive at the core in numbers that cannot be assimilated, the whole project of capitalism is put in jeopardy.

American troops can scarcely police the whole world – from Panama to Iraq, from Somalia to Bosnia – even with the acquiescence of the United Nations. Making the world safe for capital is a quixotic undertaking.

Concluding comments

Having reviewed where we stand in our research I conclude that the emerging world city paradigm has not only been productive of interesting research hypotheses but is sufficiently robust to guide our efforts in the years ahead. Our work has only just begun.

I use the term 'paradigm' advisedly. What I still called 'hypothesis' in 1986 has been fleshed out into a solid research paradigm which allows us to explore in a number of different directions. As an explicitly spatial framework it requires bifocal vision: one eye directed at the dynamic capitalist system at the core – the space of global accumulation and its articulations – and the other at the fragmented periphery of the excluded. The two must be brought together into a stereoscopic view. Or, to use another metaphor, they must be read as parts of the same story; their separate narratives hang together.

The beauty of the world city paradigm is its ability to synthesize what would otherwise be disparate and diverging researches – into labour markets, information technology, international migration, cultural studies, city building processes, industrial location, social class formation, massive disempowerment, and urban politics – into a single meta-narrative. It is said that meta-narratives are no longer fashionable (just as dualisms are considered *passé*). But surely that is only because the meta-narrative of capital remains largely invisible. *Without a counter-narrative to place into high relief, it is as if it did not exist.* The world city paradigm not only allows us to make portions of the meta-narrative of capital visible but also provides us with a basis for a critical perspective.

It allows us, for instance, to question the general validity of economic growth theory which is the foundation of development ideology. From our bifocal perspective economic growth theory is best understood as a partial, rather than a general, theory concerned with accumulation processes in the core locations of the global system. Its focus is exclusively the life situation of one-third of humanity. This failure to consider the excluded two-thirds as part of the same story gives rise to such lame and misdirected research as the World Bank's recent discussion paper: *How Adjustment Programs Can Help the Poor* (Ribe 1990). Applied research like this is not just a result of unifocal vision, but of a failure to grasp the social dynamics of an economic system that is unable to hold out the promise of a better life to the vast majority of the world's population. I have called the dualism of the excluded the Achilles' heel of capitalism. If we continue to ignore it it will bring us face to face with unimaginable grief.

NOTES

1 For an early formulation of this thesis see Barnet and Müller 1974.
2 Düsseldorf is one of several important urban centres in or adjacent to the Ruhr region, which also includes Essen and Dortmund, within a conurbation of about eight million people. In a sense the whole of the Rhein–Ruhr region may be regarded as a potential world city (Kunzmann and Wegener 1991; van der Cammen 1988).
3 Others might simply wish to include the whole of Randstad – the major Dutch conurbation – as a world city region, equivalent to Paris, London, Los Angeles, and so forth (Kunzmann and Wegener 1991; van der Cammen 1988).
4 Petrella's counting is rhetorical. His image of an archipelago of technopoles, although powerful, is misleading. If we were to rephrase his argument in terms of the world city paradigm, we would argue that a much larger fraction than one-eighth – perhaps one-third to one-half – is significantly part of the economy which conventionally we call global, with the remaining populations effectively excluded from participation and reproducing their low levels of living with few possibilities for escape into the promised land of cumulative growth (Friedmann 1992: 18–21). World cities articulate large regions of the world economy into the global system. Instead of an archipelago of city regions (technopoles), we have a chunkier, more inclusive, understanding of the world economy. But Petrella is nevertheless on the mark. A very large percentage of the world's population – possibly the majority – fails to participate in industrial capitalism and the growth impulses the system generates.

REFERENCES

Amin, Ash and Thrift, Nigel. 1992. 'Neo-Marshallian nodes in global networks', *International Journal of Urban and Regional Research*, 16(4): 571–87.

Banham, Rayner. 1974. *Los Angeles: The Architecture of Four Ecologies*. Harmondsworth: Pelican.

Barnet, R. J. and Müller, R. E. 1974. *Global Reach: The Power of Multinational Corporations*. New York: Simon and Schuster.

Castells, Manuel. 1983. *The City and the Grassroots*. Berkeley: University of California Press.

1989. *The Informational City: Information Technology, Economic Restructuring and the Urban–Regional Process*. Oxford: Basil Blackwell.

Chase-Dunn, Christopher. 1985. 'The system of world cities, AD 800–1975'. *Urbanization in the World-Economy*, ed. Michael Timberlake, pp. 269–92. New York: Academic Press.

Chung-Tong Wu. 1993. 'Hyper-growth and hyper-urbanization in southern China'. Unpublished draft.

Cohen, R. B. 1981. 'The new international division of labour, multi-national corporations and urban hierarchy'. In *Urbanization and Urban Planning in Capitalist Society*, ed. Michael Dear and Allen J. Scott, pp. 287–315. New York: Methuen.

Friedmann, John. 1966. *Regional Development Policy: A Case Study of Venezuela*. Cambridge MA: MIT Press.

 1986. 'The world city hypothesis'. *Development and Change*, 17(1): 69–84. (Reproduced as appendix in this volume.)

 1988. *Life Space and Economic Space. Essays in Third World Planning*. New Brunswick NJ: Transaction Books.

 1991. 'On the relations between economic, social, and physical planning in new urban zones: some lessons of experience and guidelines for practice'. University of California, Los Angeles: Architecture and Urban Planning: 9104.

 1992. *Empowerment: The Politics of Alternative Development*. Oxford: Basil Blackwell.

Friedmann, John and Wolff, Goetz. 1982. 'World city formation. An agenda for research and action'. *International Journal of Urban and Regional Research*, 6(3): 309–44.

Fröbel, F., Heinrichs, J., and Kreye, O. 1980. *The New International Division of Labour: Structural Unemployment in Industrialized Countries and Industrialization in Developing Countries*. Cambridge: Cambridge University Press.

Government of Singapore. 1991. *The Next Lap*. Singapore: Times Editions Ptd. Ltd.

Heskin, Allan David. 1991. *The Struggle for Community*. Boulder CO: Westview Press.

Keil, Roger and Lieser, Peter. 1992. 'Frankfurt: global city – local politics'. In *After Modernism: Global Restructuring and the Changing Boundaries of City Life*, ed. Michael Peter Smith, pp. 36–69. New Brunswick NJ: Transaction Publishers.

King, Anthony D. 1990. *Global Cities: Post-Imperialism and the Internationalization of London*. London: Routledge and Kegan Paul.

Kunzmann, Klaus R. and Wegener, Michael. 1991. *The Pattern of Urbanization in Western Europe 1960–1990*. University of Dortmund, Institut für Raumplanung, Berichte no. 18.

Lipietz, Alain. 1989. *Mirages and Miracles: The Crises of Global Fordism*. London: Verso.

Lovering, John. 1990. 'Fordism's unknown successor: a comment on Scott's theory of flexible accumulation and the re-emergence of regional economics'. *International Journal of Urban and Regional Research*, 14(1): 159–74.

Machimura, Takashi. 1992. 'The urban restructuring process in Tokyo in the 1980s: transforming Tokyo into a world city'. *International Journal of Urban and Regional Research*, 16(1): 114–28.

Mollenkopf, John H. and Castells, Manuel (eds.). 1991. *Dual City: Restructuring New York*. New York: Russel Sage Foundation.

Moran, M. 1991. *The Politics of the Financial Service Revolution*. London: Macmillan.

Parsonage, James. 1992. 'Southeast Asia's "growth triangle". A subregional response to global transformation'. *International Journal of Urban and Regional Research*, 16(2): 307–17.

Petrella, Riccardo. 1992. 'Techno-apartheid for a global underclass'. *Los Angeles Times*, Metro-section, 6 August 1992.

Piore, Michael and Sabel, Charles F. 1984. *The Second Industrial Divide: Possibilities for Prosperity*. New York: Basic Books.

Portes, Alejandro, Castells, Manuel, and Benton, Laura (eds.). 1989. *The Informal Economy: Studies in Advanced and Less Developed Countries*. Baltimore: Johns Hopkins University Press.

Ribe, Helena. 1990. *How Adjustment Programs Can Help the Poor: The World Bank's Experience*. World Bank Discussion Paper 71. Washington DC: World Bank.

Rimmer, Peter J. 1986. 'Japan's world cities: Tokyo, Osaka, Nagoya, or Tokaido megalopolis?' *Development and Change*, 17(1): 121–58.

Sandercock, Leonie. 1992. 'Community and other myths'. *Editions: Australian and International Books and Ideas*, 14 (Melbourne University).

Sassen, Saskia. 1988. *The Mobility of Labor and Capital: A Study in International Investment and Labor Flows*. Cambridge: Cambridge University Press.

   1991. *The Global City: New York, London, Tokyo*. Princeton NJ: Princeton University Press.

Sayer, Andrew. 1989. 'Postfordism in question'. *International Journal of Urban and Regional Research*, 13: 666–95.

Sklair, Leslie. 1991. *Sociology of the Global System: Social Change in Global Perspective*. Baltimore: Johns Hopkins University Press.

Smith, Michael Peter. 1992. *After Modernism: Global Restructuring and the Changing Boundaries of City Life*. New Brunswick NJ: Transaction Publishers.

Soja, Edward W. 1989. *Postmodern Geographies: The Reassertion of Space in Critical Social Theory*. London: Verso.

   1992. 'The stimulus of a little confusion: a contemporary comparison of Amsterdam and Los Angeles'. In *After Modernism: Global Restructuring and the Changing Boundaries of City Life*, ed. Michael Peter Smith, pp. 17–38. New Brunswick NJ: Transaction Publishers.

Storper, M. and Walker, R. 1989. *The Capitalist Imperative*. Oxford: Basil Blackwell.

Sudjik, Deyan. 1992. *The 100 Mile City*. London: André Deutsch.

Thrift, Nigel and Leyshon, A. L. *Making Money: The City of London and Social Power in Britain*. London: Routledge and Kegan Paul (forthcoming).

van der Cammen, Hans (ed.). 1988. *Four Metropolises in Western Europe: Development and Urban Planning in London, Paris, Randstad Holland, and the Ruhr Region*. Assen/Maastracht: Van Gorcum.

Wallerstein, Immanuel. 1974. *The Modern World System 1: Capitalist Agriculture and the Origins of the European World Economy in the Sixteenth Century*. New York: Academic Press.

Zukin, Sharon and associates. 1992. 'The bubbling cauldron: global and local interactions in New York City restaurants'. In *After Modernism: Global Restructuring and the Changing Boundaries of City Life*, ed. Michael Peter Smith, pp. 105–32. New Brunswick NJ: Transaction Publishers.

3   World cities and territorial states: the rise and fall of their mutuality

Peter J. Taylor

The studies that have been stimulated by John Friedmann's world cities hypothesis have been largely contemporary in nature, the chief exception being Anthony King's (1990) work on London as an imperial city. This general concern for the present is no accident and represents the derivation of the original study from Friedmann's initiative in linking urban hierarchies to the 'new international division of labour' (Fröbel et al. 1980). Studies of the latter argued that the world economy was entering a new era with the relocation of industrial production to the Third World, with world cities acting as the basing points of capital in this new globalized organization of production. However, the basic assumption of a social discontinuity between the present and what has gone before is in contradiction with the overall framework that world-systems analysis is sometimes thought to provide for world city studies. For this theoretical schema the emphasis is on a basic structural continuity in a single capitalist world-economy that can be traced back to around 1500 (Wallerstein 1983). Here I will approach the study of world cities from an explicitly world-systems perspective, which means, minimally, setting contemporary world cities into their *longue durée* context. If there are any benefits to be gained from this exercise it is likely that they will be two-way: as well as extending concern for world cities beyond their contemporary existence we will be focusing on the role of cities in the world-economy, a topic relatively neglected in world-systems analysis (the work of Fernand Braudel (1984) is a major exception).

Braudel identified 'world cities' in his influential work on early modern social change in Europe. These are single cities that dominate the world economy in which they operate. His sequence of such cities – Venice, Antwerp, Genoa, Amsterdam – is continued in the capitalist world economy as the economic centres of hegemonic states (what Lee and Pelizzon (1991) call hegemonic cities): Amsterdam in seventeenth-century Netherlands, London in nineteenth-century Britain, and New York in twentieth-century United States (see also Arrighi 1990). Notice the overlap, with Amsterdam appearing as both world city in its own right and as hegemonic city within a hegemonic state. It is the question of the relationship between Braudel's world city and territorial states that I take as my starting point. In terms of articulating space the former creates a functional pattern of points and flows whereas the latter defines a compartmentalized space, a political mosaic. Since both forms of spatial organization have existed concurrently throughout the era of the capitalist world economy we may assume that they have operated for their general mutual benefit.

What is this mutual benefit? At the most basic level it resides in the accumulation of capital as a taxable resource for the state in return for the provision of basic physical security for the city and its capitalists. To be sure, the questions of taxes and security are perennially contested political issues, but in the capitalist world-economy success for both city and state has involved achieving a favourable balance between extraction and protection so that accumulation can proceed in conditions of relatively predictable stability. All this is premised on a territorialization of political life, the world political map as a mosaic of defensible spaces. But this premise was by no means self-evident at the beginning of the capitalist world-economy when states saw cities as potential political rivals and cities viewed states as rapacious destroyers of capital (Pullan 1985). This is what Charles Tilly (1990) refers to as 'states versus cities' – certainly the mutuality we referred to above had to be created. This chapter is organized around the changing nature of territoriality in the modern world-system. I identify three phases – necessity, nationalization, and demise – that provide the framework for the location of world cities in a *longue durée* context.

Phase one: the necessity for territoriality

The political structure that the modern world-system inherited from medieval Europe was a very complex one. As well as political institutions with 'universal' pretensions (the Papacy and Holy Roman Empire), there was a jumble of hierarchical and areal political patterns including 'medium-sized' kingdoms (Portugal, England, France) and a wide range of small polities including duchies, bishoprics, lands of crusading knights, and city states. It is the kingdoms and the city states that are of particular interest here. The former become the vehicles for the creation of our modern territoriality, with their centralization strategies in the sixteenth century producing a 'power container', as Giddens (1985) so aptly terms the modern state. Of course, such a development threatened the political survival of all other polities above and below the container.

The city state is no exception to this political pressure, but in its incorporation into a larger entity it fundamentally transformed the nature of the emerging territorial state. This is the story of how the city/state mutality was constructed.

The model city state consisted of a single city within a wide trade network through which it accumulated wealth and used part of it to subdue the surrounding rural area. The latter becomes the 'garden' of the city, totally dependent on it economically as market and politically controlled by it (Burke 1986). At the peak of European medieval civilization in 1200 there were between 200 and 300 autonomous city states in central and northern Italy. In addition there were other cities with various degrees of autonomy, imperial and free cities in Germany, and similar relations between city and overlord elsewhere in a bewildering complexity. The most important cities formed the 'central economic spine' of Europe from northern Italy to the Low Countries. There existed, in Braudel's phrase, a 'bipolarity of capital accumulation' with competing northern and southern nodes of dense city networks. These two nodes had contrasting experiences with respect to the new centralizing states, a fact which was to determine the geoeconomic and geopolitical balance in Europe for centuries to come.

Dynastic states with their potential and actual scattering of lands, both governed and claimed, were transmuted, in varying degrees, in the sixteenth century into relatively contiguous and compact lands as territorial states (Luard 1986). These new territorial states embarked on the process of political centralization, putting all other polities under threat. Their key advantage would seem to be the ability to mobilize for war on a new scale (Mackenney 1989: 9). The first clear indication of this advantage came in the Italian wars of the 1490s when first France and then Spain were able to remove the Italian city states as major political actors from the European stage. George Modelski (1987) sees this as marking the beginning of our modern political world. The medieval city states had consolidated into just a few major city polities by the late fifteenth century but even these were no match for the power of the new territorial states. For instance the most powerful Italian state, the city empire of Venice, while managing to retain its independence was eclipsed as a major power in the new European politics that was emerging. Traditional Italian political rivalries between cities had become incorporated into a new European political rivalry based upon territorial states. This did not lead to the end of the southern node of capital accumulation of course (indeed, Genoa became one of Braudel's world cities towards the end of the sixteenth century). Rather, it fundamentally changed the political economy of the city network. Cities became politically dependent despite their continuing economic success in accumulating capital. Such dependence could be disastrous even for a world city. Genoa, under the protection of the Spanish Habsburgs, became the great banking centre of Europe – Braudel refers to its 'discreet rule over Europe' – but was brought down by the bankruptcies of its political patron in the 1620s, caused by a war that had nothing directly to do with Genoa. The lesson is clear in hindsight: allowing the future of capital to be politically dependent on war-lords is no framework for a sustained accumulation of capital.

The war that finally ended Genoa's status as world city was the Spanish attempt to quell the rebellion of its outlier in the Low Countries, the Habsburg Burgundian inheritance. In this northern node of capital accumulation the rise of territorial states was to produce a very different outcome. Habsburg policies of centralization in the 1560s precipitated the Netherlands rebellion that would ultimately create an independent state. This was a remarkable achievement; the rebels of this city-rich land were able to defeat the most powerful state in Europe. But not all of the Netherlands was freed from the Spanish crown; only the seven provinces centred upon Holland eventually consolidated their independence. This did not include the world city of Antwerp, which joined the rebellion in its early stages but was recaptured on two traumatic occasions by the Spanish army (Parker 1977). In 1576 the 'Spanish fury' saw the sacking of the city in an eight-day orgy of violence and destruction in which some 8,000 citizens were killed. The final fall of the city in 1585 was much less violent but the tribute paid to the victorious army totally crippled the economy. This political war economy was an alternative to Genoa's dependence political economy and was clearly a much worse framework: Genoa may not have controlled its destiny but this was infinitely better than being losers in a war zone.

The problem for capital in the sixteenth century was becoming quite straightforward. The rise of territorial states as a new scale of war machine was putting enhanced demands on cities and their capital that seemed likely eventually to bankrupt the whole system. Rather than mutuality between state and city, states seemed bent on destroying cities either physically or economically. This became all too true in the first half of the seventeenth century in the devastation of Germany in the Thirty Years War (Mackenney 1989: 12–13). If capital was to have security and stability for expansion a new political economy would have to be constructed. This was the achievement of the independent Netherlands republic in the seventeenth century.

With the second fall of Antwerp the major capitalists and their capital fled the city before the army entered. With two débâcles in less than a decade it was clear that major capital would not return to this vulnerable location – the final end of Antwerp as world city – but where it would relocate was by no means clear initially. At first the diaspora was scattered. Some moved to Italy, but it was not suitable since the core of economic activities was now firmly established in northern Europe. Some moved to other northern cities, notably Hamburg. For a short while this was perhaps the favourite to take over Antwerp's mantle. In the event it was Amsterdam that became the new world city. Within a decade of 1585 it was being portrayed as the 'new Antwerp'. Why? What did Amsterdam have that Hamburg did not? The answer is simple: a territorial state, a defensive shell for the accumulation of capital (Israel 1989: 36). The new United Provinces created a zone of peace in the first half of the seventeenth century that was unique in Europe: Mackenney (1989: 31) describes the new state as 'a crucial imaginative leap in overcoming the problems of scale' that were facing cities (see also Taylor 1994a: 29–31). While the Thirty Years War was destroying Germany and other countries were facing civil wars and rebellions, Dutch cities were expanding their economy behind their fortified frontier in an oasis of peace. This was the Dutch 'golden age' while the rest of Europe suffered its famous seventeenth-century 'crisis'. This 'great exception' of its time had created a new political economy that was to be of world-historical importance.

The nature of the Dutch state and the role of the world city of Amsterdam have been the subject of two important debates (Taylor 1994a). First, there have been those who have expressed doubt as to whether the United Provinces constituted a state at all (Braudel 1984; Wilson 1958) because of the degree of its political decentralization. As a product of a revolt against state centralization it is hardly surprising that the independent Netherlands were a very decentralized polity. By their victory they bucked the political tendency towards centralization and this was part of the reason for their success. They did not have the burden of the upkeep of the absolutist state and its war machine that others had to carry. But this did not make the new state an inferior instrument of security. Quite the opposite: security was costed as a necessity to be paid for but no more. The efficacy of this arrangement is to be seen in the result, the defeat of the largest state, the greatest war-machine of the era, Habsburg Spain. The degree of statehood of the United Provinces can only be doubted via a narrow definition of state that over-emphasizes the outward appearance of power rather than its actual application.

Second, given that the United Provinces was a state, what sort of state was it? The answer to this question has generated two entrenched sides.

For some the new state was the last of a series of dominant city states, Amsterdam's city state (Aymard 1982; Barbour 1963; Braudel 1984). They point to Amsterdam's dominance in size and wealth within the new state. Braudel is sometimes ambiguous on this point and hints that the Netherlands may be the first 'national state'. In fact he seems finally to come to the conclusion that the Netherlands/Amsterdam situation represented a half-way case between a city-dominated world-economy and one dominated by nation states. We would go further. Following Israel (1989), Rowen (1986), and Burke (1986) we interpret the United Provinces as much more than Amsterdam's city state. They point to the decentralized decision-making where on several key occasions Amsterdam was in the minority. In a real city state the city can hardly be outvoted! Furthermore, Amsterdam was not even the seat of government. In this polity based upon balancing interests The Hague was chosen as the capital of both the province of Holland and the United Provinces precisely because it posed no threat to other cities. This was definitely not Amsterdam's city state; rather we have a new territorial state joining Europe's inter-state system, but a very distinctive one. It was a merchant's state, its foreign policy was motivated by economic interests. Its political debates were not concerned with the glories of war to enhance the status of the sovereign; war was seen as a practical policy option to further economic ends. The result was the creation of a rival *raison d'état* to counter the dominant thinking behind states as war-machines. The state could be what we would today call an economic growth machine. A new political economy was forged linking the old economic imperatives previously found in city states with a security/war potential only found in the new territorial states. The result was the era of mercantilism where economic concerns were added to military ones in foreign policy. With mercantilism we move beyond the state as war-machine and can see recognizably 'modern' states operating beyond an extractive political economy. The Dutch as hegemon were the quintessential modern state of their age and all others who aspired to success emulated the new *raison d'état* to varying degrees in their new mercantilist policies.

Because of the disastrous experience of the world cities of Antwerp and Genoa we designate phase one in terms of the necessity of a political territoriality for capital expansion. With an appropriate new political economy imperative, territorial states could become platforms for capital expansion by combining security with opportunity (Gottmann 1973). The United Provinces as hegemonic state was the instrument for creating this outcome.

Phase two: the nationalization of territoriality

The legacy of mercantilism was to define a spatial congruence of polity and economy within the state's territory. This arrangement was transformed and deepened by the two great revolutions of the late eighteenth century: Britain's industrial revolution and France's great political revolution. The economic transformation relocated the locus of production from rural to urban areas and set in train the great industrial urbanization of the nineteenth century. A new class of world city was created, the great industrial metropolis (Manchester, England was the first of this kind). But the industrial revolution also transformed the state by building upon the pre-existing mercantilist link to economic practices and policies. Any state that wished to compete in the inter-state system had to industrialize in order to be a viable war-machine. At the same time the French-led political transformation further strengthened the territorial state by adding a cultural dimension to the power matrix: the 'people' as 'nation' enter the political stage (Billington 1980). A new spatial congruence was created linking territorial state to national economy and national homeland. This congruence has so dominated our collective imagination in the last two centuries – witness the interchangeable use of the terms 'state' and 'nation' – that 'nation-states' have come to be seen as 'natural' divisions of humanity (Taylor 1994b). And herein lies the great irony for cities. Just as production was becoming urbanized to give them greater relative economic power, they were losing any remaining political autonomy through the cultural centralization known as nationalization.

The territorial states that descended from dynastic states were by no means homogeneous culturally. For some of these states producing a 'nation' was a slowly evolving process but with the French Revolution the ideal of nationalization of territoriality was diffused across Europe. From this time onwards the idea of society was deemed to have increased in scale. The residents of states came to be converted from subjects into 'citizens', with the term redefined to mean the 'nationals' of states rather than residents of cities. This signified a reconceptualization of community as if existing at the state scale: national movements have been able to convert the residents of whole countries into what Benedict Anderson (1983) has famously called 'imaginary communities'. The physical communities of cities based upon direct contacts have been superseded by national 'communities' that can only exist in our imaginations. Using such cultural tools as language and religion plus a generous helping of invented traditions, nationalist politicians have been able to transfer basic loyalty and attachment to place from localities at the city scale to the territorial state as nation-state. From this point on there is no ambiguity in the political relationship between city and state: the state rules and commands personal 'citizen' identity, the city has minimal political power with its 'citizens' having first loyalty to state not city.

With the nation embedded in the collective consciousness, the idea of city versus state was largely eliminated in the nineteenth century world-system, allowing for the full flowering of state–city mutuality. With the state's role as economic growth machine encompassing industrialization as the universal route to development, its policies were compatible with the economic needs of rapidly growing cities. Hence, as well as the rise of nationalism contemporaries saw the nineteenth century as a unique era of great cities (Weber 1989). What was created was a mutuality combining the economic power of new cities, now as production points as well as basing points for capital, with the new political power of the states. But this was always a very unequal partnership.

Stripped of their political power great cities became creatures of the state. Purely industrial cities were soon eclipsed by capital cities, condemned to be mere reflections of their states. There had been what Lawton (1989: 2) terms 'the world urban system of the capitals of . . . states' since the establishment of territorial states in the sixteenth century, but now with the rise of the nation-state and associated expansion of state functions, this category of city came to dominate. In late nineteenth-century Britain, for instance, London reasserted its metropolitan predominance by converting into a great imperial city, relegating the original industrial metropolis, Manchester, to relative political obscurity. In general, as the nineteenth century progressed the importance of a world city was measured by the power of its state: witness the rapid rise in importance of Berlin when converted from capital of Prussia to capital of the German Empire after 1871. To the degree that there was any world city hierarchy it was a political one that simply reflected the state hierarchy in Europe: (1) London, Berlin; (2) Paris, Vienna, St Peterburg; (3) Rome.

Phase three: the demise of territoriality

The great legacy of nationalization was the incredible congruent geography exhibited across social activities. The original war-machine and political power container was now an economic growth machine with social welfare implications, a cultural entity with individual identities tied to it as nation-state, and generally accepted as the scope of 'society' (Taylor 1994b). The creation of a power–economy–culture container was never watertight, of course, and earlier theorists, notably the Marxist debaters on monopoly capital and imperialism at the beginning of this century, propagated the existence of a world society of sorts. But all this came to an abrupt halt with the great victory of national consciousness over all else in 1914: the war-machine with its numerous appendages was stronger than ever. This compartmentalizing of space ensured that there was no world-wide city economic hierarchy. There were important national and imperial hierarchies to be sure, but the capital-integrated world and its concomitant world city hierarchy that we experience now were not in place. This had to await the beginnings of the demise of territoriality as we have known it.

Despite the continuing power of the nation-state in world mentalities, it no longer circumscribes our social reality as the world cities studies have illustrated and the world-systems analysis school has theorized. The key to this changing situation is a geographical paradox within American hegemony after 1945. The two basic hallmarks of the US hegemonic political strategy have been trans-state institutions and national self-determination. In the former the USA has promoted international political and economic institutions to aid in the smooth running of both the world economy and its inter-state system. We are truly living in an age of international organization which is undermining the viability and autonomy of states. But alongside this the USA has presided over a period unprecented in the quantity of state-creation: the membership of the inter-state system more than doubled between 1945 and 1970. This was due primarily to the dismantling of European empires, of course, but the process did not stop there. The promise of self-determination was the regional politicians' dream slogan for mobilizing against existing states. Almost all existing nation-states were found to be imperfect specimens of the ideal state–nation congruence by some of their citizens. The result was what many found to be a surprising new round of national separation movements affecting even the oldest of states in Europe itself. Even in the USA the 'melting pot' ideal was ended, with the country moving towards becoming a bilingual society. Hence we come to the geographical paradox of American hegemony: concurrent tendencies towards aggregating and disaggregating states.

All of this could be accommodated in the period of 'high hegemony' (1945–70) as a social evolutionary process building on what had gone before. There was a hegemonic state in place with New York as 'hegemonic city' overseeing the world's finances, just as Amsterdam and London had done before. The 'invasion' of the world by US 'multi-national corporations' could be seen as just the latest form that hegemonic capital had found to dominate the world-economy using technological advances to control its capital more directly than British portfolio international investments and Dutch charter companies of previous hegemonies. But with the demise of US hegemony – the symbolic date is 1971 when President Nixon floated the dollar – the geographical paradox became clearly expressed as a spatial bifurcation away from the scale of the individual state. The classic case can be found in the old core of the world-economy where Britain, France, and Spain faced political separatist challenges at the same time that they were moving towards more political integration in the European Community. Three sets of literature reflected this bifurcation. First, the 'demise of the state' argument found a whole series of key issues – environmental, defence, economic – that could not be addressed adequately by the politics of individual states (Taylor 1994b, 1994c). Second, there was the rediscovery of the global as the crucial arena of activity, as in the new international division of labour literature and world-systems analysis. This problematized the idea of 'society' at the state scale and led to the third concern, the rediscovery of the local as an arena that had not been completely 'nationalized' (Agnew 1987). At its worst this bifurcation of studies could lead to a self-defeating 'battle of geographical scales', but most researchers, while focusing on one or other scale, accepted the existence of what we might call the local–global nexus: we cannot understand one without the other. World cities studies are perhaps the most explicit recognition of this necessary nexus.

The world city hierarchy is an outcome of the trans-state processes set in train by US hegemony. After about 1970 trilateralism in political practices has been complemented by a trilogy of cities at the top of a global urban hierarchy. The parallel is quite close. In the political sphere the USA is still the major power, although no longer hegemonic: its politicians are unable to dominate Western Europe and Japan as in the recent past. As a world city New York is the most important although, again, it is no longer hegemonic: its markets are unable to dominate Tokyo and London as in the recent past. These three stand on top of a global network that transcends states. All states have become vulnerable to the world market to an unprecedented degree, so that the very notion of a national economy is being despatched to history. The political economy of the state – mercantilism and industrialization – that enabled the state to attain its modern social dominance is undermined.

In addition, the state is being undermined from below. Contemporary global restructuring does not only affect the state; the 'local' does not remain unscathed. In the reordering of the division of labour world cities inevitably become major forces of attraction for international migrants. States might continue to struggle to control immigration but it is cities not countries that are becoming the prime migration goal. And within the city new identities are being formed that further erode the nation-state. Cities are no longer melting pots. From the ideal of national self-determination comes cultural assertiveness expressed concretely as multiculturalism in the city. For instance, one study shows that immigrants and their children living in London think of themselves, not as 'English' with its ethnic overtones, or even 'British' with its state identification, but rather as 'Londoners' (Western 1992). For Mlinar (1992: 2) there is a general decline in the cultural exclusiveness of territories which he represents as a 'transition from identity as an island to identity as a crossroads'. In contemporary globalization territories can no longer preserve their distinctiveness behind political boundaries; rather, new identities, he argues, 'may be formed as a unique crossroad in the flow of people, goods and ideas'. Or in our terms: cities are replacing states in the construction of social identities. Hence, alongside the erosion of national economy we can glimpse the erosion of nation-state. The incredible spatial congruence that was simultaneously a power, economic, and cultural container is clearly unravelling.

We must not go too far in this deprivileging of the state in our analysis (Taylor 1993a). It retains its role as war-machine, as any cursory look at the daily news will show. For all the erosion of their functions, states are still lethal instruments. States remain as sovereign entities on the world scene, which means that theirs is the only legitimate coercion within their territories standing as the final guarantor of all fixed capital. Hence, states retain the security function that enabled them politically to dominate cities in the first place. But even here the 'demise of the state' literature discovers crucial erosion. With the coming of inter-continental ballistic missiles (ICBMs) all states lose their basic ability to defend their population (Herz 1976). The key point, however, is the limited utility of weapons of mass destruction which means that wars, and states as war-machines, have continued unabated throughout most of the world. In addition there is another important development that may directly impinge on the defence function that states provide. Since 1945 international respect of existing international boundaries has produced a mummified world political map. Decolonization overwhelmingly en-dorsed the old European-drawn colonial boundaries and turned them into state boundaries. In Europe the solidification of the post-war settlement was achieved at Helsinki in 1975, so that for the first time in the history of the world-economy no state formally claimed the territory of any other state in continental Europe. Even the post-1989 upheavals in Eastern Europe and the former USSR have not changed international boundaries but rather have converted former provincial boundaries into new state boundaries. Boundaries have never been so firmly set in our global politics, cemented by a myriad of international agreements that constitute our trans-state political regime. And there is the irony: the integrity of states is confirmed by this trans-state world which simultaneously undermines their functions. This was one of the lessons of global reaction to the Iraqi incorporation of Kuwait in 1990–1. And where were the aggressive neighbours ready to take advantage of the breakdown of the states of Liberia and Somalia in 1992? Political competition between states ain't what it used to be!

But if state territories are now guaranteed at the trans-state level this means effectively that the original security function of the territorial state is seriously eroded. Coercion may still be required internally but the problem of outside aggressors is lessening. However, city states were always able to deal with internal dissent, they only lost their political power to territorial states because of outside threats. Hence, we can say that objectively we are reaching a situation where city states can again prosper in the world-system. We have already seen this happening in the cases of Hong Kong and Singapore. The former is soon to be absorbed into a territorial state but the mutuality between China and Hong Kong already exists economically, the political link may destroy the mutuality. Singapore is perhaps the model for the future, organizing South-east Asia but without the military, economic, and social costs of being part of a dominant territorial state in the region. Which leads us to ask whether London as world city needs Britain, or New York as world city requires to be part of the large territorial state that is the USA. In a growing trans-state world the relationship between city and state can become problematical once again.

Conclusion: what legacy are we leaving?

One interpretation of the success of 'Thatcherism' in Britain is as a declaration of independence by the south of England, the community dependent on London as a world city (Taylor 1993c). Here the mutuality between world city and territorial state is only maintained because of the size of London and its dependent regions relative to the rest of the country: deindustrialization of the north is legitimized by democracy. As Tom Nairn (1981) has pointed out, in the twentieth century Britain has acted very much like a 'city-state' with economic policies dominated by a City–Treasury–Bank of England nexus. Such an ideal outcome from the perspective of a world city cannot be expected to be widely replicated in a trans-state era. What would a strong protectionist policy resulting from a popular revolt by industrial America do for New York's role as a world city? Would capital move to a still 'free' Tokyo market? The point I am making is simply that we can no longer assume a general mutuality of interests between state and city.

If we are to return to a 'states versus cities' situation such as obtained before the seventeenth century, we can speculate on the basic differences the return of an autonomous city politics may mean for our world. From a *longue durée* perspective the most intriguing potential for change comes in terms of the limits to economic growth: the earth is not large enough for capitalism as an ever-expanding system. But the modern state has evolved as an economic growth machine, and mainstream politicians of all states see their prime purpose as boosting their country's gross national product (GNP). The state is tied to 'development'. It is hard to imagine any 'national' politician winning office on a promise of no growth or even slow growth. But city politicians in select areas have done just that.

In the mini-boom of the mid- to late-1980s some prosperous localities were becoming conscious of the disadvantages of continuous economic growth on their quality of life. Concern for such 'over-development' was a sort of aggregate 'not in my back yard' response to the continuously dynamic, changing nature of capitalism. Now such anti-growth political movements were certainly not anti-capitalist in any general sense – capital accumulation would have to continue to support their good life – but it did not have to occur in their communities. Since capital accumulation cannot go on infinitely on our finite earth and states are growth machines, it follows that in these selfish affluent city-based movements we may be seeing the beginnings of the long-awaited challenge to capitalism as a system. Without growth there can be no capitalism, the world city hierarchy might just be the structure through which a sustainable non-capitalist development is created that protects the affluent at the expense of the rest (Taylor 1993b).

REFERENCES

Agnew, J. A. 1987. *Place and Politics*. London: Allen and Unwin.
Anderson, B. 1983. *Imagined Communities: Reflections on the Origin and Spread of Nationalism*. London and New York: Verso.
Arrighi, G. 1990. 'The three hegemonies of historical capitalism'. *Review*, 13: 365–408.
Aymard, M. 1982. 'Introduction'. In *Dutch Capitalism and World Capitalism*, ed. M. Aymard, pp. 1–17. Cambridge: Cambridge University Press.
Barbour, V. 1963. *Capitalism in Amsterdam in the 17th Century*. Ann Arbor: University of Michigan Press.
Billington, J. H. 1980. *Fire in the Minds of Men*. London: Temple Smith.
Braudel, F. 1984. *The Perspective of the World*. London: Collins.

Burke, P. 1986. 'The city-state'. In *States in History*, ed. J. Hall, pp. 137–53. Oxford: Basil Blackwell.

Fröbel, F., Heinrichs, J., and Kreye, O. 1980. *The New International Division of Labour: Structural Unemployment in Industrialized Countries and Industrialization in Developing Countries*. Cambridge: Cambridge University Press.

Giddens, A. 1985. *The Nation State and Violence*. Cambridge: Polity Press.

Gottmann, J. 1973. *The Significance of Territory*. Charlottesville, VA: University Press of Virginia.

Herz, J. A. 1976. *The Nation-state and the Crisis of World Politics*. New York: McKay.

Israel, J. I. 1989. *Dutch Primacy in World Trade, 1585–1740*. Oxford: Clarendon Press.

King, A. D. 1990. *Global Cities: Post-Imperialism and the Internationalization of London*. London: Routledge and Kegan Paul.

Lawton, R. 1989. 'Introduction'. In *The Rise and Fall of Great Cities*, ed. R. Lawton, pp. 1–19. London: Belhaven.

Lee, R. and Pelizzon, S. 1991. 'Hegemonic cities in the modern world-system'. In *Cities in the World-system*, ed. R. Kasaba, pp. 43–54. New York: Greenwood Press.

Luard, E. 1986. *War in International Society*. London: Tauris.

Mackenney, R. 1989. *The City-State, 1500–1700*. London: Macmillan.

Mlinar, Z. 1992. 'Introduction'. In *Globalization and Territorial Identities*, ed. Z. Mlinar, pp. 1–15. Aldershot: Avebury Press.

Modelski, G. 1987. *Long Cycles in World Politics*. London: Macmillan.

Nain, R. 1981. *The Break-up of Britain*. London: New Left Books.

Parker, G. 1977. *The Dutch Revolt*. Harmondsworth: Penguin Books.

Pullan, B. 1985. 'The role of the state and the town in the general crisis of the 1590s'. In *The European Crisis of the 1590s*, ed. P. Clark, pp. 285–300. London: Allen and Unwin.

Rowen, H. H. 1986. *John de Witt*. Cambridge: Cambridge University Press.

Sassen, Saskia. 1994. *Cities in a World Economy*. Thousand Oaks CA: Pine Forge/Sage.

Taylor, P. J. 1993a. 'States in world-systems analysis: massaging a creative tension'. In *Transcending the State–Global Divide*, ed. R. Palan and B. Gills, pp. 107–24. Boulder CO: Lynne Rienner Publishers.

1993b. 'The last of the hegemons: British impasse, American impasse, world impasse'. *Southeastern Geographer*, 33: 1–23.

1993c. 'The meaning of the North: England's "foreign country" within?' *Political Geography*, 12: 136–55.

1994a. 'Ten years that shook the world? The United Provinces as the first hegemonic state'. *Sociological Perspectives*, 37: 25–46.

1994b. 'The state as container: territoriality in the modern world-system'. *Progress in Human Geography*, 18: 151–62.

1995. 'Beyond containers: inter-nationality, inter-stateness, inter-territoriality'. *Progress in Human Geography*, 19: 1–14.

Tilly, Charles. 1990. *Coercion, Capital, and European States, AD 990–1990*. Oxford: Basil Blackwell.

Wallerstein, I. 1983. *Historical Capitalism*. London: Verso.

Weber, A. F. 1899. *The Growth of Cities in the Nineteenth Century*. New York: Cornell University Press.

Western, J. 1992. *A Passage to England*. Minneapolis MN: University of Minnesota Press.

Wilson, C. 1958. *Mercantilism*. London: Historical Society.

4   On concentration and centrality in the global city

Saskia Sassen

Place and production in the global economy

One of the central concerns in my work has been to look at cities as production sites for the leading service industries of our time, and hence to recover the infrastructure of activities, firms, and jobs that is necessary to run the advanced corporate economy. Specialized services are usually understood in terms of specialized outputs rather than the production process involved. A focus on the production process in service industries allows us (a) to capture some of the locational characteristics of these industries; and (b) to examine the proposition that there is a producer services complex which, while catering to corporations, has distinct locational and production characteristics. It is this producer services complex more so than headquarters of firms generally that benefits and often needs a city location.

We see this dynamic for agglomeration operating at different levels of the urban hierarchy, from the global to the regional. At the global level, a key dynamic explaining the place of major cities in the world economy is that they concentrate the infrastructure and the servicing that produce a capability for global control. The latter is essential if geographic dispersal of economic activity – whether factories, offices, or financial markets – is to take place under continued concentration of ownership and profit appropriation. This capability for global control cannot simply be subsumed under the structural aspects of the globalization of economic activity. It needs to be produced. It is insufficient to posit, or take for granted, the awesome power of large corporations.

By focusing on the production of this capability we add a neglected dimension to the familiar issue of the power of large corporations. The emphasis shifts to the *practice* of global control: the work of producing and reproducing the organization and management of a global production system and a global market-place for finance, both under conditions of economic concentration. Power is essential in the organization of the world economy, but so is production: including the production of those inputs that constitute the capability for global control and the infrastructure of jobs involved in this production. This allows us to focus on cities and on the urban social order associated with these activities.

Much analysis and general commentary on the global economy and the new growth sectors does not incorporate these multiple dimensions. Elsewhere I have argued that what we could think of as the dominant narrative or mainstream account of economic globalization is a *narrative of eviction* (Sassen 1993, 1994a). Key concepts in the dominant account – globalization, information economy, and telematics – all suggest that place no longer matters and that the only type of worker that matters is the highly educated professional. This account privileges the capability for global transmission over the concentrations of built infrastructure that make transmission possible; information outputs over the workers producing those outputs, from specialists to secretaries; and the new transnational corporate culture over the multiplicity of cultural environments, including reterritorialized immigrant cultures, within which many of the 'other' jobs of the global information economy take place. In brief, the dominant narrative concerns itself with the upper circuits of capital, not the lower ones, and with the global capacities of major economic actors, not the infrastructure of facilities and jobs underlying those capacities. This narrow focus has the effect of evicting from the account the *place*-boundedness of significant components of the global information economy.

The intersection of globalization and the shift to services

To understand the new or sharply expanded role of a particular kind of city in the world economy since the early 1980s, we need to focus on the intersection of two major processes. The first is the sharp growth in the globalization of economic activity; this has raised the scale and the complexity of transactions, thereby feeding the growth of top-level multinational headquarter functions and the growth of advanced corporate services. It is important to note that even though globalization raises the scale and complexity of these operations, they are also evident at smaller geographic scales and lower orders of complexity, as is the case with firms that operate regionally. Thus while regionally oriented firms need not negotiate the complexities of international borders and the regulations of different countries, they are still faced with a regionally dispersed network of operations that requires centralized control and servicing.

The second process we need to consider is the growing *service intensity* in the organization of all industries (Sassen 1991: 166–8). This has contributed to a massive growth in the demand for services by firms in all industries, from mining and manufacturing to finance and consumer services. Cities are key sites for the production of services for firms. Hence the increase in service intensity in the organization of all industries has had a significant growth effect on cities in the 1980s. It is important to recognize that this growth in services for firms is evident in cities at different levels of a nation's urban system. Some of these cities cater to regional or subnational markets; others cater to national markets, and yet others cater to global markets. In this context, globalization becomes a question of scale and added complexity.

The key process from the perspective of the urban economy is the growing demand for services by firms in all industries, and the fact that cities are preferred production sites for such services, whether at the global, national, or regional level. As a result we see in cities the formation of a new *urban economic core* of banking and service activities that comes to replace the older, typically manufacturing oriented, core.

In the case of cities that are major international business centres, the scale, power, and profit levels of this new core suggest that we are seeing the formation of a new urban economy. This is so in at least two regards. First, even though these cities have long been centres for business and finance, since the late 1970s there have been dramatic changes in the structure of the business and financial sectors, as well as sharp increases in the overall magnitude of these sectors and their weight in the urban economy. Second, the ascendance of the new finance and services complex, particularly international finance, engenders what may be regarded as a new economic regime, that is, although this sector may account for only a fraction of the economy of a city, it imposes itself on that larger economy. Most notably, the possibility for superprofits in finance has the effect of devalorizing manufacturing insofar as the latter cannot generate the superprofits typical in much financial activity.

This is not to say that everything in the economy of these cities has changed. On the contrary, they still show a great deal of continuity and many similarities with cities that are not global nodes. Rather, the implantation of global processes and markets has meant that the internationalized sector of the economy has expanded sharply and has imposed a new valorization dynamic: that is, a new set of criteria for valuing or pricing various economic activities and outcomes. This has had devastating effects on large sectors of the urban economy. High prices and profit levels in the internationalized sector and its ancillary activities, such as top-of-the-line restaurants and hotels, have made it increasingly difficult for other sectors to compete for space and investments. Many of these other sectors have experienced considerable downgrading and/or displacement, as, for example, neighbourhood shops tailored to local needs are replaced by upmarket boutiques and restaurants catering to new high-income urban élites.

Though at a different order of magnitude, these trends also became evident during the late 1980s in a number of major cities in the developing world that have become integrated into various world markets: São Paulo, Buenos Aires, Bangkok, Taipei, and Mexico City are only a few examples. Also, here the new urban core was fed by the deregulation of financial markets, ascendance of finance and specialized services, and integration into the world markets. The opening of stock markets to foreign investors and the privatization of what were once public sector firms have been crucial institutional arenas for this articulation. Given the vast size of some of these cities, the impact of this new core on the broader city is not always as evident as in central London or Frankfurt, but the transformation is still very real.

It is important to recognize that manufacturing remains a crucial sector in all these economies, even when it may have ceased to be a dominant sector in major cities. Indeed, several scholars have argued that the producer services sector could not exist without manufacturing (Cohen and Zysman 1987; Markusen and Gwiasda 1994). In this context it has been argued, for example, that the weakening of the manufacturing sector in the broader New York region is a threat to the city's status as a leading financial and producer services centre (Markusen and Gwiasda 1994). A key proposition for these and other authors is that producer services are dependent on a strong manufacturing sector in order to grow. There is considerable debate about this issue (Drennan 1992; Noyelle and Dutka 1988; Sassen 1991). Drennan (1992), a leading analyst of the producer services sector in New York City, argues that a strong finance and producer services sector is possible in New York notwithstanding decline in its industrial base, and that these sectors are so strongly integrated into the world markets that articulation with the larger region becomes secondary.

Sassen (1991), in a variant on both positions, argues that manufacturing indeed feeds the growth of the producer services sector, but that it does so whether located in the area in question, somewhere else in the country, or overseas. Even though manufacturing – and mining and agriculture, for that matter – feeds growth in the demand for producer services, their actual location is of secondary importance in the case of global-level service firms: thus whether manufacturing plants are located offshore or within a country may be quite irrelevant as long as it is part of a multinational corporation likely to buy the services from those top-level firms. Second, the territorial dispersal of plants, especially if international, actually raises the demand for producer services. This is yet another meaning, or consequence, of globalization: the growth of producer service firms headquartered in New York, London, or Paris can be fed by manufacturing located anywhere in the world, as long as it is part of a multinational corporate network. Third, a good part of the producer services sector is fed by financial and business transactions that either have nothing to do with manufacturing, as is the case in many of the global financial markets, or for which manufacturing is incidental, as in much merger and acquisition activity, which is centred on buying and selling firms rather than the buying of manufacturing firms as such.

Some of the data for New York and London, two cities which experienced heavy losses in manufacturing and sharp gains in producer services, illustrate this point. New York lost 34 per cent of its manufacturing jobs from 1969 to 1989 in a national economy that overall lost only 2 per cent of such jobs, and there was actually manufacturing growth in many areas. The British economy lost 32 per cent of its manufacturing jobs from 1971 to 1989, and the London region lost 47 per cent of such jobs (Buck, Drennan, and Newton 1992; Fainstein et al. 1993; Frost and Spence 1993). Yet both cities had sharp growth in producer services and raised their shares of such jobs in total city employment. Further, it is also worth noting the different conditions in each city's larger region: London's region had a 2 per cent decline compared to a 22 per cent job growth rate in the larger New York region. This divergence points to the fact that the finance and producer services complex in each city rests on a growth dynamic that is somewhat independent of the broader regional economy (a sharp change from the past, when a city was presumed to be deeply interdependent with its hinterland).

The formation of a new production complex

According to standard conceptions about information industries, the rapid growth and disproportionate concentration of producer services in central cities should not have happened. Because they are thoroughly embedded in the most advanced information technologies, producer services could be expected to have locational options that bypass the high costs and congestion typical of major cities. But cities offer agglomeration economies and highly innovative environments. The growing complexity, diversity, and specialization of the services required has contributed to the economic viability of a free-standing specialized service sector.

The production process in these services benefits from proximity to other specialized services. This is especially the case in the leading and most innovative sectors of these industries. Complexity and innovation often require multiple highly specialized inputs from several industries. The production of a financial instrument, for example, requires inputs from accounting, advertising, legal expertise, economic consulting, public relations, designers, and printers. The particular characteristics of production of these services, especially those involved in complex and innovative operations, explain their pronounced concentration in major cities. The commonly heard explanation that high-level professionals require face-to-face interactions, needs to be refined in several ways. Producer services, unlike other types of services, are not necessarily dependent on spatial proximity to the consumers, i.e. firms served. Rather, economies occur in such specialized firms when they locate close to others that produce key inputs or whose proximity makes possible joint production of certain service offerings. The accounting firm can service its clients at a distance, but the nature of its service depends on proximity to specialists, lawyers, and programmers. Moreover, concentration arises out of the needs and expectations of the people likely to be employed in these new high-skill jobs, who tend to be attracted to the amenities and lifestyles that large urban centres can offer. Frequently, what is thought of as face-to-face communication is actually a production process that requires multiple simultaneous inputs and feedbacks. At the current stage of technical development, immediate and simultaneous access to the pertinent experts is still the most effective way, especially when dealing with a highly complex product. The concentration of the most advanced telecommunications and computer network facilities in major cities is a key factor in what I refer to as the production process of these industries.[1]

Further, time replaces weight in these sectors as a force for agglomeration. In the past, the pressure of the weight of inputs from iron ore compared with unprocessed agricultural products was a major constraint pushing toward agglomeration in sites where the heaviest inputs were located. Today, the acceleration of economic transactions and the premium put on time have created new forces for agglomeration. Increasingly this is not the case in routine operations. But where time is of the essence, as it is today in many of the leading sectors of these industries, the benefits of agglomeration are still extremely high – to the point where it is not simply a cost advantage, but an indispensable arrangement.

This combination of constraints suggests that the agglomeration of producer services in major cities actually constitutes a production complex. This producer services complex is intimately connected to the world of corporate headquarters; they are often thought of as forming a joint headquarters–corporate services complex. But in my reading, we need to distinguish the two. Although it is true that headquarters still tend to be disproportionately concentrated in cities, over the last two decades many have moved out. Headquarters can indeed locate outside cities, but they need a producer services complex somewhere in order to buy or contract for the needed specialized services and financing. Further, headquarters of firms with very high overseas activity or in highly innovative and complex lines of business tend to locate in major cities. In brief, firms in more routinized lines of activity, with predominantly regional or national markets, appear to be increasingly free to move or install their headquarters outside cities. Firms in highly competitive and innovative lines of activity and/or with a strong world market orientation appear to benefit from being located at the centre of major international business centres, no matter how high the costs.

Both types of firms, however, need a corporate services complex to be located somewhere. Where this complex is located is probably increasingly unimportant from the perspective of many, though not all, headquarters. From the perspective of producer services firms, such a specialized complex is most likely to be in a city rather than, for example, a suburban office park. The latter will be the site for producer services firms but not for a services complex. And only such a complex is capable of handling the most advanced and complicated corporate demands.

Elsewhere (Sassen 1994), a somewhat detailed empirical examination of several cities served to explore different aspects of this trend towards concentration. Here there is space only for a few observations. The case of Miami, for instance, allows us to see, almost in laboratory-like fashion, how a new international corporate sector can become implanted in a site. It allows us to understand something about the dynamic of globalization in the current period and how it is embedded in place. Miami has emerged as a significant hemispheric site for global city functions, although it lacks a long history as an international banking and business centre as is typical of such global cities as New York or London.

The case of Toronto, a city whose financial district was built up only in recent years, allows us to see to what extent the pressure towards physical concentration is embedded in an economic dynamic rather than simply being the consequence of having inherited a built infrastructure from the past, as one would think was the case in older centres such as London or New York.[2] But Toronto also shows that it is certain industries in particular that are subject to the pressure towards spatial concentration, notably finance and its sister industries (Gad 1991).

The case of Sydney illuminates the interaction of a vast continental economic scale and pressures towards spatial concentration. Rather than strengthening the multipolarity of the Australian urban system, the developments of the 1980s – increased internationalization of the Australian economy, sharp increases in foreign investment, a strong shift towards finance, real estate, and producer services – contributed to a greater concentration of major economic activities and actors in Sydney. This included a reduction in such activities and actors in Melbourne, for a long time the centre of commercial activity and wealth in Australia (Daly and Stimson 1992).

Finally, the case of the leading financial centres in the world today is of continued interest, since one might have expected that the growing number of financial centres now integrated into the global market would have reduced the extent of concentration of financial activity in the top centres.[3] One would further expect this outcome given the immense increases in the global volume of transactions. Yet the levels of concentration remain unchanged in the face of massive transformations in the financial industry and in the technological infrastructure upon which this industry depends.[4]

For example, international bank lending grew from US $1.89 trillion in 1980 to US $6.24 trillion in 1991 – a fivefold increase in a mere ten years. Three cities (New York, London, and Tokyo) accounted for 42 per cent of all such international lending in 1980 and for 41 per cent in 1991, according to data from the Bank of International Settlements, the leading institution world-wide in charge of overseeing banking activity. There were compositional changes: Japan's share rose from 6.2 per cent to 15.1 per cent; the UK's share fell from 26.2 per cent to 16.3 per cent; while the US share remained constant. All increased in absolute terms. Beyond these three, Switzerland, France, Germany, and Luxembourg bring the total share of the top centres to 64 per cent in 1991, which is just about the same share these countries had in 1980. One city, Chicago, dominates the world's trading in futures, accounting for 60 per cent of worldwide contracts in options and futures in 1991.

The space economy of the centre

Today there is no longer a simple, straightforward relation between centrality and such geographic entities as the downtown, or the central business district. In the past, and up to quite recently in fact, the centre was synonymous with the downtown or the central business district. Today, the spatial correlate of the centre can assume several geographic forms. It can be the central business district, as it largely still is in New

York City, or it can extend into a metropolitan area in the form of a grid of nodes of intense business activity, as we see in Frankfurt (Keil and Ronneberg forthcoming).

Elsewhere (1991) I have argued that we are also seeing the formation of a transterritorial 'centre' constituted via digital highways and intense economic transactions; I argued then that New York, London, and Tokyo could be seen as constituting such a transterritorial terrain of centrality with regard to a specific complex of industries and activities. And at the limit we may see terrains of centrality that are disembodied, that lack any territorial correlate, that are in the electronically generated space we call cyberspace. Certain components of the financial industry, particularly the foreign currency markets, can be seen as operating partly in cyberspace.[5]

What is the urban form that accommodates this new economic core of activities? Three distinct patterns are emerging in major cities and their regions in the developed countries. First, in the 1980s there was a growing density of work-places in the traditional urban centre associated with growth in leading sectors and ancillary industries. This type of growth also took place in some of the most dynamic cities in developing countries, such as Bangkok, Taipei, São Paulo, Mexico City, and, toward the end of the decade, Buenos Aires. Second, alongside this central city growth came the formation of dense nodes of commercial development and business activity in a broader urban region, a pattern not evident in developing countries. These nodes assume different forms: suburban office complexes, *edge cities*, and *exopoles*. Though in peripheral areas, these nodes are completely connected to central locations via state-of-the-art electronic means. Thus far, these forms are only rarely evident in developing countries, where vast urban sprawl with a seemingly endless metropolitanization of the region around cities has been the norm. In developed countries, the revitalized urban centre and the new regional nodes together constitute the spatial base for cities at the top of transnational hierarchies. Third is the growing intensity in the local-ness or marginality of areas and sectors that operate outside that world market-oriented subsystem, and this includes an increase in poverty and disadvantage. This same general dynamic operates in cities with very diverse economic, political, social, and cultural arrangements.

A few questions spring to mind. One question here is whether the type of spatial organization characterized by dense strategic nodes spread over the broader region does or does not constitute a new form of organizing the territory of the 'centre', rather than, as in the more conventional view, an instance of suburbanization or geographic dispersal. Insofar as these various nodes are articulated through cyber-routes or digital highways they represent the new geographic correlate of the most advanced type of 'centre'. The places that fall outside this new grid of digital highways are peripheralized; one question here is whether it is so to a much higher degree than in earlier periods, when the suburban or non-central economic terrain was integrated into the centre because it was primarily geared *to* the centre.

Another question is whether this new terrain of centrality is differentiated. Basically, is the old central city, still the largest and densest of all the nodes, the most strategic and powerful node? Does it have a sort of gravitational power over the region that makes the new grid of nodes and digital highways cohere as a complex spatial agglomeration? From a larger transnational perspective these are vastly expanded central regions. This reconstitution of the centre is different from agglomeration patterns still prevalent in most cities that have not seen a massive expansion in their role as sites for global city functions and the new regime of accumulation thereby entailed. We are seeing a reorganization of space–time dimensions in the urban economy.

It is under these conditions that the traditional perimeter of the city, a kind of periphery, unfolds its full industrial and structural growth potential. Commercial and office space development lead to a distinct form of decentralized reconcentration of economic activity on the urban periphery. This geographic shift has much to do with the locational decisions of transnational and national firms that make the urban peripheries the growth centres of the most dynamic industries. It is distinctly not the same as largely residential suburbanization or metropolitanization.

We may be seeing a difference in the pattern of global city formation in parts of the United States and in parts of Western Europe (Keil and Ronneberg forthcoming; Sassen 1994). In the United States major cities such as New York and Chicago have large centres that have been rebuilt many times, given the brutal neglect suffered by much urban infrastructure and the imposed obsolescence so characteristic of US cities. This neglect and accelerated obsolescence produce vast spaces for rebuilding the centre according to the requirements of whatever regime of urban accumulation or pattern of spatial organization of the urban economy prevails at a given time.

In Europe urban centres are far more protected and they rarely contain significant stretches of abandoned space; the expansion of workplaces and the need for intelligent buildings necessarily will have to take place partly outside the old centres. One of the most extreme cases is the complex of La Defense, the massive, state-of-the-art office complex developed right outside Paris to avoid harming the built environment inside the city. This is an explicit instance of government policy and planning aimed at addressing the growing demand for central office space of prime quality. Yet another variant of this expansion of the 'centre' on to hitherto peripheral land can be seen in London's Docklands. Similar projects for recentralizing peripheral areas were launched in several major cities in Europe, North America, and Japan during the 1980s.

Conclusion: concentration and the redefinition of the centre

The central concern in this chapter has been to examine the fact of locational concentration of leading sectors in urban centres. This concentration has occurred in the face of the globalization of much economic activity, massive increases in the volume of international transactions, and revolutionary changes in technology that neutralize distance.

The specific issues discussed provide insights into the dynamics of contemporary globalization processes as they materialize in specific places. Concentration remains a critical dimension particularly in the leading sectors such as financial services. The production process in these industries is one reason for this, and the continuing concentration of the most advanced communications facilities in major cities is a second important reason. There are, however, a multiplicity of spatial correlates for this concentration, and in this sense we see emerging a new geography of the centre, one that can involve a metropolitan grid of nodes connected through advanced telematics. These are not suburbs in the way we conceived them twenty years ago, but a new form or space of centrality.

NOTES

1   The telecommunications infrastructure also contributes to concentration of leading sectors in major cities. Long-distance communications systems increasingly use fibre optic wires. These have several advantages over traditional copper wire: large carrying capacity, high speed, more security, and higher signal strength. Fibre systems tend to connect major communications hubs because they are not easily spliced and hence not suitable for connecting multiple lateral sites. Fibre systems tend to be installed along existing rights of way, whether rail, water, or highways (Moss 1986). The growing use of fibre optic systems thus tends to strengthen the major existing telecommunication concentrations and therefore the existing hierarchies.

2   In his study of the financial district in Manhattan, Longcore (1993) found that the use of advanced information and telecommunication technologies has a strong impact on the spatial organization of the district because of the added spatial requirements of 'intelligent' buildings (see also Moss 1991). A ring of new office buildings meeting these requirements was built over the last decade immediately around the old Wall Street core, where the narrow streets and lots made this difficult; furthermore, renovating old buildings in the Wall Street core is extremely expensive and often not possible. The occupants of the new buildings in the district were mostly corporate headquarters and the financial services industry. These firms tend to be extremely intensive users of telematics, and availability of the most advanced forms typically is a major factor in their real-estate and locational decisions. They need complete redundancy of telecommunications systems, high carrying capacity, often their own private branch exchange, etc. With this often goes a need for large spaces. For instance, the technical installation backing a firm's trading floor is likely to require additional space the size of the trading floor itself.

3   Furthermore, this unchanged level of concentration has happened at a time when financial services are more mobile than ever before: globalization, deregulation (an essential ingredient for globalization), and securitization have been the key to this mobility, in the context of massive advances in telecommunications and electronic networks. One result is growing competition among centres for hypermobile financial activity. In my view there has been an overemphasis on competition in general and in specialized accounts on this subject. As I have argued elsewhere (Sassen 1991: ch. 7), there is also a functional division of labour among various major financial centres. In that sense we can think of a transnational system with multiple locations.

4   Much of the discussion about the formation of a single European market and financial system has raised the possibility (and even the need if it is to be competitive) of centralizing financial functions and capital in a limited number of cities, rather than maintaining the current structure in which each country has its own financial centre.

5   This also tells us something about cyberspace – often read as a purely technological event and in that sense a space of innocence. The cyberspaces of finance are spaces where profits are produced and power is thereby constituted. Insofar as these technologies strengthen the profit-making capability of finance and make possible the hypermobility of finance capital, they also contribute to the often devastating impacts of the ascendance of finance on other industries, on particular sectors of the population, and on whole economies. Cyberspace, like any other space, can be inscribed in a multiplicity of ways: some benevolent or enlightening; others, not (see Sassen 1993).

REFERENCES

Buck, N., Drennan, M. P., and Newton, K. 1992. 'Dynamics of the metropolitan economy'. In *Divided Cities: New York and London in the Contemporary World*, ed. Susan Fainstein, Ian Gordon, and Michael Harloe. Cambridge MA: Basil Blackwell.

Cohen, Stephen S. and Zysman, John. 1987. *Manufacturing Matters: The Myth of the Post-Industrial Economy*. New York: Basic Books.

Daly, M. T. and Stimson, R. 1992. 'Sydney: Australia's gateway and financial capital'. In *New Cities of the Pacific Rim*, ed. E. Blakely and T. J. Stimpson, ch. 18. Berkeley: University of California, Institute for Urban and Regional Development.

Drennan, M. P. 1992. 'Gateway cities: the metropolitan sources of US producer service exports'. *Urban Studies*, 29(2): 217–35.

Fainstein, S., Gordon, I., and Harloe, M. (eds.). 1993. *Divided Cities: Economic Restructuring and Social Change in London and New York*. New York: Basil Blackwell.

Frost, M. and Spence, N. 1992. 'Global city characteristics and central London's employment,' *Urban Studies*, 30: 547–58.

Gad, Gunter. 1991. 'Toronto's financial district'. *Canadian Urban Landscapes* 1: 203–7.

Keil, Roger and Ronneberg Klaus (forthcoming). 'The city turned inside out: spatial strategies and local politics'. In *Financial Metropoles in Restructuring: Zurich and Frankfurt En Route to Postfordism*, ed. Hansruedi Hitz.

Longcore, T. R. 1993. 'Information technology and world city restructuring: the case of New York City's financial district'. Unpublished thesis, Department of Geography, University of Delaware.

Markusen, A. and Gwiasda, V. 1994. 'Multipolarity and the layering of functions in the world cities: New York City's struggle to stay on top'. Paper presented in Tokyo at the conference 'New York, Tokyo, and Paris', October 1991. *International Journal of Urban and Regional Research*, 22: 239–67.

Moss, M. 1986. 'Telecommunications and the future of cities'. *Land Development Studies*, 3: 33–44.

1991. 'New fibers of urban economic development'. *Portfolio: A Quarterly Review of Trade and Transportation*, 4(1): 11–18.

Noyelle, T. and Dutka, A. B. 1988. *International Trade in Business Services: Accounting, Advertising, Law and Management Consulting*. Cambridge MA: Ballinger Publishing.

Sassen, Saskia. 1991. *The Global City: New York, London, Tokyo*. Princeton NJ: Princeton University Press.

(co-curator) 1993. 'Trade routes'. Catalogue for an exhibition at the New Museum of Contemporary Art, New York City.

1994a. *Cities in a World Economy*. Thousand Oaks CA: Pine Forge/Sage.

1994b. 'Analytic borderlands: race, gender and nationality in the new city'. In *Re-presenting the City*, ed. A. King. London: Macmillan.

Part 2

Cities in systems

5 Cities in global matrices: toward mapping the world-system's city system

David A. Smith and Michael Timberlake

Last November in the Mississippi Delta, William White, an African-American tractor driver on the old Miley Plantation, harvested a few hundred acres of cotton. Several months later in the Los Angeles downtown garment district, a man's dress shirt was made from some of this same cotton. Rosa Gomez, an undocumented Guatemalan immigrant put the final stitches into the shirt, operating a state-of-the-art Japanese-produced sewing machine. Ms Gomez had recently arrived in Los Angeles, only one month after her family fled economic deprivation and political terror in the barrios of Guatemala City. They left their homeland about the same time that the cotton was being harvested near Clarksdale, Mississippi. Now the Guatemalan seamstress completed the shirt in a cramped, hot, noisy factory employing about thirty other Latino men and women, run by Mr Su-Hoon Kim, himself an immigrant from Korea. Mr Kim's factory is located in a high-rise building owned by an Anglo family that has long been part of the Los Angeles political élite. Mr Kim, one of a dozen small Asian-American subcontractors in this building, makes shirts for a major US sportswear company which markets them under its brand name at malls and department stores across North America, and exports them under its label to Europe and Japan. These expensive shirts are designed by 'famous name' fashion specialists who work out of much newer, more comfortable, high-rise office buildings located at the edge of the apparel district, closer to the financial centre of Los Angeles.

Clearly Rosa, her sewing machine, Mr Kim, and the shirt are part of a very complex, hierarchically stratified industrial production complex in the Los Angeles garment district. Within this small area of a few square miles is a world characterized by high levels of inequality, structured by race, ethnicity, and gender. However, it is impossible to understand this slice of economic activity without conceptualizing it as the locus of global connections: this complex is at the confluence of various flows of people, materials, machines, capital, and information that all come together in Los Angeles. Los Angeles qualifies as a world city in terms of the global reach of its industries, in terms of its role as a design and finance centre for the Pacific Rim, and in terms of the presence of millions of people from an enormous variety of racial and ethnic backgrounds. As a world city Los Angeles increasingly requires, paradoxically, the simultaneous presence of major global economic actors in business and finance on the one hand, and low-wage manufacturing on the other. Downtown Los Angeles provides a combination of Third World living and working conditions and First World opulence. Within blocks of the business, financial, government, and cultural core of its downtown area lies the teeming squalor of the garment district: low, eight to twelve storey run-down buildings housing an estimated 5,000 small factories that employ the nearly 120,000 workers primarily responsible for the production of 'the California look'.

Tracing the flow of cotton as it becomes a shirt, the immigration of Rosa Gomez and Su-Hoon Kim, the importation of the factory machinery, and the shipping of the finished products to wholesalers and retailers, relates Los Angeles to other locales. It situates Los Angeles in a global system of geographical places, linked on the basis of the migration of people, the organization of production, and other economic linkages in which the apparel industry is involved. Conceptualizing urban areas as central nodes in multiplex networks of economic, social, demo-graphic, and information flows gives us an analytical tool that allows us to conceptualize what 'world cities' are and to map their structural relationships.

In this chapter we begin to identify these structural relationships – the linkages among remote locales that tie them together into a global network. Guided by theoretical considerations suggested by global political economy theories (e.g. world-systems theory) and urban ecology, and by the methodological logic of network analysis, we consider the myriad ways in which cities and other locales are interconnected by flows of people, commodities, capital, and informa-tion. We suggest a typology of flows, and then we move toward operationalizing some of these conceptual linkages by identifying the kinds of data that are required if we are to develop maps of the world-system's city system that begin to match the sophistication of our theorizing about it.

Cities in the world-system

The relations among cities in the world-system are myriad, numerous, and complex, but they are observable. By studying the structure of these relationships and the way they change over time, we stand to learn a great deal more about the nature of the world-system itself. Moreover, locating particular cities within the structure of the world city system in terms of the roles they occupy in global networks will provide a new basis for comparing cities and understanding their morphology.

We understand cities to be situated in a hierarchic network of global economic and political arrangements. At the global level, the primary political units are nation-states, and their behaviour is clearly inseparable from the world economic order. Although the world-system is thus politically fragmented, it constitutes a relatively coherent hierarchically arranged economic system stratified into a 'core', 'semiperiphery', and 'periphery' (see Wallerstein 1974a and 1974b). Social relations within regions (e.g. countries or cities), broadly speaking, are powerfully shaped by how those regions are situated in the world economy and by the character of the particular nation-state. Nevertheless, as suggested above, cities can be considered somewhat separately from nations because, although their interrelations are often mediated by nation-states, they are in direct and frequent contact with one another through the various city-to-city flows. It is our view that the nature of these interrelations (e.g. frequency, strength, importance, dominance/subdominance) undergirds the structure of the world-system, reproducing its hierarchy, and powerfully shaping social life in particular regions. The niche a city occupies in the world-system will deeply affect the nature of that urban area, but this niche is subject to change as world-system cycles and trends rearrange the global order, disrupting the aforementioned 'flows' among cities, and therefore altering the interrelations among locales (see also Smith and Timberlake 1993).

World cities, commodity chains, and global economic restructuring

While there is little debate that the contemporary capitalist world economy has been in operation for several hundred years (Chase-Dunn 1989), many social scientists claim that the second half of the twentieth century has witnessed a great deal of global restructuring, perhaps even the rise of a 'new international division of labour' (NIDL) (Fröbel, Heinrichs and Kreye 1980). Here we make no effort to adjudicate the thornier debates about how new the NIDL really is (Walton 1985) or whether the changes are so great that the dynamics of global capitalism have been essentially transformed (Ross and Trachte 1990). Rather, we are more interested in: (1) the ramifications that the concrete patterns of global economic restructuring have for global cities; and (2) the usefulness of conceptual language that emerged from the debate over the nature of changes in the global division of labour, in particular the recent elaboration of the idea of global 'commodity chains'.

The intellectual foment over the nature of global economic restructuring has led scholars to recognize the need to basically reconceptualize the role of industrialization in economic development. Today rising levels of 'industrialization' may be a better gauge to a country's supply of low-wage workers than a sign of incipient prosperity. As manufacturing becomes increasingly prevalent throughout the poorer countries of the periphery, it is important to recognize that it has differential impacts on economic growth and social welfare. It is important to examine closely the nature of industrial activities and the specific linkages connecting manufacturing enterprises to global markets and local, state, and global capital. While some less-developed parts of the world are primarily 'export platforms' for simple low-technology, labour-intensive goods made by poorly paid, unskilled workers, 'industrial upgrading' in some of the newly industrialized countries (NICs) has led to a shift from commodities like textiles, garments, or footwear to 'higher value-added items that employ sophisticated technology and require a more extensively developed, tightly integrated local industrial base' (Gereffi 1992: 92). This idea, which in many ways parallels the 'value chain' of economist Michael Porter (1990) or the 'production chain' of geographer Peter Dicken (1992), draws on Hopkins and Wallerstein's (1986) formulation of a commodity chain as a 'network of labor and production processes whose result is a finished commodity' (1986: 159). Gereffi and Korzeniewicz (1990) conceptualize these chains as consisting of a number of 'nodes' that comprise the pivotal points in the production process. These include the extraction and supply of raw materials, the stage(s) of industrial transformation, the export of goods, and the marketing of finished products. Each node is itself a network connected to other nodes which perform related activities; local, regional, and world economies are seen as ever more intricate web-like structures of these chains. Ultimately, global inequality is defined by the positions that societies, regions, firms, or localities occupy in these multiplex networks of world-wide economic production and exchange. Differential profits and surpluses are generated up and down the chains, with the 'higher order' functions of marketing of products and the co-ordination and control of the integrated networks likely to be the most lucrative. This conceptual approach to identifying inter-locale linkages is reminiscent of earlier work seeking to identify global systems of cities.

Hill, drawing on the work of Wallerstein, McKenzie, and that of Stephen Hymer (1972) suggests that scholars focus attention on 'global production systems' linking places across the globe in an increasingly integrated vertical division of labour: a 'spider's web' of production. Large cities housing global corporate and financial headquarters become the centres for the global system, exercising control not only within organizational structures of the transnational corporations, but also across entire 'production systems consisting of innumerable operating units, ranging from transnational corporations to small parts shops, all linked by technology and organization in the manufacture of a final product' (Hill n.d.: 15). Conceptualizing cities in this way leads us to think of urban areas as nodes in a multilayered network that comprises the world city system. This helps draw attention to the overall morphology of the world city system and the changing relative positions of cities within this 'spider's web', and this suggests that research might be aimed at examining the whole global urban network, or at least large chunks of it. Next we discuss briefly several important efforts to understand cities in the context of the world-system.

Studies of cities in the global context

Case-oriented research on some of the world's huge cities has largely substantiated John Friedmann's notion that there is a distinct category of 'global' or 'world cities' housing activities and organizations that exert international co-ordination and control. Important examples include Anthony King's work on London, Robert Ross and Kent Trachte's book that includes examination of New York City, and Saskia Sassen's comparative study of New York, London, and Tokyo. All are concerned with describing how these cities' roles in the world economy shape social and cultural life within each metropolis. King (1990) provides evidence showing how Britain's (and London's) changing international roles are mirrored in the architecture, infrastructure, opportunity structure, and patterns of metropolitan expansion of London. Ross and Trachte (1990) stress the effects that the contraction of the world economy, and the relative decline of the USA in the world-system, has on the development of a growing low-skilled, low-wage labour pool in New York City. They argue that, though the lives of this segment of the New York working class have become increasingly harsh and tenuous, the group as a whole is far from marginal, nor is it 'residual': 'instead it is tied to the capital accumulation process as it unfolds in the modern world-economy'. Sassen's comparative analysis locates New York, Tokyo, and London in the global system in terms of their similar roles in the world economy (Sassen 1991). Moreover, she links their global structural similarities to social conditions within them, thus illustrating the importance of knowing about global processes in order better to understand local social patterns.

It is misleading to think that only a few 'global cities' are tied to the world-system. Other urban areas as well 'articulate' with the global political economy, and the work of Feagin and his associates has indicated how this articulation operates through relatively concrete transactions linking actors, hierarchically, in different cities (see Feagin 1988; Feagin and Smith 1987; Hill and Feagin 1987). Rodriguez and Feagin (1986) compare three pairs of cities (one pair in each of three hegemonic periods since the sixteenth century), with each consisting of the world financial centre and a major production city for each of the three hegemonic eras, yielding Amsterdam/ Leiden, London/Manchester, and New York/Houston. They show how the fate of each city was interwoven with the other in the pair and, simultaneously, with the processes and structures of the world-system as a whole. World-system processes shape the growth and nature of particular cities, but the global system as a whole is influenced by the development of these cities too (Rodriguez and Feagin 1986: 218).

There are a few notable attempts to identify global urban hierarchies on the basis of quantitative data. Chase-Dunn's (1985) listing of the world urban hierarchies for the last 1,200 years was based on the population rank size rule of urban primacy, which holds that in a normal, well-integrated system of cities, the statistical distribution of cities by population size is lognormal. His data allow him to argue that changes in the distribution are linked to the dynamics of competition between power centres competing for hegemony in geopolitics and the world economy. The data on which his analyses are based are probably quite accurate. Nevertheless, population rank size does not directly tell us about how a city is interlinked in a system of cities. Instead, it assumes linkage on the basis of theories in urban geography and sociology's human ecology about functional integration, functional role, and population rank size. Thus, as opposed to the relational analysis of the 'globalized' case studies mentioned above, Chase-Dunn's is an attributional analysis that does not actually demonstrate that a particular rank entails certain relations with cities of other ranks or with the world system as a whole. David Meyer's quantitative work begins to overcome these shortcomings by using data that are more relational to portray large chunks of a global system of cities. Examples include his study of the distribution of international bank branches linking cities in Latin America to the world's financial centres and to each other (Meyer 1986). More recent efforts examine other large areas of the world

(Meyer 1991a and 1991b). In directly examining linkages among cities, Meyer's work leads in the right direction: toward the study of the entire world-system of cities, examining many types of important flows among them. But is this even remotely possible?

Conceptualizing linkages among the world's cities

Any effort to map relations among cities requires that we clearly specify criteria for identifying the kinds of relationships likely to be most important. The discussion so far has implied that the various flows among cities are primarily of an economic nature, but it is easy to think of other ways in which cities are interlinked. For example, political relations may exist among cities, cultural ties most certainly can be conceived, as can relations involving social reproduction – social ties that transcend purely economic or political realms. We can further classify potential flows into mutually exclusive categories based on their general material form. Thus we can conceive of flows of human population, flows of material objects that humans have produced (including potential energy), and flows of information (symbols). We can now produce a four- by three-cell table on the basis of cross-classifying the four purposes of flows with the three forms the flows may take.

The resulting classification scheme is shown in table 5.1. We have included examples in each cell that suggest more concrete operational-izations of each of the twelve conceptual categories of flows depicted in the table. Economic linkages among cities in the human form include flows of labour, sales and producer-services personnel, and managers. When people migrate or immigrate from one city to another in order to find employment they represent labour flows. Roza Gomez, our Los Angeles garment factory seamstress is an example. When a manager travels from corporate headquarters to the site of a branch plant in another city, that represents an economic flow in the human form. The primary material objects linking cities can be traced in the flow of commodities, both in the production process and in the distribution process. Some cities house important value-added processes for commodities that are shipped into the city from other urban locales. Cotton fabric is shipped daily to Mr Kim's shirt factory, where Ms Gomez works. Other cities house break-of-bulk transportation facilities for moving commodities to smaller cities where they will be purchased by consumers. Examples of economic flows taking the form of symbolic communication include business telecommunications (e.g. telephone calls, fax and telex messages), mail orders, business related mail, and so on.

Table 5.1 *Conceptualizing inter-city linkages: a typology*

Function	Form		
	Human	Material	Information
Economic	labour, managers, lawyers, consultants	capital, commodities	business phone calls, faxes, telex messages, technology transfer, advertisements
Political	troops, diplomats, social workers	military hardware, foreign aid	treaties, political threats
Cultural	exchange students, dance troupes, rock concerts, theatre	paintings, sculpture, artefacts	feature films, videos, phono albums (CDs)
Social reproduction	families, Red Cross, community organizers	remittances, foreign aid	post cards, night phone calls

We will not go through all the categories in such detail, but a look at table 5.1 provides an idea of other types of flow that might be found. In principle, detailed information on many different kinds of flow could be used to produce many different kinds of charts of the world-system of cities, or they could be used to produce one or a few overall maps of the system. Before discussing in more detail issues related to data content, we will now turn to the issue of data analysis.

Network analysis

Formal network analysis of exchange patterns provides a rigorous way to operationalize theoretical conceptions about the global economy. A number of existing studies use this methodology to measure world-system structure (Nemeth and Smith 1985; Smith and White 1992; Snyder and Kick 1979; Steiber 1979). But no one has used formal network analysis to look at world cities and the global urban system, despite its obvious appeal as a potential tool for exploring the structured patterns of flows that define the world-systems' city system. Given appropriate data (a daunting issue, discussed below), network analysis allows us simultaneously to examine multiple types of flows between many pairs of cities, such that the complex structure of interrelationships between cities in an entire network becomes apparent. This methodology offers a particularly close 'fit' with theories that emphasize the defining character of world cities as nodes in global flows of people, commodities, capital, information, and so on.

Two broad types of network analytic measures seem particularly appropriate. The first is a standard tool used in previous network analyses of general world-system structure. Block-modelling operationalizes the idea of structural or relational equivalence between actors (in the previous analyses, nations) in a network (flows of international trade, people, information, investment, etc.). The goal of block-modelling is to sort actors into broad groups that relate to other nodes in ways that are similar. Snyder and Kick (1979) and Nemeth and Smith (1985) used the widely available CONCOR (Convergence of Iterated Correlations) computer program (see White, Boorman, and Breiger 1976) which measured structurally equivalent positions. More recently Smith and White (1992) used a relational distance algorithm (REDI) (see White and Reitz 1989) which more accurately captures the idea of similar roles. Block-modelling could be used to sift and sort cities into analogous types of 'levels' in the world-city hierarchy.

A second especially promising network concept is that of centrality. Recent sociological work using this notion links centrality in communities or inter-organizational networks with power, prestige, and economic success (Burt 1982; Galaskiewicz 1979; Laumann, Galaskiewicz, and Marsden 1978; Laumann and Pappi 1976). Anthropologists and geographers have taken the lead in examining centrality in trade networks between places (for example, see Hage and Harary 1981; and Pitts 1965, 1979). Network methodologists point out that there are several ways to conceptualize centrality (Burt 1982; Freeman 1979), each measured differently and appropriate to distinct substantive problems. Drawing on graph theory, Freeman (1979) distinguishes between three types of point centrality: (1) 'degree', (2) 'betweenness', and (3) 'closeness'. The most widely available programs for indexing centrality in networks are designed only to handle the presence or absence of ties between actors or nodes. But Doug White (n.d.) is currently developing algorithms that allow researchers to measure centrality using quantitative data (that include the amount or value of the exchange) on (1) direct flow ('outflow and inflow'), (2) betweenness ('egress and ingress'), and (3) polar centrality ('source and sink'). How would these relate to global cities? Probably the most relevant measure would be a gauge of 'betweenness' in global networks, since this would best capture the way world cities control and broker various types of international exchanges. This formal property would seem to operationalize the major thrust of Sassen's image of these places as centres for 'coordination and control'. Polar centrality might also have utility. We would suppose that world cities would be central 'sources' of information and capital flows, for instance, while they are simultaneously central 'sinks' for certain types of migrants and high-tech equipment. The crucial point here is that these formal techniques provide a potentially valuable analytical tool: they are logically compatible with the relational imagery of theoretical discussions of world cities in the world-system, and quantitative analysis would naturally complement qualitative case studies. Further, the formal conceptualizations offered by network analysis (e.g. types of 'equivalence' or 'centrality'), regardless of whether they are applied to actual data or not, provide a precise, concise language for describing the relationships between places: analysis that might promote better theoretical formulations about global cities and urban systems.

Toward operationalizing the world city hypothesis

By now we hope the reader is convinced that the logic of network analysis offers a powerful tool for charting the world-system's city system. Our conceptualization of key categories of flows among cities in the global system (table 5.1) is fairly obvious and straightforward. And the broad theoretical idea of global cities linked together in various types of international networks suggests that this methodology should be useful. But how we do move from analogies and generalities to a specific operationalization combining theory, method, and data?

A quick overview of a previously successful effort of international network analysis provides a research exemplar: network analysis of the modern world economy. Wallerstein and other world-system theorists have developed a relationally based structural conception of the global system (see especially Evans 1979; Wallerstein 1974a, 1979). Though there is a considerable debate about specifics, there is a relative consensus among world-system proponents about basic elements. Among the key characteristics of world-system structure is the existence of a core–semiperiphery–periphery hierarchy, the importance of various mechanisms of 'unequal exchange', the possibility of both upward and downward 'mobility' of countries over historical time, and the rise and demise of 'hegemonic' powers. The crucial flow channelling and maintaining this entire system is global economic exchange.

In order to examine world-system structure using network analysis several researchers have used 'block-modelling' techniques that sort nations into discrete strata based on various measures or international interaction, which verifies elements of the core–semipheriphery–periphery model (Snyder and Kick 1979; Nemeth and Smith 1985; Smith and White 1992). The most ambitious and theoretically grounded of these efforts has used data on a variety of basic commodity flows to gauge the changing structure of the global system at multiple time points between 1965 and 1980 (Smith and White 1992). This provides evidence of upward mobility of some nations (Brazil, South Korea) and downward mobility by others (India, Pakistan). By reanalysing international trade data using the derived blocks it is possible empirically to examine various types of asymmetrical exchanges in the global system, including economic flows that approximate notions of 'unequal exchange' (and to see changes in these patterns over the years consistent with the rise of a 'new international division of labour'). Finally, the use of multidimensional scaling to graphically depict the data visually clearly shows the declining hegemony of the United States, with West Germany, especially, challenging it by 1980.

The first step in network analysis of the world city system is to have some well-defined notions about its structure. Just as in literature about the world-system, there are disputes and disagreements about the nature of global cities and the structural hierarchy they assume. Much of the writing is case specific, and offers only fragmentary suggestions about the configuration of a global city system (see above). Fortunately, the version of 'the world city hypothesis' provided by Friedmann (1986) provides both general principles and particular positioning for specific cities that can be tested. Friedmann's first hypothesis argues that 'integration with the world economy', formulated with specific reference to Wallerstein's world capitalist system as 'a single (spatial) division of labour', is the key to understanding structural changes within world cities. In particular, focus should centre on 'relations that link the urban economy into the global system of markets for capital, labor, and commodities' (Friedmann 1986). Hypothesis two claims that 'key cities throughout the world are used by global capital as "basing points" in the spatial organization and articulation of production and markets'. Friedmann fleshes out this hypothesis very concretely by offering a table of 'primary' and 'secondary' world cities in both 'core countries' and 'semiperiphery countries' (Friedman, table A.1) and a schematic drawing of 'the hierarchy of world cities' complete with an array of key 'linkages' (Friedmann, figure A.1).

Although others may quibble over the categorization and placement of particular cities in Friedmann's scheme, it provides a particularly rich starting point for network-based research. First, it is quite clear about the types of relations that are important. Flows of capital, economic commodities, and labour migration are most obvious. But we also must consider other types of relations that facilitate the movement of these basic elements of the world economy. Here information links become critical, since they facilitate world cities' co-ordination and control over the world-system. Business travellers, as well as all the forms of telecommunication, are crucial sinews holding this system together.

If we have systematic data of city-to-city flows and connections on these sorts of measures, testing Friedmann's model becomes relatively easy. Various sorts of structural or relational equivalence algorithms would be used to partition cities into blocks which would classify places that are formally similar in the multiplexity of their ties to all other places. Using these techniques we would expect to find that London, New York, and Tokyo would cluster together as dominant first-ranked world cities: despite dealing with somewhat distinct hinterlands and using distinct cultural forms and social institutions to exert power and control, these three key urban areas should be integrated into global networks in broadly similar ways. An interesting question for block-modelling, in this case, is what other cities (Los Angeles? Paris?) might also fit into this block? This approach could also provide intriguing information about secondary and tertiary world cities. Since it looks at similar patterns of flows independent of geographic regions, there may be some interesting clusters of lower-level core cities with peripheral/semiperipheral metropolises (perhaps Miami, Rio/São Paulo, and Seoul all occupy a single middle layer of the world city system – if so, should we look for structural similarities between their internal structures?).

Measures of network centrality would also be relevant. If global cities are 'basing points' and/or 'centres for co-ordination and control' of global production and markets, the degree to which they are at the centre of flows of people, material, and information is extremely important. Scalar measures of centrality could help us to determine the relative dominance of global cities; measures taken at multiple points in time could provide a strong predictor of cities changing their positions in the world city hierarchy. Has Tokyo been steadily increasing its degree of centrality in financial and information networks over the past thirty years? Has New York's central position declined or held steady? Can we identify the secondary centres of emerging importance by gauging increases in their level of centrality? Various measures of centrality could also help to verify or dismiss the lines that indicate important 'linkages' in Friedmann's figure. Thus, through theoretically grounded network analysis we can actually test empirically some of central claims of 'the world city hypothesis'.

A proviso on data

The previous section sketches out some ideas about using network methodology to assay theories about the world city system. There is, however, a pragmatic consideration that must be raised. Finding data on actual flows of people, materials, and information between global cities may present a particularly daunting task. Further, the nature of network analysis makes missing data particularly problematic.

Because of the way quantitative data are gathered and compiled, there is an absolute dearth of relational data on all social phenomena. There is growing theoretical interest in the various social sciences on how social structures are generated through the relationships and linkages between people, localities, institutions, nations, etc. (see, for example, Tilly 1984). But statistical information still tends to be collected in the attributional form. That is, the data report values on the characteristics of particular units (e.g. an individual's income, a city's population, a nation's gross national product) rather than information about their relationship to others (in terms of either connections or flows). Therefore, it is very difficult to obtain data on international flows or links between social units (whether these entities are cities, regions, organizations, corporations, or nations). So while it is easy to get attributional data on various nation-states, and there are some good network data at the inter-national level (commodity trade flows, for instance, see Smith and White 1992), compilations of networks of interactions or flows between world cities are not readily available. This does not mean that these data do not exist or that pulling them together into a usable format is impossible; it does mean that this may require much hard work.

This effort is compounded by a methodological issue. While network analysis is a powerful tool for understanding social structure, it has some stringent data requirements. Other types of statistical analysis use relatively simple, standardized ways of adjusting for 'missing cases'. But incomplete data in network matrices is much more difficult to accommodate. Although there are some techniques that attempt to deal with this problem, lack of data on the flows between any units of a network mean that relational analysis can never adequately capture its multiplex structure in totality. The inclusion of information on a single unit can fundamentally alter the configuration of a network.

The importance of complete matrices of data, coupled with a serious problem of data availability, make it incumbent on us to suggest some possible sources of relevant information. Economic flows in the human form can be of several kinds. Labour migration is one. When people move over long distances it is often employment related. Periodic surveys of national populations for certain periods of time may allow us to piece together a world-system map of labour flows. Of course, accurate counts of migrants will not be available for many countries in the world, and when they are, cities of origin may not be coded. Yet the study of migration is central to demographic inquiry, and involving experts in this research area may yield data allowing us to begin to chart a migration-based world city system map.

Travellers form other strands in the web linking the world's cities. Corporate emissaries, government trade and commerce representatives, and independent entrepreneurs, for example, move among cities, greasing the wheels of production, finance, or commerce through face-to-face contact. Airline data may provide good estimates of the way in which cities are linked by the movement of people. Relatively accessible data are available on US air travel in a form suitable for network analysis. These data consist of systematic estimates of origins and destinations for travel among domestic cities. International air travel data may also be available for the larger cities in the world. Of the data leads we have uncovered so far, air travel patterns are the most promising. In the form of origination and destination information, they would constitute the kind of relational data that network analysis requires.

Economic flows in their material form may be operationalized by describing commodity chains linking geographic locales. The required data are the cities of origin and destination of commodities. Once again, the complete data for all the world's large cities probably do not exist at the present time, but we can begin to piece together a partial map of the world's city system by using the data that are available and making efforts to develop new sources. For example, in the USA, a commodity flow survey will be ready for analysis around 1995. The survey will provide a complete network database (from systematic sampling of commodity flows) on the value and number of commodity flows by zip code. These forthcoming data provide exciting possibilities. Once again, the obvious shortcoming is that they will allow researchers to produce only partial maps of the world city system. But we have just begun to explore the possibilities. It is quite likely that other commodity flow data for locales are being collected by governments and international agencies (e.g. the EEC). Moreover, it is important to begin the task of mapping the world city system even though only incomplete data are available at the present time.

Communication among actors in geographic locales remote from one another takes place in the absence of face-to-face contact. Firms, businesses, and business people with far-flung operations and interests use telephone calls, telex and fax messages, telegraph, and mail for such purposes. In principle, it is possible to sample the volume by locale of origin and destination of some of these communications from existing records. The telephone bills most of us receive indicate that data are kept, at least temporarily, in a form suitable for network analysis. Scholars of the communications industry and the major telecommunications corporations themselves may be willing to co-operate in generating the necessary data to begin to map the global inter-city information network.

These few example of how we might utilize some of the concepts posited as linkages among the world's cities illustrate both the possibility of such an endeavour and the great difficulties involved.

Conclusions

Our theoretical understanding of the world-system, including our theorizing specifically about world city systems, is permeated with network analogies. Moreover, other areas of social scientific inquiry have been considerably advanced by recent efforts to apply formal network analytic procedures using quantitative, relational data (for examples see Fischer 1982; Wellman and Berkowitz 1988). These facts suggest that efforts to begin the empirical project of identifying the world-system's city system are overdue. Our discussion suggests at least three important conclusions about such a task.

Firstly, a project aimed at producing truly complete and comprehensive maps of the world's city system will require a collaborative effort among a fairly large number of experts from a range of backgrounds. Ideally, these experts would include government officials (e.g. researchers in agencies regulating commerce), industry representatives, and scholars in a number of fields (demography, economic geography, communications, and international political economy). It is a big job that will require interdisciplinary co-operation, but one that needs to be done.

A second conclusion is less obvious, more theoretical, and perhaps more interesting. People tend most easily to grasp social realities that are immediately observable in their everyday experiences. As a result families, communities, and workplaces, along with many other locally circumscribed social, political, economic, and cultural institutions, are familiar topics of social science research. But our discussion of concrete operationalization of the linkages between global cities makes it clear that a world network of cities is no more abstract than these more mundane social groups (for instance, families). It consists of specific physical units (albeit inhabited by very large numbers of people) bounded in time and space, and linked to one another by readily observable interactions (e.g. telephone calls, bank loans, commodity shipments, travel). Of course, the world city system exists on a global scale, making it much larger and more spatially extensive than other objects of social scientific inquiry (families, communities, institutions, etc.). But these qualities do not make it less 'real' nor its structure and dynamics less observable. Mapping out its structure presents a challenge for collecting and compiling data analogous in some ways to the problems faced by astronomers in charting the galactic structures of the universe. But there *is* a world city system 'out there' to study: we need to begin systematically by gathering the information needed to map its contours.

Finally, the fact that it exists at the global level and involves the activities of many millions of people, and arguably, everyone on earth, makes knowledge of the world-system's city system extremely important. This knowledge could potentially move well beyond the arcane esoterica of academic understanding. As Alger poignantly argues, 'The cities of the world are inhabited by people in desperate need of knowledge that would enable them to cope with the multifaceted dimension of world-wide relationships of everyday life' (Alger 1990: 493). Understanding the world city system, how it is structured, how it changes and impacts on peoples lives, is 'policy-relevant'. Or it should be! The more we understand about the ways that global processes and structures work, the greater the prospects that people will be able to influence change for the common good. Otherwise we all remain at the mercy of the impersonal logic of the contemporary world-system. It is our responsibility to describe the global structures of the world city system as accurately and clearly as possible and, hopefully, in ways that are relevant to ordinary people's everyday experiences. We should keep in mind that the point is not just to interpret the world, but to create the capacity to change it.

REFERENCES

Alger, C. 1990. 'The world relations of cities: closing the gap between social science paradigms and everyday human experience'. *International Studies Quarterly*, 34: 493–518.

Burt, R. 1982. *Toward a Structural Theory of Action: Network Models of Social Structure, Perception, and Action.* New York: Academic Press.

Chase-Dunn, C. 1985. 'The system of world cities, AD 800–1975'. In *Urbaniza-*

tion in the World Economy, ed. M. Timberlake, pp. 269–92. New York: Academic Press.

1989. *Global Formation*. New York: Basil Blackwell.

Dicken, P. 1992. *Global Shift: The Internationalization of Economic Activity*. 2nd edn. New York: Guilford Press.

Evans, P. B. 1979. *Dependent Development: The Alliance of Multinational, State, and Local Capital in Brazil*. Princeton NJ: Princeton University Press.

Feagin, J. R. 1988. *The Free Enterprise City*. New Brunswick NJ: Rutgers University Press.

Feagin, J. R. and Smith, M. P. 1987. 'Cities and the new international division of labor'. In *The Capitalist City*, ed. M. P. Smith and J. R. Feagin, pp. 3–34. Oxford: Basil Blackwell.

Fischer, C. 1982. *To Dwell Among Friends: Personal Networks in Town and City*. Chicago: University of Chicago Press.

Freeman, L. C. 1979. 'Centrality in social networks: conceptual clarification'. *Social Networks*, 1: 215–39.

Friedmann, J. 1986. 'The world city hypothesis'. *Development and Change*, 17(1): 69–84. (Reproduced as appendix of this volume.)

Fröbel, F., Heinrichs, J., and Kreye, O. 1980. *The New International Division of Labour: Structural Unemployment in Industrialized Countries and Industrialization in Developing Countries*. Cambridge: Cambridge University Press.

Galaskiewicz, J. 1979. *Exchange Networks and Community Politics*. Beverly Hills CA: Sage.

Gereffi, G. 1992. 'New realities of industrial development in East Asia and Latin America: global, regional, and national trends'. In *States and Development in the Asian Pacific Rim*, ed. Richard Appelbaum and Jeffrey Henderson, pp. 85–112. Beverly Hills CA: Sage.

Gereffi, G. and Korzeniewicz, M. 1990. 'Commodity chains and footwear exports in the semiperiphery'. In *Semiperipheral States in the World-Economy*, ed. W. Martin, pp. 45–68. Westport CT: Greenwood Press.

Hage, P. and Harary, F. 1981. 'Mediation and power in Melanesia'. *Oceania*, 52: 124–35.

Hill, R. C. (n.d.) 'The spider's web: global theories of urban development'. Unpublished manuscript, Department of Sociology, Michigan State University.

Hill, R. C. and Feagin, J. R. 1987. 'Detroit and Houston: two cities in global perspective'. In *The Capitalist City*, ed. M. P. Smith and J. R. Feagin, pp. 155–77. New York: Basil Blackwell.

Hopkins, T. and Wallerstein, I. 1986. 'Commodity chains in the world-economy prior to 1800'. *Review*, 10(1): 157–70.

Hymer, S. 1972. 'The multinational corporation and the law of uneven development'. In *Economics and World Order*, ed. J. W. Bhagwati, pp. 113–40. New York: Macmillan.

King, A. 1990. *Global Cities: Post-Imperialism and the Internationalization of London*. London: Routledge and Kegan Paul.

Laumann, E. O., Galaskiewicz, J., and Marsden, P. 1978. 'Community structures as interorganizational linkages'. *Annual Review of Sociology*, 4: 455–84.

96   *David A. Smith and Michael Timberlake*

Laumann, E. O. and Pappi, F. 1976. *Networks of Collective Action: A Perspective on Community Influence Systems.* New York: Academic Press.

Meyer, D. 1986. 'World system of cities: relations between international financial metropolises and South American cities'. *Social Forces*, 64(3): 553–81.

1991a. 'The formation of a global financial center: London and its intermediaries'. In *Cities in the World-System, Studies in the Political Economy of the World-System*, ed. K. Resat, pp. 97–106. New York: Greenwood Press.

1991b. 'Change in the world system of metropolises: the role of business intermediaries'. *Urban Geography*, 12(5): 393–416.

Nemeth, R. and Smith, D. A. 1985. 'The political economy of contrasting urban hierarchies in South Korea and the Philippines'. In M. Timberlake, *Urbanization in the World-Economy*, pp. 169–82. Orlando FL: Academic Press.

Pitts, F. 1965. 'A graph theoretic approach to historical geography'. *Professional Geographer*, 17(5): 15–20.

1979. 'The medieval river trade network of Russia revisited'. *Social Networks*, 1: 285–93.

Porter, M. 1990. *The Competitive Advantages of Nations.* New York: Free Press.

Rodriguez, N. P. and Feagin, J. R. 1986. 'Urban specialization in the world system. *Urban Affairs Quarterly*, 22: 187–220.

Ross, R. and Trachte, K. 1990. *Global Capitalism: The New Leviathan.* Albany: State University of New York Press.

Sassen, S. 1991. *The Global City: New York, London, Tokyo.* Princeton NJ: Princeton University Press.

Smith, D. A. and Timberlake, M. 1993. 'World cities in the world-system: a political-economy/network approach'. In *New Perspectives in Urban Sociology. Research in Urban Sociology*, vol. 3. ed. R. Hutchinson, pp. 181–207. JAI Press.

Smith. D. A. and White, D. 1992. 'Structure and dynamics of the global economy: network analysis of international trade 1965–1980'. *Social Forces*, 70(4): 857–93.

Snyder, D. and Kick, E. 1979. 'Structural position in the world system and economic growth, 1955–1970: a multiple network analysis of transnational interaction'. *American Journal of Sociology*, 84: 1097–1126.

Steiber, S. 1979. 'The world system and world trade: an empirical explanation of conceptual conflicts'. *Sociological Quarterly*, 20: 23–36.

Tilly, C. 1984. *Big Structures, Large Processes, Huge Comparisons.* New York: Russell Sage Foundation.

Wallerstein, I. 1974a. *The Modern World System I: Capitalist Agriculture and the Origins of the European World Economy in the Sixteenth Century.* New York: Academic Press.

1974b. 'The rise and future demise of the world capitalist system: concepts for comparative analysis'. *Comparative Studies in Society and History*, 16(4), 387–415.

1979. *The Capitalist World Economy.* New York: Cambridge University Press.

Walton, J. 1985. 'The third "new" international division of labor'. In *Capital and*

Labor in the Urbanized World, ed. J. Walton, pp. 3–14. Beverly Hills CA: Sage.

Wellman, B. and Berkowitz, S. D. (eds.). 1988. *Social Structures: A Network Approach*. Cambridge: Cambridge University Press.

White, D. (n.d.). 'Measuring role distance: structural and relational equivalence'. Unpublished paper presented at the Social Network Colloquium, University of California, Irvine.

White, H., Boorman, S., and Breiger, R. 1976. 'Social structure from multiple networks: 1. Block models of roles and position'. *American Journal of Sociology*, 81: 730–80.

White H. and Reitz, K. 1983. 'Graph and semigroup homomorphisms on networks of relations'. *Social Networks*, 5: 193–224.

6 World cities, multinational corporations, and urban hierarchy: the case of the United States

Donald Lyons and Scott Salmon

Introduction

From the moment the term was initially coined, world cities have been associated with the concentration of power and wealth within a global context (Geddes 1968; Hall 1966). Such centres; 'cities with international destinies', have always been at the core of the world economy (Braudel 1984). During the tumultuous decades following 1960, changes in the organization of international economic activity and in the nature of advanced corporate and financial services have prompted scholars to identify a system of world cities that appear to operate as global nodes for international business decision-making and corporate strategy formulation (Cohen 1981). This international urban system has been recognized in the world city hypothesis as a hierarchy of urban places ranked on the basis of their integration with the world economy. At the apex of the hierarchy are the global cities: sites of rapidly increasing concentrations of corporate power, international finance, and higher-order producer services (Friedmann 1986).

Although its principal exponents have always insisted that the world city concept was not a theory but a hypothesis in need of empirical verification, the world city idea, and its associated assumptions about the nature of urban development, has been absorbed rapidly into the lexicon of urban studies. This in itself should occasion little surprise; the concept has provided a useful heuristic for those struggling to conceptualize the complex linkages of the new global economy. However, history has repeatedly reminded us that the evolution of cities and their role in the process of capital accumulation is characterized by a continuous restlessness (see Braudel 1984; Harvey 1986; Knox 1991), and world cities are no exception.

This chapter suggests that recent changes in the organization of economic activity within the US urban hierarchy indicates that the original conception of the world city, as defined by the world city hypothesis, must be at least partially revised. We argue that there is some evidence that the increased globalization of the world economy is redefining linkages within the US urban hierarchy and, in the process, expanding the global control potential of some cities further down the hierarchy. This chapter focuses on the changing geography of corporate control, indicated by corporate headquarter concentration, and examines the spatial structure of linkages between corporate headquarters and their major financial and producer service providers. The chapter concludes with a reassessment of the impacts of continuing globalization on the evolution of the US urban hierarchy.

Globalization and the centralization of corporate control

In their seminal statement of the world city hypothesis, Friedmann and Wolff (1982) explicitly linked the emergence of world cities to the restructuring of the world economy, the spatial organization of the new international division of labour, and, in particular, the strategies of the transnational corporation (also see appendix). Essentially, the hypothesis is predicated on the recognition of what Amin and Thrift (1992: 574–5) have described as the shift from an international to a global economy, which is characterized by the growth of increasingly integrated global production networks orchestrated and controlled by large multinational corporations. World cities are the command centres of this new global economy: 'basing points' in the spatial organization and articulation of production and markets. As such, world cities are characterized by the relative concentration of economic functions, primarily those of management, banking and finance, legal services, accounting, technical consulting, telecommunications, and computing.

For Friedmann and Wolff (1982) the defining feature of the world city is its functional importance for capital. Based on the growing centralization of corporate control functions, and the resulting linkages, it is possible from within this framework to arrange cities into a complex global hierarchy. Particular cities within the hierarchy perform specific roles. Some carry out management or headquarter functions, others are financial centres, while still others articulate regional and/or national economies with the global system. Truly 'world' cities are likely to perform all these tasks simultaneously (see appendix). This notion of an urban hierarchy, based not on size but on function, has been integral to the world city concept from its inception.

An early and influential formulation of this idea is to be found in Robert Cohen's (1981) examination of the way in which the emergence of the new international division of labour, the competitive strategies of multinational corporations, and the associated transformation of specialized corporate services contributed to the emergence of a new hierarchy of world cities in the USA. Cohen's study revealed that by the mid-1970s an extremely limited number of cities within the US urban hierarchy were functioning as global centres of business and corporate services. Moreover, as these centres emerged as dominant world cities (primarily New York and San Francisco), even the international activities of firms headquartered outside these cities were increasingly linked to financial institutions and corporate services located within them (Cohen 1981: 304–5). Cohen argued that future developments within the world economy, notably the ongoing inter-nationalization of capital and the growing dependence of corporations on advanced business services, would lead to a further concentration of corporate and financial decision-making in existing world cities over the following decade. These trends, he suggested, would further exacerbate uneven urban development in developed nations by drawing decision-making activities away from national or regional centres to the world cities.

More recently, Sassen has extended these arguments, suggesting that transformations in the world economy, underway since the 1960s, have produced a new global economic order characterized by a complex duality of spatial dispersion and global integration in the organization of economic activity. This combination, she suggests, has 'created a new strategic role for major cities' (Sassen 1991: 3). The territorial dispersal of economic activity associated with globalization, creates a need for expanded centralized control and management. The new, global city has emerged as a highly concentrated command point in the organization of the world economy, operating not only as a focus of corporate control but also as a site for post-industrial production in specialized business and producer services and financial innovation (Sassen 1991: 126). Thus, reiterating the basic tenets of the world city hypothesis, at the core of her approach lies the now familiar pairing of globalization of activity with centralization of control: 'The fundamental dynamic posited here is that the more globalized the economy becomes, the higher the agglomeration of central functions in a relatively few sites, that is the global cities' (Sassen 1991: 5).

Although the notion that a growing centralization of corporate control has accompanied the process of globalization serves as some-thing of an axiom for the world city hypothesis, the precise form that this centralization assumes, and its impact on other cities in the urban hierarchy, is not immediately clear. Seeking to understand the changing relationship between the US urban hierarchy and the global economic system, we take the question of the centralization of corporate control as our conceptual and empirical entry point.

At the scale of the individual firm, the most significant site of control is the corporate head office. Corporate headquarters are considered important because they control the fiscal resources of the corporation and decide the level and allocation of the corporate budget between component units. Typically, headquarter offices are the nerve centres of the corporation, processing and transmitting information within the organization and between other high-level organizations located outside the corporation (Dicken 1992). This administrative structure generates a system of economic relations that locates production in some places and control in others (Browett 1984; Green 1987). Consequently, our initial approach to understanding the evolution of corporate control within the US urban hierarchy is to consider the changing geography of corporate headquarter location.

The changing geography of corporate headquarters

Although traditionally, the relocation of corporate headquarters (either via physical relocation or as the result of mergers and acquisitions) involved a movement from regional to national centres (as the world city hypothesis suggested), there are indications that this pattern is breaking down, in the USA at least (Holloway and Wheeler 1991; Lyons 1994). In fact, there is mounting evidence suggesting that recent shifts in corporate headquarter location within the USA may have resulted in a shift down the urban hierarchy rather than towards world city status (Borchert 1978; Holloway and Wheeler 1991; Semple 1973; Semple and Phipps 1982). What is less clear is the nature of this dispersal and the impact of the increased globalization of economic activity on the US urban hierarchy. Certainly New York has continued to lose much of its corporate base during the last thirty years, and the other US world cities – Chicago, Los Angeles, and San Francisco – do not seem to have increased proportionately. Obviously, an enormous concentration of headquarter and corporate service functions remains in New York, but for the world city hypothesis to be correct we would expect this concentration to be increasing rather than decreasing. Thus, our initial hypothesis addresses the question of corporate headquarter location. If the fundamental assumptions of the world city hypothesis, concerning the centralization of corporate control, are correct we would expect to find an increased concentration of corporate head-quarters among US global cities.

To test this hypothesis we gathered information on the corporate headquarter location of the largest 250 US corporations for 1974, 1982, and 1989. Corporate headquarter concentration was defined by summing the proportional contribution of each corporation's assets, sales, profits, market, and employment for the top 250 publicly traded corporations listed by *Forbes*, and broken down by metropolitan area (*Forbes* 1975, 1983, 1990). The areal unit of analysis is the Consolidated Metropolitan Statistical Area (CMSA) as defined by the 1990 *Statistical Abstract of the United States* (US Department of Commerce 1990). The boundaries of the metropolitan areas were standardized by projecting their 1989 boundaries back to 1974.

To analyse shifts in corporate headquarter and producer service concentration across different types of metropolitan region and to identify potential US world cities we employed Noyelle and Stanback's (1984) classification of US cities. This well-known taxonomy, based on location quotients for employment by economic sector, classifies the 140 largest metropolitan areas into two major classes and several sub-categories (see figure 6.1). Each type of diversified centre provides a variety of service functions, with the widest range and greatest degree

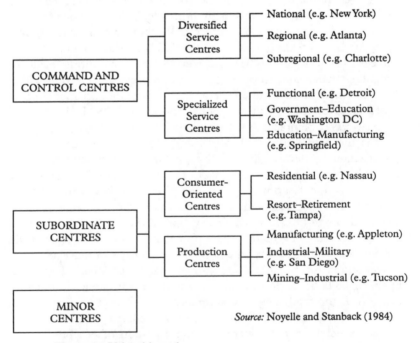

Figure 6.1 Urban hierarchy

Table 6.1 *Concentration of corporate control by metropolitan type: 1974, 1982, 1989*

Type	Forbes 1974	Forbes 1982	Forbes 1989	Change 74–89	Increasing Centres (%)
Command centres	**96.1**	**96.7**	**95.0**	**−1.1**	57
Diversified					
National	59.6	58.4	48.7	−10.9	25
New York	**43.5**	**39.8**	**32.0**	**−11.5**	
National (excl. NY)	16.1	18.6	16.7	0.6	33
Regional	17.9	21.0	24.0	6.1	58
Subregional	1.3	1.7	3.5	2.2	75
Specialized					
Functional	16.4	14.4	16.1	−0.3	46
Govt (education)	0.9	0.5	2.6	1.7	100
Education	0.1	0.0	0.0	0.1	00
Manufacturing industry (military)	0.0	0.7	0.0	0.0	00
Subordinate centres	**1.3**	**0.4**	**0.9**	**−0.4**	33
Manufacturing	1.3	0.4	0.9	−0.4	33
Minor centres	**2.6**	**2.9**	**4.1**	**1.5**	56

Source: Forbes (1975, 1983, 1990).

of sophistication found among the diversified national centres at the apex of the urban hierarchy. Since these diversified national centres (New York, Chicago, Los Angeles, and San Francisco) are the largest and most complex US cities, it is among these cities that 'global city characteristics' are most likely to be observed. Service functions among specialized command and control centres are directed toward a particular set of industrial sectors. Subordinate centres are medium-sized metropolises with few of the sophisticated services found in larger metropolitan regions. A final category, minor centres, was employed to account for metropolitan regions that were too small to be covered by the Noyelle and Stanback classification but were home to the head-quarters of at least one of the top 250 corporations.

From table 6.1 we can see the changing concentration of corporate control amongst metropolitan centres in the USA between 1974 and 1989. Although the highest concentration of corporate headquarters continues to be found among the four diversified national metropolitan regions, New York, Chicago, Los Angeles, and San Francisco (48.7 per cent of the top 250 in 1989), only Los Angeles recorded an increase in concentration. The majority of the declines were concentrated in New York (−11.5 per cent), although as Harper (1987) points out, New

York continues to be the most important centre for corporate headquarter locations. The major beneficiaries of New York's demise were a select group of smaller regional diversified cities (6.1 per cent), in particular Atlanta, Dallas/Fort Worth, Philadelphia, and St Louis. Specialized functional centres, the third major category of metropolis in which corporate headquarters are concentrated, remained relatively stable at approximately 16 per cent of the total. Subregional diversified and government-educational centres (particularly Washington DC) and minor centres recorded some growth, although their overall concentrations remain minor. Within the various categories of metropolis, the fortunes of individual metropolitan centres varied widely. Almost all categories of metropolis had both increasing and decreasing corporate centres (column five) suggesting that changing corporate headquarter influence is selective across and within types of metropolitan region. For example, even within the rapidly expanding diversified regional centre category 42 per cent of metropolises declined.

At first glance, the apparent dispersal of corporate headquarters within the USA from 1974 to 1989 appears to contradict the widely held assumption that a growing concentration of corporate control accompanies globalization. Much of the confusion here stems from the inherently unstable nature of urban spatial hierarchies (Friedmann 1993; Storper and Walker 1989), including the corporate headquarter hierarchy.

Generally, changes in metropolitan corporate headquarter concentration in the USA result from the balance of *in situ* growth or decline of corporations and, to a lesser extent, technological innovations that have reduced the friction of distance (Borchert 1978; Holloway and Wheeler 1991; Lyons 1994). Increase in corporate concentration is an outcome of a continuous struggle by existing and new corporations to capture new growth opportunities as older opportunities decline. Cities that maintain their position do so by continuing to capture a greater balance of propulsive industries to counter declining industries (Storper and Walker 1989). For example, while the balance of growth and decline in New York was strongly negative, it captured significant gains in corporate concentration among four of the top ten increasing sectors in which corporations expanded,[1] while recording major declines in six of the ten declining sectors.

Similar, though considerably less extreme, levels of growth and decline among the top ten most important growing and declining sectors were recorded among the other diversified national cities (Lyons 1994). Given that the diversified national cities have historically been major focuses for corporations, even prior to the emergence of a global economy (Amin and Thrift 1992), we would expect that declining sectors would be concentrated among these cities. Thus, while the overall pattern suggested a decreased concentration, growth among many of the most rapidly expanding sectors is still concentrated among diversified national cities – our potential US world cities. This lends some support to the suggestion that global cities have emerged as important centres of innovation and as production sites for new and expanding business and producer service functions (Sassen 1991).

Despite the evidence of some growth among the diversified national centres of cities, their overall decline in concentration and the rapid increase among a select number of diversified regional centres cannot be ignored. It suggests that, for the USA at least, widely held assumptions concerning globalization, corporate control, as measured by corporate headquarter location, and urban hierarchy may be in need of revision. It is evident that on the basis of corporate headquarter concentration global city primacy is either dispersing throughout the upper end of the US urban hierarchy or a small number of regional cities are emerging as global cities in their own right. How these newly emerging centres interact with the global economy and whether they can truly be defined as global is taken up in the next section.

A changing role for world cities?

Cohen (1981) has argued that, while a number of smaller regional cities are important as corporate headquarter centres, they tend to house the headquarters of corporations primarily involved in national rather than international markets and therefore cannot be termed world cities. Focusing on the concentration of international banking and the extent to which a centre's corporations operate in foreign or domestic markets, Cohen identified only two truly global centres: New York and San Francisco. Wheeler's (1986) conclusion that the dispersion of higher-order financial services throughout the US urban hierarchy has proceeded at a much slower rate than the headquarters of other large corporations tends to support this view. Moreover, Wheeler suggests that corporations tend to proceed up the urban hierarchy for their advanced service and banking needs. Echoing these points, Friedmann argues that the driving force of world city growth is found in the rapid expansion of the international finance, transport, communications, and high level business services such as advertising, accounting, insurance, and legal sectors in these cities (see appendix). Recently he has suggested that the expansion of these services occurred to facilitate new problems of co-ordination that emerged from the increasing globalization of the economy (Friedmann 1993).

Of particular importance here, especially in terms of the world city hypothesis, is the relative significance of financial and advanced business services in the organization and management of the world economy, i.e. the degree to which advanced business services have assumed responsibility for the deployment and manipulation of multinational capital. Sassen (1991: 87), for example, argues that transformations in the composition of the global economy and the accompanying shift to services and finance have brought about a renewed importance for world cities as sites for the production of certain types of services, marketing, and innovation. The production and consumption of the specialized producer and financial services in world cities constitutes a major element of global control. Moreover, the internationalization of corporate mergers, acquisitions, and financial transactions make world cities relatively neutral centres for the management and co-ordination of international transactions and consequently help to solve the conflicts that emerge in an era of global management in a world of territorially defined political interests.

If these suppositions are accurate it may indicate that the role of world cities within the US urban hierarchy is changing. Based on the evidence presented in the previous section it is possible that the world cities exercise their function of global control via the agglomeration of advanced producer and financial services rather than simply on the basis of corporate headquarter concentration. Following Sassen's (1991) argument that developments in global telecommunications have enabled dispersal while reinforcing the centralization of control it is possible that, although corporate headquarters appear to be dispersing, they remain dependent on the global centres for those specialized business and financial services vital for the manipulation of multinational capital. Thus, the function of the global city may be to 'broker' or mediate the global links of corporations located in cities throughout the nation rather than to physically 'house' the headquarters of these corporations. If this is the case it becomes important to examine the nature of the linkages between cities within the US urban hierarchy and the world economy – in particular to draw a distinction between those cities that dominate global transactions and those that simply participate.

Accordingly, we posit a secondary research hypothesis: although US regional centres are expanding their corporate headquarter function, their global linkages continue to be 'brokered' by the diversified national cities. If these cities perform such a 'brokering' role, we would expect:

Table 6.2 *Proportional concentration of corporate headquarters and business service*

Type	HQs	AUD	LEGAL	INSB	MBR	INVB	FORB
Diversified							
National	58.4	54.0	68.1	78.8	74.2	98.2	43.6
New York	**39.8**	**33.7**	**50.4**	**62.0**	**48.0**	**94.4**	**28.8**
National (excl. NY)	18.6	20.3	19.7	16.8	26.2	3.7	14.7
Regional	21.0	29.7	24.4	15.3	15.3	1.2	2.5
Specialized							
Functional	14.4	10.4	4.2	2.9	8.1	0.0	0.0
Other	6.2	6.0	3.3	3.2	2.6	0.6	0.6
Foreign		0.0	0.0	0.0	0.0	0.0	53.4

Notes: HQs: Proportion of corporate headquarters in 1982
AUD: Auditors
LEGAL: Legal Council
INSB: Insurance Brokers
MBR: Major Banking Relationships
INVB: Investment Banking
FORB: Foreign Banking
Source: Zehring (1983), *Forbes* (1983).

(a) a positive balance between the proportion of corporate headquarters concentrated among diversified national cities, or at least New York, and the extent of concentration of higher order service corporations;

(b) conversely, a negative balance between the proportion of corporate headquarters concentrated among smaller cities (regional, sub-regional, diversified, and specialized functional), and the extent of concentration of higher order service corporations; and

(c) an increase in concentration among diversified national cities over time.

To investigate this hypothesis we compiled information on the metropolitan location of the major producer and financial service providers for each of the top 250 corporations for 1982 and 1989 from *The Corporate Finance Bluebook* (Dun and Bradstreet 1990; Zehring 1983). Specifically, the location of corporate auditors, legal council, insurance brokers, major commercial bank links, investment bank(s), and major foreign banking relationships were identified. The degree of producer and financial service concentration was measured by summing the number of corporations that obtained each of these services from a provider broken down by metropolitan area (tables 6.2 and 6.3). For example, in 1982 54 per cent of corporations obtaining services from audit providers located in diversified national centres.[2] The resultant levels of concentration for each service were then compared with the degree of corporate headquarter concentration (table 6.2, data column one). Thus, for example, in 1982 national diversified centres accounted for 58.4 per cent of corporate concentration and 54.0 per cent of auditor concentration.

Generally in 1982, among the four diversified national centres, our would-be world cities, the balance between corporate headquarter concentration and the financial/producer service companies was strongly positive only in New York (table 6.2). This positive balance is most evident for many of the highest level financial needs of corporations measured here by insurance brokers (62.0 per cent versus 39.8 per cent), major banking relationships (48.0 per cent versus 39.8 per cent), and investment banking requirements (94.4 per cent versus 39.8 per cent). The balance between headquarter concentration and the slightly lower-order auditing and legal services is less extreme, probably because these service needs tend to be provided locally. For foreign banking, the quintessential higher order function of the world city, all categories of metropolis utilized foreign banks more than US banks. Even New York corporations tended to utilize overseas banking outlets more than local banks (28.8 per cent versus 39.9 per cent). To the extent that foreign banking needs are met within the USA, however, they are provided almost exclusively within the diversified national centres and, in particular, by New York banks. Smaller corporate centres, in particular the diversified regional and specialized functional centres, utilized few local sources for the highest financial needs (i.e. investment banking, major banking relationships, and foreign banking) in 1982. They do tend to utilize locally available sources for their auditing and legal services, however.

While these results lend some support to the notion that US global cities may be performing a 'brokering' role, they fall well short of providing conclusive proof. Moreover, the idea that higher order services might concentrate at the upper end of the hierarchy is hardly a novel one. For the 'brokering' hypothesis to have any real validity, we should be able to demonstrate that the degree of concentration of these higher order services, especially banking services, has increased over time.

Contrary to our initial expectations, both New York and the other diversified national centres provide higher order services for fewer corporations in 1989 than in 1982 (table 6.3). This result is consistent across the entire range of higher order services for New York, and holds true for four of the six types of services among the remaining diversified national centres (auditors, insurance brokers, major banking relationships, and foreign banking). On the other hand, the number of

Table 6.3 *Shifts in proportional concentration of corporate headquarters and business services firms, 1989*

Type	HQs	AUD	LEGAL	INSB	MBR	INVB	FORB
Diversified							
National	48.7	44.5	58.3	61.4	66.5	93.0	40.2
Change since 1982		−	−	−	−	−	−
New York	**32.0**	**26.5**	**38.3**	**44.8**	**44.1**	**83.8**	**26.4**
Change since 1982		−	−	−	−	−	−
National (excl. New York)	16.7	17.8	20.0	16.6	22.4	9.2	13.7
Change since 1982		−	+	−	−	+	−
Regional	24.0	32.1	25.8	27.6	17.1	3.5	2.6
Change since 1982		+	+	+	+	+	+
Specialized							
Functional	16.1	11.5	6.7	5.5	10.3	0.7	0.0
Change since 1982		+	+	+	+	+	*
Other	11.1	11.9	9.1	5.5	5.9	1.4	0.0
Change since 1982		+	+	+	+	+	−
Foreign						1.4	57.3
Change since 1982						+	+

Notes: HQs: Proportion of corporate headquarters in 1982
AUD: Auditors
LEGAL: Legal council
INSB: Insurance brokers
MBR: Major banking relationships
INVB: Investment banking
FORB: Foreign banking

Change since 1982:
+ increased concentration
− decreased concentration
* no change
Source: Dun and Bradstreet (1990). *Forbes* (1990).

corporations utilizing locally provided higher order services among diversified regional and specialized functional centres has increased during the 1980s. Indeed, even among the smallest corporate head-quarter centres, some increase in the amount of higher order services provided locally was recorded.

These results suggest, contrary to our hypothesis, that the 'brokering' role of US world cities, as indicated by the diversified national centres, is actually declining. Clearly, part of the growth of services in regional centres is related to the overall transformation of both the US and global economies. Most cities have expanded their producer and service sectors as entrepreneurs take advantage of the new opportunities to service the increased needs of local corporations. While much of this expansion may initially be focused on the organization of regional or national markets there is no inherent reason to expect that some service providers would not expand into the provision of international services over time. Needless to say, such expansion would be on a much smaller scale than that documented for the major global cities (Sassen 1991), but the increased connectivity of the economy and the world in general, combined with the global range of many economic opportunities and markets, is likely to affect cities at all levels of the hierarchy.

It should be pointed out also that the decreased use of New York and other diversified national centres for higher order services, and the increased use of services provided among the regional centres, are relatively minor. New York in particular continues to provide many of the higher order services for large numbers of corporations, and the ratio of absolute concentration, especially for investment banking, foreign banking, and major banking relationships, remains heavily in favour of New York. What we may be witnessing in the growth of concentration among regional centres is the effect of a series of 'globalizing' trends similar to those of the world city but on a much smaller scale.

Conclusion

The evidence presented in this chapter suggests that the widely recognized relationship between the globalization of economic activity and the centralization of corporate control over that activity does not seem to have found expression in spatial terms. Examining the patterns of corporate headquarter location between 1974 and 1989 it was evident that the trend towards agglomeration in the nation's largest centres is being reversed. The continuing process of globalization notwithstanding, corporate headquarter agglomerations are no longer the exclusive prerogative of world cities, at least US world cities (i.e. diversified national centres).

As illuminating as these trends are, they do raise the question of whether corporate headquarter location can still be considered an accurate indication of the locus of corporate control. Drawing on the work of numerous scholars who have pointed to the significance of the rapid emergence of higher level business services in the world cities, we speculated that the dispersal of corporate headquarters might be symptomatic of a shift in the organizational locus of corporate control rather than in geographical location. Thus we hypothesized that US diversified national cities may be emerging as 'brokers', mediating and orchestrating the global linkages of multinational corporations, headquartered in lower order centres, through the agglomeration of advanced business and producer services.

However, on the basis of the data concerning shifts in the proportional use of business and producer service firms by large corporations, the evidence was hardly convincing. In fact, it was apparent that New York and the other major centres were actually providing higher order services for fewer corporations over the period studied. Corporations located in regional and specialized functional centres appeared increasingly to be turning towards local providers of advanced business services during the 1980s. Apparently the mediating role of the US diversified national centres is actually declining, even though the absolute differences in concentration of higher order business services remain large.

It may be that we are witnessing the birth of a select set of new potential 'global cities' within the USA. This is certainly suggested by the inability of the remaining diversified national centres (i.e. Los Angeles, San Francisco, and Chicago) to capitalize on the decreases in New York and the rapid expansion of a select few diversified regional centres. Lord's (1987, 1992) work on the US banking industry lends some support to this interpretation. He points to the rapid increase in asset concentration among banks in smaller centres, such as Atlanta, Charlotte, and Boston, due to state deregulation and a series of inter-state banking acquisitions during the 1980s.

On the other hand, what we may be observing are the effects of the continuing globalization of the US economy. As a result of a number of changes taking place in the US and the world economy as a whole, the primacy of the USA's diversified national or world cities may be eroding. Clearly, corporations no longer need physically to locate their head-quarters in the largest cities in order to manage their international operations, but it also seems they are no longer finding the need to conduct their operations 'through' these cities either. Regional centres, further down the urban hierarchy, may now be sufficiently integrated into the world economy to function as command centres in their own right. In this way, rather than being 'brokered' by the global centres, the fortunes of cities lower in the urban hierarchy are now much more directly linked to developments within the world economy than ever before.

Certainly, there is nothing preordained about an individual city's position within the structure of the US urban hierarchy. The case of Houston is instructive here. Houston expanded rapidly during the late 1970s and early 1980s to become the diversified regional centre with the highest level of corporate headquarter concentration. Yet a few years later it had dropped to sixth place among this group. Although Houston's boom was closely allied to the fortune of the oil industry, the inability of many of its corporations to adjust to changing circumstances points to the volatile nature of changing corporate influence among new, rapidly expanding centres. If this is the case it would imply that the globalization of economic activity is not so much reconcentrating economic power within the current structure of the US hierarchy as remaking that hierarchy in the process.

From this perspective, the patterns we have observed may also suggest a change in the nature of the linkages between global cities and the world-system. It is apparent that US corporations are increasingly utilizing foreign banks for much of their foreign banking transactions – bypassing New York in the process. Intuitively this makes considerable sense, especially if market penetration, rather than utilization of cheap labour, is the goal of globalization. As US corporations expand their overseas operations, their knowledge, expertise, and business contacts increase also. Similarly, financial corporations in the host country develop a wider range of services and the necessary experience to deal with the needs of US corporations. Hence, in an effort to streamline linkages it is likely that as a corporation becomes more established overseas, the need for a 'broker' may decrease and be replaced by a series of direct contacts. If this is the case then the function of the global city in the future may not be so much to provide the conduit for national capital as it expands overseas, but to serve as the 'host' for international capital as it flows into the (national) hinterland of that global city. Thus while the primacy of the global cities is apparently being eroded in the USA, the process of globalization may actually be reinforcing the role of peripheral world cities in facilitating the penetration of foreign capital.

ACKNOWLEDGEMENT

The authors would like to acknowledge the research assistance of Brad Lagano in the Department of Geography, SUNY – Binghamton, and also wish to thank the editors for their helpful comments on an earlier draft. They are all, of course, absolved of any responsibility for the outcome. The authors alone are responsible for the content of this chapter.

NOTES

1   SIC 621, security brokers; SIC 211, cigarettes; SIC 633, fire, marine, and casualty insurance; and SIC 603, savings institutions (SIC: Standard Industrial Classification).
2   This does not necessarily imply that the head office of the audit provider was located in that city, only that the service was provided in that city.

REFERENCES

Amin, A. and Thrift, N. 1992. 'Neo-Marshallian nodes in global networks'. *International Journal of Urban and Regional Research*, 16(4): 571–87.

Borchert, J. R. 1978. 'Major control points in American economic geography'. *Annals of the Association of American Geographers*, 68: 214–32.

Braudel, F. 1984. *The Perspective of the World*. London: Collins.

Browett, J. 1984. 'On the necessity and inevitability of uneven spatial development under capitalism'. *International Journal of Urban and Regional Research*, 8: 155–75.

Cohen, R. B. 1981. 'The new international division of labour, multi-national corporations and urban hierarchy'. In *Urbanization and Urban Planning in Capitalist Society*, ed. M. Dear and A. J. Scott, pp. 287–315. New York: Methuen.

Dicken, P. 1992. *Global Shift: The Internationalization of Economic Activity*. 2nd edn. New York: Guilford Press.

Dun and Bradstreet. 1990. *Corporate Finance Bluebook*. Skokie IL: National Register Publishing Co.

Forbes. 1975. The *Forbes* 500s, 15 May: 155–96.

1983. A summary of the 500s rankings, 9 May: 266–305.

1990. The *Forbes* 500s annual directory, 30 April: 222–434.

Friedmann, J. 1986. 'The world city hypothesis'. *Development and Change*, 17(1): 69–84. (Reproduced as appendix in this volume.)

1993. 'Where we stand: a decade of world city research'. Paper presented to the World Cities in a World System conference, 1–3 April, Sterling VA. (Reproduced as ch. 2 in this volume.)

Friedmann, J. and Wolff, G. 1982. 'World city formation: an agenda for research and action'. *International Journal of Urban and Regional Research*, 6: 309–44.

Geddes, P. 1968. *Cities in Evolution*. New York: Howard Fertig.

Green, M. B. 1987. 'Corporate-merger-defined core–periphery relations for the United States'. *Growth and Change*, 18: 12–35.

Hall, P. 1966. *The World Cities*. London: Weidenfeld and Nicolson.

Harper, R. 1987. 'A functional classification of management centers of the United States'. *Urban Geography*, 8: 540–9.

Harvey, D. W. 1986. *The Urbanization of Capital*. Oxford: Basil Blackwell.

Holloway, S. R. and Wheeler, J. O. 1991. 'Corporate headquarters relocation and changes in metropolitan corporate dominance, 1980–1987'. *Economic Geography*, 67: 54–74.

Knox, P. L. 1991. 'The restless urban landscape: economic and sociocultural change in the transformation of metropolitan Washington, DC'. *Annals of the Association of American Geographers*, 81: 181–209.

Lord, J. D. 1987. 'Interstate banking and the relocation of economic control points'. *Urban Geography*, 8: 501–19.

1992. 'Geographic deregation of the US banking industry and spatial transfers of corporate control'. *Urban Geography*, 13: 25–48.

Lyons, D. 1994. 'Changing patterns of corporate headquarter influence 1974–1989'. *Environment and Planning A*, 26: 733–47.

Noyelle, T. J. and Stanback, T. M. 1984. *The Economic Transformation of American Cities*. Totowa NJ: Rowman and Allanheld.

Sassen, S. 1991. *The Global City: New York, London, Tokyo*. Princeton NJ: Princeton University Press.

Semple, R. K. 1973. 'Recent trends in the concentration of corporate headquarters'. *Economic Geography*, 49: 309–18.

Semple, R. K. and Phipps, A. G. 1982. 'The spatial evolution of corporate headquarters within an urban system'. *Urban Geography*, 3: 258–79.

Storper, M. and Walker, R. 1989. *The Capitalist Imperative*. Oxford: Basil Blackwell.

US Department of Commerce. 1990. *Statistical Abstract of the United States*. Washington DC: US Government Printing Office.

Wheeler, J. O. 1986. 'Corporate spatial links with fiscal institutions: the role of the metropolitan hierarchy'. *Annals of the Association of American Geographers*, 76: 262–74.

Zehring, K. 1983. *The Corporate Finance Bluebook*. New York: Zehring Publishing.

7 Transport and the world city paradigm

David J. Keeling

Introduction

The world city paradigm posits a distinct role for certain cities in articulating regional and national economies in the global system (Friedmann 1986). World cities develop hierarchical relationships that rise and fall over time according to their control and mediary functions in the system. As commanding nodes in the world economy, world cities are defined by dense patterns of interaction between people, goods, and information. A rapidly expanding and sophisticated global network of transport services and infrastructure facilitates this interaction. In turn, the globalization of finance, production, labour, service, cultures, and information has given impetus to, and has helped to shape, extraordinary advances in transport provision. Thus, the role of transport in the evolving world city system is both crucial and fundamental.

Although much research has addressed world city formation and the genesis, growth, and change of the world city system, we still do not have a clear appreciation and understanding of either the dynamics or the role of transport in shaping world cities. Few studies have examined theoretically or empirically how, why, or where transport linkages function in the world city system. Moreover, little attention has been paid to the way control and mediary functions of world cities are helping to shape global, regional, and local transport networks and services.

This chapter moves toward addressing these issues by examining several important components of the transport–world city nexus. Firstly, a framework is established for analysing transport's role in the world city system. Secondly, broad trends in global transportation are analysed by focusing on the contemporary international airline network. Thirdly, the potential regional and global implications of the transport–world city nexus are discussed and two possible development scenarios are considered. Finally, an agenda for future research is proposed.

A framework of analysis

Despite transport's key role in the world city system, the relationship between transport and world cities has proved extremely difficult to conceptualize. Theory suggests a strong correlation between good transport linkages and urban integration at the national, regional, and global levels (Owen 1987). The importance of transport in the evolution of the capitalist world economy, for example, is implicit in Wallerstein's (1983) world systems theory. Transport also plays a pivotal role in modernization theory, from which models of network growth have been developed to help explain the economic development of a country and its incorporation into the world economy (Taaffe and Gauthier 1973). Yet the driving forces behind the mutual interdependence and bi-directionality of the transport–world city relationship have remained conceptually elusive. A narrow, explicitly economic approach has dominated attempts to theorize the transport–urban growth nexus. Such an approach argues that transport's role is merely to foster inter-regional or inter-urban linkages for the purpose of economic growth and expansion (Dugonjic 1989). If we are to move beyond an economically determined framework of analysis, specific cultural, political, social, and environmental components must be incorporated into our conceptualization of the transport–world city relationship.

Furthermore, there is a contradiction in the theoretical literature concerning the principles that are shaping the space–time relationships of global activities. The 'footloose' qualities of administrative and information (transactional) activities argue for geographic dispersion in a variety of places. Advances in transport and communication technology have removed many of the spatial and temporal barriers to activity decentralization and, in some ways, have made cities such as Rapid City in South Dakota as competitive as New York for certain types of information-based activities. In contrast, the world city hypothesis suggests that specialized international, regional, and domestic activities tend to concentrate in a few dominant cities. These world cities organize and exert tremendous control over national, regional, and multinational economies (Friedmann and Wolff 1982; see also Friedmann's discussion in the appendix). Thus, a theoretical paradox exists, particularly at the national level, concerning transport's role as both a centralizing and decentralizing development force. An examination of global links to world cities can shed light on the interplay between these seemingly contradictory forces.

Figure 7.1 provides a starting point for theoretical and empirical analyses of transport's role in the world city system. It suggests a highly

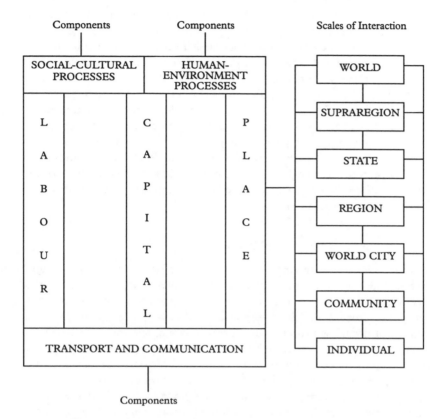

Figure 7.1 A framework for analysing the transport–world city nexus

generalized set of central relationships at work in and among world cities. Place, global capital, and the international division of labour are central pillars in the world city system. Interaction between these three components over space and through time is inextricably intertwined with, and conditioned by, social, cultural, political, and environmental processes. Transport and communication function as the foundation upon which the central pillars of the world city system rest. Transport helps to shape the negative, positive, and neutral spatial impacts of these interrelated processes and, in turn, is shaped by these impacts. Transport facilitates the movement of people, goods, and information through the system and functions as a necessary, though not sufficient, component of world city and world economy genesis, growth, and change.

Detailed analyses of interaction among world cities can take place at a variety of scales. We may choose to focus on an individual, a community, a specific world city, a macro-region, or the global system itself. Each of these scales of interaction is intimately connected with the others. Changes at the individual level can have a ripple effect throughout the system, just as global changes can have an impact at every level down to the individual. The purpose of the framework, however, is not to establish definitive boundaries for interaction or to suggest that these are the only relationships between components that matter. Interaction between and among all components is fluid, dynamic, and occurs on multiple scales. The framework's purpose is merely to guide our analysis of transport's role in the world city system and to suggest specific pathways of interaction that may prove to be useful avenues of research.

Global links to world cities

World cities are connected by hierarchies of transport networks and services that provide both vertical and horizontal linkages at a number of different scales. Not only are world cities connected to other major cities of equal, greater, or lesser importance, they also are connected to a variety of urban and rural centres at the regional and local levels. These connections are facilitated at the global and regional levels primarily by air transport, telecommunications circuits, and non-voice data transfer systems. Airline linkages offer the best illustration of transport's role in the world city system for five reasons: (i) global airline flows are one of the few indices available of transactional flows or inter-urban connectivity; (ii) air networks and their associated infrastructure are the most visible manifestation of world city interaction; (iii) great demand still exists for face-to-face relationships, despite the global telecommunications revolution (Heldman 1992; Noam 1992); (iv) air transport is the preferred mode of inter-city movement for the transnational capitalist class, migrants, tourists, and high-value, low-bulk goods; and (v) airline links are an important component of a city's aspirations to world city status.

For many cities attempting to compete in the global economy, the phrase 'direct flight to London' (or New York or Tokyo) has become a metaphor for success. Non-stop air service to major world cities symbolizes both the globalization of society and trade and the emergence of an information-based economy (Abbott 1993). The movement and interaction of people and information have become equally as important as the movement of goods. For example, the port of Portland in Oregon has argued that non-stop air service between Portland and London or

Frankfurt is vital to the continued growth of Oregon's economy. Direct air links to advanced technology centres in Europe would create a potential for expansion comparable to the growth experienced in Pacific Rim trade (Oregon International Trade Institute 1992).

Similar arguments are being made by local boosters, trade organizations, local governments, and other interested parties in cities around the world. Direct connections into the global airline and world city system are perceived to endow certain competitive advantages upon urban areas. Nashville officials are touting the city's recent successful bid for a non-stop flight to London as a direct pipeline into the world economy. And planners in Denver believe that new airport infrastructure and direct air links to world cities will give Denver's essentially static, regionally oriented economy a revolutionary transactional and global dimension (Goetz 1992; Noel 1989).

In addition to the economic impetus to world city connectivity, the perception of a particular world city's attractiveness for other activities also plays a powerful role in determining global airline connections. London, Paris, and New York, for instance, are three of the most important tourist destinations in the world today. Tourism, as the fastest growing global industry, will continue to exert tremendous influence over the international airline network. Historical inertia also plays a crucial role in determining links between world cities. As traditional destinations for international labour, domestic and foreign migrants, and investment capital, many world cities continue to exert control and mediary functions based on historic colonial or neo-colonial relationships (King 1990). The volume of weekly flights between Sydney and London, for example, is driven more by familial and tourist relationships than by economic considerations alone.

The purpose of analysing the global airline network is not to define a rigid rank order of world cities. Hierarchies of world city connectivity are dynamic, fluid, and extremely plastic. A city's position in the network rises and falls depending on myriad factors, including supply and demand, government regulation, the influence of emerging regional trade blocs, historical inertia, local circumstances, and changing perceptions of place. Rather, by taking a snapshot of the network in space and time, the analysis suggests that certain cities control and dominate flow throughout the network. Moreover, empirical data can help our theorization of the transport–world city nexus by raising questions about why certain city pairs are linked together. Twenty years ago, for example, Tokyo had just regional and local connections on a non-stop, daily basis, yet today it is an important international hub and world city (O'Connor and Scott 1992).

Table 7.1 *Number of cities over one million population with direct airline service to major world cities*

Population (millions)	+15	10–15	5–10	3–5	2–3	1.5–2	1–1.5	Total
No of cities by category	5	8	17	35	53	48	100	266
Rank City								
1 London	5	5	14	24	21	23	33	125
2 Paris	5	7	14	26	21	17	29	119
3 Frankfurt	5	7	14	26	22	15	27	116
4 New York	4	6	13	23	22	16	31	115
5 Moscow	3	5	13	16	17	19	29	102
6 Amsterdam	4	7	12	21	17	14	25	100
7 Zurich[a]	4	6	14	13	15	13	19	84
8 Los Angeles	5	5	9	20	13	10	18	80
9 Miami	2	6	4	13	14	10	18	67
10 Tokyo	4	7	14	18	6	9	9	67
11 Bangkok	3	5	10	12	6	8	17	61
12 Singapore	3	5	12	13	8	7	12	60
13 Cairo	2	2	8	10	6	10	15	53
14 Hong Kong	4	3	10	10	7	7	7	48
15 Bombay	4	3	8	9	4	5	11	44
16 Rio de Janeiro	3	4	3	13	6	9	5	43
17 São Paulo	2	5	3	12	5	8	6	41
18 Sydney	4	4	6	8	2	4	5	33
19 Buenos Aires	2	5	1	9	6	4	4	31
20 Johannesburg	1	2	2	4	4	7	0	20

Note: [a] population less than one million.
Source: Official Airline Guide (1992), United Nations (1992).

The global airline network

In order to analyse and map the dominant linkages in the global airline network, and to identify those cities that seem to exert control over global connectivity, a matrix was created of scheduled air service to and from 266 cities whose metropolitan populations exceeded one million. Only non-stop and direct flights (the same plane but with one or more stops *en route*) between city pairs were captured, as an almost endless permutation of connections is possible using one or more plane changes. The global airline network was divided into seven regions (North America, South America, East Asia, West Asia/Middle East, Africa, Europe, and Oceania), and the dominant cities in each region were analysed and mapped. International and domestic flight frequencies between city pairs within each region and between regions determined the regional and global dominance of a city.

From the matrix emerges the functioning of the global airline system, and with it a working hypothesis of the world city system's functional hierarchy. The data revealed twenty cities that dominate their respective regional hinterlands and function as major hubs in the global air network (table 7.1). These cities enjoy high levels of connectivity, not only to urban centres with populations over one million, but also to smaller regional and domestic cities. City-pair flight data provide a clear pattern of connectivity among cities of equal status (horizontal linkage), and between cities of equal and lesser status (vertical linkage), at a variety of regional scales.

Service frequencies and city-pair linkages suggest a global airline network divided into three distinct levels. At the top of the hierarchy of spatial articulations sit the cities that are the subject of Saskia Sassen's (1991) recent research: the command and control centres of the global economy – New York, London, and Tokyo. These cities contain many branch, regional headquarters, and head offices of major national and multinational corporations, as well as offices or representatives of most of the world's major banks. Thus, New York, London, and Tokyo account 'for most large business dealings on a world scale' (Thrift 1989: 70). They function as centres for interaction between and among the transnational capitalist class, tourists, the economic élite, and others.

A map of international air connections clearly illustrates the major global linkages between New York, London, and Tokyo, and the role the cities play as dominant global hubs (figure 7.2). Together, these three world cities receive 36.5 per cent of the total global non-stop flights to the world airline network's twenty dominant cities (table 7.2). They also control 27 per cent of the total intra-regional flights and 38.7 per cent of the total domestic flights to the twenty dominant cities. Although flights outside a world city's own region are quite limited compared to the volume of intra-regional and domestic flights, by any measure London, New York, and Tokyo dominate the international airline network. Notice, however, that Tokyo ranks only fourth in the total number of global non-stop flights (table 7.2), and tenth in the number of 'millionaire' cities served (table 7.1). Moreover, Tokyo is not the dominant regional hub in East Asia. Singapore and Hong Kong are the most important centres of Asian regional traffic, but Tokyo is the dominant city from that region in the world city hierarchy. This highlights the dominance of the Japanese economy in the Asian region, as well as its importance in the global system.

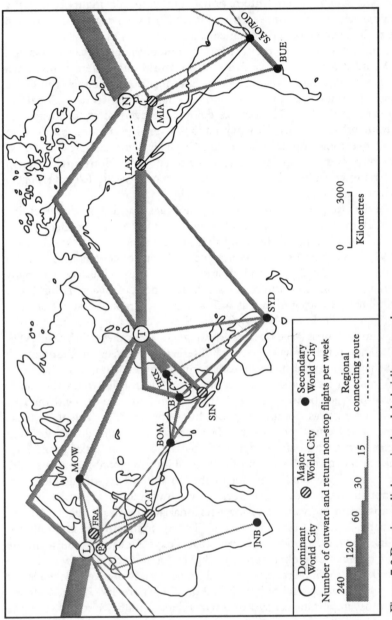

Figure 7.2 Dominant linkages in the global airline network

Table 7.2 *Total number of non-stop flights per week to the major world cities, 1992*

City	Global	Regional	Domestic
London	775	3,239	1,063
New York	644	634	8,837
Paris	565	2,264	1,436
Tokyo	538	401	1,814
Frankfurt	482	1,376	771
Miami	311	1,389	2,146
Cairo	277	34	114
Los Angeles	245	419	7,150
Bangkok	231	483	307
Amsterdam	229	1,593	0
Singapore	221	831	0
Hong Kong	154	713	0
Zurich	147	1.258	155
Sydney	144	89	1,541
Rio de Janeiro	93	44	933
Moscow	87	400	1,430
Bombay	64	111	313
São Paulo	64	97	1,418
Buenos Aires	52	336	414
Johannesburg	40	108	450

Source: Official Airline Guide (1992).

At the second level of spatial articulation sit the zonal or regional centres such as Paris, Frankfurt, Amsterdam, and Zurich in Europe, Miami and Los Angeles in North America, Singapore in East Asia, and Cairo in North Africa. These cities serve as important links in the global economy but are responsible for specific zones rather than for interaction at the global scale. An analysis of the total number of cities world-wide with non-stop or direct flights to the global network's twenty dominant cities illustrates the role of zonal centres (table 7.3). For example, Miami dominates North and South America, and Cairo is the major link between Africa and the Middle East. In East Asia, Singapore controls connectivity with 831 non-stop flights each week serving 39 cities, more than twice as many flights and cities served than Tokyo. Paris clearly is the dominant hub for Africa, with connections to 61 cities, as well as for continental Europe. In terms of global connectivity, however, Paris certainly ranks alongside London and New York. Paris is the second most connected of the matrix's twenty major world cities (table 7.1). It has the second highest total of non-stop regional connections and the third highest total of global connections (table 7.2), and it is the

Table 7.3 *Number of cities with direct flights to major world cities by region, 1992*

City	North America	South America	East Asia	West Asia Mid-East	Africa	Oceania	Europe	Total international	Total domestic
London	43	6	12	25	34	6	116	242	17
New York	45	20	7	12	6	1	40	131	126
Tokyo	18	3	18	8	1	13	19	80	38
Paris	17	11	13	24	61	4	93	223	53
Frankfurt	34	10	14	24	28	4	76	190	19
Amsterdam	26	9	11	21	25	2	86	180	0
Zurich	12	4	10	14	21	0	80	141	2
Miami	58	30	0	0	0	0	13	101	61
Singapore	6	0	39	17	3	11	20	96	0
Los Angeles	33	10	16	0	1	8	12	80	103
Cairo	4	0	5	23	16	0	30	78	9
Moscow	9	4	14	23	14	0	51	115	108
Bangkok	6	0	24	19	1	8	23	81	17
Hong Kong	7	0	36	9	2	7	8	69	0
Bombay	3	0	9	20	7	0	11	50	31
Sydney	5	2	15	3	1	14	9	49	53
Johannesburg	1	1	2	1	23	0	13	41	25
Rio de Janeiro	9	12	2	0	4	0	13	40	41
São Paulo	12	13	2	0	0	0	13	40	63
Buenos Aires	9	19	0	0	1	2	9	40	41

Source: Official Airline Guide (1992).

second most globally connected city in the world airline system (table 7.3). Yet Paris has only 19 non-stop flights per week to Tokyo and only 58 non-stop flights each week to New York. These data suggest that Parisian connectivity relates more to historic colonial, cultural, and political ties than to contemporary global economic control and mediary functions.

Finally, there are the regional cities such as Moscow, Hong Kong, São Paulo, and Sydney. Although these tertiary level cities host many corporate offices and foreign banks, their influence is primarily regional and domestic in nature. Sydney, for example, is the major regional hub for Oceania, and Johannesburg functions as the dominant hub for southern Africa. In the case of Moscow and Johannesburg, political conditions have limited regional and global connectivity. The future position of these cities in the world city hierarchy may alter over the coming decade as economic (Russia) and political (South Africa) circumstances change.

To summarize, the analysis of the global air transport network has revealed the existence of a few dominant hubs dispersed around the world. Traffic at the global level seems to be quite limited and concentrated on a few dominant world cities. The greatest number of flights are medium- or short-haul in nature, which highlights the importance of regional and domestic connectivity. For example, nine of the top ten city pairs are either regional or domestic in terms of number of flights (table 7.4). Only the London–New York sector has a volume of weekly flights sufficient to rank in the top ten.

At the regional and domestic levels, a system of three major subnetworks exists. The North American subnetwork is centred on New York and, to a lesser degree, Los Angeles and Miami, with an extension reaching out to the peripheral realm of South America. Europe is dominated by London and Paris, although Amsterdam, Frankfurt, and Zurich function as important centres. The European subnetwork also extends beyond its continental limits, with connections to the Middle East, Africa, and Oceania. Finally, the East Asian subnetwork is focused on Tokyo, Hong Kong, and Singapore, with extensions to Oceania, South Asia, and West Asia. All three of these subnetworks overlap in their connectivity to the peripheral regions of the world system – Oceania, South America, the Middle East/West Asia, and Africa.

Regional implications of the transport–world city nexus

A regional perspective on world city linkages is particularly important as world cities are becoming increasingly disarticulated from their host

Table 7.4 *Number of non-stop outbound and return flights per week between city pairs*

Rank	City pair		No. of flights
1	New York	– Miami	846
2	London	– Paris	760
3	London	– Amsterdam	461
4	New York	– Los Angeles	405
5	Singapore	– Kuala Lumpur	342
6	Singapore	– Jakarta	308
7	Hong Kong	– Taipei	298
8	London	– New York	242
9	London	– Frankfurt	235
10	Hong Kong	– Bangkok	233
11	Singapore	– Bangkok	223
12	Los Angeles	– Mexico City	196
13	Tokyo	– Honolulu	175
14	London	– Zurich	170
15	Amsterdam	– Paris	160
16	Frankfurt	– Paris	156
17	Tokyo	– Hong Kong	133
18	Amsterdam	– Frankfurt	125
19	Tokyo	– Los Angeles	122
20	New York	– Paris	119
21	Singapore	– Hong Kong	104
22	Singapore	– Tokyo	94
23	Bangkok	– Tokyo	83
24	São Paulo	– Buenos Aires	80
25	London	– Tokyo	76
26	London	– Los Angeles	75
27	Frankfurt	– Moscow	71
28	Miami	– Los Angeles	70
29	New York	– Tokyo	66

Source: Official Airline Guide (1992).

countries (Thrift 1989). For example, it can be argued that the majority of Argentina's population is largely irrelevant to Buenos Aires' internationally oriented economy. Indeed, much attention in recent years has focused on bifurcated development in both Western, industrialized states (Champion and Townsend 1990) and less-developed countries (Carlevari 1993). At the same time, emerging regional trade blocs in Europe (EC), South America (MERCOSUR), North America (NAFTA), and South Asia (ASEAN) suggest that intra-regional relationships could play a dominant role in the world city system in the decades ahead. Patterns of transport growth and change in these regions raise some important questions concerning the possible development impetus of world cities at both regional and local scales. Two possible scenarios are suggested by these network patterns: (i) development focused on the major world cities (centralized), or (ii) development that disperses the benefits of world city processes to the regional hinterland (decentralized).

Centralized development

The first scenario assumes a spatial strategy that focuses on major urban centres. Urban concentration and specialization help to determine transport development patterns, which in turn have an enormous impact on world city relationships with regional hinterlands. Many transport policies are influenced heavily by the tremendous economic and political power of world cities. As a result, policies more often than not reflect the needs of the world city as if they were identical to the needs of the state or region. The French and British national transport systems, for example, focus almost exclusively on the national capital city. Little attention is given to transverse inter- and intra-regional connectivity outside the ambit of the capital city's control.

In Britain, the infrastructure associated with the Eurotunnel project is focused solely on London. The development implications of Eurotunnel for the less developed areas of Wales, Scotland, or northern England have received scant attention in British transport policies. Thus, the development impetus of Eurotunnel will be focused on London and its immediate hinterland, an area already considered economically 'over-heated' compared to the rest of Britain. Exacerbating this problem, the British government has hindered the decentralization of international air flights from the heavily congested London area by being reluctant to grant foreign airlines landing rights at Manchester, Glasgow, and other regional airports.

Centralized development is most evident in countries where a world city or primary urban centre overwhelmingly dominates the state. In Argentina, Buenos Aires controls the political, economic, cultural, and social processes of the entire nation. Transport and regional development policies in Argentina have been formulated and implemented based on the premise that what is good for Buenos Aires is good for Argentina. The capital city captures all international air traffic, with the exception of a few weekly flights to contiguous countries from a handful of interior cities. The result has been a reinforcement of a dendritic pattern of transport whereby almost all global, regional, and national interaction is focused on Buenos Aires. In a classic example of centralized development, Argentina has become a bifurcated state, split between the wealthy world city and the impoverished maldeveloped interior (Keeling 1993).

Decentralized development

The second scenario assumes a development pattern composed of growth axes and chains of urban centres. Such a pattern offers the possibility of reversing the relative disarticulation of world cities from regional hinterlands (Williams 1992). Integrated, multimodal transport networks are fundamental to this process and could help to diffuse the development impetus of world cities both vertically and horizontally throughout a region.

In Japan, a linear chain of urban development with associated hinterlands seems to be growing between Osaka and Tokyo (Rimmer 1986). Osaka is connected to Tokyo and intermediate urban centres by a new high-speed train. Osaka also has a new 24-hour international airport that is attracting traffic away from the heavily congested and inconvenient Tokyo Narita airport. Eleven regional and thirteen international cities now have non-stop or direct flights to Osaka, compared with only a handful of cities ten years ago. Both air and surface transport are thus playing a crucial role in helping spread the development impetus of both Tokyo and Osaka along the urban corridor linking the two centres.

Several countries in Europe are developing an integrated, multimodal, inter-city surface and air transport network that embraces entire countries and regions in an interlocking, grid-based system of interaction. In Germany, the economic impetus of Frankfurt, Munich, Berlin, and the Koln-Essen agglomeration is spreading through the region along growth axes and chains of urban connections. Moreover, future regional development plans in Europe are based on an evolving European high-speed rail network that links primary and secondary cities together in interlocking chains of urban connectivity. Similarly, in other regions around the world, both air and surface transport are playing a fundamental role in rearticulating world cities with their regional and local hinterlands.

Conclusion: an agenda for research

Transport and communication have played a critical role in shaping the evolving world city system. In turn, world cities have been instrumental in shaping global, regional, and local transport and communication networks. World cities have also encouraged extraordinary advances in the technology and infrastructure necessary to facilitate the movement of people, goods, and information through the system. This symbiotic relationship suggests, along with issues raised in the preceding pages, that future research on the transport–world city nexus ought to focus on five important areas.

Firstly, geohistorical analyses are needed of transport's role in the evolution of individual world cities and the world city system. How has transport conditioned the development of a city's control and mediary functions in local, regional, and global arenas of interaction over space and through time? Secondly, world city analyses would benefit from a greater appreciation of the real constraints to global and regional transport development. How will Paris, Berlin, and London be affected by the disparate national transport policies of France, Germany, and Britain, policies developed against the backdrop of the European Community's drive toward regional development and integration? How is the articulation of Lagos, Cairo, Buenos Aires, or São Paulo with the world economy being hindered by the lack of integrated, multimodal, regional, and national transport systems which are so crucial to the development process? Thirdly, analyses of the transport–world city nexus would benefit from GIS-based (Geographic Information Systems) data on traffic patterns related to world city interaction on a variety of scales. Fourthly, we need to analyse transport–world city relationships against the backdrop of emerging regional trade blocs. Patterns of transport development in these regions could provide important indicators on the likely future relationships of world cities at both regional and global levels.

Finally, transport and communication ought to play a central role in theories and models concerned with world city genesis, growth, and change. Transport is not merely a non-interactive process whereby inanimate objects move through the system without purpose or design. It is the product of individual, community, and institutional desires to move about and communicate. The decisions that are made about movement and communication help to shape global, regional, and local transport networks. Reciprocally, these networks play a critical role in shaping pathways of interaction between and among individuals, institutions, and places. Incorporating transport more fully into the world city paradigm could enrich our understanding of world city processes. It could also facilitate an exciting dialogue among those concerned with forging theoretical and empirical links between the global, the regional, and the local.

ACKNOWLEDGEMENTS

The author thanks the editors and Anthony King, David Meyer, Robert Harper, and David Simon for their constructive comments and criticisms on this chapter's initial drafts.

REFERENCES

Abbott, Carl. 1993. 'Through flight to Tokyo: sunbelt cities and the new world economy, 1960–1990'. In *Urban Policy in Twentieth-Century America*, ed. Arnold R. Hirsch and Raymond A. Mohl, pp. 183–212. New Brunswick NJ: Rutgers University Press.

Carlevari, Isidro. 1993. *La Argentina: Estructura Humana y Económica*. Buenos Aires: Ediciones Macchi.

Champion, A. G. and Townsend, A. R. 1990. *Contemporary Britain: A Geographical Perspective*. London: Edward Arnold.

Dugonjic, V. 1989. 'Transportation: benign influence or an antidote to regional inequality?' *Papers of the Regional Science Association*, 66: 61–76.

Friedmann, John. 1986. 'The world city hypothesis'. *Development and Change*, 17(1): 69–84. (Reproduced as appendix in this volume.)

Friedmann, John and Wolff, Goetz. 1982. 'World city formation. An agenda for research and action'. *International Journal of Urban and Regional Research*, 6(3): 309–44.

Goetz, Andrew R. 1992. 'Air passenger transportation and growth in the US urban system, 1950–1987'. *Growth and Change*, 23(2): 217–38.

Heldman, R. K. 1992. *Global Telecommunications: Layered Networks' Layered Services*. New York: McGraw-Hill.

Keeling, David J. 1993. 'Transport and regional development in Argentina: structural deficiencies and patterns of network evolution'. *Yearbook of the Conference of Latin Americanist Geographers*, 19: 25–34.

King, Anthony. 1990. *Global Cities: Post-Imperialism and the Internationalization of London*. London: Routledge and Kegan Paul.

Noam, E. 1992. *Telecommunications in Europe*. Oxford: Oxford University Press.

Noel, Thomas J. 1989. 'Unexplored western skies: Denver International Airport'. Paper given at the 29th annual meeting of the Western History Association. Tacoma, WA, 13 October.

O'Connor, K. and Scott, A. 1992. 'Airline services and metropolitan areas in the Asia-Pacific region'. *Review of Urban and Regional Development Studies*, 4: 240–53.

Official Airline Guide. 1992. *Worldwide Edition, January*. Oak Brook IL: Reuben H. Donnelly.

Oregon International Trade Institute. 1992. *Air Cargo Imports from Europe to the Portland Region*. Portland OR: OITI.

Owen, W. 1987. *Transportation and World Development*. Baltimore MD: Johns Hopkins University Press.

Rimmer, Peter J. 1986. 'Japan's world cities: Tokyo, Osaka, Nagoya, or Tokaido megalopolis?' *Development and Change*, 17(1): 121–58.

Sassen, Saskia. 1991. *The Global City: New York, London, Tokyo.* Princeton NJ: Princeton University Press.

Taaffe, Edward J. and Gauthier, Howard L. 1973. *Geography of Transportation.* Englewood Cliffs NJ: Prentice-Hall.

Thrift, Nigel. 1989. 'The geography of international economic disorder'. In *A World in Crisis?* ed. Ronald J. Johnston and Peter J. Taylor, pp. 16–78. Oxford: Basil Blackwell.

United Nations. 1992. *Demographic Yearbook, 1991.* New York: United Nations Publishing Division.

Wallerstein, Immanuel. 1983. *Historical Capitalism.* London: Verso.

Williams, Richard. 1992. 'European spatial planning and the cityport system'. In *European Port Cities in Transition,* ed. Brian S. Hoyle and David A. Pinder, pp. 59–79. London: Belhaven Press.

8   The world city hypothesis: reflections from the periphery

David Simon

Introduction

In the decade since John Friedmann and Goetz Wolff (1982) launched the world city hypothesis with their 'agenda for research and action' on what one might call the political economy of the global urban system, much attention has been focused on the still smallish group of global control centres of the world economy. The hypothesis itself stimulated a fair level of academic work and debate, although somewhat less than might have been hoped in view of the increasingly intense integration of the world capitalist system. Moreover, this system is structured by inequality between immense power and profound weakness, in which vast wealth coexists with, and depends on, deepening immiseration and marginalization *within* world cities as much as any other class of city or territorial unit. In the words of Friedmann and Wolff (1982: 322):

They become the major points for the accumulation of capital and 'all that money can buy'. They are luxurious, splendid cities whose very splendour obscures the poverty on which their wealth is based. The juxtaposition is not merely spatial; it is a functional relation: rich and poor define each other.

The phenomenon of 'globalization', itself necessarily now the subject of intense debate, more nuanced conceptualization, and more refined application (e.g. King 1991; Robertson 1992), has heightened awareness of the increasing concentration of formative political, economic, social, and cultural processes and practices on a world scale. These may have very different features and agendas from their smaller-scale counterparts and are much less subject to the control of individual governments, to which their interests may in any case be directly antagonistic. Particularly within the fields of critical social theory and cultural studies, much attention has also been devoted to the articulation between globalization and localization as consequence, coincidence, or as conscious cultural practice.

Nevertheless, much of the literature on world cities has originated from very different, often eclectic or politically naive, perspectives without any reference to the world city hypothesis or its conceptual underpinnings. This is evident from the different attempts at defining world cities (see below). This volume is therefore very timely in several respects. First, work broadly within the framework of the world city hypothesis can be evaluated against the other material just referred to. Second, enough time has elapsed to permit refinement of the world city hypothesis on its own terms. Third, the world today is a very different place from a decade ago and we need to think through the effects of the dramatic changes in the world system that have occurred over this period. The most obvious developments to consider are, on the one hand, the demise of the former Soviet Union and the near total eclipse of state socialism as a mode of production outside China, North Korea, and Cuba, and on the other, the impact of structural adjustment and economic recovery programmes in many Third World countries. Fourth, we need to engage with recent assertions on the relevance of post-modernism for the Third World and the questions of identity and representation which therefore arise. Although its central theme is refinement of the world city hypothesis in the light of research on the principal cities of sub-Saharan Africa, this chapter will touch on all of these issues.

The world cities hypothesis

It is useful at the outset briefly to remind ourselves of the essence of this hypothesis, which comprises seven loosely linked 'theses' (Friedmann 1986). The first of these highlights the importance of a city's integration with the world economy for understanding its role in the international division of labour and for analysing internal structural change. The remaining theses outline the principal features of world cities as global control centres and 'basing points' for international capital accumulation. As such, the emphasis is very much on political economy rather than on political institutions and processes or on cultural (re)production, issues which have risen in prominence in world city research in the last decade.

On the basis of the hypothesis, Friedmann distinguishes a taxonomy of world cities (see appendix table A.1 and figure A.1) which, as he points out, has three significant features:

- all but two of the primary world cities (São Paulo and Singapore) are located in core countries;
- European world cities are difficult to classify because of their relatively small size and often specialized functions;

- the list of secondary cities is suggestive rather than definitive, because in core countries they are often smaller and more specialized than primary cities, while in semi-peripheral countries they are mostly capital cities, the relative international importance of which depends greatly on the 'strength and vitality of the national economy which these cities articulate'.

Although I am in broad agreement with these propositions, I would like to explore these issues further. Apart from pointing out the inconsistency of Johannesburg's classification in Friedmann's table A.1 and figure A.1 respectively, I will focus on the notion that only cities in the core and semi-periphery can be regarded as world cities.[1] At one level, research on sub-Saharan Africa, the outer periphery of the world economy, supports this contention. On the other hand, however, it also suggests that the seven 'theses' in themselves are inadequate for specifying or defining world cities.

The political economy of world city formation

Underpinning the world city hypothesis is the political economy of the global urban system. In developing this theme, it is necessary to examine the interplay between national political economies and the world system, i.e. between national and international capital, states and international organizations. Since world cities are generally primate cities (and, where they exist, also other national metropolises), these represent one important arena in which the issues can fruitfully be examined. This reflects the roles of such cities as political capitals and transactional crossroads between internal and external relations, as well as the related factors of their size, economic complexity and centrality, and their attractiveness to new migrants from within and beyond the country. Irrespective of how internationally marginal a country is, its capital and/or principal industrial and port centres are far more closely integrated into the world economy than its inter-mediate and small centres. Primate, and especially world, cities might also be revealing elements of international convergence in the way that production, circulation/distribution, and consumption are organized and regulated as these processes become increasingly globalized. These developments are also manifest in elements of their built environments. This is not to argue, however, that convergence is all-embracing, uniform, or ubiquitous; aspects of divergence will continue to be evident. Primate cities are therefore reliable barometers of national and international politico-economic processes, and the (dis)-articulation between them.

In my recent book (Simon 1992), I sought to advance our understanding and conceptualization of post-colonial urban development by examining capital and other major cities in terms of their mode of incorporation into (i.e. their national and international functions within) the world economy. This represents arguably the most fruitful approach to elucidating how they operate and the processes through which their built environments have been socially constructed and reconstructed over time. On account of its unwanted status as the poorest, most marginal continental region within the current world economy, sub-Saharan Africa provided the case study.

The task necessitated the development of a conceptual framework, grounded in political economy but sensitive to human agency and social and cultural expression. This framework was designed to integrate five scales of analysis, namely the global, continental regional, national, urban, and intra-urban, and yet be flexible enough to explore the pivotal role of these cities in the interrelationships between them. Needless to say, no ready-made, off-the-peg, theory could be pressed into action. Several related global level paradigms were interwoven to inform the analysis. I rejected strict 'world-systems theory', as formulated and elaborated by Immanuel Wallerstein, as rather too economistic and deterministic, not least because the role of the state is at times unfairly marginalized. This is also true of different social groups within countries and territories (Peter Taylor's personal comment), although there have been recent attempts to focus world-systems theory at the level of the household (e.g. Smith and Wallerstein 1992). However, juxtaposing the generic roles of capital (both international and national) and the state, yielded a very useful perspective into which the constructs of colonialism and post-colonialism could be melded. These, in turn, provided the immediate umbrella under which the theories of colonial and post-colonial urban development were further developed, and the relationships between these and the respective urban forms elucidated. The urban and intra-urban levels were then related back to the world scale through a consideration of different permutations of the globalization thesis, and the extent to which the process of increasingly globalized production and especially consumption could be said to be leading to cultural convergence and, ultimately, the evolution of a global culture.

The very nature of culture and human agency seems to rule out the notion of a single homogeneous culture, although many globalized cultural forms in specific spheres and contexts are emerging.[2] The near universal adoption of specific aspects of (generally) Western material culture does not automatically presage overall cultural hybridization, while convergence may equally well spawn new counter-cultures, either spontaneously or through conscious articulation. Some of these issues will be returned to below.

The wider schema comprises the world system or global political economy and the role, or principal mode of production, of individual countries and regions within the international division of labour. Cities are not autonomous units but human artefacts, i.e. culturally, technologically, and environmentally modified manifestations of the system that produces them. In much of sub-Saharan Africa the dominant mode of production since the colonial period has been capitalism. Colonization of the continent in the late nineteenth century was predicated on the needs of European industrial capitalism and the associated imperial ambitions of the major powers. Within the evolving world economy, sub-Saharan Africa's principal roles became those of a raw material supplier and a captive market for manufactured goods; functions that, apart from some import substituting industrialization, the continent has generally been unable to transcend in the few short decades since decolonization. This is central to Africa's progressive peripheralization and current crisis.[3]

It was in the European settlement colonies (South Africa, Namibia, Kenya, Zimbabwe, and to a far lesser extent Senegal) that indigenous land dispossession was most extensive and labour exploitation most intense. Ironically, these countries have among the most diversified and sophisticated economies today, but even they still rely mainly on primary and semi-processed, rather than on manufactured, goods for the bulk of their export revenue. In other words, Africa remains the only large and populous continent without a true newly industrializing country (NIC) which, seemingly, is another reason for its marginality to global circuits of commercial, industrial, and financial capital. South Africa has many characteristics of a NIC and, but for the distortions of the apartheid system and the effects of its increasing international isolation on that account until 1989–90, would already have attained true NIC status. In most African countries independence was followed by progressively greater direct and indirect state involvement in the economy, in an effort to catalyse development and to promote greater localization (indigenization), a politically popular strategy intended to reduce external economic control, create employment, and (usually also) to enlarge the indigenous capitalist classes. Even these measures failed to promote sophisticated industrialization, and they are now generally viewed as important contributors to Africa's economic plight, and are being reversed in favour of 'market forces'. I have recently elaborated on these issues elsewhere (Simon 1993). This backdrop of regional and national modes and relations of production within the world economy informs my analysis of the continent's cities.

Most African cities have experienced rapid growth but only limited economic transformation since independence. There are few industrial cities on the continent, and those which do exist remain geared primarily to the import substitution of consumer non-durables and durables rather than to large-scale export or the production of capital goods. Given the absence of NICs this is not surprising. In most cases commerce is still more important than manufacturing.

At the same time, however, the service sector has been growing in significance and sophistication in most capital cities. While much of this growth has been in producer services, the insurance and personal service element has also been dynamic. Perhaps more than any other, it is the communications subsector which has assumed progressively greater importance in the age of high technology and telecommunications. This provides the instant linkages to other capital cities and centres of the world economy, and has entrenched the sharpening distinction between the system of core cities which controls the international circuits of commercial, industrial, and financial capital, and the cities of the semi-periphery and periphery. So, paradoxically, just as the world is becoming ever more tightly integrated and interconnected by virtue of advances in aviation and telecommunications technology, it is also becoming increasingly differentiated in relative terms and, in the case of most of sub-Saharan Africa (SSA), also in absolute terms.

Inextricably bound up with the communications subsector is the range of activities we could best classify as producing, consuming, and reproducing culture in the broadest sense. These include the print and broadcasting media, film, video and associated industries, music, theatre, art, and other forms of formal culture production. As elsewhere, these are heavily concentrated in Africa's primate cities, although their reach or scope[4] remains overwhelmingly national or subcontinental. As Friedmann points out in his chapter in this volume, global 'cultural services' are increasingly located in world cities.

The few exceptions in SSA to the general trends just outlined are the cities which, like the metropolitan complex centred on Johannesburg (the Pretoria–Witwatersrand–Vereeniging (PWV) region) and Nairobi, have developed significant service sectors and levels of international connectivity. Details of this can be found in Simon (1992), but I will summarize the situation with reference to two unconventional yet illuminating variables, the number of secretariats of international organizations (table 8.1) and the volume of air traffic (table 8.2).

Table 8.1 *African cities with the greatest number of secretariats of international organizations*

City	Principal secretariats				Secondary secretariats				Grand Total
	A	B	C	Total	A	B	C	Total	
Nairobi	0	30	69	*99*	0	2	4	*6*	*105*
Dakar	0	25	33	*58*	0	5	1	*6*	*64*
Addis Ababa	0	10	38	*48*	0	1	3	*4*	*52*
Tunis	0	17	21	*38*	0	1	2	*3*	*41*
Abidjan	0	13	24	*37*	1	0	2	*3*	*40*
Cairo	4	18	14	*36*	1	1	0	*2*	*38*
Lagos	1	14	13	*28*	1	1	1	*3*	*31*
Accra	0	13	14	*27*	0	0	1	*1*	*28*
Ouagadougou	0	5	19	*24*	0	1	1	*2*	*26*
Harare	0	4	10	*14*	1	0	7	*8*	*22*
Yaoundé	0	8	10	*18*	0	3	0	*3*	*21*
Some comparisons:									
Asia									
Bangkok	5	12	77	*94*	1	1	3	*5*	99
Manila	2	26	50	*78*	2	4	7	*13*	91
Kuala Lumpur	2	19	30	*51*	1	1	0	*2*	53
New Delhi	5	11	22	*38*	2	3	1	*6*	44
Jakarta	1	6	29	*36*	0	3	3	*6*	42
Seoul	1	7	9	*17*	2	1	2	*5*	22
Latin America and Caribbean									
Buenos Aires	3	42	24	*69*	1	7	6	*14*	83
Mexico City	3	31	40	*74*	2	1	5	*8*	82
Santiago	0	18	51	*69*	2	1	5	*8*	77
Caracas	0	25	41	*66*	2	3	5	*10*	76
Bogotá	1	18	10	*29*	2	1	3	*6*	35
São Paulo	1	11	8	*20*	2	0	0	*2*	22
Europe									
Brussels	90	299	592	*981*	13	43	45	*101*	1082
Paris	155	257	368	*780*	33	49	43	*125*	905
London	130	137	233	*500*	9	11	20	*40*	540
Rome	18	19	388	*425*	6	6	9	*21*	446
Geneva	73	44	244	*361*	15	7	27	*49*	410
North America									
New York	17	26	188	*231*	10	7	34	*51*	282
Washington DC	18	19	120	*157*	8	6	17	*31*	188
Montreal	12	6	19	*37*	3	2	5	*10*	47
Ottawa	5	4	15	*24*	1	0	1	*2*	26

Notes: (1) International organizations include all non-profit bodies, whether governmental or non-governmental.

(2) Secretariats located in differently named suburbs/districts are not always included.
(3) A: International organizations with global or inter-continental membership (i.e. UIA *Yearbook* categories A–C).
     B: Regionally defined membership organizations, representing at least 3 countries in a particular continent or subcontinental region (i.e. UIA *Yearbook* category D).
     C: Other (including funds, foundations, religious orders etc., i.e. UIA *Yearbook* categories E, F, R).
Source: UIA (1990), vol. II table 10.

Given assertions about the growing importance of non-state actors in organizing and regulating human activities, one interesting variable is the extent to which individual cities serve as headquarters for such bodies (table 8.1). African cities compare reasonably well with those in other regions of the Third World in terms of the total number of secretariats based there. However, when the data are disaggregated, Africa loses out heavily. Unlike Latin American and Asian cities, Nairobi (Africa's most popular location) has no headquarters of global membership organizations. At the same time, however, we must remember the overwhelming extent to which such organizations are still headquartered in world cities of the North, symbolizing their continued grip on global power.

The progressive expansion of civil aviation reflects continued growth in business and international tourism. The data in table 8.2 are revealing of the relative insignificance of sub-Saharan African (SSA) airports relative to those in the NICs, in particular, and the primary gateways of the North. Cairo is Africa's busiest airport, while Johannesburg is SSA's primary gateway, reflecting the airport's hub functions for the southern African region and its importance for both business and tourist travellers, reflected in the large number of domestic passengers and volume of freight and post handled. Nairobi has gained its position by virtue of being East Africa's gateway and a stopover *en route* to South Africa from Europe. This latter function has fallen away significantly since the recent introduction of non-stop flights to South Africa with the new Boeing 747–400 series, while the phasing out of sanctions against South Africa since 1991 has greatly increased the number of foreign airlines and flights serving Johannesburg. Lagos is surprisingly unimportant, given the country's vast population and considerable potential in view of its economic situation. It is important to note the scores on the different variables.

The PWV's pre-eminence reflects South Africa's economic sophistication and the wealth of the white minority and new black middle classes,

Table 8.2 *Volume and nature of commercial traffic through selected African airports, 1988*

Airport	Aircraft movements (000)		Passengers (000)		Freight (000 tonnes)		Mail (000 tonnes)		Number of airports served directly		Number of airlines serving	
	Total	International	Total	International	Total	International	Total	International	Total	African	Total	African
Abidjan	16.7*	–	854*	–	19.5*	–	0.2*	–	26	14	20	11
Accra	6.3	5.3	287*	251	11.2	11.2	0.6	0.6	12	7	11	5
Addis Ababa	13.1	4.8	445	236	43.4	17.5	1.1	0.9	18	10	11	4
Cairo	63.7	47.6	6,690	5,392	102.1	99.7	–	–	69	11	46	10
Dakar	10.9†	9.3†	662†	621†	17.2†	17.2†	0.6†	0.6†	35	11	19	11
Johannesburg	65.3*	21.5*	4,538*	1,537*	118.8*	81.7*	11.7*	5.2*	25	16	19	8
Lagos	47.6*	12.2*	2,972*	740*	26.4*	–	0.9*	–	29	14	20	7
Nairobi	20.4*	15.0*	1,348*	1,056*	38.5*	37.4*	2.1*	2.0*	47	19	30	13
Some comparisons:												
Hong Kong	87.4	87.0	15,227	15,227	694.1	694.1	18.4	18.4	–	–	–	–
Chicago O'Hare	712.4	36.9	56,773	4,059	737.2	310.3	273.0	17.3	–	–	–	–
London Heathrow	330.4	244.2	37,510	30,659	642.1	635.3	65.3	58.6	–	–	–	–
Tokyo Narita	100.8	96.3	14,657	13,893	1,202.7	1,194.0	23.9	22.6	–	–	–	–

Notes:

1 Passenger, freight, and mail data are bidirectional but exclusive of transit traffic.

2 Africa includes mainland only.

* 1987

† 1986

– not available

Source: Calculated from ICAO, *Air Traffic 1988* and *Traffic by Flight Stage 1988.*

while Nairobi's position is due to its relative sophistication, the consequent location there of the headquarters of two UN agencies, and the attractive effect this has had on other international organizations, both international governmental organizations (IGOs) and nongovernmental organizations (NGOs). In other words, Nairobi has assumed a supranational role in the sphere of information flows and associated diplomatic and financial transactions. However, on account of a wide range of other problems and limitations, the city is still a considerable way short of becoming even a continental city, let alone a true world city, despite being dubbed the 'world capital of the environment' by some IGO officials.

The definition and nature of world cities

At this point it is appropriate to consider the question of what the prerequisites for world city status actually are. Inevitably there is no unanimity on the subject. Perhaps the most basic criterion might be population. For example, Peil (1991) claims that Lagos, with an estimated 4–5 m. inhabitants, is a world city on this basis alone. For me this is inadequate: not only does it beg the problematic question of what critical threshold to use but it also takes no account of the fact that several modestly sized cities, e.g. Washington DC and Geneva, do fulfil true global roles whereas many far larger conurbations (including Lagos) patently do not. In their initial essay on the world city hypothesis, Friedmann and Wolff (1982: 310) were explicit that population could *not* be used, since this more accurately reflects than determines a city's economic and political role. However, Janet Abu-Lughod (chapter 10 in this volume) rightly draws attention to the importance of the extent (even more than the actual proportions) of population diversity in world cities.

A second and far more widely used criterion is the existence of a major industrial and manufacturing base which exports a significant share of its output. It is certainly true that many longstanding world cities, e.g. London, New York, and the Rhine–Ruhr, attained their positions at least partly on that basis. However, it would certainly not be true of Washington DC and Geneva. Hence this, too, is clearly inadequate on its own.

In the contemporary world it is becoming increasingly clear that the three most important criteria relate to:
(a) the existence of a sophisticated financial and service complex serving a global clientele of international agencies, transnational corporations (TNCs), governments and national corporations, and NGOs;

(b) the development of a hub of international networks of capital and information and communications flows embracing TNCs, IGOs, and NGOs; and

(c) a quality of life conducive to attracting and retaining skilled international migrants i.e. professionals, managers, bureaucrats, and diplomats. In this sense, quality of life embraces not only physical and aesthetic aspects of the environment but also broader considerations such as perceived economic and political stability, cosmopolitanism, and 'cultural life'.

The first and second criteria just mentioned are very closely related and correspond to what Gottmann (1989: 62) calls concentrations of 'brainwork-intensive' industries which he perceives as the hallmark of transactional cities. His list of current world cities is revealing and comprises seven on which there has long been agreement, i.e. London, Paris, Moscow, New York, Tokyo, Randstad Holland, and the Rhine–Ruhr (presumably with Frankfurt as core), together with three relative newcomers, Washington DC, Beijing, and Geneva. He sees another set of cities (Chicago, Los Angeles, San Francisco, Montreal, Toronto, Osaka, Sydney, and debatably also Zürich), as approaching world city status, but specifically excludes Mexico, São Paulo, and Seoul, three of the most dynamic metropolises of the South (cf. Kowarick and Campanario 1986: 63–4). Surprisingly, Singapore and Hong Kong do not even rate a mention in this schema. With the possible exception of Beijing, therefore, all Gottmann's world cities are in the North, a fact clearly related to his rather loaded and contestable assertion that Third World cities are only now beginning their industrial revolution (Gottmann 1989: 62). The contrast with Friedmann's schema and list (see appendix) is notable, but reflects their very different conceptual underpinnings.

Friedmann and Wolff (1982) argue that world cities are undergoing economic restructuring, a process they discuss by grouping economic activities into six clusters:

- the strongest dynamism arises from the growth of a primary cluster of 'high level business services' (management, banking, legal services, accounting, technical consulting, higher education, etc.);
- a secondary cluster involves other fast-growing services, the demand for which is derived from the primary cluster. These include real estate, construction, hotel and catering establishments, private police, and domestic services;
- thirdly, international tourism is often fast-growing. This overlaps with the second cluster to a large extent but depends on international economic cycles;

- the fourth cluster comprises manufacturing industries, which are generally regarded as being in decline;
- government services comprise the fifth cluster, with concern and responsibility for the reproduction of the world city;
- sixthly, they distinguish the 'informal' or 'floating' sector, and ascribe a residual role to those who do not have regular or income earning activities.

This classification is helpful in building up a profile of world cities, although some doubt must remain as to whether they do specify them uniquely. Similar trends are readily observable in a wide range of cities not vying for 'world' status. The principal difference, it seems to me, lies in the absolute scale, relative importance, specialization, and growth rates of the respective clusters. Further work would be required to 'calibrate' the appropriate rates.

Newly published data on air pollution in mega-cities of the world (defined as having populations of at least 10 m. projected for the year 2000), highlight the problems of unique definition of world cities (table 8.3). Of course, mega-cities are not the same as world cities. Even here, however, major differences emerge, for example, in the ratio of cars to population, in average population density, the extent of the physical urban area, and in current population growth rates. Even among the primary core world cities, there are marked disparities between, say, London and Los Angeles. Since motor vehicle emissions are one of the principal sources of urban air pollution, the number of registered vehicles can be regarded as a crude proxy for air quality, subject to climatic conditions, average incomes, cultural values, urban structure, and vehicle use patterns. Nevertheless, actual air pollution data are now available. To the extent that generalization across the different variables in figure 8.1 is possible, primary core world cities appear now to have lower average air pollution levels than those of secondary world cities or mega-cities in the NICs or proto-NICs. This is often a result of more stringent abatement legislation and enforcement in the former (and therefore also the relocation of some heavily polluting industries to major cities in the NICs). Air pollution problems closely reflect the rate and extent of industrialization and vehicle use together with urban size. Hence, in the context of Africa's global economic peripherality, it is noticeable that there are no African cities in table 8.3. In addition, wood, coal, and charcoal smoke from the hearths of low income and other residents without access to electricity, gas, or paraffin, comprises a major component of air pollution in most large Third World cities – a problem directly related to the proportion of urban poor in each case. Such pollution thus tends to decline in relative (and perhaps also

Table 8.3 *Mega-cities: selected data*

City	Population (m.) 1990	Population (m.) 2000	Registered motor vehicles	Area (km²)
Bangkok	7.16	10.26	1,760,000 ('88)	1,565
Beijing	9.74	11.47	308,000 ('91)	16,800
Bombay	11.13	15.43	588,000 ('89)	603
Buenos Aires	11.58	13.05	1,000,000 (est.)	7,000
Cairo	9.08	11.77	939,000 ('90)	214*
Calcutta	11.83	15.94	500,000 ('89)	1,295
Delhi	8.62	12.77	1,660,000 ('89)	591 (81)
Jakarta	9.42	13.23	1,380,000 ('87)	590‡
Karachi	7.67	11.57	650,000 ('89)	3,530 (82)
London	10.57	10.79	2,700,000 ('88)	1,579†
Los Angeles	10.47	10.91	8,000,000 ('89)	16,600
Manila	8.40	11.48	510,000 ('88)	636°
Mexico City	19.37	24.44	2,500,000 ('89)	2,500
Moscow	9.39	10.11	665,000 ('89)	994
New York	15.65	16.10	1,780,000 ('90)#	3,585
Rio de Janeiro	11.12	13.00	n/a	6,500
São Paulo	18.42	23.60	4,000,000 ('90)	8,000
Seoul	11.33	12.97	2,660,000 ('89)	1,650
Shanghai	13.30	14.69	147,700 ('90)	6,300
Tokyo	20.52	21.32	4,400,000 ('90)	2,162

Notes:
1 Mega-cities defined as projected to have > 10 m. population by the year 2000.
2 The following cities have been omitted from the study: Dacca, Lagos, Osaka, Tehran, while South Africa's PWV complex is not mentioned.
* Cairo Governate only
‡ Metro Jakarta
† Greater London
° Manila only
New York City only

Source: UNEP/WHO (1992).

absolute) importance, while vehicle emissions generally rise, with increasing average urban incomes. Nevertheless, no direct mechanistic reading is possible, and the data show just how complex the picture actually is when considering a range of variables.

The issue of classification inevitably raises two vital questions. Firstly, as discussed above, is a heavy industrial base a prerequisite for world city status? Put differently, in terms of national modes of production, can a world city arise in a state which has not attained at least NIC status? Secondly, in the context of key features of the contemporary world economy (international mobility of capital and new technologies,

	Sulphur dioxide	Suspended particulate matter	Lead	Carbon monoxide	Nitrogen dioxide	Ozone
Bangkok	◔	●	●	◔	◔	◔
Beijing	●	●	◔	○	◔	●
Bombay	◔	●	◔	◔	◔	○
Buenos Aires	○	●	◔	○	○	○
Cairo	○	●	●	●	○	○
Calcutta	◔	●	◔	○	◔	○
Delhi	◔	●	◔	◔	◔	○
Jakarta	◔	●	●	●	◔	●
Karachi	◔	●	●	○	○	○
London	◔	◔	◔	●	◔	◔
Los Angeles	◔	◐	◔	●	●	●
Manila	◔	●	●	○	○	○
Mexico City	●	●	◐	●	◐	●
Moscow	○	●	◔	●	●	○
New York	◔	◔	◔	●	◔	●
Rio de Janeiro	●	●	◔	◔	○	○
São Paulo	◔	●	◔	●	●	●
Seoul	●	●	◔	◔	◔	◔
Shanghai	◐	●	○	○	○	○
Tokyo	◔	◔	○	◔	◔	●

● Serious problem, WHO guidelines exceeded by more than a factor of two

◐ Moderate to heavy pollution, WHO guidelines exceeded by up to a factor of two (short-term guidelines exceeded on a regular basis at certain locations)

◔ Low pollution, WHO guidelines are normally met (short-term guidelines may be exceeded occasionally)

○ No data available or insufficient data for assessment

Figure 8.1 Air quality indicators for twenty mega-cities world-wide, based on a subjective assessment of data records
Source: After fig. 4.2 in UNEP/WHO (1992).

changing global divisions of labour, etc.) is it possible for major cities to develop tertiary and quaternary functions without a heavy industrial base? The discussion above would seem to indicate – as asserted by Friedmann (1986) – that world cities are found only in core and semi-peripheral countries. However, the second question requires a positive answer, exemplified best by Singapore and Hong Kong. These admittedly atypical city states have become continental, and in some respects also global, centres of accumulation and communication, with the emphasis increasingly on selected hi-tech sectors, transport, financial markets, and the business and personal services sectors.

Nairobi is one (by no means outstanding) example of how a significant supranational hub of transactional functions can evolve without a major industrial base. Moreover, at least in terms of the total number of international organizational headquarters, an important indicator of transactional networking and hub functions, Montreal and Ottawa do not rank more highly than a number of Third World metropolises. However, when the data are disaggregated, a crucial difference becomes evident, namely, that Montreal has more headquarters of global membership organizations. In terms of telecommunications and air passenger links, together with quality of life, the Canadian cities almost certainly also have an advantage. Such ambiguities simply underline my earlier point about the complexity of the issue and the inadequacy of using any single criterion as the basis for definition. At least two of the factors discussed above, together with a favourable image and quality of life, are likely to be necessary. Finally, one can concur with Gottmann's (1989: 64) assertion that globalization in urban terms is increasing, in that

Every substantial city nowadays aspires to a world role, at least in some specialty. This makes them expand linkages abroad, participating in more networks. All these trends contribute, little by little, to building up and intensifying the global weave of urban networks.

There is also every likelihood that the number of world cities will increase over time, as he suggests, but the mere development of a particular, specialized global role is clearly *not* a sufficient condition for becoming a world city. For various reasons many major cities, and even mega-cities (as defined above), will not attain such status.

This leads neatly back to the 'world city hypothesis' and the work of John Friedmann (Friedmann 1986; Friedmann and Wolff 1982). He is careful to describe the seven theses comprising the hypothesis as constituting primarily 'a framework for research. It is neither a theory nor a universal generalization about cities, but a starting-point for political enquiry' (Friedmann 1986). While extremely useful in this context, the theses do not actually *define* world cities. Rather, they provide an admirable summary of the features of all major cities with significant supranational roles, of which true world cities are only a subset. Given Friedmann and Wolff's (1982: 310–11) emphasis on the form and strength of integration into the world economy and the extent of such spatial dominance, this is surprising, but perhaps reflects their concern with the evolutionary process of 'world-cities-in-the-making' rather than with a finite set of existing world cities at a given point in time.

However, even Friedmann's (1986) refinement of distinguishing primary and secondary world cities within both the global core and semi-periphery does not adequately avoid this drawback. For example, all the 'theses' apply to Nairobi, which remains some way short of either continental or world city status. Moreover, although Kenya is the dominant economic power in East Africa, it does not yet even come close to forming part of the semi-periphery. Its status remains unambiguously peripheral in politico-economic and other terms. This is more generally true of SSA's primate cities. For example, as stated earlier, the 'cultural services' (to use Friedmann's term) produced or located there seldom reach continental, let alone global, markets.

In a very different context, Friedmann and Wolff (1982: 310) raised the empirical problem of how far Soviet and Chinese cities could be included within this schema. Although essentially empirical in nature, this question highlights the point that cities which are supposedly the manifestations of state socialism, may nevertheless be tied into the international capitalist economy in strong and influential ways. Of course, we now have to consider this issue anew with respect to Moscow and St Petersburg, in particular, given the consequences of the dramatic end to state socialism in the former Soviet Union (something I do not attempt here). Nevertheless, this point serves as a salutary reminder of the magnitude and rapidity of change that is possible within the apparently highly structured and institutionalized world system. Not only has the 'mode of production' in the former USSR collapsed totally but the global role of Moscow has also shrunk markedly despite the city and Russia being open to Western capitalist penetration as never before.

In some respects, urban diversity in sub-Saharan Africa has actually increased since independence, rather than decreased. However, similar conflicts over access to the means of production and especially of social reproduction are occurring throughout the continent. Class, ethnicity, religion, and other potential cleavages combine or are operationalized in different contexts as means of engendering both unity and division, harmony and conflict. Urban form reflects the intertwined social relations of production and reproduction. Thus rapid urban growth, inadequate shelter provision and the consequent proliferation of irregular housing, unemployment and underemployment, and the mushrooming of 'informal' or petty commodity activities, are the norm in sub-Saharan Africa and beyond. At the same time, capitalists continually seek out the most profitable avenues for rapid accumulation which, given the prevailing conditions in many African countries, may well be through the commercialization of irregular housing markets. This process often exploits the poorest and weakest urban dwellers.

A dialectic of cities: whose world cities and for whom?

This forces us to consider the issue of conflicting and divergent interests in the city. Whose cities are they and whom do they serve? How is control or regulation organized and by whom? How are different identities and representations scripted? What is the relevance of the 'new' discourses of post-modernism and globalization in a Third World context? As discussed throughout this paper, globalization is obviously of fundamental import to analysis of world cities and of the way in which the various parts of the Third World are embedded and incorporated on the basis of differing – and changing – degrees of exploitation and unequal exchange. However, much of the earlier writing on the subject was vague and used 'globalization' in simplistic, all-encompassing terms. The importance of specifying the context and precise meanings of analysis has now become abundantly clear.

By contrast, the connections between globalization and post-modernism, especially as they pertain to research on, and representations of, the Third World, are far from clear and are only now beginning to come under serious and critical scrutiny. One of the problems, again, is that post-modernism is a flexible friend, to and for which different meanings attach in the various arts and social sciences. Certainly, critical writing on post-modernity by Featherstone (1991), Harvey (1989), Soja (1989), and others within First World geography and cognate disciplines has simply tended to assume universal applicability, without considering some of the implications and problems inherent in our unequal world. Given that many of the writers concerned have long pedigrees as radicals and have worked on the political economy and internationalization of capital, this is all the more surprising and remarkable. As recently pointed out, this assumption of universal relevance has applied as much to the erstwhile Second World as to the Third World (Bradshaw 1990; Sidaway 1990, 1992; Simon 1989, 1992). Massey (1993) has also referred to the need for an understanding of the 'power-geometry' of time–space compression. In a very post-modern way, then, this situation raises fundamental questions of (non-/mis)representation and Euro-American bias. In a somewhat different context, Sanders (1992) has raised the issue of Eurocentrism in research on, and representation of, African urbanization. While we should certainly be ever vigilant, her argument is not exactly new and is actually less convincing today than in earlier work, as it does not cover the full range of recent literature.

Along with King (1991, 1992), I have felt hitherto that the condition of post-modernity could have only marginal relevance, at best, to the Third World, since it presupposes the existence of modernity. Yet, beyond the enclaves of international capitalism – of which world cities are such fundamental lynchpins – modernity cannot be said to have been more than partially experienced. The principal exceptions are the widespread consumption of aspects of (primarily) material culture, and the impress of modern state forms and their associated ideologies and instruments of enforcement. However, there is still a vast difference between the situation and experiences of modernity of most Third World citizens and those of their First World counterparts.

Nevertheless, Folch-Serra (1989) and Slater (1992a, 1992b) have written convincingly on the need to re-examine such positions. There are several strands to their arguments, which can be summarized as follows:

1 In as much as post-modernism relates to a multiplicity of discourses, dialectics, and representations, reinterpreting and re-presenting the 'other' (in this case the Third World in all its diversity) should find a ready place within critical thought in this paradigm. It cannot simply be marginalized or ignored.

2 There are, in any case, important 'schools' of post-modern discourse emerging in parts of the Third World, especially among Latin American literary writers in the genre of Gabriel Garcia Marquez. Not only are they very influential within their own region, but their work pre-dates much concern in the North with post-modernism, and is having an important impact on world literature. We must hear these voices, give them a space, and consider carefully their representations and the identities expressed through these media.

In this light – and without offering a firm position of my own - we should debate these issues in much greater detail in the context of our specific concerns in this volume. At this stage I shall do no more than pose some central questions:

1 Is there really a plurality of discourses or a new hegemony?

2 How serious is Euro-Americocentrism in academe:

    (a) in mainstream social thought and theory

    (b) in relation to (post-)modern problematics?

3 What implications do these issues have for our conceptualizations of globalization, and more specifically, of the world city hypothesis?

4 Is the concept of a world city even universally relevant and meaningful?

As with the concept of 'globalization', we need to avoid slipshod terminology and the imputing of all-embracing characteristics to world cities. The nature of space and place is contested, both within and between individual cities. We must interrogate our assumptions, disaggregate our categories, and address the questions of whose city and for whom. For many, the disjuncture between aspirations and opportunities is – and is likely to remain – great. While it is difficult to postulate a firm figure for the percentage of urban poor in world cities, it is likely to be significantly higher – perhaps even the majority – in Third World metropolises. This situation again reflects the strength of their respective national economies and the nature of their insertion into the world system. The aspirations of the poor to a more adequate standard and quality of life cannot be ignored. Their perceptions of what is appropriate and desirable are likely to be very different to those of even progressive and activist planners and populist politicians.

In this context, it is worth quoting Garau's (1989: 72–3) useful schema, which contrasts the (obviously stereotyped and ungendered) views on functions and priorities held by four key groups of inhabitants of big Third World cities, namely, the poor, the affluent and semi-affluent national residents, non-national businesspeople and expatriates, and visitors/tourists:

Urban poor

Functions: The city is a tough place, but better than most, and certainly preferable to the village of origin. It is the best opportunity around to save some money to buy security (i.e. land) and to ensure children a better future through formal education.

Priorities (in descending order): income opportunity, prices, schools, housing, transport (emphasis on availability and affordability).

Affluent and semi-affluent national residents

Functions: The city is the place to be, for a great many reasons. It provides the best services, easy access to government and business contacts, and a gateway to the external world.

Priorities: status, income, security, availability of cheap labor (emphasis on quality of life and cost-quality trade-offs of goods and services).

Non-national business people and expatriates

Functions: The city is a good place to extract the highest possible profit in the shortest possible time, to win brownie points with headquarters, to save good money, and/or to enjoy a privileged life-style while it lasts.
Priorities: political and social stability, security, urban services, schools, housing, amenities, labor markets (emphasis on availability and reliability of services and quality of goods, with prices a marginal factor).

Visitor/tourist

Functions: The city has atmosphere, relaxation, a touch of the exotic, good shopping, and all the amenities need[ed] for a good holiday or a short stay.
Priorities: accommodation and transport, security, amenities, shopping, attractions, availability of 'essential' goods and services (emphasis on trade-offs between price and quality of services).

Massey (1993) has recently made a similar point in the context of London and other localities in general. Naturally, Garau's schema could usefully be disaggregated further to bring out the differential needs, experiences, and aspirations of specific subgroups within these four categories. Perhaps the most obvious of these are male and female-headed households, children, the elderly, and ethnic groups within the urban population. In other words, world (and other) cities are experienced differently according to people's gender, age, class, ethnicity, and nationality, in addition to their individual personalities.

Concluding remarks

Post-colonial cities in sub-Saharan Africa and other continental regions of the South represent a rich arena for research geared to practical issues of policy and planning, as well as at the level of theory. Insights derived from the complexity and dynamism of many Third World urban societies deserve to inform general urban and social theory far more than hitherto. The value of research into development paths diverging out of a common colonial experience is enhanced by the differential changes being wrought to the inherited structures and forms by increasingly powerful forces of globalization, instant communications, and the growing importance of international financial capital.

The Third World is becoming increasingly differentiated. On the one hand, some countries (the NICs and proto-NICs) are expanding the semi-periphery of the world economy, while some key cities in the NICs are becoming important continental and global financial centres in their own right (e.g. Singapore, Hong Kong and, to a lesser extent, São

Paulo). On the other hand, with very few exceptions, the countries of sub-Saharan Africa seem destined to remain very largely in the new global periphery, suffering growing urbanization and poverty together with economic stagnation, marginalization, and environmental degeneration. Such a fate is contested, with whatever means available, by Africa's nation-states. However, there is an inherent contradiction between the interests of individual nation-states, the territories of which are spatially bounded (see Taylor, chapter 3 in this volume), and the international capitalist system, led by TNCs and global economic institutions.

However, this is too simple a dichotomy; as I said earlier, the inequality and poverty at all scales *within* the core, semi-periphery, and periphery are just as important as those *between* these entities, however construed and constructed. As illustrated in several chapters in this book, and expressed so eloquently in the quotation from Friedmann and Wolff in my introduction, deprivation and disempowerment within primate and world cities go hand in hand with wealth and power. The fortunes of individual cities rise and fall, as do the divides between rich and poor within and between them.

In the context of current, more nuanced, writings on globalization and the post-modern conversations addressing questions of identity and representation, we should ponder the 'construction' of the world city hypothesis, both to sharpen its definitional clarity and to examine how its political economy articulates with the social and cultural realms of plurality, difference, meaning, and otherness.

In chapter 12, Tony King argues that the city is above all a representation – an imagined environment – so that our concern should focus on where and by whom that culture is produced. While I accept the basic point, I disagree with the superlative 'above all'; the city is, of course, also a very concrete entity. However, that physical form is socially and culturally constructed, and is then also imbued with diverse, even multiple and conflicting, meanings ('imagined environments') by people – from different positions within the same 'culture' as much as from different cultures.

Hence we should ponder whether the notion of a world city has any meaning – and if so, what – for different groups of world city inhabitants, especially the impoverished shanty dwellers and pavement people of Mexico City, Bombay, or Johannesburg. Yet, to end on a suitably post-modern note, even if the answer should be entirely negative (which it may well be), this would not negate the validity of our enterprise in this regard or, indeed, preclude these cities from functioning as world cities. It would only underscore the need for us to be conscious of the boundedness of our constructs in every sense. The current concern, in post-modern jargon, with reflexivity or positionality is healthy and valuable in moderation. However, if taken to extremes, it displaces other modes of analysis and results in self-indulgent exceptionalism, precluding any possibility of agreement on observable social conditions or processes, and thus precipitating an inability to move forward from analysis to (social) action. This really would be a case of throwing the baby out with the bathwater. For example, as widely evidenced even in this volume, colleagues working on world cities in the North so easily make unjustified implicit and explicit universalizing assumptions about the global relevance or uniqueness of our constructs. This does not, however, negate the value of such work; rather it requires that we become more self-conscious and less ready to impute or ascribe universal 'truths' based on Euro/Americo – and ethnocentric – experience, paradigms, and research.

ACKNOWLEDGEMENTS

A grant from the British Academy enabled my participation in the conference and this is gratefully acknowledged. I am grateful to conference participants, Paul Knox, Peter Taylor, James Sidaway, and Rob Potter for helpful comments on earlier drafts, while Justin Jacyno drew figure 8.1.

NOTES

1   In their parallel work, Armstrong and McGee (1985: 44–52) go even further. Their hierarchical model of economic organization in the world system distinguishes global centres – located in the North – very clearly from 'national metropolises', the principal metropoles of Third World societies.
2   Armstrong and McGee (1985) provide one of the earlier discussions of this process, in the context of convergence and divergence in Third World urbanization. Together with O'Connor's (1983) narrower notion of Westernization and indigenization of post-colonial urban form in tropical Africa, this remains apposite today.
3   The contrast with the dynamic economic development in the SE Asia–Pacific Rim region is marked. It is thus in no sense coincidental that there is no African equivalent of the 'kotadesatie' process whereby specialized industrial development is giving rise to 'extended metropolises' with increasingly important international roles (Ginsberg et al. 1991).
4   In this respect it has become fashionable to speak of the consumption of culture. While a very vivid image appropriate to our consumer culture, I find this concept too limited – and limiting – on the whole. Our relationship with cultural forms is far more profound and subtle.

REFERENCES

Armstrong, W. and McGee, T. G. 1985. *Theatres of Accumulation: Studies in Latin American and Asian Urbanisation*. London: Methuen.

Bradshaw, M. 1990. 'New regional geography, foreign area studies and Perestroika'. *Area*, 22(4): 315–22.

Featherstone, M. 1991. *Consumer Culture and Postmodernism*. London and Newbury Park CA: Sage.

Folch-Serra, M. 1989. 'Geography and post-modernism: linking humanism and development studies'. *Canadian Geographer*, 33(1): 66–75.

Friedmann, J. 1986. 'The world city hypothesis'. *Development and Change*, 17(1): 69–84. (Reproduced as appendix in this volume.)

Friedmann, J. and Wolff, G. 1982. 'World city formation. An agenda for research and action'. *International Journal of Urban and Regional Research*, 6(3): 309–44.

Garau, P. 1989. 'Third world cities in a global society viewed from a developing nation'. In *Cities in a Global Society*, ed. R. V. Knight and G. Gappert, pp. 68–78. London and Newbury Park CA: Sage.

Ginsburg, N., Koppel, B., and McGee, T. G. (eds.). 1991. *The Extended Metropolis: Settlement Transition in Asia*. Hawaii: University of Hawaii Press.

Gottmann, J. 1989. 'What are cities becoming the centres of? Sorting out the possibilities'. In *Cities in a Global Society*, ed. R. V. Knight and G. Gappert, pp. 58–67. London and Newbury Park CA: Sage.

Harvey, D. 1989. *The Condition of Postmodernity*. Oxford: Basil Blackwell.

ICAO. *Air Traffic 1988* (Series AT, no. 29). United Nations: International Civil Aviation Organization.

ICAO. *Traffic by Flight Stage 1988* (Series TF, no. 103). United Nations: International Civil Aviation Organization.

King, A. D. (ed.). 1991. *Culture, Globalization and the World-System*. London and SUNY, Binghamton: Macmillan.

1992. 'Identity and difference: the internationalization of capital and the globalization of culture'. In *The Restless Urban Landscape*, ed. P. Knox, pp. 83–110. Englewood Cliffs NJ: Prentice-Hall.

Kowarick, L. and Campanario, M. 1986. 'São Paulo: the price of world city status'. *Development and Change*, 17(1): 159–74.

Massey, D. 1993. 'Power geometry and a progressive sense of place'. In *Mapping the Futures: Local Cultures, Global Change*, ed. J. Bird, B. Curtis, T. Putnam et al., pp. 59–69. London: Routledge and Kegan Paul.

O'Connor, A. 1983. *The African City*. London: Hutchinson.

Peil, M. 1991. *Lagos: The City and its People*. London: Belhaven.

Robertson, R. 1992. *Globalization: Social Theory and Global Change*. London and Newbury Park CA: Sage.

Sanders, R. 1992. 'Eurocentric bias in the study of African urbanization: a provocation to debate'. *Antipode*, 24(3): 203–13.

Sidaway, J. 1990. 'Post-Fordism, post-modernity and the Third World'. *Area*, 22(3): 318–19.

1992. 'In other worlds: on the politics of research by "First World" geographers in the "Third World"'. *Area*, 24(4): 403–8.

Simon, D. 1989. 'Colonial cities, postcolonial Africa and the world economy: a reinterpretation'. *International Journal of Urban and Regional Research*, 13(1): 68–91.

1992. *Cities, Capital and Development: African Cities in the World Economy*. London: Belhaven.

1993. 'Debt, democracy and development: sub-Saharan Africa in the 1990s'. Paper presented at the British–Dutch–Nordic conference on Global Change, Structural Adjustment and Access to Economic, Political, Social and Environmental Resources, University of Amsterdam, 29–31 March.

Slater, D. 1992a. 'On the borders of social theory: learning from other regions'. *Environment and Planning D: Society and Space*, 10(3): 307–27.

1992b. 'Theories of development and politics of the post-modern – exploring a border zone'. *Development and Change*, 23(3): 283–319.

Smith, J. and Wallerstein, I. (eds.). 1992. *Creating and Transforming Households: The Constraints of the World-Economy*. Cambridge: Cambridge University Press.

Soja, E. 1989. *Postmodern Geographies: The Reassertion of Space in Critical Social Theory*. London: Verso.

UIA. 1990. *Yearbook of International Organizations 1990/91*. 2 vols. Union of International Associations.

UNEP/WHO. 1992. *Urban Air Pollution in Megacities of the World*. Oxford: Basil Blackwell.

9 Global logics in the Caribbean city system: the case of Miami

Ramón Grosfoguel

Studies of urbanization processes in the Caribbean in the past two decades tend either (1) to consider urbanization processes in the Caribbean outside of a global context (e.g. Hope 1986), or (2) to consider the local urban dynamics of urbanization apart from the Caribbean city system (e.g. Cross 1979; Portes and Lungo 1992; Potter 1989). The limitations of the studies that examine Caribbean urbanization are also to be seen in the literature on Miami. This literature tends to analyse Miami in relation to the Caribbean and Latin America in terms of the Cuban presence, but does not consider it as a world city (e.g. Allman 1987; Didion 1987; Garreau 1981; Grenier and Stepick 1992; Mohl 1983; Porter and Dunn 1984; Portes and Stepick 1993).

The Caribbean city system refers to a regional division of labour that produces transnational linkages between the most important Caribbean cities; this regional division of labour is based on the movement of commodities, capital, and people across cities. A movement which challenges traditional boundaries. This movement produces a hierarchical division of labour among the region's cities in terms of three distinctive roles: core, semi-periphery, and periphery.

The purpose of this chapter is to analyse the historical–structural developments that explain the emergence of Miami as a world city within the Caribbean city system during the 1970s and 1980s. Within the Caribbean city system, Miami is conceptualized as a core city. I will structure my analysis of this city according to three global logics: that of capitalist accumulation, the geopolitical military, and the geopolitical symbolic logic. The literature on world cities formation normally considers the first but tends to overlook the two geopolitical logics, namely, the military and the symbolic. This chapter is an attempt to incorporate the symbolic and military logics into the analysis of the formation of world cities. The paper is divided into five sections: (1) the theoretical framework; (2) the peculiar history of Miami which contributed to its eventual transformation into a world city; (3) the capitalist restructuring of the last twenty years and its effects on Miami's role in the Caribbean region; (4) the unique processes that explain why Miami emerged as a world city as opposed to New Orleans; and (5) the conclusion.

The global logics of world cities: theoretical overview

Debates about world cities very often emphasize the spatial aspect of the logic of capitalist accumulation, or what has been called an 'international division of labour in the world economy (Braudel 1984; Chase-Dunn 1985; Friedmann 1986, see appendix; Friedmann and Wolff 1982; Sassen 1991). World cities are usually conceptualized as nodal points of co-ordination, command, control, and management of global capitalist production and/or trade (Friedmann and Wolff 1982; Sassen 1988). In contemporary capitalism they are cities from which transnational capital or international banks co-ordinate, supervise, control, or manage capital investments in one or several regions. So, for example, world cities can control and manage capital investments over the entire world (e.g. New York, Tokyo, or Paris), over only one region (e.g. Houston, Sydney), or mediate between a core power and a peripheral region (such as semi-peripheral world cities like Singapore, Johannesburg, and São Paulo). Although these conceptualizations are very fruitful for understanding the role of world cities in the capitalist world economy, they do not adequately consider other global logics which also explain their emergence and their multiple functions in the world-system.

One such logic is the geopolitical military/security strategies of core states within the inter-state system. Certain world cities play a strategic military/security role over other regions; they centralize some of the military commands and co-ordinate a core state's global security strategy. These strategies have a spatial component in that they make use of strategic locations within specific regions.

Another logic refers to the geopolitical symbolic strategies of core states. These are ideological/symbolic strategies developed by core states to gain symbolic capital (Bourdieu 1977) within a region. This symbolic capital is usually exercised *vis-à-vis* the development model of another core state or of a challenging peripheral state, for example, by the 'showcasing' or presentation of a city or an ethnic group within a city as 'successful stories' to ideologically 'conquer the minds' of other people within a peripheral region.

The capital accumulation logic, the military logic, and the symbolic logic correspond, respectively, to the structural relations of exploitation, domination, and hegemony within the world system. The actual entanglement and interfacing of these structuring logics can lead to different scenarios, namely, instances where these logics can enforce or contradict each other. The conceptualization of the relationship among these structuring logics reveals neither full autonomy nor full reduction of one to another. Rather, the relationships among them are conceptualized here as semi-autonomous and historically contingent, where the dominance of one logic over another is dependent upon the particular historical–structural context (Kontopoulos 1993).

World cities, I will argue, reproduce simultaneously the three logics over a specific region or the entire globe. These cities perform functions of economic control, military domination, and ideological influence over other regions. These are not abstract logics, but instead are concretely inscribed in real life by such actors as transnational corporations, military organizations, intelligence agencies, communication and media enterprises, and foreign policy officials. Depending on which global logic dominates, some world cities will have a primary economic, military, or symbolic role. Thus, the concept of 'command and control' used in the literature about world cities (Friedmann and Wolff 1982) needs to be analytically expanded so as to include these geopolitical logics. Due to the literature's emphasis on world cities as economic articulators, cities with a dominant political–military function of control and command over the world system, such as Washington DC, are excluded from the world city analysis. By reconceptualizing world cities in this way, we can account better for the variety of world cities within the world-system, and for the multiple functions world cities can simultaneously articulate.

Now that the theoretical assumptions underlying this chapter have been presented, I now proceed to analyse the case of Miami.

The historic background: Miami

Since early in the sixteenth century south Florida has played an important military/security role for the core powers in the Americas. South Florida was an important military outpost; it was used as part of the strategy to defend the Spanish fleets that carried gold and silver from Mexico to Europe.

By the early nineteenth century south Florida was still a Spanish military stronghold with a walled city, St Augustine. By the mid-nineteenth century, after the USA snatched Florida from the Spaniards, it was largely an unpopulated territory with several military outposts, including Fort Myers, Fort Lauderdale, and Fort Dallas (now Miami)

(Portes and Stepick III 1993). Although many local Indians had been killed some groups managed to survive.

Miami was formally founded in 1896 as a tourist resort for wealthy families from the north-east. However, its role as an important geopolitical military location continued, guarding core power interests in the Caribbean region. By 1898, during the Hispanic-American war, Camp Miami was a strategic outpost for US regional operations. During the Second World War dozens of airfields were built. By 1942 the Army Air Corps occupied Miami Beach, renting more than a hundred tourist hotels to provide shelter for soldiers stationed there (Mohl 1983: 60). Since Nazi submarines were moving around Caribbean waters Miami served as a rearguard to protect the Caribbean region from military aggression.

With the construction of new military bases in other parts of the Caribbean, some of the military operations in Miami were reduced. However, it has continued to play a central role in the operations of intelligence agencies in the Southern Hemisphere. After the Cuban revolution anti-communist operations were established by intelligence agencies in Miami. Miami became the centre for the counter-revolutionary activities of the anti-communist Cuban exiles. During the early 1960s the University of Miami had the largest CIA station in the world, second only to their headquarters in Virginia (Grenier and Stepick III 1992: 11). An alliance was established in the early 1960s between the CIA, the Mafia displaced from Cuba after the revolution, and the Cuban exiles (Garreau 1981: 174; US House of Representatives 1979: 149–95). Millions of dollars circulated in Miami as part of these operations, helping to subsidize many Cuban-owned businesses that served as fronts for CIA operations. These alliances had three important consequences for the future development of the city: Miami became the undisputed 'drug capital' of the world (Mohl 1983: 77); it functioned as the centre for a successful Cuban ethnic economy (Portes and Bach 1985); and lastly, it became the centre for the control and co-ordination of CIA operations in Central America and the Caribbean during the 1970s and 1980s (Cockburn 1987: 53–76; Dickey 1987: 156–9). During the 1980s the operations for the Contra war and El Salvador's civil war pumped Miami with millions of dollars once again. Specifically, the Contras not only received millions of dollars a year from the US government but also raised a fortune through drug smuggling, which was laundered through a dozen or so companies in Miami (Lernoux 1984: Sklar 1988: 294). In the early 1980s federal officials calculated that around 28 billion dollars' worth of illegal drugs entered the USA through Miami each year (Mohl 1983: 77). It is currently the number one industry in the city.

After the Cuban revolution the US core state developed ideological/symbolic strategies to diminish communist influence over the region. These strategies developed in response to the US need for a 'successful capitalist model' to gain symbolic capital *vis-à-vis* the Soviet model exemplified by Cuba. Puerto Rico became the 'showcase' of capitalism for Latin America and the Caribbean (Grosfoguel 1992). Miami became another capitalist showcase, but in a different manner. Thousands of members of the Cuban political and economic élites moved to Miami. Refugees escaping communism had a more powerful symbolic/ideological function than any anti-communist manifesto. Cuban refugees became symbols of the struggle between the two superpowers. In order to have an ideological effect on the Cubans that remained on the island as well as on the entire Caribbean region, the US state developed specific policies to make them a 'success story'. Otherwise they could have become a powerful weapon for communist propaganda during the Cold War years. Pedraza-Bailey (1985: 16–17) develops this point:

In America, all the political migrations that took place during the peak years of the Cold War – the Hungarians, Berliners and Cubans – served an important symbolic function. In this historical period of the Cold War, West and East contested the superiority of their political and economic systems. Political immigrants who succeeded in the flight to freedom became touching symbols around which to weave the legitimacy needed for foreign policy.

As with the Hungarian refugees several years before, the USA developed a Cuban refugee programme to facilitate the successful incorporation of the Cuban élites into the receiving society (Pedraza-Bailey 1985). Part of the strategy was to resettle thousands of Cuban refugees outside Miami. The goal was to release the local economy from 'overpopulation' pressures, guaranteeing the successful incorporation of those that stayed in Miami. During the 1960s and early 1970s around one billion dollars were invested in education, bilingual programmes, food, health care, and securing jobs in a population of less than 600,000 people. Some of the welfare programmes implemented in the late 1960s as a response to the African-American social unrest were already in place as a result of the earlier experience with the Cuban refugees. In addition, between 1968 and 1979 Cubans received around 46.9 per cent (47.6 million dollars) of the total dollar amount of loans issued by the Small Business Administration (SBA) in Miami compared to just 6.3 per cent (6.4 million dollars) for the African-Americans during the same period (Porter and Dunn 1984: 197). The Cubans received 66 per cent of the total number of loans while blacks received just 7.9 per cent (ibid.). By 1977 around one-third of Cuban small businesses were subsidized by the SBA. If we add that the CIA had on their Miami payroll around 12,000 Cubans in the early 1960s (being one of Florida's largest employers) (Grenier and Stepick 1992: 11) in addition to the capital and entrepreneurial skills that the Cuban bourgeoisie brought with them, it is easy to understand why they became a successful business community. A conservative estimate of the total amount of social capital transferred by the US state to the Cuban community would be approximately 1.3 billion dollars (one billion from the refugee programme, more than 50 million dollars from the SBA in Miami, and around 250 million dollars from the CIA payroll and subsidies to Cuban businesses). The Cubans (around 700,000 people by 1975) received in a matter of fifteen years close to half of the total amount of the US foreign aid that Brazil (a country of more than 100 million people) received between 1945 and 1983 (US Bureau of the Census 1984: 810).

It is the US core state's symbolic and military strategies during the first Cold War challenge of US domination in the Caribbean that provides the historical background for the emergence of Miami as a world city in the late 1970s and early 1980s. As we will see strategic cities provide better political, social, and infrastructural conditions for the control and management of global capital.

The contemporary period: global capitalist restructuring after 1973

The oil crisis of 1973 was part of a long-term crisis that started with the end of the gold standard and the breakdown of the post-war Bretton–Woods agreements. The inflation created by both of these events together with the labour–capital Fordist agreements increased the cost of production in the core economies. Transnational industries responded with new strategies to cope with the crisis. The mobility of capital to peripheral and semi-peripheral areas in search of cheaper labour and lower costs of production was the strategy pursued by many transnational corporations; this had the effect of reducing the number of manufacturing jobs in core economies (Sassen 1988). Similarly, by 1978 regional banks in the USA were doing better than the larger Chicago and New York money centre banks. *Business Week* (1978: 66) reported that:

Return on average assets – the most important measure of a bank's profitability – stood at 0.72 per cent at the regionals, compared with 0.48 per cent for the titans, which include Citcorp, Chase Manhattan, Manufacturers Hanover, J. P. Morgan, Chemical, Bankers Trust, and the two Chicago giants, Continental Illinois and First Chicago.

Thus, both transnational industries and global banks decentralized their operations, paying more attention to regional and peripheral processes. Rather than having a centralized headquarters from which global investment strategies were co-ordinated, multinational industries and global banks opened regional headquarters in strategic cities around the world. This is the global context that explains the emergence of new world cities in the global economy after 1973. Consequently, as global capital intensified manufacturing investments in peripheral regions like the Caribbean Basin, there was a need for a closer and more direct supervision over capital investments. New York, where many multinational global headquarters concentrate, became a weaker location for close management of Caribbean investments. Within this context Miami emerged as an alternative to New York. Miami is an example of a recently formed world city. It became an international banking and trade centre exercising functions of control and the management of global capital for the entire Caribbean Basin. As the core city of the entire region it acquired the title 'capital of the Caribbean'.

As part of the same process of global capitalist restructuring, after 1973 the mainland labour-intensive industries in the USA had moved to new peripheral regions like the Dominican Republic, Haiti, and Jamaica in search of cheaper labour. Puerto Rico experienced deindustrialization of the labour-intensive industries and a reindustrialization of highly skilled manufacturing industries. The island was transformed into a centre for capital-intensive industries, with San Juan providing business services not only to these operations, but also to industries located on other Caribbean islands. San Juan became a semi-peripheral world city sharing with Miami the role of capital management and control over the other islands' industrial processes.

It is from a world-system perspective that we can better understand these changes. The transformations in Miami form part of a single process of capital restructuring in the entire Caribbean city system that transformed the regional division of labour. Before 1973 most of the Caribbean islands were agrarian or mining enclaves exporting primary products to the core economies. In the post-1973 period capitalist restructuring produced a 'new international division of labour' within the Caribbean Basin. Caribbean countries are now exporters of manufactured consumer goods. The industrialization of peripheral cities like Port-au-Prince, Santiago de los Caballeros, Kingston, and Port of

Spain now form part of the same regional division of labour that transformed Caguas, Manatí, or Humacao (in Puerto Rico) into capital-intensive industrial cities and turned Miami and San Juan into financial and producer service centres.

By 1977 some fifty-five multinational corporations had located their regional headquarters for Latin America and the Caribbean in the Miami area. By 1980 these regional headquarters increased to more than a hundred (Mohl 1983: 75). Among them are such conglomerates as Exxon, Gulf Oil, Texaco, Dow Chemical, International Harvester, ITT, DuPont, Alcoa, General Electric, Goodyear, Uniroyal, and American Express (Mohl 1983: 75).

In 1977 there were just ten Edge Act banks in Miami (Baer 1985: 221). Five of them were subsidiaries of banks with headquarters in New York and two in California. There were no foreign banks in the area. The liberalization of US international banking regulations over Edge Act corporations and foreign bank agencies, together with Miami's proximity and infrastructure in relation to Latin America and the Caribbean, dramatically transformed the city in a few years. By 1983 there were forty-two Edge Act banks, forty foreign bank agencies, and eight foreign bank representative offices in Miami (Baer 1985: 221). Even regional banks located in the area developed a more sophisticated core of international departments. Miami became second only to New York as an international banking centre in the USA (Grenier and Stepick III 1992: 2).

In the 1960s Miami was a point of entry for US imports from Latin America. Imports, measured in tons of cargo, exceeded exports by three to one (Cruz 1985: 165). However, by the early 1970s exports started surpassing imports. In 1972 exports represented 55 per cent of the total tonnage of cargo, which had almost doubled since 1960 from 411,000 to 800,000. This reflected the new role of Miami as a trade export centre for US capital goods to Latin America. In 1982, out of a total of 3.1 million tons of cargo, 70 per cent were exports and 30 per cent imports (Cruz 1985: 165). That same year the port of Miami had the largest Caribbean and Latin American market shares among all the ports of the USA. This market represented 91.2 per cent of Miami's total market (6.8 billion dollars), followed by Houston with 26.5 per cent (4.6 billion), Tampa with 23.1 per cent (0.5 billion dollars), New Orleans with 14.1 per cent (2.6 billion dollars), and New York with 10.8 per cent (3.4 billion dollars) (Lipner 1985: 163). Around 40 per cent of Miami's trade was with the Caribbean (Lipner 1985: 162). Miami exceeds Houston in the number of banks and financial institutions with a Latin American and Caribbean base and its airport accounts for a larger proportion of its exports. The trade with this region is of such magnitude that in 1992 the US Custom Service moved the Andean/Caribbean help desk from Washington DC to Miami. Miami has 35 per cent of the total US trade with the Caribbean Basin (Bamrud 1992). From a tourist and retirement haven in the 1960s Miami has emerged as a centre of international trade and finance.

Why Miami and not New Orleans?

New Orleans was a more important trade centre than Miami in 1960 (Grenier and Stepick III 1992: 9). The global logic of capital accumulation is necessary, but not sufficient, to explain the relocation of banks and transnational corporation regional headquarters for the Caribbean and Latin America from New York to Miami rather than New Orleans, or to explain the displacement of New Orleans as the country's principal trade outlet with Latin America. Economic processes are always embedded in political, social, and cultural processes. To exercise functions of management and control of global capital you need more than just economic structures. This is where the geopolitical strategies discussed above are necessary to understand the economic transformation of Miami. The rest of this chapter attempts to explain this relocation.

The Cuban connection

The massive flow of Cuban exiles after the revolution in 1959 has changed the socio-cultural landscape of Miami. Today Miami is a bilingual city where you find more stores with signs saying 'We speak English' than those saying '*Se habla español*'. The Spanish-speaking population grew from just 20,000 in 1950 to 50,000 in 1960, 300,000 in 1970 (23.6 per cent of the total population in the Miami Metropolitan area), and 581,000 in 1980 (35.7 per cent of the total population for the Standard Metropolitan Statistical Area) (Mohl 1983: 70). Nowadays Latinos compose over half of the population of Miami; Anglos have decreased from 85 per cent of the total population in 1950 to just 30 per cent by 1990 (Grenier and Stepick III 1992: 5). The Miami Metropolitan area has the largest proportion of foreign-born residents (35.3 per cent) of any US city, even larger than Los Angeles (22.3 per cent) and New York (21.3 per cent) (Grenier and Stepick III 1992: 4). With the entrance of thousands of Jamaicans, Haitians, Puerto Ricans, Nicaraguans, Dominicans, and Salvadoreans during the 1980s, Miami has become the most desirable migration point in the Caribbean Basin (Grenier and Stepick III 1992: 14).

But large Spanish-speaking populations exist in other cities of the USA. Thus, what has transformed Miami is not just the presence of the Spanish-speaking community but the presence, with the assistance of the US federal government, of an economically successful Cuban community. The Cuban revolution uprooted and transplanted to Miami an entire national bourgeoisie. This event not only relocated some of Cuba's established networks with the Caribbean and Latin America, but also created new ones. One of these niches within the Miami area since the early 1960s has been the import/export business. Cubans were the first to start the trend toward exports to the Caribbean region (Garreau 1981: 201; Grenier and Stepick III 1992: 9–10; Mohl 1983: 78). In my own fieldwork I found several Cuban owners of import/export businesses who explained that friends and relatives who had established themselves in Costa Rica, Venezuela, Puerto Rico, and other Caribbean Basin countries provided the initial linkage to their trade within the region. Their knowledge of the culture and language facilitated their access to these markets. Once the linkage was established the business proliferated. Between 1970 and 1980 the number of import/export businesses in Miami tripled to over 300. Cubans started selling consumer goods in the 1960s. Now, however, they export whole factories (Garreau 1981: 200–1). Cuban-owned banks also started financing these trade activities. By the mid-1980s Latins owned 40 per cent of Miami's banks.

The presence of the counter-revolutionary Cuban élites in Miami, and the CIA operations linking them with other anti-communist élites within the Caribbean Basin, gave Miami an exalted position as a safe haven for their capital and families. After the Nicaraguan revolution in 1979 Miami was the initial location where the Somoza family established their operations. During the Salvadorean civil war in the 1980s the economic élites not only moved their families to the Miami area, but also transferred their capital to Miami-based banks. Regional élites, escaping political turmoil or economic instability, found in Miami a large Spanish-speaking community and the political and economic stability unavailable in their country of origin.

In addition, the Latin ambience of the city attracted the upper-middle classes of the region to purchase luxury goods that were too expensive or simply unavailable in their countries of origin. Miami became the shopping district for the élites of Latin American and the Caribbean Basin (Garreau 1981: 177; Grenier and Stepick III 1992: 2). During the oil boom of the 1970s and early 1980s Venezuelan élites reinvested most of their profits in Miami. Now, most of the tourists come to Miami from the South rather than the North.

Miami's social relations with the Caribbean are unique compared to those of other cities in the USA. The transnational social networks fostered by Cubans who settled during the 1960s, together with US geopolitical strategies, are one of the reasons for the relocation of many banks and transnational corporations to the Miami area. They facilitate investments and trade with Latin America for the internationally oriented corporations. But today there is an additional advantage: the presence of a large pool of second-generation young professional Cubans with bilingual and bicultural skills. Although the upper level of Miami's financial community is controlled by Anglos, Cubans constitute a significant number of the middle and lower management level employees (Perez 1992: 104). This facilitates significant business transactions with the region. Anglo middle classes have become redundant to the new Latin-oriented businesses in the city. The rapid flight of Anglo middle-class sectors from Miami during the 1980s has consolidated the Cubans' increased dominance over these positions (Mohl 1983: 71).

Thus Cubans transformed the geographic orientation of Miami's economy, from a city looking North for tourists and the retired to one looking South for trade and investments (Mohl 1983: 172). It is no wonder the *Wall Street Journal* referred to the Cubans as 'the Phoenicians of the Caribbean' (Mohl 1983: 176).

Foreign investments

Foreigners have been investing in Miami on an unprecedented scale. Not only Latin élites, but the Mafia and transnational corporations also have invested sizeable amounts of laundered money in south Florida's real-estate markets. This has created a real-estate boom, which partially insulated the area from some of the negative effects of the 1982 recession. In 1980 alone property sales to tax-free Netherlands Antilles corporations totalled one billion dollars in Dade county (Mohl 1983: 76). According to Charles Kimball, an economist researching the real-estate markets in south Florida, 40 per cent of all property sales over 300,000 dollars in the Miami area are paid with illegal cash money (Garreau 1981: 190). Half of these investments are from anonymous offshore corporations while the other half is drug money. It is suspected that billions of dollars from the Medellin cartel are invested in south Florida. In 1979 the Federal Reserve found an excess of 5.4 billion dollars of untraceable cash money arriving in Florida's banks from other parts of the world (Garreau 1981: 175). This flow of cash money is another source of attraction for banks to the area.

Institutional and physical infrastructure

Miami has more advanced facilities in communications, port, airport, and business services than any country in Latin America and the Caribbean. Part of the advanced infrastructural conditions are due to the historical development of the city as a major tourist resort for North American tourism. Airports, seaports, and communications were originally a result of the tourist economy. However, the city's infrastructural orientation toward Latin America is a result not just of market forces but is also due to the history of the Miami area as a geopolitical military location for core powers' domination over the region. The CIA invested millions of dollars after 1959, thus improving infrastructural communications and the social networks of Miami with the Caribbean Basin (Arguelles 1982: 31; Didion 1987: 90–1). The transnational headquarters and international banking that proliferated in Miami after 1975 took advantage of these facilities for their own operations. In a sense they inherited a whole infrastructure built originally for purposes different to those for which they are currently used.

Another reason for the relocation of many internationally oriented businesses in Miami was the institutional formation of a free trade zone (FTZ). The largest FTZ in the USA is located near Miami's international airport. Approximately 200 companies involved in international trade located there by the early 1980s (Mohl 1983: 76). Most of these are import/export companies that store, manufacture, assemble, or re-export goods from abroad without paying customs tariffs (Mohl 1983: 76). This has provided international banking and transnational headquarters with an attractive institutional environment for trade and capital investments in the Caribbean Basin.

The three factors outlined above are crucial for understanding the relocation in Miami of many North American banks and corporations' regional departments and headquarters for Latin America and the Caribbean. The post-1973 global restructuring of capitalism, jointly with geopolitics, infrastructural/institutional facilities, and transnational networks, provides a more comprehensive explanation of these geographical shifts. A good example is DuPont's relocation of its Latin American headquarters from Wilmington (Delaware) to Miami.

According to Kenneth Trelenberg, a DuPont executive, the area of Coral Gables in Miami was selected after considering eight other cities: Mexico City, San José, Bogotá, Caracas, São Paulo, Rio de Janeiro,

Buenos Aires, and San Juan (Garreau 1981: 201). They used eighteen criteria in a scorepoint analysis to decide which city could best serve as the capital of its Latin American operations. This is how Trelenberg described the selection process (as quoted by Garreau 1981: 201–2):

Buenos Aires and Bogotá were disqualified because of concern for the personal safety of employees transferred to those cities ... Caracas was disqualified because of operational problems. That is, visa difficulties, acute shortage of hotel rooms, tax clearances needed for departure, and so forth ... San José and San Juan are somewhat isolated and lacking in direct air service to other locations in the area, so they were wiped out.

The remaining four cities – Mexico City, Coral Gables [in the Miami area], São Paulo, and Rio – were surveyed and rated using the following criteria:

Number one, political stability and good business climate;

Number two, centrality of location;

Number three, regional air-transportation service;

Number four, telecommuncations and mail service;

Number five, ability to maintain area perspective ... We have major subsidiaries in Mexico City and São Paulo and in Buenos Aires. There was fear that there would be trouble with the local management maintaining its local perspective and the division management maintaining a regional perspective. The fear was that the regional management would always be telling them what to do ..

The sixth category was ease of expatriate adjustment and living. In other words, living conditions ..

The seventh was operating costs.

These first seven criteria were so important that they were assigned double weight. The remaining eleven criteria were secondary. Out of a total score of 100, Coral Gables in Miami had 87, followed by Rio with 70, São Paulo 60, and Mexico 55. According to Trelenberg (Garreau 1981: 202) 'the reasons those others bombed out, primarily were poor communications from that city to other cities in Latin America – not to the United States, but to other cities in Latin America – and poor air connections'.

These communication facilities, transportation infrastructure, and political stability were due both to Miami's original tourist-oriented economy and its geopolitical role. In addition, the Cuban connection and the core state's geopolitical strategies created a good business climate for the relocation of transnational corporations' Latin American and Caribbean regional headquarters to Miami as part of the post-1973 global capital restructuring. As a result, by the late 1970s Miami was transformed into a world city with functions of global control and management of capital flows across the region. In many studies about urbanization processes in the Caribbean (e.g. Cross 1979; Hope 1986;

Portes and Lungo 1992; Potter 1989) Miami is not even mentioned. These studies have reified nation-state boundaries by not conceptualizing Caribbean cities as a city system. In contrast, the world-city approach outlined in this chapter provides a more comprehensive explanation for the regions's urban transformations.

REFERENCES

Allman, T. D. 1987. *City of the Future*. New York: The Atlantic Monthly Press.
Arguelles, Lourdes. 1982. 'Cuban Miami: the roots, development and everyday life of an émigré enclave in the US national security'. *Contemporary Marxism*, 5: 27–43.
Baer, Donald E. 1985. 'Economic relations between Latin America and Miami'. In *External Debt and Development Strategy in Latin America*, ed. A. Jorge, J. Salazar-Castillo, and F. Diaz-Pou, pp. 221–5. New York: Pergamon Press.
Bamrud, Joachim. 1992. 'Customs-move praised'. *International Business Chronicle*, 3(1): 9.
Bourdieu, Pierre. 1977. *Outline of a Theory of Practice*. Trans. Richard Nice. Cambridge: Cambridge University Press.
Braudel, F. 1984. *The Perspective of the World*. London: Collins.
Business Week. 1978. 'The fancy Dans at the regional banks'. 17 April: 66–8.
Chase-Dunn, Christopher. 1985. 'The coming of urban primacy in Latin America'. *Comparative Urban Research*, 11(1–2): 14–31.
Cockburn, Leslie. 1987. *Out of Control*. New York: The Atlantic Monthly Press.
Cross, Malcolm. 1979. *Urbanization and Urban Growth in the Caribbean*. Cambridge: Cambridge University Press.
Cruz, Robert D. 1985. 'Forecasting the economic interaction between Latin America and Miami'. In *External Debt and Development Strategy in Latin America*, ed. A. Jorge, J. Salazar-Castillo, and F. Diaz-Pou, pp. 165–70. New York: Pergamon Press.
Dickey, Christopher. 1987. *With the Contras*. New York: Simon and Schuster Inc.
Didion, Joan. 1987. *Miami*. New York: Pocket Books.
Friedmann, John. 1986. 'The world city hypothesis'. *Development and Change*, 17(1): 69–84. (Reproduced as appendix in this volume.)
Friedmann, John and Wolff, Goetz. 1982. 'World city formation. An agenda for research and action'. *International Journal of Urban and Regional Research*, 6(3): 309–44.
Garreau, Joel, 1981. *The Nine Nations of North America*. Boston: Houghton Mifflin Company.
Grenier, Guillermo and Stepick III, Alex. 1992. 'Introduction'. In *Miami Now!*, ed. Guillermo Grenier and Alex Stepick III, pp. 1–18. Gainsville: University Press of Florida.
Grosfoguel, Ramón. 1992. 'Puerto Rico's exceptionalism: industrialization,

migration and housing development'. Ph.D. thesis, Department of Sociology, Temple University.

Hope, Ronald. 1986. *Urbanization in the Commonwealth Caribbean*. Boulder: Westview Press.

Kontopoulos, Kyriakos. 1993. *The Logics of Social Structures*. Cambridge: Cambridge University Press.

Lernoux, Penny. 1984. 'The Miami connection – Mafia/CIA/Cubans/banks/ drugs'. *The Nation*, 18 February: 186–98.

Lipner, J. Kenneth. 1985. 'Past and present trade activity in Miami'. In *External Debt and Development Strategy in Latin America*, ed. A. Jorge, J. Salazar-Castillo, and F. Diaz-Pou, pp. 161–4. New York: Pergamon Press.

Mohl, Raymond. 1983. 'Miami: the ethnic cauldron'. In *Sunbelt Cities: Politics and Growth since World War II*, ed. R. M. Bernard and B. R. Rice, pp. 58–99. Austin: University of Texas Press.

Pedraza-Bailey, Silvia. 1985. *Political and Economic Migrants in America: Cubans and Mexicans*. Austin: University of Texas Press.

Perez, Lisandro. 1992. 'Cuban Miami'. In *Miami Now!*, ed. Guillermo Grenier and Alex Stepick III, pp. 83–108. Gainsville: University Press of Florida.

Porter, Bruce and Dunn, Marvin. 1984. *The Miami Riot of 1980: Crossing the Bounds*. Lexington MA: Lexington Books, D. C. Heath and Company.

Portes, Alejandro and Bach, Robert. 1985. *Latin Journey: Cuban and Mexican Immigrants in the United States*. Berkeley: University of California Press.

Portes, Alejandro and Lungo, Mario (eds.). 1992. *Urbanización en el Caribe*. San José: FLACSO.

Portes, Alejandro and Stepick III, Alex. 1993. *City on the Edge: The Transformation of Miami*. Berkeley: University of California Press.

Potter, Robert B. (ed.). 1989. *Urbanization Planning and Development in the Caribbean*. London: Mansell.

Sassen, Saskia. 1988. *The Mobility of Labor and Capital: A Study in International Investment and Labor Flows*. Cambridge: Cambridge University Press.

  1991. *The Global City: New York, London, Tokyo*. Princeton NJ: Princeton University Press.

Sklar, Holly. 1988. *Washington's War on Nicaragua*. Boston MA: South End Press.

US Bureau of the Census. 1984. *Statistical Abstract of the United States 1985* (105th edn.). Washington DC: Government Printing Office.

US House of Representatives. 1979. 'Investigation of the assassination of President John F. Kennedy'. Appendix to *Hearings before the Select Committee on Assassinations*, US House of Representatives, 95th Congress, Second Session, X, Washington DC: US Government Printing Office.

10 Comparing Chicago, New York, and Los Angeles: testing some world cities hypotheses

Janet Lippman Abu-Lughod

Introduction

Much of the literature generated out of the powerful 'world cities hypothesis' (more accurately, a *set* of complex and suggestive hypotheses) framed by Friedmann and Wolff (1982) and Friedmann (1986, see appendix) has tended to emphasize *similarities* among world cities, attributing these congruencies to global changes in economic organization, labour flows, and finance capital. Sassen (e.g. 1988) has made significant contributions to this new literature by examining the flows of capital and labour between countries of the Third World and the largest American cities, and her most recent book (1991) has highlighted similarities in such historically and culturally divergent settings as New York, London, and Tokyo, attributing them to the global processes of economic restructuring and the impact of transnational finance capital and the 'trade' in money.

In the past decade there have also been some excellent studies of the effects of global economic restructuring on specific world cities. On New York, for example, there is, in addition to Sassen (1989), the article by Ross and Trachte (1983) and a book edited by Mollenkopf and Castells (1991). Early on, Soja, Morales, and Wolff (1983) tried to trace the effects of the international economy on Los Angeles; and Allardice et al. (1988) and Squires et al. (1987) have published somewhat less satisfying studies of the changing economy of Chicago.

Most work on world cities, however, has been neither 'comparative' nor 'historical', although some promising signs of change have appeared in the past few years. A recent co-authored work by Fainstein et al. (1992) has attempted to go beyond the implicit generalizations of world city theory to explore *how* 'common causes' originating at the international level have had different effects in London and New York. And Fainstein's later book (1994) stresses the commonalities that grow out of the work of international city builders in those two cities today. In addition Soja's recent attempt to compare New York with Los Angeles (in Mollenkopf and Castells 1991), albeit empirically thin, is another promising step in this direction. The field now seems ready for a deeper investigation of the variable effects of global forces.

This chapter presents some tentative findings from a large-scale comparative and historical study of New York, Chicago, and Los Angeles that I am currently undertaking. The study explores how the reactions and fates of each of these American 'world cities' have been contingent not only on world-system forces over time, but on the specificities of their individual historical trajectories, their strategic locations within the American and world systems, and their dominant demographic mixes. Furthermore, I am finding that the historically evolved 'civic cultures' and repertoires for politically mediated conflict resolution in each city have tended to shape and modify the responses each has made, even to common problems that may have been generated at the international level.

My study has adopted the research strategy of 'closest comparisons' (Abu-Lughod 1971, 1975) as the best way to gain a concrete understanding of variations in world-city development. I believe that only by holding macro-culture and the basic context of national political and economic organization relatively constant, albeit affected by an evolving world economy, is it possible to unravel what makes world cities different, not only from non-world cities, but from one another.

Why select New York, Los Angeles, and Chicago?

In addition to the obvious fact that these three cities are the centres of the largest metropolitan regions of the United States today and therefore have a prima facie claim to world city-ness, they are of intrinsic interest. Each constitutes a quintessential example of the type of city that developed in successive eras of American history. Historians, economists, and sociologists have conceptualized these ideal types as the 'mercantile' city of the eighteenth and early nineteenth centuries; the 'industrial' city of the late nineteenth and early twentieth centuries; and the 'corporate', 'post-industrial', or 'informational' city of the twentieth and twenty-first centuries (Castells 1989; Gordon 1978; Hill 1977). Not only did each experience its maximum formation during one of these successive eras, but it is possible to encapsulate the historical epochs of urbanization in the USA over the past century and a half through case studies of these leading (and largest) exemplars of their types.[1] Furthermore, the moment of each city's maximum growth coincided with a particular geographic structure of the world system and the USA's role in it. Although details cannot be given here, a brief overview may help set the

Table 10.1   *Population of the largest secondary cities, as percentage of the city that ranked first, 1790–1900*[*]

City	1790	1830	1860	1890	1910	1990
Philadelphia	First	74	52	42	33	22
New York	75	First	First	First	First	First
Chicago	0	0	10	44	46	38
Los Angeles	0	0	0	2	7	49

Note: [*] These figures, because they include only the populations living within the city boundaries, become less and less meaningful over time, as 'metropolitan' and then 'saturation' forms of urbanization break the mould of the city as a discrete place. (For a fuller discussion of saturation urbanization, see ch. 6 of my *Changing Cities* (1991).)

scene.[2] Table 10.1 shows the 'moment' in history when each city came to the fore in the American urban system.

New York: the quintessential 'mercantile city'

At the time of the American revolution, the three largest American cities were Philadelphia, New York, and Boston (in that order), significantly all northern ports with strong shipping connections to the metropole. Once New York recovered from her wartime population losses, however, she began to rival Philadelphia and by 1810 had outstripped her to become the largest city in the country, a primacy she has never lost. During the second third of the nineteenth century New York became triply hegemonic. By 1860 New York was not only the most important port of the USA, at a time when deep-draft steamships significantly altered the time–cost schedule of international trade, but it was the key entry point connecting the USA to a 'world system' which was then focused almost exclusively on the Atlantic. Its location at the juncture of both the Erie Canal and, by mid-century, the rail routes to the midwestern 'frontier' of the American interior made it the key nexus between the international and continental systems. During that period New York was also the 'port of entry' for the largest inflow of (European) immigrants ever received, at a moment in American history when dispersal of immigrants to rural areas had begun to slow down. Furthermore, just before the Civil War New York had become the prime industrial and financial centre of the country where both technological and social inventions were concentrated. To its existing strengths as a commercial city, then, it added significant industrial strength. In addition, New York, in its capacity as chief financial centre, handled both the credit for and trans-shipment of the southern cotton crop. With the 'opening' of the midwest other primary products were also financed through and shipped from New York. It is no wonder, then, that New York should have reached its moment of overwhelming primacy within the American urban system by the turn of the twentieth century.

Chicago: the quintessential 'industrial city'

Founded in the 1830s this tiny fort expanded dramatically in the course of the nineteenth century, reaching its apogee to become the 'second city' in the American urban system by the 1920s. In 1890 Chicago's population was equal to that of Philadelphia and, by the turn of the century, it had pulled considerably ahead of that city. There were obvious reasons for this. Between the 1880s and the 1920s the dominant theme in American development was internal expansion and consolidation. Paradoxically, the external hinterland of the United States contracted *vis-à-vis* the world system, while the consolidation of the internal hinterland took place at an astounding rate. Virtually every city that would eventually be important in the twentieth century had been founded by 1890 when the continental urban system was essentially completed. While Chicago lacked direct sea access to the world system it was a key point in linking the farther west with New York via rail and a canal and river system, and in tying the midwest to the Caribbean via the Mississippi river. Large-scale steam-powered industrial production and long-distance managers, monopoly capitalism (initiated in the railroads), and the futures market for agricultural commodities raised in the great granaries of the midwest (Cronon 1991), propelled Chicago to eminence. Large-scale immigration from Eastern Europe and later of former slaves from the stagnating post-bellum South fed Chicago's population increases.

Los Angeles: the quintessential 'post-industrial city'[3]

Until California was taken from Mexico in the middle of the nineteenth century, Los Angeles was a very small town that served as the central place for the surrounding large cattle ranches owned by Mexicans. In 1850 California was admitted as a state in the union, and 'Anglos' increased their presence. However, it was not until the arrival of rail lines (from San Francisco in the 1870s and from Chicago about 1885) that the slow process began of transforming a small Spanish town into the sprawling metropolitan region of today.

Heavily subsidized rail transport prices stimulated internal migration and associated agricultural production geared to eastern markets. The most dramatic spurt in growth, however, had to await the decade of the 1920s when the population doubled. By then highways had begun to transform the spatial system of US urbanization, and internal migration westward, combined with Mexican and Asian immigration, started to inflate growth. (Water supply became critical at this point.) The major factor underlying this growth had come in the preceding decade. Los Angeles was located some miles inland and, until the First World War, it lacked a true international port. Construction of its federally subsidized harbour was completed in 1914, thus allowing it to compete effectively with San Francisco with its finer natural harbour. The expanded port facilities linked Los Angeles by sea to the east coast and to Europe beyond via the Panama Canal, which was also completed in that year. It was not until the Second World War, however, when the Pacific became a primary war zone, that Los Angeles, well positioned in what was to become the new focus of a changing world system, the Pacific, was thrust to a hegemonic position. Population exploded from three sources linked to this: internal migration from east (mostly from the midwest) to west; Mexican migration; and, most recently, migration from many parts of Asia. In 1990, Los Angeles displaced Chicago as 'second city' in the US urban system.

Theoretical framework and rationale

While to some extent all three of these world cities are now examples of the evolving form of urban economy variously termed 'post-industrial', 'informational', 'corporate', or 'late capitalist', their specific histories, geographic locations, and demographic mixes have led to different characteristics and trajectories of transformation, as we have seen in the brief historical vignettes above. That is why systematic comparisons along a set of common and theoretically defensible axes not only can advance our understanding of the problems these three archetypal cities now face, but can yield a deeper theoretical understanding of the nature of cities themselves.

In *Changing Cities* (Abu-Lughod 1991) I set forth a general theory about urban location and growth, applying it not only to the origin and development of early cities, but to their later manifestations and the changing character of cities in the USA. The theory integrates three basic variables:

- internal economic developments and restructuring through social and technological inventions;
- changes in external connections to regional and (even) world-system hinterland;[4]
- demographic spurts from natural increase and migration.

These three variables constitute powerful analytic tools for explaining not only earlier examples of urbanization, but those of the contemporary period. And these variables constitute the major dimensions on which a comparative narrative will have to be constructed. But before one can do this it is perhaps necessary to specify more precisely just what we mean by 'world city'.

Operationalizing the world city

Selecting which American cities to include in a comparative study was not totally unproblematic, even though the three I chose now constitute the three largest metropolitan regions in the USA. No one has ever raised an objection to including New York. However, while acknowledging that Chicago is big, some questioned whether it is really a world city,[5] and others suggested that San Francisco, while smaller than Los Angeles, is really 'more worldly'.[6] Washington DC was also proposed, on the grounds that political power, in this day and age, cannot be ignored. To defend my selection I needed a clearer operational definition of a 'world city'.

Just what makes a major metropolitan region a 'world city'? This question requires the evaluation of possible 'indicators' of world city status. Guided by theory, two demographic and five economic indicators were considered.[7]

Demographic indicators

Size

Large size is a necessary but not sufficient indicator. The 1990 census recorded consolidated metropolitan regional (CMSA) populations of 18 million for New York, 14.5 million for Los Angeles, and over 8 million for Chicago, which easily places them at world city rank.[8] However, Mexico City, as well as a goodly number of other densely settled cities in the Third World, have populations that far exceed those of Chicago and Los Angeles, without assuring them of world city status by other criteria.

Table 10.2   *Percentage of CMSA population that is Black, Asian, or Hispanic** (New York, Chicago, and Los Angeles 1990)*

Race/Ethnic	New York	Chicago	Los Angeles
Black (non-Hispanic)	18.2	19.2	8.5
Hispanic	15.4	11.1	32.9
Asian	4.8	3.2	9.2
American Indian	0.3	0.2	0.3
Total minority	38.7	33.7	50.9

Note: * The category of Hispanic still presents difficulties, since in some 1990 census data I have examined small percentages of Hispanics report themselves as black or Asian, a larger percentage report white, but an overwhelming majority classify themselves as 'other', thus confounding American racial categories.

Diversity

A second demographic criterion for identifying a world city is its 'cosmopolitan character'. The population must be drawn from diverse sources. By this criterion New York and Los Angeles clearly qualify, since they are the two American urban regions with the highest proportion of foreign-born residents (20 and 27 per cent respectively). The Chicago region (with 11 per cent) is somewhat less dependent upon foreign immigration. Simply distinguishing between native- and foreign-born, however, is inadequate. On these grounds Tijuana would qualify whereas Chicago might not. Rather, one must supplement native/foreign with the range of the 'mixture', on the assumption that world cities are 'cosmopolitan' in that they draw on a wide variety of demographic sources. This diversity characterized all three cities.[9]

In addition, minorities constitute at least a third of the population in all three CMSA regions. Minority representation is even greater in the centre cities where these groups are concentrated, since all three cities have more than half of their populations classified as members of 'minority' groups, figures boosted in Los Angeles and New York by recent immigration from abroad.[10] This introduces another caveat. Today the centre city populations of many large American cities, especially those in the South and in the declining 'rust belt', are predominantly minority, but this does not necessarily make them 'world cities'. Diversity seems more important than absolute numbers. (See table 10.2.)

Economic indicators

Thus far we have examined only demographic indicators, but the hypotheses about world cities stress the degree to which their local economies are integrated with the international economy. Many of the hypothesized consequences of world city-ness are presumed to follow from that integration. Operationalizing this dimension, however, is very difficult.

Foreign trade, shipping, and air freight

While theoretically one would expect that the tonnage and value of commodities involved in international trade would be important measures of globalization, the actual figures reveal so many anomalies that one must use this crude measure with caution. Geographic position, more than anything else, determines the flow of imports and exports through specific ports. Thus, Chicago's Custom House, with direct access to only one water-adjacent foreign country (Canada),[11] cannot be expected to process as much international shipping as the major coastal sea-port regions. Because of its location many of the commodities originating at Chicago terminals that are destined for overseas will be trans-shipped through more coastal ports.

Nor, more surprisingly, are the ports of the New York and Los Angeles regions hegemonic in the American system. For example, raw figures for 1988–90 indicate that both Houston and New Orleans outranked the New York region on foreign tonnage, and Los Angeles ranked only tenth. Chicago's rank among American ports was even lower (58th in 1988, 44th in 1989, and 59th in 1990). Comparing only those three cities on raw tonnage of imports and exports, the range is narrowed somewhat, as table 10.3 shows.

Therefore, such figures are best used in time series for the same city, rather than for cross-city comparisons, and they must, of course, now be supplemented with similar information on air freight, where the three cities do somewhat better (see table 10.4). Furthermore, given the shift to containerization, it is probably useless to try to compare the pre- and post-Second World War periods.

Control exercised through corporate headquarters

In the theory of the world city, however, the 'economic' factor that occupies a privileged position is not production or even handling but 'control', especially over decision-making in transnational firms and

Table 10.3   *Raw tonnage of ship-borne freight imported and exported from the ports* of New York, Los Angeles, and Chicago, 1989*

Region	Raw tons imported	Raw tons exported
New York	47,121,436	7,179,929
Los Angeles	13,492,146	11,261,409
Chicago	3,162,718	1,078,530

Note: * Chicago includes Chicago, Peoria, East Chicago, Gary, Davenport, and Rock Island; New York includes Albany but not New Jersey ports; Los Angeles includes Los Angeles, Port san Luis, Long Beach, El Segundo, Ventura, Port Hueneme, Capitan, and Marro.
Source: US Army Corps of engineers, Navigation Data Center, Waterborne Commerce Statistics Center, *Annuals of 1991 and 1992*.

Table 10.4   *Enplaned revenue tons of freight passing through airports of New York, Los Angeles, and Chicago, 1990–1*

Regional airports	1990	1991
New York/Newark	462,297	419,361
Los Angeles*	368,240	364,644
Chicago	304,959	292,179
Total (large hubs)	3,001,217	2,960,604

Note: * Includes the Hollywood/Burbank, Long Beach, Los Angeles International (almost all), and Orange County airfields.
Source: US Department of Transportation, Federal Aviation Administration, Research and Special Programs, *Airport Activity Statistics of Certified Route Air Carriers*, annual reports for 1990 and 1991. Unfortunately, the data do not distinguish between domestic and foreign destinations.

concerning international operations. Over the years several measures have consistently been employed as indicators of this. All use some variant based upon the location of headquarters for large corporations of various kinds. According to these criteria, the three top-ranking 'world cities' in the USA are clearly New York (with a long, albeit decreasing, lead), followed by Chicago, and then Los Angeles.

For example, by the end of the 1980s of the 500 largest corporations in the USA (most of them with transnational connections), the New York metropolitan region was home headquarters for 138; Chicago occupied second place with 42; and Los Angeles ranked third with only 25. New York's dominance among transnational corporations was even more pronounced. Of the 100 firms receiving the most foreign revenues,

Table 10.5   *Number of firm headquarters in cities and suburbs of New York, Chicago, and Los Angeles by type of firm, 1990–1*

Type of firm	% in three	New York	Chicago	Los Angeles
Manuf. (n=200)	37	42	17	14
Advert. (n=50)	82	34	5	2
Finance (n=50)	54	20	6	1
Div. services (n=50)	34	8	3	6

Source: 1990 estimated by author from data contained in tables reproduced in Rand McNally's *1992 Commercial Atlas and Marketing Guide*, pp. 48–9, but data appeared originally in *Fortune Magazine*, 22 April 1991 and 3 June 1991, and in *Advertising Age*, 25 March 1991. The totals are only approximate.

40 were headquartered in New York city or its suburbs. And in 1986 some 55 per cent of the $137 billion foreign revenues received by these top 100 transnational corporations went to the 40 with headquarters in the New York region.[12]

The degree of centralized dominance, however, varied with the type of business. Large firms engaged in retail trade, commercial banking,[13] insurance, utilities, and transportation were least concentrated, while headquarters of manufacturing, advertising, and diversified financial companies (all earmarked by theory as exercising 'control' functions) were most likely to be concentrated in the three world cities and their extended suburban regions. Table 10.5 shows the number of headquarters of the 200 largest manufacturing companies and of the largest 50 of the other types of companies that in 1990 and 1991 were located in the New York, Chicago, and Los Angeles metropolitan areas.

Predominance of producer and corporate services in the mix

Economic restructuring is hypothesized to concentrate producer and corporate services within world cities, thus enhancing their hegemony. Counteracting this trend has been the recent decentralization of such services around metropolitan cores. Suburbanization *per se*, however, has not undermined the dominance of metropolitan centres in these all important sectors, despite the brouhaha over 'edge city' (Garreau 1991). Alex Schwartz (1992: 276–96) compared New York, Chicago, and Los Angeles in this regard. Analysing data from the *Corporate Finance Bluebook*,[14] he tabulated entries for the 1,452 companies in the CMSA's of New York, Chicago, and Los Angeles that provide actuarial, auditing, banking, investment banking, and legal services to corporations. He found that 54 per cent of them were located in the New York region, 26 per cent were in the Chicago area, and 20 per cent were in the Los Angeles area (Schwartz 1992: 282). Although by then more than half of the corporate service firms were physically located in 'suburbs', the firms located in the central cities were nearly twice the size of those located in the suburbs.[15] Chicago proved to be most centralized and that city has continued to outstrip Los Angeles in the volume and control over at least these five types of producer services.

Presence of international 'markets'

Another economic criterion which, if Sassen (1991) is correct, has become increasingly important in distinguishing 'world cities' from other mega-cities, is the presence of international investment, commodity, and financial markets. Significantly, Los Angeles is, to my knowledge, the only one of the three that does not host at least one important international exchange. New York, of course, is home to the major US stock market exchanges and to a limited number of pricing markets for world commodities (notably sugar, oil, and gold). But Chicago still contains the all-important agricultural commodities/futures markets which have hitherto been overlooked in discussions of world cities. Whereas normally one thinks of exchange markets in terms of industrial/service firms and of monetary instruments, it is important to remember that agricultural commodities still constitute the chief export of the USA, earning the largest trade surplus and thus helping to reduce the imbalance in its international accounts.[16] What is somewhat less well known is that the Chicago Mercantile Exchange, which used to specialize in pork bellies, now has a subsidiary – the International Monetary Market – which sets futures on all international currencies.[17] This is a quintessential world-city function.

Transnational investments

The presence of international markets is only one indicator of global integration. Transnational investment flows to and from the USA are also important. To some extent this is captured by the presence in world cities of the headquarters of large multinational firms that invest abroad. However, the globalization of the American economy works in not one, but two ways. International involvement is also signalled by the degree to which American world cities attract investment from abroad. A 'world city' not only extends its global reach via transnational and giant

Table 10.6   *Foreign direct investment (in $m.) in USA and in the states of New York/New Jersey, Illinois, and California, 1981 and 1988 (gross book value)*

Place	$m.	$m.	% increase
	1981	1988	1981–8
NY/NJ	14,744	43,922	198
Illinois	5,646	19,491	245
California	20,404	48,270	136
Three-state total	40,494	110,853	174
US total	178,003	385,734	117
Three-state share	22.8%	28.8%	26%

Source: Values have been computed by the author from data in table no. 1392, US Government (1992) *Statistical Abstract of the United States 1991*, p. 795, based on US Bureau of Economic Analysis (1990), *Survey of Current Business* (July 1990) and 'Foreign direct investment in the United States operations of US affiliates of foreign companies (Preliminary 1988 estimates)'.

Table 10.7   *Employment (in thousands) by foreign firms in the USA and in New York/New Jersey, Illinois, and California, 1981 and 1988*

Place	1981	1988	% increase 1981–8
NY/NJ	345.2	571.2	65.5
Illinois	113.6	224.2	97.4
California	248.4	388.3	56.3
Three-state total	707.2	1,183.7	67.4
US total	2,402.3	3,662.6	52.5
Three-state share	29.4%	32.3%	10.0%

Source: Values have been computed by the author from data in table no. 1392, US Government (1992) *Statistical Abstract of the United States 1991*, p. 795, based on US Bureau of Economic Analysis (1990), *Survey of Current Business* (July 1990) and 'Foreign direct investment in the United States operations of US affiliates of foreign companies (Preliminary 1988 estimates)'.

corporations but is commensurately an object of interest to other global investors.

Thus far I have been unable to locate data on direct foreign investments in specific CMSAs, but I have found such material by states for the period between 1981 and 1988, when foreign investments in the USA rose rapidly. From these data it is clear that even if *we* may have some reservations about which American urbanized regions are truly of world significance, foreign investors do not share our doubts. They single out New York–New Jersey, Illinois, and California[18] as the preferred outlets for their investments. About 30 per cent of all foreign investments went to the three states in which our world cities were centred, and fully a third of all employees of foreign-owned firms were concentrated there. Between 1981 and 1988 foreign investments in these states grew at a rate that far exceeded the total growth rate in foreign investments, which means that during this period foreign investments became increasingly concentrated in them (see tables 10.6 and 10.7).

While additional information is needed to make the criteria for 'world city' status more precise, the evidence thus far suggests that the selection of Chicago, New York, and Los Angeles can be defended not only on theoretical and historical grounds, but on current empirical grounds as well.

What are the consequences of being a world city?

The most interesting and challenging parts of the world city hypotheses advanced by Friedmann and Wolff deal not with the characteristics of the cities *per se*, but with the consequences entailed by their greater integration into and dominance of the world system. This is one of the chief contributions of their work. However, it is in this section of their article that premature generalizations are most prevalent. A comparative analysis of Chicago, Los Angeles, and New York allows us to specify a more precise model for how forces generated at the international level actually play themselves out differently 'on the ground' in cities with different forms of articulation with the international system and, even more significantly, with different physical structures, demographic compositions, and political traditions of inter-ethnic, inter-class, and intra-regional conflict resolution. In this chapter I can raise only a few issues that need further investigation.

One of the major hypotheses of Friedmann and Wolff (1982) concerns the growing gap between rich and poor in today's world cities. This is expressed by their powerful metaphor of the 'citadel' and the 'ghetto'. A number of questions arise concerning this, each of which warrants more controlled empirical investigation.

1 Are inequalities greater in today's world cities than they were in earlier times? Friedmann and Wolff imply that they are.

2 Are they greater than those in non-'world cities'? Again, following their logic, they should be.

3 And if they are, by what mechanisms are such inequalities linked to increased integration with the global economy and its restructuring?

Sassen (1988) suggests a number of ways, but they are more general than ones that operate only in world cities.

Many of the propositions about inequality have obvious face validity, especially if one looks only at the centres of the world cities where rich and poor tend to be juxtaposed in dramatic fashion. But if we include the larger metropolitan regions in which these centre cities are embedded, would we really find greater inequalities today than existed in earlier times and in other places? Given the 'flight' of the middle classes from centre cities throughout the USA, it is essential to include suburban and exurban areas when testing the hypothesis that there has been a dichotomization of classes in post-industrial world cities. I plan to investigate this more closely in the three urbanized regions.[19]

We then come to the question: to what can these inequalities be attributed? Assuming we do verify the proposition that, even when entire urbanized regions are examined, class dichotomization has grown greater, are we justified in attributing this bifurcation to the globalization of their economies? Here again, this is a matter for empirical investigation. There is some collinearity that definitely contaminates the causal chain.

It is now fairly well established that the 'long' 1980s (the decade of the 1980s plus or minus a few years) witnessed a redistribution of wealth in the USA as a whole, and not just in the few urbanized places singled out as world cities.[20] The work of Mishel and Frankel (1991) documents the roles that taxation and transfer payments have played in bringing about this redistribution of income/wealth, suggesting that the growing gap between rich and poor in the USA is due only in part to the decline of unions and the restructuring of production processes. Nor can such inequalities be attributed solely to international economic integration. Investigations by Shaikh and Bakker (forthcoming) suggest that restructuring has not had automatic and uniform effects on the redistribution of wealth in the six advanced capitalist countries they studied (USA, Canada, Britain, Germany, Sweden, and Australia). National policies have a major effect on how incomes are distributed. One would have to disentangle these variables.

Friedmann and Wolff's metaphor of the citadel and the ghetto, however, was intended to have meaning not only in socio-economic space, but in physical space and in power relations as well. It denotes spatial segregation and an antagonistic relationship between the two 'camps' – one that requires walls and fortifications to keep some in and others out. In order to study this one needs to compare the three cities on the dimensions of ecological structure and civic culture, both of which are deeply embedded in the historical specificities of the cities.

Socially and ecologically, Chicago and Los Angeles are both more bipolar and sharply segregated by race/ethnicity than is New York, even though Harlem remains the largest black ghetto in the USA. The white–black/north–south divide of Chicago is paralleled in Los Angeles by an equally sharp Anglo–Latino split between west and east. By contrast, the spatial distributions of racial and ethnic groups in New York are more chequered, and the existence of 'intervening' ethnic and racial groupings makes the city less subject to neat polarization. This must have some effect on the social and political civic culture of New York.[21]

Civic cultures do not merely exist; rather, they evolve gradually over the years, as groups struggle and negotiate for the sharing of power. In the course of this process mechanisms for conflict resolution are honed. I suspect that not only ethnic and racial divisions, but the degree and type of unionization may turn out to be important variables in shaping the different civic cultures in the three cities. New York, with its long-standing profusion of very small firms, has never depended upon coalitions of large unions to effect a redistribution of political power. Therefore, wheeling and dealing, pay-offs, and Tammany Hall politics may all have played some role in keeping New York from massive civil strife, or at least tamping down the fire.[22] In contrast, the strength of large industrial unions in Chicago has tended to intensify confrontational politics, a tradition that has perhaps carried over into racial and ethnic polarities.[23] Los Angeles, in marked contrast to the other two cases, began as a non- or anti-union town, with clear Anglo dominance and control.[24] It may be that recent confrontations in that city reveal less about class and ethnic divisions (which, indeed, are paralleled in New York and Chicago) than they do about the city's lack of experience in negotiating and adjudicating disputes before they reach epic proportions.

Summing up progress thus far

In this exploratory essay I have tried to outline a project which is still in embryonic form. It is clear that the framing of many of the questions raised owes a significant debt to the world city hypotheses set forth more than a decade ago by Friedmann and Wolff. If I appear to cavil with details or criticize the work of other scholars working on global cities, it is only because they have stimulated such concerns. Only when the research is completed will it be possible to frame a fuller theory.

In this chapter I have also had to omit a discussion of the policy implications of the comparative inquiry I am advocating. Let me end, however, on a more practical note. Urban policy prescriptions will be unrealistic unless they take into account the unique histories and contexts of world cities. Policies suited to New York may be quite different to those suited to Chicago or to Los Angeles. Causal comparative analysis can not only deepen our understanding of world cities in the world system but potentially can offer some helpful guidelines for making realistic policy recommendations.

NOTES

1 It is not accidental that in the field of urban sociology, scientific paradigms have changed in part because they derived from these different exemplars, a process I trace briefly in *Changing Cities* (1991). Here I might simply point out that the first phase of urban sociology, as it developed toward the end of the nineteenth century, took poverty and housing as its central foci and used the large social survey as its chief method because New York and London were its chief 'cases'. The second phase of urban sociology, developed by the Chicago School with its dual concern for ecological structure and neighbour-hood studies, was not unconnected to its object of study. Today, a third paradigm is evolving in what some practitioners are calling the 'LA School'; its preoccupation with non-spatial networks in urban life is not unrelated to that case.

2 A number of sources have been consulted to compile the brief historical vignettes that follow. These have been cited in the references and will not be enumerated here.

3 Like many others, I have grave reservations about this term and use it only for denotational purposes. In actual fact, the Los Angeles region is now one of the most industrialized in the nation.

4 In *Before European Hegemony: The World System AD 1250–1350*, I examined international linkages among major cities to demonstrate how internal political economies and external relations interacted to determine the rise and fall of particular places during the Middle Ages. I am recommending a similar analysis for nineteenth- and twentieth-century American cities.

5 Significantly, Chicago was conspicuously absent from Friedmann and Wolff's long list of 'world cities' (1982: 310), although the authors claim the omission was unintentional!

6 The best study of the US urban hierarchy (Noyelle and Stanback 1984) listed New York, Los Angeles, Chicago, and San Francisco as 'national nodal' centres, even though on all operational variables except the value of banking deposits, San Francisco fell well below the top three.

7 Although I focused on major American centres, Third World mega-cities were considered as implicit correctives.

8 All other major metropolitan areas in the USA fall considerably below these totals, with San Francisco and Philadelphia around six million and all others below five million.

9 Boosters of each compete over *which* city includes the 'most' nationalities.

The claims are all in the range of 160–80, suggesting that this is a current asymptote.

10 Good sources on ethnic diversity in Los Angeles include those by Ong (1990) and by Sabagh (forthcoming). In 1992 the New York City Department of City Planning released a report on *The Newest New Yorkers* based on the 1990 census. These data form the basis for Mollenkopf's *Social and Political Atlas for New York City* (1993).

11 One can predict that if the 'axis' of US trade is partially deflected from east–west to north–south under NAFTA, Chicago's role as a 'border port' will expand.

12 See Drennan's chapter in Mollenkopf and Castells (1991), esp. pp. 36–7.

13 But in 1986 six of the nation's ten largest banks with foreign deposits were located in New York City, and 'together they had 85% of those foreign deposits, up from their 1976 share of 69%'. Quoted from Drennan in Mollenkopf and Castells (1991): 37.

14 The *Corporate Finance Bluebook* (serial since 1983) is an annual directory of major US companies.

15 Median sales volume of city-located firms and the median number of employees per city firm were almost twice as high as in suburban-located firms (Schwartz 1992: 283).

16 According to Omvedt (1975), as quoted in Worseley (1984: 166):

> The American economy is absolutely dependent on agricultural exports. Not steel, not transistor radios, nor even old armaments, but wheat, corn, rice and soya beans are the major products it has to sell to the world. In 1973, US exports of $17.7 billion overcame a trade deficit of $7.6 billion in other areas ... In 1972–73 the US share of world food exports have risen to 43.9 per cent of wheat, 57.1 per cent of animal feed grain, 58.1 per cent of oilseeds ... The US is also the major seller on the world market of ... that pre-eminently Asian crop, rice.

The 1977 edition of the Chicago Board of Trade's pamphlet, *Grains*, notes that the 'US is by far the world's largest exporter of wheat and wheat products ... [comprising] nearly 44% of all [world] wheat exports' (p. 11), and is 'the largest producer of soybeans, growing ... some 80% of average annual world production ... making soybeans the nation's leading agricultural dollar-earner abroad' (pp. 16–17).

Grain has always been the most important item in international trade, and earlier 'world cities' and their 'merchants' were always crucial in this. Joseph Wechsberg's (1966) fascinating account, *The Merchant Bankers*, is relevant in this regard, as is William Cronon's (1991) *Nature's Metropolis: Chicago and the Great West*, which gives a wonderful account of exactly *how* midwest grains became commodified in Chicago in the mid-1800s. See also Wayne Broehl (1992) for a history of the wheat trader, Cargill, the largest private corporation in America.

17 As one might expect from Chicago's prior role in the national economy (see Cronon 1991), the Chicago Board of Trade handles the commodity markets for corn, oats, soybeans, soybean oil and meal, and wheat, and the Chicago Mercantile Exchange still handles cattle, hogs, pork bellies, and lumber. What is less commonly recognized, however, is that the Chicago Board of Trade also sets international prices for silver (copper, gold, and platinum are

priced in New York), as well as such monetary instruments as US Treasury and Municipal Bonds and Notes. Furthermore, the International Monetary Market of the Chicago Mercantile Exchange not only prices US Treasury Bills but determines futures rates for most important foreign currencies. Details on the evolution of the MERC appear in a fascinating book by Bob Tamarkin (1993).

18 Since data for New York and New Jersey are combined and there is little foreign investment in Illinois except in the Chicago region, state figures can serve as reasonable urban–region surrogates. However, statewide data from California combine the southern Los Angeles–San Diego urbanized region with the northern urbanized region around San Francisco.

19 The complexity of the New York case is explored in Harris's article in Mollenkopf and Castells (1991). Thus far I have considerable 'raw' data on income differentials between Chicago and its suburban counties and on Los Angeles and its outlying counties, but these remain only incompletely analysed.

20 See, *inter alia*, Mishel and Frankel (1991) and Shaikh and Bakker (forthcoming).

21 My students and I have just completed a micro-study of the East Village of Manhattan. See Abu-Lughod et al. (1994). Among our findings was the extreme importance of the social diversity *within* the neighbourhood which led to a very complex 'ecology of games' with shifting alliances and coalitions – the antithesis of the 'dual city' phenomenon found in Chicago and Los Angeles.

22 I do not claim that New York has been free from conflict. Certainly it has had its share, e.g. the Astor Place riot of 1830 (Buckley 1988), the Draft riot of 1863 (Berstein 1990), the Tompkins Square riot of 1874 (Gutman 1965), all the way down to the Harlem riots of 1936 and 1943, as well as the Bedford–Stuyvesant blow-up of 1964, which was the first in the long series of urban explosions in the late 1960s. However, these never polarized the city, as did the Chicago race riots of 1919 and later, or as the Watts and East South Central riots of Los Angeles have done.

23 This is not to say that Chicago politics were devoid of bosses and horse-trading!

24 Certainly, there is nothing in Mike Davis's *City of Quartz* (1990) that would refute this description.

REFERENCES

Abu-Lughod, Janet. 1971. 'Cities (North African) blend the past to face the future'. *African Reports*, June.
    1975. 'The legitimacy of comparisons in comparative urban studies: a theoretical position and an application to North African cities'. In *The City in Comparative Perspective*, ed. J. Walton and L. Masotti, pp. 17–39. Repr. 1976, London: Sage.
    1989. *Before European Hegemony: The World System A.D. 1250–1350*. New York: Oxford University Press.

1991. *Changing Cities*. New York: Harper/Collins.

Abu-Lughod, Janet and Mele, Christopher. 1992. *Working Bibliography of New York, Chicago and Los Angeles*. Center for Studies of Social Change: New School for Social Research.

Abu-Lughod, Janet et al. 1994. *From Urban Village to East Village: The Battle for New York's Lower East Side*. Oxford: Basil Blackwell.

Allardice, David, Weiwel, Wim, and Wintermute, Wendy. 1988. 'Chicago, Illinois: reaping the benefits of size and diversity'. In *Economic Restructuring of the American Midwest*, ed. Richard D. Bingham and Randall Weberts, pp. 75–102. Cleveland: Federal Reserve Bank.

Bernstein, Iver. 1990. *The New York City Draft Riots*. New York: Oxford University Press.

Broehl, Wayne. 1992. *Cargill: Trading the World's Grain*. Hanover and London: University Press of New England.

Buckley, Peter. 1988. *The Astor Place Riot*. New York: Oxford University Press.

Castells, Manuel. 1989. *The Informational City: Information Technology, Economic Restructuring and the Urban–Regional Process*. Oxford: Basil Blackwell.

Chicago Board of Trade. 1977. *Grains: Processing, Production, Marketing*. Chicago: Board of Trade.

Corporate Finance Bluebook. Skokie IL: National Register Publishing Company (serial publication).

Cronon, William. 1991. *Nature's Metropolis: Chicago and the Great West*. New York: W. W. Norton.

Cutler, Irving. 1976. *Chicago: Metropolis of the Mid-Continent*. Dubuque: Kendall/Hunt.

Davis, Mike. 1990. *City of Quartz: Excavating the Future in Los Angeles*. London and New York: Verso.

Fainstein, Susan. 1994. *The City Builders: Property, Politics and Planning in London and New York*. Oxford UK and Cambridge US; Basil Blackwell.

Fainstein, Susan, Gordon, Ian, and Harloe, Michael (eds.). 1992. *Divided Cities. New York and London in the Contemporary World*. Oxford: Basil Blackwell.

Fogelson, Robert. 1967. *The Fragmented Metropolis: Los Angeles, 1850–1930*. Cambridge, MA: Harvard University Press, reprinted University of California Press, 1993.

Friedmann, John. 1986. 'The world city hypothesis'. *Development and Change*, 17(1): 69–84 (Reproduced as appendix in this volume.)

Friedmann, John and Wolff, Goetz. 1982. 'World city formation. An agenda for research and action'. *International Journal of Urban and Regional Research*, 6(3): 309–44.

Garreau, Joel. 1991. *Edge City: Life on the New Frontier*. New York: Doubleday.

Gordon, David. 1978. 'Capitalist development and the history of American cities'. In *Marxism and the Metropolis*, ed. W. Tabb and L. Sawers, pp. 25–63. New York: Oxford University Press.

Gutman, Herbert. 1965. 'The Tompkins Square riot in New York City on January 13, 1874'. *Labor History*, 6: 45–70.

Hill, Richard Child. 1977. 'Capital accumulation and urbanization in the United States'. *Comparative Urban Research*, 4: 39–60.

Israilevich, Philip and Mahidhara, Ramahohan. 1990. 'Chicago's economy: twenty years of structural changes'. *Economic Perspectives: A Review from the Federal Reserve Bank of Chicago*, 14: 15–23.

Jackson, Kenneth. 1984. 'The capital of capitalism: the New York metropolitan region, 1890–1940'. In *Metropolis 1890–1940*, ed. Anthony Sutcliffe, pp. 319–53. Chicago: University of Chicago Press.

Mayer, Harold and Wade, Richard. 1969. *Chicago: Growth of a Metropolis.* Chicago: University of Chicago Press.

Mishel, L. and Frankel, D. M. 1991. *The State of Working America.* Armonk NY: M. E. Sharpe Inc.

Mollenkopf, John. 1990. 'New York: the great anomaly'. In *Racial Politics in American Cities*, ed. R. Browning, D. Marshall, and D. Tabb. New York: Longman.

    1993. *Social and Political Atlas for New York City.* New York: Simon and Schuster.

Mollenkopf, John and Castells, Manuel (eds.). 1991. *Dual City: Restructuring New York.* New York: Russell Sage Foundation.

New York City. 1992. *The Newest New Yorkers.* New York: Department of City Planning.

Noyelle, Thierry J. 1989. *New York's Financial Markets.* Boulder CO: Westview Press.

Noyelle, Thierry J. and Stanback, Thomas M. 1984. *The Economic Transformation of American Cities.* Totowa NJ: Rowman and Allanheld.

Omvedt, Gail. 1975. 'The political economy of starvation'. *Race & Class*, 17: 111–30.

Ong, Paul. 1990. *The People of Los Angeles.* Los Angeles: Morris McNeill Inc.

Rand McNally. 1992 and 1993. *Commercial Atlas and Marketing Guide.* New York: Rand McNally.

Ross, Robert and Trachte, Kent. 1983. 'Global cities and global classes: the peripheralization of labor in New York City'. *Review*, 6(3): 393–431.

Sabagh, Georges. 'Los Angeles: a world of new immigrants: an image of things to come?' In *Migration Policies in Europe and the United States*, ed. Giacomo Luciani. Netherlands: Kluwer Academic Publishers (forthcoming).

Sassen, Saskia. 1988. *The Mobility of Labor and Capital: A Study in International Investment and Labor Flows.* Cambridge: Cambridge University Press.

    1989. 'Finance and business services in New York City: international linkages and domestic effects'. Paper prepared for UNESCO (Mimeo).

    1991. *The Global City: New York, London, Tokyo.* Princeton NJ: Princeton University Press.

Schwartz, Alex. 1989. 'The decentralization of advanced service industries in the New York metropolitan area'. Ph.D Dissertation, Rutgers University.

    1992. 'Corporate service linkages in large metropolitan areas: a study of New York, Los Angeles, and Chicago'. *Urban Affairs Quarterly*, 28(2): 276–96.

Shaikh, Anwar and Bakker, Ida (eds.). *The Post-War Struggle Over the Social Wage: An Empirical Study of Six Advanced Countries.* Unpublished book manuscript (forthcoming).

Soja, Edward, Morales, Rebecca, and Wolff, Goetz. 1983. 'Urban restructuring:

an analysis of social and spatial change in Los Angeles'. *Economic Geography*, 59(2): 195–230.

Squires, Gregory, Bennett, Larry, McCourt, Kathleen and Nyden, Philip. 1987. *Chicago: Race, Class, and the Response to Urban Decline*. Philadelphia: Temple University Press.

Tamarkin, Bob. 1993. *The MERC: The Emergence of a Global Financial Powerhouse*. New York: Harper/Collins.

Tobier, Emanuel. 1984. *The Changing Face of Poverty: Trends in New York City's Population in Poverty: 1960–1990*. New York: Community Service Society of New York.

US Army Corps of Engineers, Navigation Data Center. *1989 Port and State Tonnage Ranking Reports*, as reproduced in the 1991 Annual, updated by *1991 Port and State Tonnage Ranking Reports*.

US Bureau of Economic Analysis. 1990. 'Foreign direct investment in the United States operations of US affiliates of foreign companies (preliminary 1988 estimates)'. *Survey of Current Business*, July 1990.

US Department of Transportation, Federal Aviation Administration. *Airport Activity Statistics of Certified Route Air Carriers*. Annual reports for 1990 and 1991.

US Government. 1992. *Statistical Abstract of the United States 1991*. Washington DC: Government Printing Office.

US Riot Commission. 1968. *Report of the National Advisory Commission on Civil Disorders*. New York: Bantam Books.

Wechsberg, Joseph. 1966. *The Merchant Bankers*. New York: Pocket Books.

Worseley, Peter. 1984. *The Three Worlds: Culture and World Development*. London: Weidenfeld and Nicolson.

11 'Going global' in the semi-periphery: world cities as political projects. The case of Toronto

Graham Todd

At one time a beneficiary of tariffs which encouraged the formation of an import substitution manufacturing zone in southern Ontario, Toronto's subsequent rise to world city status has been based on the city's disproportionate national share of business and commercial services. Growing out of the intensive manufacturing of the Fordist era, the city's globally oriented service sector is the legacy of a now defunct Keynesian interventionism that sought to promote national economic development through a comprehensive industrial policy. This chapter explores the recent transformation of Toronto to the status of a world city by examining these sectoral shifts and the long-standing and pivotal role of finance capital in the national economy. The emergence of a new economic space of predominantly finance-based accumulation has coincided with the cultural transformation of the city through increased international and internal migration, and has provoked conflict over the direction of local economic development.

David Gordon (1988) reminds us that the historical process of the integration of the world economy is far from complete. But as many observers have noted, there has been a considerable expansion of the global circulation and investment of capital and of the movement of migrant populations (Sassen 1988, 1991; Stafford 1992). These phenomena can be connected to the period of almost continuous economic crisis that began in the 1970s and which spurred foreign direct investment (FDI) and saw the rise of competing industrial capitals in the newly industrialized countries (NICs). Through these interconnected processes of the movement of capital and productive populations, globalization has played itself out in particular ways in the various places and locales of international capitalism. At such a 'conjectural moment' any attempt to reflect critically on the process of globalization must engage its specific political and social dimensions in order to avoid merely chronicling – or fetishizing – the expanding scope of the circulation of capital.

In the developed core states the political hegemony of capital, crisis-induced restructuring, and the secular rise in the rate of unemployment have all been subjected to a similar form of mystification. Both negative and positive trends in various national economies have come to be portrayed as resulting from unavoidable global economic forces. In Canada and elsewhere this discourse is associated with neo-conservatism and was the mainstay of policies designed to enhance trade and competitiveness throughout the 1980s. But global competitiveness in manufacturing proved more difficult to achieve than global integration of financial markets and related services. In Toronto the response to globalization took the form of sectoral restructuring, involving rapid growth in business and commercial services and the relative decline of industrial manufacturing. The service sector rapidly replaced manufacturing as the main 'pillar' of accumulation.

In this context one of the theoretical tasks of critical geography and political economy must be to reveal the extent to which the process of 'going global' is organized locally and is strategically linked to the political struggle being waged by capital from above – both as an integral part of and as a reaction to economic crisis. 'Local' in this sense introduces a spatial reference which goes beyond the level of the firm or sector, but is more concrete and particular than the nation-state structures that are normally the object of inquiry in political economy. Both in the study of international political economy, and in analyses which concentrate more exclusively on national economic development, there is a need to address more specifically the places and sites, or 'spaces of accumulation' (Létourneau 1990: 310) of capitalist economies at the level of the city – if for no other reason than their role as significant agglomerations of fixed capital. In the restructured North American economy cities are increasingly the focal point for new forms of spatial disparity in a services-dominated regime of accumulation (Létourneau 1990). By pointing out the empirically specific social impact of globalization, and its strategic importance for capitalism, the world city hypothesis provides the analytical tools 'to link the urbanization process with global economic forces' (Friedmann 1986, see appendix). For these reasons the research framework of the world city hypothesis offers valuable insights into how local social formations with established modes of regulation or social structures of accumulation are globalized as part of a new strategy of capital accumulation.

This sort of critical perspective is especially important in an era in which the economic policy imperatives of nation-states are almost exclusively focused on the promotion of the global competitiveness of their respective economies. Together with the need for freer markets, this policy agenda has achieved the status of orthodoxy. The potentially most important contribution of the world city hypothesis for the study of specific national–political–economic formations (in this case Canadian) and international political economy lies in the refocusing of critical attention on the actually existing local, historical, and material conditions of the 'world historic' process of globalization. The approach provides a richly descriptive means of situating Toronto within the global hierarchy of world cities. In keeping with the general theme of the other chapters, a second aim will be to reflect upon the various conceptual elements which make up the theoretical framework within which the development of world cities may be described and analysed.

By referring to the specific domestic context of Toronto I wish to make explicit the political dimensions of the process by which the local political economy has been globalized. My argument here is that the processes identified with globalization are best understood as part of a specific implementation of what Bob Jessop (1990), in Gramscian language, refers to as an 'economic accumulation strategy and a hegemonic political project'. An accumulation strategy 'defines a specific economic growth model complete with its various extra-economic preconditions, and also outlines a general strategy appropriate to its realization' (Jessop 1990: 198). The pursuit of globalization certainly qualifies as such a strategy. A hegemonic political project seeks to resolve the more abstract problems of conflicts between particular and general interests by mobilizing political support and appealing to common-sense understandings of the economy. The various policies associated with the notion of global competitiveness (a freer market, a smaller state, increasingly 'recommodified' delivery of social services) are on the verge of achieving the status of 'common-sense' requirements for a national economy to function effectively. By connecting globalization with social and political developments 'on the ground', the world city hypothesis counters the mainstream tendency to view the recent growth in the global connections in the world economy in aggregate terms, and affords some critical distance on the local politics of 'going global'.

This chapter is organized into three main sections. I begin with a discussion of specific factors affecting the development of the Canadian political economy at the national and international levels. Focusing on Toronto, the second section then describes the impact of economic restructuring on the country's urban system and the growth of the service sector. I also examine the ways in which the city has been incorporated into the international economy through elevated levels of immigration. The third section discusses a series of examples of local socio-spatial conflict in a world city. Finally, I consider briefly some of the methodological implications of the world city approach to studying the phenomenon. Throughout the chapter I refer to the main arguments of the world city hypothesis, which is framed here as a set of working hypotheses or an 'agenda for research' (Friedmann and Wolff 1982).

The political economy of the rich periphery

Several different approaches to international political economy have engaged questions of spatial and regional ordering and hierarchy in the attempt to explain the social relations of Canadian and international capitalism. World-systems theory, which the world city hypothesis appropriates in a specific way, speaks of core and periphery. Dependency theory conjures a spatial referent in its description of *dependencias* as satellites arrayed around the core economies. With appropriate modifications, dependency theory has been used to explain the development and under-development of the Canadian economy (Clement 1977; Panitch 1981). Building on the staples thesis of Harold Innis, dependency theorists argued that Canada was a rich dependency where relatively advantageous class relations contributed to higher than average wages for Canada's proletariat, and a mobilized working class was able to win gains from the state.

Glenday (1989) uses trade data and a theoretical framework adopted from Wallerstein and Braudel in order to argue that Canada occupies a semi-peripheral position in the world economy: in an unequal economic position with the twelve core countries, yet advantaged in its trading with other countries. Over the 1970s and 1980s, however, the import/ export ratio for end products and the balance of trade in specific sectors showed that Canadian trading patterns with developed core countries became less unequal, and that the country had moved higher up within the semi-periphery as productivity and trade balance gains were made. But improvements in export profile do not take into account the high degree of foreign control in the economy. As the title of Glenday's article would have it, Canada occupies an 'ambiguous position in the world-economy'. For Glenday, in such semi-peripheral countries the state is more autonomous and can become a more effective actor in structuring the economy than in the periphery proper, where weak state structures inhibit the implementation of national development policy, or in the core where autonomy is not as great. Semi-peripheral states are better able to move up in the world hierarchy during periods of crisis since they can maintain surpluses with peripheral states where they sell end-products, and with core states where they sell raw materials and minimally fabricated goods.

Following this line of reasoning then, if during the present crisis period the Canadian economy is becoming more closely integrated into the core of the world economy, then the Canadian state will begin to shed its traditionally more interventionist role in an effort to take advantage of the global economic environment. In general, at the level of the nation-state, free trade agreements such as NAFTA and the Maastricht initiatives accomplish precisely this task and are 'typical of the new policy environment pushing states to adopt market-based and trade-centred policies in the 1990s' (Drache and Gertler 1991: 3). As Marjorie Cohen has noted (1991), the application of these sorts of policies in Canada – specifically, trade liberalization – has done little to eliminate regional disparity since it only exacerbates the problem of the concentration of manufacturing industry and high-end services in southern Ontario and Quebec, and reliance on resource extraction in the rest of the country. As Canada has moved higher in the hierarchy of world trade and Toronto has solidified its role as the country's centre for international finance and business services, there has been no consequent 'restructuring of the economy to encourage a better integration between resource producing sectors and the manufacturing and services sectors' (Cohen 1991: 99).

The 'permeable' nature of Canadian Fordism – as Jane Jenson (1989) has termed it – punctuated by regionalism, language differences, the decentralized federal structure of the Canadian state, and the concentration of economic activity in southern Ontario, has meant that class compromise and the mode of regulation have often been mediated by various fractions of the state. The breakdown of the Canadian Keynesian/Fordist compromise (the so-called 'National Policy') of the postwar era coincided with a greater decentralization of economic development policy and the adoption of continental free-trade policy. This transition has strengthened the political economic forces which underlie the long-standing and pronounced regional disaggregation of the Canadian economy and has contributed to recent constitutional tensions (Brodie 1990).

Canadian political economist William Carroll (1986, 1990) rejects dependency theory, and has attempted to document the powerful global reach of Canadian capital throughout the world economy. Despite empirical problems in demonstrating Canada's role as a middle-level imperial power on the basis of FDI flows, Carroll has documented the impressive conglomerate concentration of Canadian capital (1990). Carroll's work and that of others suggests that the sphere of circulation and the finance fraction of capital is relatively over-developed within Canadian capitalism (cf. Mahon 1977). Partly because of this financial concentration the globalization of the Canadian economy has had a remarkably local character, since the space of accumulation of the new global capitalism is geographically concentrated in the nation's largest cities (Economic Council of Canada 1991). At the national level the conflict arising out of the restructuring of the Canadian economy has been made all the more politically complex for the federal government because of the high proportion of domestic economic activity that has centred on Toronto and the 'Golden Horseshoe' around the western end of Lake Ontario. The political focus on international markets and trade as a national economic strategy has obscured the growing regional and inter-urban economic disparity. The distinction must be made between the effects of *international trade*, which has been a mainstay of Canadian economy since beaver pelts were the main export, and *globalization* in which accumulation takes place through the internationalization of investment and finance.

Toronto: 'FIRE' at core of the semi-periphery

Toronto serves as Canada's undisputed financial and commercial services centre. The headquarters, labour force, and fixed capital of international firms in the finance, insurance, and real estate (FIRE) sector are all concentrated in Toronto. The shift to a post-Fordist economy and the strategic creation of a globally oriented urban space for financial services has decidedly tilted the balance of national economic development in new sectors such as specialized business services and flexible manufacturing in favour of the country's best contender for world city status. In comparison, Montreal and Vancouver, the two next largest urban centres in the country, serve much more specialized niches in the national economy and function as regional centres in the North American context. As Goldrick (1992) has shown Toronto's more globally oriented role has served as an impetus to organize local capital. When Montreal and Vancouver sought special tax status under federal legislation as international banking centres, state and private capital interests in Toronto successfully and powerfully lobbied to have the policy changed in its early stages. Montreal and Vancouver have been unable to attract the same level of headquarters and command and control functions as Toronto. This is partly because banking, financial, and corporate headquarters functions are part of an internal corporate decision-making process 'characterized by monopoly power that is hard to break' (Harvey 1989b: 49). Of the 56 foreign banks in Canada, 42 have head offices in Toronto, as do half of Canada's top 50 foreign-owned companies. The executive functions of Canada's top five banks and the headquarters of six of the ten largest life insurers in the country were located in Toronto. Toronto was also the site of the head office, management, and corporate control functions for 193 of the top 500 Canadian corporations (Board of Trade of Metropolitan Toronto 1991: 119). In a trade-driven and predominantly foreign-owned economy many of these companies have extensive international connections mediated by specialized service sector firms. In essence, Canadian capital has organized itself around Toronto and sees little reason to change.

In his elaboration of the world city hierarchy, John Friedmann (1986) ranks Toronto within the system of secondary core-country cities, along with other secondary North American centres such as Miami, Houston, and San Francisco. But what makes Toronto and the surrounding region distinct from these urban areas is the city's predominant role in the national economy and the financial system of a G7 country. Because of the peculiarities of national development, Toronto's role in the global economy extends beyond that of many comparably sized cities elsewhere in the world. The historically close ties between productive and financial capital have lent globalization a special significance with respect to financial services in Canada. All of the top six Canadian chartered banks have close links and large equity holdings in real estate development firms, and the Canadian Imperial Bank of Commerce holds its own real estate development subsidiary, CIBC Developments. New legislation enabling 'universal' banks which can engage directly in insurance activities, trust operations, and securities and investment services has not only created greater scope for financial accumulation but has also affected the hegemony of finance capital in the national economy by opening up the industry to foreign firms, thus 'aiding in the consolidation of transnational financial capital' (Carroll 1990: 282).

Following Sassen (1991: 172), a rough measure of the financial concentration within the Canadian economy can be provided by stock market capitalization figures. With equity market capitalization of over $Can 300 bn. in 1989, representing well over 50 per cent of GNP, the relative weight of financial sector activity in the Canadian economy places the country well apart from other advanced industrialized nations such as France or Germany, and closer to those national economies where global cities such as New York, Tokyo, and London mediate massive volumes of international financial transactions. The concentration of Canadian financial and money market activities in Toronto, which is also the site of the country's largest stock exchange, has meant that the city has rapidly become the space for a significant amount of national and international command and control functions within the global regime of finance-based accumulation. Originally planning to capitalize on Pacific Rim connections in Vancouver, the Japanese giant Daichi Bank relocated its Canadian headquarters in Toronto, presumably to be in closer proximity to the hub of the country's financial industry. According to Maureen Farrow, an analyst with Coopers and Lybrand, Toronto's financial markets rank fourth overall in North America and eleventh world-wide in terms of total capitalization. Financial flows in Canadian money markets, concentrated almost exclusively in Toronto, now exceed $Can one trillion, and transactions on the Toronto stock exchange in 1991 reached $Can 67 bn. (Binhammer 1993).

The insertion of Toronto into the international financial services economy provided an important but spatially delimited mechanism of growth. By the end of the 1980s the central area of the City of Toronto had been transformed into an economic space servicing the requirements of global financial capital. On Nigel Thrift's classification Toronto, along with seventeen other cities, was a 'first order international financial centre' by 1983 (1987: 209). The resulting employment growth in the service sector provided a demand 'pull' to the 'push' of investment into real estate development that the socio-spatial dynamic and the political and economic crisis of Fordism had encouraged. Toronto's unrivalled position in the national economy has been as important a factor in propelling the city to the status of a 'second tier' world city as have been global linkages to the world economy. The process of 'going global' during the 1980s was facilitated by the previous success of the city in establishing and maintaining its position as the financial centre of the country. During the 1960s, when industrial plants were leaving Toronto's downtown core, the office sector of banking, finance, business, and commercial services had been organized under the guidance of the Redevelopment Advisory Commission to usurp this role from Montreal. The strategy turned on redeveloping the central business district to fit with a restructured space of accumulation.

The social space of globalization (1): service sector and urbanization

The regionally and locally fragmented character of development in national economies, to say nothing of the international economy, would seem to vitiate claims of consistent or systemic logic in capitalist development. But one constant is the deployment of a variety of forms of producer and business services firms in an increasingly complex social, technical, and spatial division of labour. Friedmann's third thesis reminds us that the 'driving force' behind the specific economic structures underlying urban social change and the development of the world city 'is found in a small number of expanding sectors' (see appendix). In Toronto, as elsewhere, service sector growth has been the primary engine of urban economic development since the 1960s. Recent analysis has demonstrated the link between locationally specific services and the need for greater global (or national, regional) control capacity (Economic Council of Canada, 1991; Sassen 1991). In Canada, service sector employment accounted for 59.9 per cent of the labour force by 1981. In Toronto the effect of this 'sectorial restructuring' was even more pronounced: by 1985 the service producing sector accounted for 71.8 per cent of employment in the Toronto census metropolitan area (CMA) (Municipality of Metropolitan Toronto 1986).

For Britton (1991) certain trends in the development of the service economy are common to all capitalist countries. The increasing integration of various factors of commodity production, together with the circulation and marketing of finished products and the valorization of surplus in new forms of financial instruments, all require the increased use of labour outside of the strict bounds of 'production' in order to maximize accumulation. The increasing division of labour allows service labour to be differentially incorporated into production following patterns specific to the commodity or process in question and designed to maximize profits. For example, resource extraction and primary manufacturing will incorporate the 'indirect labour' of service workers differently than the production of consumer electronics, which requires the development of software/firmware and extensive R & D work.

The service sector 'class' also contributes to local, national, and international accumulation by deepening and broadening markets through the creation of new service products and the international extension of markets and capital. The increasing autonomy of financial capital co-exists with a convergence of industrial, commercial, and investment capital functions in large conglomerate and franchise organizations which organize service inputs into separate, semi-autonomous companies that 'on-sell' services to franchisees, owner-operators, or other divisions of the corporation, in addition to selling services as an 'out-sourcing' establishment in the general market (Britton 1991). Evidence of intra-corporate linkages and sectoral interdependence reveals the process of service sector growth to be one that is firmly connected to the general development of capitalist economies rather than an isolated moment of economic growth in response to market signals. The growth of services does not so much reveal some inexorable 'logic of capital', as it does, on a realist interpretation, the systemic manner in which capitalist social relations shape the process of economic restructuring.

The gendered aspect of service sector employment is a significant part of the new urban space of accumulation. In tandem with the sectoral restructuring of the economy there has been a marked increased in the participation rate of women in the workforce in Canada (44 per cent in 1975, 54 per cent in 1985). The employment structure of the service sector is particularly important to women since almost 83 per cent of female employment in Canada is in services, a much higher concentration than that of men (Myles 1991: 355). The concentration of service activities in urban areas indicates the strong connection between sectoral restructuring, the internationalization of the economy, and the changing gender division of labour. Continued structural discrimination in earnings and the high proportion of female part-time workers has meant that wage polarization both between women and men and amongst female workers has increased as a result. These developments have partly enabled sectoral growth. Just as with an earlier phase of the 'administrative revolution' of clerical work, the transformation of urban economies has played itself out at the cultural level in terms of the construction of appropriate gender roles in the work-force (Lowe 1987; Rose 1989).

The spatial dimensions of the expansion of the service economy are complex and contradictory, and are rendered more complicated by the close connection of services and finance with real estate development. Evidence from a recent study of the service sector in Canada indicates that while computer and telecommunications equipment may have loosened restrictions on location, a high proportion of employment, especially in the areas of financial and business intermediary services, had remained concentrated in the central business districts (CBD) of the largest urban areas (Economic Council of Canada 1991). Services growth has also led to decentralization or 'multinucleation' of office nodes in most major North American cities, and Toronto is no exception to this trend (Municipality of Metropolitan Toronto 1986). While routinized clerical tasks, such as data entry and payroll, are located in suburban office nodes, corporate decision-making and higher end legal and accounting services remain in the core CBD. This decentred nodal development pattern of office 'parks' and 'campuses' has far outstripped the creation of new 'flex-spec' industrial districts in large urban centres. While local economic development agencies in such cities as Toronto and Montreal may advocate the (re)creation of a fast disappearing industrial base or the introduction of high-tech production, the market forces at work in spatial development are creating an entirely different post-Fordist, or post-modern landscape of tourist attractions, convention facilities, world trade centres, and a fragmented network of malls and office developments stretched out like a 'net of mixed beads' from the CBD (Pivo 1990; Soja 1989).

In fact this sort of spatial restructuring represents a thoroughgoing social 're-regulation' of the space of accumulation in which a new infrastructure for the creation of new forms of value replaces an older obsolete form. Saskia Sassen's analysis alerts us to the fact that in order to comprehend and theorize the complexities of globalization, post-Fordist restructuring, and the internationalization of the state, we must take into account the impact of locally situated configurations of economic and political institutions on the functioning of the global economy. The transformed space of accumulation that is being constituted within the metropolitan centres of the national economy does presage new directions in the development of Canadian capitalism, but the shift of economic activity into the service sector does not represent some benign technological transformation to a 'post-indus-trial' society. Rather, the process reflects a changed set of political and economic strategies for accumulation, with profound implications for workers and for local communities. In this light the new office towers, conference centres, sports and entertainment complexes, and luxury commercial and residential projects which are being constructed in the downtown cores and suburban hinterlands of major cities can be seen as part of the ongoing effort to create the local political and economic space required for a development strategy which is ever more global in its reach, and thoroughly commodifying in its intent.

The social space of globalization (2): immigration and cultural change

The formation of world cities depends not only on the sectoral transformations that form the 'infrastructure' for the globalization of capital flows, but on a parallel expansion in the migration of labour. Toronto's predominant role in the internationalization of the Canadian economy is made evident in immigration trends as well. In relative terms Toronto rivals New York and London as a destination point for international migration. Three-quarters of a million immigrants are expected to settle in the Toronto area between 1990 and 1995 (Canada 1990). Recent figures show that 36 per cent of the population of the municipality of Metropolitan Toronto is foreign-born (Statistics Canada 1989: tables 1 and 10) – a comparatively high level. King's figures for Greater London, for example, show approximately 20 per cent of the population of foreign origin in 1981 (1990: 139–42). Together, Toronto, Montreal, and Vancouver are the destination for 80 per cent of immigrants to Canada, with Toronto alone receiving 32 per cent. When internal migrants are included the importance of Toronto as a destination point for migration both internationally and domestically is evident. As a result, the cultural make-up of the city has been substantially altered to the point where in the Toronto CMA over 60 per cent of the population is of other than French or English origin (*Globe and Mail*, 24 Feb. 1993: A14).

The extent and impact of undocumented or 'uncontrolled' international migration in Canada has been much more subdued in comparison to the USA and Europe, partly due to its relative geographical isolation. Refugee claims, however, have risen to unforeseen numbers in recent years, sparking criticism of this *de facto* form of immigration as a 'queue-jumping' tactic in the face of restrictive immigration policy (Creese 1992: 129). Throughout the 1980s international migration to Canada was relatively high, with combined immigrant and refugee levels reaching almost 1 per cent of the total population, a figure more than twice that of comparable migrant destination countries such as the USA and Australia (Frideres 1992; Stoffman 1993). These figures have been seized upon by conservative think-tanks such as the C. D. Howe Institute, but a less examined factor in the international labour migration picture has been the massive increase in 'non-immigrant work permits' which reflects the growing use of migrant labour in the Canadian economy. In fact 'more foreign workers are being admitted as migrants (temporary transient labour) than as immigrants (permanent settler labour)' (Bolaria 1992: 224).

While a pronounced bias towards 'business immigrants', and technically skilled professionals has been maintained, the strictly policed immigration system has been unable to cope with changing push and pull factors influencing global migration patterns. In addition, as the restructuring of the Canadian economy has proceeded, the manner in which immigrant labour has been incorporated into the social structure has changed significantly. During the 1950s and 1960s the proportion of the population of immigrants from 'non-traditional sources' that had attended university was almost twice that of the non-immigrant population. But recent immigrants have had lower levels of educational attainment than the general population.

While Canadian immigration policy has in the past contributed to the brain drain in Third World countries of origin, economic restructuring has changed the typical immigrant's education and employment prospects. Immigrant workers are now over-represented in the rapidly expanding small business sector and in declining older firms and increasingly are integrated into the work-force on a part-time basis (usually with more than one job) (Stafford 1992). Whether the segmented migrant and immigrant labour is contributing to the overall polarization of the Toronto (and Canadian) labour markets, or whether this labour is being inserted into a previously existing set of social relations, is in many ways a moot point, since it is obvious that in Toronto, as elsewhere, immigrant and foreign transient workers are being strategically incorporated into what is best described as a new regime of accumulation.

The politics of the new space of accumulation

Local political conflict has gone hand in hand with the world city development in Toronto. During the 1980s a housing 'crisis' coincided with a real estate boom. At its peak in 1989 commercial construction comprised 32 per cent of all construction within the entire Greater Toronto Area (GTA). At the same time residential construction consisted largely of suburban 'monster homes' and condominiums. While this speculative boom in commercial real estate and residential 'real estate investment' was occurring, the vacancy rate for rental housing was below 1 per cent and low income accommodation was virtually unavailable. Taken together with the patterns of growth in the CBD of Toronto during the 1980s this kind of spatial development indicates a pronounced shift of capital into the secondary circuit of capital. In terms of outcomes in social costs and political conflict, the indicators are consistent with Freidmann and Wolff's (1982) world city hypothesis. As Friedmann points out, in a world city social needs for welfare, transportation, housing and the like are 'increasingly arrayed against other needs that arise from transnational capital for economic infrastructure and from dominant élites for their own social reproduction' (see appendix).

Besides serving as the national financial capital Toronto is at once the primary site of Canada's declining 'Fordist' manufacturing economy, and the location of the pronounced spatial restructuring process related to the transition to 'post-Fordism' in manufacturing. 'Going global' has created conditions for social and political conflict in this context as well. While the concentration of domestic and international activity in Toronto made it one of the most profitable real estate markets in North America in the 1980s, growing unemployment and spreading deindustrialization led to a series of conflicts over plant closures and property redevelopment. In one study of deindustrialization, just under one-half of plant closures were attributed to capital mobility (Norcliffe, Goldrick, and Muszunsky 1986). In a period of intensive restructuring, 'mobility' must be understood to include both international and inter-sectoral movements of capital for reinvestment in domestic FIRE or service-related activities.

In Toronto spatial conflict and class polarization have intensified as new means of producing value, centred in the service sector, displace Fordist forms based primarily in industrial manufacturing. The empirical dimensions of spatial restructuring in the Toronto region (GTA) in the 1980s emerge in construction figures for the period. While commercial construction doubled through the 1980s, industrial plant construction underwent a slight decline in the same period. In terms of country-wide construction trends, the concentration of commercial building capital in the GTA is an indication of Toronto's ascendancy at the national level and its connection to what has been called the 'international property market' (Thrift 1987: 223). In 1989, at the peak of the boom, over \$3 bn. worth of commercial construction took place in the GTA, a figure which represents over 40 per cent of the total amount of commercial construction for the entire country, more than double the city's population share. Within the CMA the greatest concentration of this activity was within the central area of the City of Toronto where 53 per cent of the total commercial construction for the area took place (Board of Trade of Metropolitan Toronto 1991).

The effects of restructuring have been most visible in those parts of the GTA where industrial and manufacturing activity have traditionally been the highest. In East York for example, where a high concentration of more Fordist activities has kept the employment share for warehousing and manufacturing among the highest in the Metropolitan area (33 per cent in 1988, down from 42 per cent in 1981), industrial construction fell from a high of a 57 per cent share of total construction in the area in 1981 to a low of 0.6 per cent in 1988. During the same eight-year time period commercial buildings rose from a 6.9 per cent share of total construction in 1981, to a high of 43 per cent in 1988. And in just four years total manufacturing sector employment in the area fell almost 20 per cent during the post-recession period between 1983 and 1987, while office employment grew 43 per cent to comprise a 30 per cent employment share (Municipality of Metropolitan Toronto 1989: table E-2.2).

In the City of Toronto proper, the railway lands and harbour front create a unique situation for expanded high-density office development. Just south of Toronto's CBD and at points contiguous with it, the harbour front and the railway lands comprise together almost 300 acres located in the prime central area of Toronto. The 1969 official plan, which had advocated the intensive spatial restructuring of the CBD, 'was designed to ensure the primacy of the down town core within the metropolitan region by encouraging redevelopment of the water front for residential, commercial and recreational purposes' (Desfor, Goldrick, and Merrens 1989: 491). But in 1972 the federal government presented the City of Toronto with nearly 100 acres on the central waterfront, intended as a balanced mix of development and open park space. The fragmentation and potential intra-state conflict represented by these two modes of development was largely avoided, however, since the intensification of the downtown core that took place in the twilight of the Fordist regime bypassed the waterfront area. By 1978, though, Harbourfront Corporation, a state development agency, had been created, and the spatial restructuring of the declining industrial district began in earnest.

Under an emerging post-Fordist regime of flexible accumulation, intensive waterfront development *à la* Manhattan gave way to intensive luxury condominium and marina development *à la* Miami, with a commercial component modelled on other successful development emphasizing spectacle, 'cultural programming', and consumption. To employ the Gramscian language introduced at the outset, as an *economic accumulation strategy* flexible accumulation implies precisely this sort of development. As David Harvey notes, 'given the grim history of deindustrialization and restructuring that left most major cities in the advanced capitalist world with few options except to compete with each other, mainly as financial, consumption, and entertainment centres' (1989a: 92).

The railway companies, Canadian National (CN) and Canadian Pacific (CP), also made successful use of the emphasis on entertainment and spectacle in pushing their own development plan. By sponsoring the construction of the publicly funded stadium project on the west end of the land package, the SkyDome, with free land and site improvements, they were able to bargain for their plan approval during the drawn-out construction process by threatening to withdraw their support. As a result of this 'linkage strategy' they achieved their long-term goal of integrating the east end of the railway lands into the high-density commercial development in the CBD. The most recent plan allows for extraction of maximal rents by developing space equivalent of six-and-a-half Empire State Buildings, just south of the now over-built CBD (*Globe and Mail*, 3 July 1990: A10). In terms of its strategic economic value the development will certainly serve to offset the earlier structural devaluation of the now 'over-accumulated' industrial capital on the site.

The intransigence of the city and the developers regarding the 'Greenlands Report' on the area is of course not surprising but does represent a further instance of world city politics impinging on local alternatives. Faced with attempts to single out the railway lands as the site for innovative spatial development of an environmentally 'sustainable' community, developers have sought to link the site to the CBD. In a hostile response to the report, the law firm acting for CN Real Estate stressed the need for adherence to the present 'agreements' – which CN wrested from City Council under duress – and the requirement for consistent zoning in the Central Area. The developers and their lawyers hope to forestall any attempt to develop the site according to land use principles that run counter to the logic of capital circulation. While any spatial development on the site has the potential to create profit, only intensive, commercial, high-rise space can function effectively as a rent-generating financial instrument on the global property market. It is this 'global city infrastructure' which developers in Toronto are intent on providing. In order to ensure this outcome the hegemonic political project of the local élite has been one which appeals to the common sense economic appeal of developing Toronto as a 'world class' international city.

Conclusion: a world city on the edge

These examples clearly indicate the strategy of spatial restructuring, intensification, and re-commodification of urban space pursued in Toronto during the 1980s. In addition to the mutations in the built environment, there has been a major sectoral recomposition of the labour force. Sectoral shifts of employment and economic growth coincided with the critical restructuring of Fordist industry and a pronounced shift of investment into real estate, which had the effect of intensifying the social and spatial importance of the service sector. Service sector growth in the local economy and the resulting office space demand was the legacy of a period of high manufacturing productivity and intensive Fordist accumulation. The concentration of Canadian economic activity in the Toronto economy allowed the city to attain the threshold of an international service centre for capital – a world city.

The main growth industries in Canada's largest city have been those which are most involved with mediating the social reorganization of the economy. There is a sense here in which the service sector is seen to be helping to secure and regulate accumulation through its role in an emerging privatized institutional mode of regulation. The conceptual tools of the regulation school are useful here in demonstrating how new modes of economic development may be established. The analysis of Fordism demonstrates how specific sectors can shape development and capture the 'high ground', establishing models of growth that are generalized throughout the economy. Rather than a monolithic state–market dyad, the emerging regime of accumulation appears less unitary and more chaotic, where economic development is shaped by the entire configuration of relevant institutions such as the local state, land markets, the family, etc. Viewed in this way regulation theory is quite amenable to the analysis of local regimes of accumulation and the ways in which these locales are subject to the structuration of global capitalism. As Storper and Walker note: 'regimes of accumulation are established only as the result of territorially differentiated class practices and distributional outcomes. The territory is essential to the marshalling of social, political, and institutional resources needed [for] ... growth and development' (1989: 215).

In Storper and Walker's view such a territorially specific regime of accumulation, or 'technological ensemble' – of institutions, processes, and resources – serves to mediate between the specifically local characteristics of development and the global economy. This may be a useful starting point for conceiving of the global dimension to service sector development. International economic activity grows apace with developments in those key growth sectors of producer services and information technology which allow 'some cities ... [to] function as command points in the organization of the world economy, as sites for the production of innovations in finance and advanced services for firms, and as key marketplaces for capital' (Sassen 1991: 338). Sassen (1991) and other observers such as Thrift (1987) and King (1990), working in the area of urbanization and global economics, implicitly or explicitly concur with the third observational proposition of the world city hypothesis: that the establishment of increasingly important international connections in the world economy is linked to the process of urbanization, and to the world-wide growth of service economies. In Toronto, as a specific national and urban territory with clear domestic advantages in the key sectors of business and financial services, capital was able to 'marshal' the resources necessary for a new economic accumulation strategy.

In this view the economy is not merely moving towards a market-based deregulation. In fact the emerging 'global economy' would exhibit an increasing degree of private regulation. That is, if by 'regulation' one intends the configuration of institutions, both private and public, which serve to regularize a regime of accumulation. If deregulation in the global economy involves the 'disarming of the nation state' (Bienefeld 1992), it also involves the proliferation of non-state collective actors which provide producer services and co-ordination and control capacity to capital. If this view of the global city is any indication then, beyond the important changes in production relations, what 'going global' has meant is a wholesale social reorganization of the economic institutions of capitalism in which economic regulation is increasingly co-ordinated through the private bureaucracy of the service sector. For Saskia Sassen the co-ordination and global control capacity of capital is contingent upon this sort of local social structure. Going global has required the creation of an entire infrastructure where this activity can occur. Because of its role within the national economy Toronto was well positioned to capitalize on this process as a strategy of economic growth.

Following Friedmann, I have utilized the world city hypothesis here as a series of connected theses and observational propositions. As an agenda for research it includes empirical generalizations, paradigmatic models of the likely combinations of empirical findings, and a critical methodology. The world city hypothesis allows us to conceive of the phenomenon of the global city in the context of capitalist economic development strategies and their unintended consequences at both the local and the more 'aggregate level' of the global economy. If the world city hypothesis is considered as theory, then a more precise description of how the various interrelated theses are connected to one another is required. As far as the critical and practical aspirations of the approach go, the world city hypothesis can certainly inform partisan progressive planning in the face of the economic hegemony of capital.

A further question involves considering whether too great a focus on geography, information, and technology inevitably leads us into a Weberian-oriented social science which eschews agency for an evolutionary perspective on the stages of capitalist growth. I disagree. Without engaging the new flexible work organization and information technologies, progressive forces risk being left behind, speaking a language of emancipation that no longer corresponds to the reality of the working world. To return to my point about hegemonic projects made at the outset: it is only by actively seeking a theoretical alternative to the mainstream account of globalization with the explanatory power to make sense to people, that viable counter-hegemonic projects can be conceived. Just as the contradictions between the rhetoric and practice of the actually existing 'global economy' must be part of the analysis of world city formation, so too must the praxis of local politics figure in our understanding of globalization. As part of a critical approach one must imagine counter-hegemonic political projects and alternative narratives of globalization at the 'analytical borderlands' of economics, culture, and politics (Sassen 1993). This kind of account of the global economy would be less focused on the internationalization of financial markets and more rooted in the experience of place and labour.

Just as any explanation of Toronto as a global city must take into account regional imbalance in the national economy and other factors 'exogenous' to the process of urban development (such as NAFTA and foreign ownership in the Canadian economy) and their impact on Toronto's place in the national and global urban hierarchy, so the analysis of the global political economy must consider the local social structures on which it depends. While the specific space of accumulation within Toronto plays its role in regulating Canadian capitalism, so do the peculiar socio-spatial and economic structures of whole networks of world cities work to create the historical and material circumstances necessary for globalization. What is specific and unique about Toronto in the Canadian economy is precisely what places it on a par with other important centres in the world economy, as one of the specific locales making possible the process of globalization.

REFERENCES

Bienefeld, M. 1992. 'Disarming the nation-state'. *Studies in Political Economy*, 37: 31–58.

Binhammer, H. 1993. *Money, Banking and the Canadian Financial System*. Toronto: Nelson Publishing.

Board of Trade of Metropolitan Toronto. 1991. *Metropolitan Toronto Business and Market Guide*. Toronto: Board of Trade.

Bolaria, B. S. 1992. 'From immigrant settler to migrant transients: foreign professionals in Canada'. In *Deconstructing a Nation: Immigration, Multiculturalism and Racism in '90s Canada*, ed. V. Satzewich, pp. 211–27. Halifax: Fernwood Publishing.

Britton, S. 1991. 'Services and national accumulation'. *International Journal of Urban and Regional Research*, 15(3): 415–31.

Brodie, J. 1990. *The Political Economy of Canadian Regionalism*. Toronto: Harcourt Brace Jovanovich.

Canada. 1990. *Minutes of the Proceedings and Evidence of the House of Commons Standing Committee on Labour, Employment and Immigration*. Issue no. 48.

Carroll, W. 1986. *Corporate Power and Canadian Capitalism*. Vancouver: University of British Columbia Press.

  1990. 'Néo-libéralisme et recomposition du capital financier'. In *Politique et régulation: modèle de développement et trajectoire canadienne*, ed. G. Boismenu and D. Drache, pp. 275–308. Montreal: Méridien.

Clement, W. 1977. *Continental Corporate Power*. Toronto: McClelland and Stewart.

Cohen, M. 1991. 'Exports, unemployment and regional inequality: economic policy and trade theory'. In *The New Era of Global Competition: State Policy and Market Power*, ed. D. Drache and M. Gertler, pp. 83–102. Montreal: McGill-Queens.

Creese, G. 1992. 'The politics of refugees in Canada'. In *Deconstructing a Nation: Immigration, Multiculturalism and Racism in '90s Canada*, ed. V. Satzewich, pp. 123–43. Halifax: Fernwood Publishing.

Desfor, G., Goldrick, M., and Merrens, R. 1989. 'A political economy of the waterfrontier: planning and development in Toronto'. *Geoforum*, 20(4): 486–501.

Drache, D. and Gertler, M. 1991. 'The world economy and the nation-state: the new international order'. In *The New Era of Global Competition: State Policy and Market Power*, ed. D. Drache and M. Gertler, pp. 3–25. Montreal: McGill-Queens.

Economic Council of Canada. 1991. *Employment in the Service Economy*, Ottawa: Economic Council of Canada.

Frideres, J. 1992. 'Changing dimensions of ethnicity in Canada'. In *Deconstructing a Nation: Immigration, Multiculturalism and Racism in '90s Canada*, ed. V. Satzewich, pp. 47–67. Halifax: Fernwood Publishing.

Friedmann, J. 1986. 'The world city hypothesis'. *Development and Change*, 17(1): 69–84. (Reproduced as appendix in this volume.)

Friedmann, J. and Wolff, G. 1982. 'World city formation. An agenda for research and action'. *International Journal of Urban and Regional Research*, 6(3): 309–44.

Glenday, D. 1989. 'Rich but semiperipheral: Canada's ambiguous position in the world-economy'. *Review*, 12(2): 209–61.

Goldrick, M. 1992. 'Global restructuring of financial services: the Canadian struggle for a national policy'. Paper presented to the International Canadian Studies Association. Jerusalem, Israel.

Gordon, D. 1988. 'The global economy: new edifice or crumbling foundations?' *New Left Review*, 168: 24–64.

Harvey, D. 1989a. *The Condition of Postmodernity*. Oxford: Basil Blackwell.

1989b. *The Urban Experience*. Baltimore: Johns Hopkins University Press.

Jenson, J. 1989. '"Different" but not "exceptional": Canada's permeable Fordism'. *Canadian Review of Sociology and Anthropology*, 26(1): 69–94.

Jessop, B. 1990. *State Theory: Putting Capitalist States in their Place*. Pennsylvania: Pennsylvania State University Press.

King, A. 1990. *Global Cities: Post-Imperialism and the Internationalization of London*. London: Routledge and Kegan Paul.

Létourneau, J. 1990. 'La reconfiguration de l'espace d'accumulation nord-américain'. In *Politique et régulation: modèle de développement et trajectoire canadienne*, ed. G. Boismenu and D. Drache, pp. 309–55. Montreal: Méridien.

Lowe, G. 1987. *Women in the Administrative Revolution*. Toronto: University of Toronto Press.

Mahon, R. 1977. 'Canadian public policy: the unequal structure of representation'. In *the Canadian State: Political Economy and Political Power*, ed. L. Panitch, pp. 165–98. Toronto: University of Toronto Press.

Municipality of Metropolitan Toronto. 1986. 'The changing Metropolitan economy'. *Metropolitan Plan Review*, report no. 2.

1989. 'Statistical series: employment and labour force'. Toronto: Metropolitan Toronto Planning Department.

Myles, J. 1991. 'Post-industrialism and the service economy'. In *The New Era of Global Competition: State Policy and Market Power*, ed. D. Drache and M. Gertler, pp. 351–66. Montreal: McGill-Queens.

Norcliffe, G., Goldrick, M., and Muszunsky, L. 1986. 'Cyclical factors, technological change, capital mobility, and deindustrialization in Metropolitan Toronto. *Urban Geography*, 6(3): 413–36.

Panitch, L. 1981. 'Dependency and class in Canadian political economy'. *Studies in Political Economy*, 6: 7–34.

Pivo, G. 1990. 'The net of mixed beads: suburban office development in six metropolitan regions'. *APA Journal*, Autumn: 457–69.

Rose, D. 1989. 'A feminist perspective of employment restructuring and gentrification: the case of Montreal'. In *The Power of Geography: How Territory Shapes Social Life*, ed. J. Wolch and M. Dear, pp. 118–38. Boston: Unwynn Hyman.

Sassen, S. 1988. *The Mobility of Labour and Capital: A Study in International Investment and Labour Flows*. Cambridge: Cambridge University Press.

1991. *The Global City: New York, London, Tokyo*. Princeton NJ: Princeton University Press.

1993. 'Analytic borderlands: economy and culture in the global city'. Paper presented to the summer school on International Political Economy, Political Science Dept. and Faculty of Environmental Studies, York University.

Soja, E. 1989. *Postmodern Geographies: The Reassertion of Space in Critical Social Theory*. London: Verso.

Stafford, J. 1992. 'The impact of the new immigration policy on racism in Canada'. In *Deconstructing a Nation: Immigration, Multiculturalism and Racism in '90s Canada*, ed. V. Satzewich, pp. 69–92. Halifax: Fernwood Publishing.

Statistics Canada. 1989. *Dimensions: Profile of the Immigrant Population*. Catalogue no. 93–155. Ottawa: Minister of Supply and Services.

Stoffman, D. 1993. *Toward a More Realistic Immigration Policy for Canada*. Toronto: C. D. Howe Institute.

Storper, M. and Walker, R. 1989. *The Capitalist Imperative*. Oxford: Basil Blackwell.

Thrift, N. 1987. 'The fixers: the urban geography of international commercial capital'. In *Global Restructuring and Territorial Development*, ed. J. Henderson and M. Castells, pp. 203–33. London: Sage.

Part 3

Politics and policy in world cities: theory and practice

12   Re-presenting world cities: cultural theory/ social practice

Anthony D. King

Introduction

In this chapter I want to address a number of issues: the notion of the world or global city as a representation; the location and context within which this representation has been constructed and circulated; whether the concept represented by the terms 'world city' and 'global city' is the same and the terms interchangeable, or whether each signals a different set of assumptions and contextual presuppositions with which the object is defined.

If, for the present, we accept that there is indeed some reality which the term 'world city' represents, I want to look at this principally as a cultural space and see what recent work in social and cultural theory suggests about it, and how this theory might be deployed to say something about the spaces and built environments of the world city. What is the significance of such a world city as a real or potential site for the construction of new cultural and political identities, or for processes of cultural transformation in general? And what relevance might it have, either for the persistence or modification of existing local, regional, or national identities and cultures, or alternatively, for the construction of new transnational ones? Let me begin by clarifying the terms I have introduced.

In the words of James Donald (1992: 6):

'the city' does not just refer to a set of buildings in a particular place. To put it polemically, there is no such *thing* as *a* city. Rather, *the city* designates the space produced by the interaction of historically and geographically specific institutions, social relations of production and reproduction, practices of government, forms and media of communication, and so forth.

Donald suggests that by calling this diversity 'the city', we ascribe to it a coherence or integrity which it does not have.

The city, then, is above all a representation. But what sort of representation? By analogy with the now familiar idea that the nation provides us with an

215

'imagined community,' I would argue that the city constitutes an *imagined environment.*

It is what is involved in that imagining, 'the discourses, symbols, metaphors and fantasies through which we ascribe meaning to the modern experience of urban living', which, for Donald, is 'as important a topic for the social sciences as the material determinants of the physical environment' (1992: 6).

This current concern with representation, with what Barnes and Duncan (1992) refer to as the 'discourses, texts and metaphors' through which the city is represented, has cautioned us against the danger of making monolithic claims and totalizing constructions. It has also, in the process, opened up the opportunity for otherwise marginalized voices, alternative representations, to be heard from below. Equally important, it has redirected our attention from the object of discourse (the city) to the subject constructing it (the author). Ulf Hannerz, one of the more prolific authors on the notion of world or global culture (including world cities) has suggested that there are principally four categories of people who play major roles in the making of contemporary Western world cities: the transnational management class, Third World populations, expressive specialists (or cultural practitioners), and tourists (1993). He also refers to the media, who have a special relationship with world cities (1992).

Though I shall make use of Hannerz's categories below, the principal omission from his list is that of the authorial subjects themselves, the academics and scholars who, by exercising their power to name, not only construct the category and the criteria used to define it, but also identify the places to which it refers. That the construction of the category 'world city' is based primarily on an interpretation of some aspects of what are referred to as 'economic data' does not disguise the fact that 'world city' is essentially a *cultural construct,* constituted at a particular time and in particular spaces of the Western academy. We might ask where, by whom, and for what purposes is this cultural construct produced?[1] I shall return to this theme below.

We might begin by reflecting on, and distinguishing between, a variety of different concepts: 'the city', 'the world', the 'world-class city' (as in 'world-class' athlete), 'cities in the world', 'cities of the world', 'world cities' (*à la* Friedmann), and 'city worlds'. It is the latter, 'city worlds', which scholars actually think about and construct; some of these 'city worlds' are 'world cities'. And just as Gayatri Spivak writes of 'the worlding of the world',[2] we might also speak of the 'citying of the city'. Indeed, it would not be inappropriate in the context of our discussion, in terms of what is seen by the West as the resurgence of religious fundamentalism and the cultural regions in the world where our present set of 'world cities' is *not* located, to include in this list the 'worldly city'; and to ask whether the world's 'world cities' are, in fact, the most worldly of the world's cities (King 1994).

What these reflections show us is that, in addition to working with imagined constructs of 'the city', we are also working with imagined constructs of 'the world'. 'World-class city' (or, indeed, cities 'out of this world'), for example, already assume a positionality, a standard from which the rest are to be measured – but a standard of what, and according to whom?

The problem with thinking about 'the city' is not only that it is in fact many cities, consisting of many representations, but rather that 'the city' reifies an imagined object, drawing boundaries around it, cutting it off from and excluding those economic, social, cultural, political, religious, administrative relations and flows without which 'the city' would not exist at all. Unlike 'the great wen', the metaphor with which William Cobbett characterized London, 'city' makes no reference to the body on which Cobbett's excrescence lived. Cities can be distinguished by a large number of criterial attributes (King 1994), only some of which refer to the geographical, economic, political, cultural, climatic, or other kinds of contextual space (such as inland, industrial, socialist, Islamic, or winter) which supposedly helps to account for their existence. But cities also exist under scores of quite different metaphors: sin city, holy city, drug city, city of angels, and many more. In this context the number of meanings which 'world city' might have are infinite.

The problem with the term 'world', or 'global city', is that it has been appropriated, perhaps hijacked, to represent and also reify not only just one part of a city's activity (not the only, or even the largest one) but also has been put at the service of only one particular representation of 'the world' – the world economy. Having myself made use, in a somewhat indiscriminate way (King 1990), of both world and global city terms and concepts (which I refer to in more detail below) I am inclined to think, in retrospect, that both are somewhat greedy in what they have appropriated under these labels. As with any over-ambitious theory, they occlude as much, if not more, than they reveal.

An argument can and, indeed, has been made (as in Friedmann and Wolff 1982; King 1990; Sassen 1991; and others) that a particular world city has, in relation to a particular economic and administrative sphere, global control capability: but this neither exhausts the function or meaning of the city in relation to the world economy, in relation to 'the world' nor, more importantly and pointedly, the significance or meaning of 'the world' to the city. If it did, God (literally) help us. To begin with, capitalism is essentially a cultural system before it is an economic one. Both the system (or systems, as it exists in many forms) and the subjects which inhabit it, and which it inhabits, have to be constructed. People are not born to consume.

However, discourse theory, in focusing solely on *discursive* representations, the way the city is spoken, read, or written (Macdonald 1986), takes our analytical attention away from two other representational levels. The first is the way the built environment, the physical and spatial form of the city, is *itself* a representation of economic, social, political, and cultural relations and practices, of hierarchies and structures, which not only represent but also inherently constitute these same relations, hierarchies, and structures of everyday social life. Here, I refer only to the spatialization, or materialization, of these social relations: the way they inscribe themselves in the physical world and which have economic, social, physical, and behavioural effects.

The second is another symbolic level constituted through visual representation, the semiotic domain where visual signifiers refer to some other signified. This level, as we well know, is a murky area, because such visual representations can have infinite meanings, many interpretations, depending on the subjectivity of the viewing self. I distinguish between these first and second levels by suggesting that a hospital building, for example, may be understood as a material or spatial representation of social discourses about health (and, indeed, is a constituent element of those discourses); a hospital designed in a particular place and at a particular period in time, in Gothic style, say, may be an attempt on the part of its patrons or its architect to fuse the discourses about health with those of religion. Each of these two levels of real physical and material representation is a necessary prerequisite for the third level: the mental constructs which form the discourses (as in the paragraph by Donald above) in which the hospital is subsequently represented (Wolff 1992).

Here we might draw attention to the immense amount of symbolic capital (Bourdieu 1977) there is invested in the site, form, history, associations, and cultural meaning of buildings which, as dramatic events in and outside world cities have reminded us, represent and help to constitute whole regimes of economic, political, and cultural power. Within the space of six months, the demolition of the Babri mosque in Ayodhya, the dynamiting of Bombay's stock exchange, the symbolic attack on New York's World Trade Center, and the massive explosion in the vicinity of the Hong Kong Bank in the City of London (all undertaken by ideological, religious, or, in the last case, anti-colonial inspired insurgents), demonstrate the extent to which the world city's 'signature architecture' has upstaged the state's (and the world's) more sober debating chambers as the appropriate site to conduct an alternative international politics.[3] With security controls now blanketing airports, symbolic world city buildings have become (with the active, conscious, concentrated, and complicit co-operation of the global media) the obvious site for contesting ideological and cultural regimes, a politics of spectacle beamed into 'the privacy of your own home'.

My third term, 'culture', is often used in an everyday sense in two ways: as 'way of life' and to refer to the 'expressive arts'. For the purposes of this chapter, I shall refer to an earlier conceptualization and collapse this distinction between what, in crude terms, we may call older 'anthropological' notions of culture (ways of life, values, beliefs) and 'humanistic' ones (expressive arts, media). By suggesting that culture (in the sense of art, literature, film, music, architecture, practices of representation of all kinds) both draws from, and participates in, the construction of culture as a way of life, as a system of values and beliefs which, in turn, continues to affect culture as a creative, representational practice, we can bridge what is often seen as a gap between these different meanings (King 1991: 2).

The term 'world city' has been around at least since the later eighteenth century, used by Goethe, apparently, to refer to the cultural eminence of Paris and Rome (Gottman 1989: 62). However, given that the language Goethe spoke does not, with the term '*Stadt*', distinguish between 'town' and 'city', his reference to '*Weltstadt*' may be treated as a neologism necessitated by the German language. In this chapter I am assuming that the meaning attached to it is that given by Friedmann in 1982. I am also assuming that by 'world cities in a world-system' we are also using, at least in relatively loose if not necessarily orthodox sense, Wallerstein's conceptualization of a 'world-system'. Although both of these concepts have obvious relevance for the understanding of cultural phenomena, this is not an aspect which is particularly well developed in either of them.

'Global' – a term used by Sassen, myself, and others – is, I believe, used interchangeably with 'world cities'; the semantic shift in 1990 probably reflecting the increased frequency of use, as well as the growing consciousness of transnational social, cultural, political, and religio-ideological movements (from ecological concerns to those of peace) characteristic of the 1980s. 'Global' may, however, also reflect the social theoretical debate on globalization, by Robertson (1992) and others, gathering pace from the mid-1980s, and premised on totally different (or complementary) bases to the world-system paradigm. The distinction between the two paradigms I would describe principally in terms of the focus of globalization theory on questions of culture, identity, and meaning in representations of 'the world as a single place', compared to the economic and political, neo-Marxist emphasis of the world-system perspective, irrespective of the fact that both theorizations would be denied as totalizing meta-narratives by disciples of the post-modern.

Globalization

Theories of globalization have been used to refer to a number of processes. A recent account by McGrew (1992), which refers especially to the writings of Giddens (1990), Harvey (1989), Rosenau (1980), Robertson (1992), Wallerstein and others, and from which much of the following is drawn, refers especially to the multiplicity of linkages and interconnections that transcend the nation-state (and, by implication, the geographically defined societies which make up the inter-state system). Resulting from the development of global networks of communication and knowledge, and systems of global production and exchange, there appears to be a diminishing grip of local circumstances on people's lives: goods, capital, people, knowledge, images, fashions, beliefs, flow across territorial borders, and there is said to be, for some at least, a profound reordering of time and space in social life. Globalization is seen to be the intensification of global connectedness, the constituting of the world as one place. In Giddens' words, it concerns 'the intersection of presence and absence, the interlacing of social events and social relations "at a distance" with local contextualities' (cited in McGrew 1992: 67).

In discussions of globalization there is considerable slippage between the discourse on 'globe talk' or 'global babble' (Abu-Lughod 1991) and the object/subject which it is seen to affect – whether this is the nation-state, locality, or the individual subject. Where globalization in Robertson's (1992: 8) terms can mean 'consciousness of the world as a whole' the subject can be collective as well as individual, and the ensuing debate may be about individual, or group cultural or political identity.

Yet globalization in this sense is neither historically nor geographically even: McGrew, for instance, writes specifically of 'Western globalization'. He sees it as not historically inevitable but occurring to a greater or lesser extent at different times and under different historic conditions. As Frost and Spence ask, 'Are the forces which have created global cities in recent times merely a single phase of development?' (Frost and Spence 1993: 557). Given that deregulation of financial markets can only occur once and, like other decisions, is likely to occur as a response to developments in other financial centres, the answer seems to be 'yes'. But it is also the case that, with intensive competition between different global cities, the possibilities of deglobalization have also to be faced.

Globalization is also seen to have a 'differential reach', with its consequences not uniformly experienced across the globe. Hegemonic states in the inter-state system work to impose a form of world order which attempts to encourage openness and interdependence, but which also reinforces inequalities of power and wealth both between states and across them.

Initially, popular wisdom saw the outcome of globalization as a process of cultural homogenization on a global scale. More recent interpretations by McGrew (1992: 74–5) are expressed in terms of five polarized oppositions, and emphasize not only the uneven but also the essentially dialectic nature of the process. The results of globalizing influences, whether economic, political, or cultural are seen as being inherently contingent on the time, place, and circumstances where they apply. McGrew states these oppositions as follows:

1 *Universalism vs. particularism.* As globalization universalizes different spheres of modern social life (the nation-state, consumer fashions, etc.), it simultaneously encourages *particularization*, by relativizing both place and locale, so that the construction of difference and uniqueness results (e.g. in the resurgence of nationalism and the highlighting of ethnic difference).

2 *Homogenization vs. differentiation.* Just as globalization produces a certain kind of 'sameness' to surface appearances and social institutions across the globe (city life, technologies, bureaucratization, etc.) it also results in the rearticulation of the global as a response to local circumstances (people interpret the same thing differently).

3 *Integration vs. fragmentation.* Although globalization creates new communities which unite people across the national boundaries of the world (international trade unions, multinational companies, etc.) it also fragments and divides within and across traditional nation-state boundaries. Thus labour becomes fragmented along local, sectional, national, ethnic, and racial lines.

4 *Centralization vs. decentralization.* As globalization facilitates concentrations of power, information, and knowledge (transnational companies, etc.), it also provokes local resistances which are also decentralizing (new social movements).

5 *Juxtaposition vs syncretization.* Globalization, by compressing time and space, forces the juxtaposition of civilizations, ways of life, and social practices. While this leads to the hybridization of ideas, values, knowledge, institutions, cultural practices (from cuisines to architecture) it also reinforces cultural and social prejudices and boundaries.

Applying McGrew's insights to the understanding of the spatial and environmental dynamics of contemporary world cities is suggestive. Above all, they suggest that whatever is existing in 'the present' is certainly not going to be the end product; space, like the forces which produce it, is constantly in flux. Not least, the powerful forces of globalization and internationalization (two quite different processes) on major world cities also result in the intensification of cultural nationalisms both in and outside those cities. I refer not just to the xenophobic responses of the right but also to the 'reinvention of tradition' and the 'vernacular' by the cultural élites. It is worth quoting Robertson (1992) at this point: 'In a nutshell, globalization involves the universalization of particularism not just the particularization of universalism. While the latter process does involve the thematization of the issue of universal (i.e. global) "truth", the former involves the global valorization of particular identities' (1992: 130). Robertson sees the contemporary concern with civilizational and societal (as well as ethnic) uniqueness, as exemplified by the increasing emphasis placed on identity, tradition, and indigenization, as being largely premised on globally diffused ideas:

Identity, tradition, and the demand for indigenization only make sense *contextually*. Moreover, unique cannot be regarded simply as a thing-in-itself. It largely depends both upon the thematization and diffusion of 'universal' ideas concerning the appropriateness of being unique *in a context*, which is an empirical matter, and the employment of criteria on the part of scholarly observers, which is an analytical issue. (Robertson 1992: 130)

Globalization, seen in this way, does not result in homogeneity but in a deepening of particularity. According to this, each world city increasingly becomes the same to the extent that each one becomes increasingly different. The logic of globalization theory, therefore, is in a sense to deny its own existence. As far as the world city is concerned, it is to recognize that there is indeed a category, but culturally and in many other ways, each one is different.

Migration and its cultural effects

In the loose kind of 'globe talk' about the multiculturality of cities, attention is often drawn to the mere presence of 'other' nationalities and language groups. That one city has representatives from 102 nations or language groups, and another from 192, is somehow taken as a 'sufficient and necessary' condition of its multiculturality. This question needs addressing both in more detail and with more sophistication.

It might be useful to imagine, from a demographic viewpoint, an idea of what a 'perfect' world city would be: for example, one whose population was composed of a minimum number of representatives (say 1,000) of each nation-state, and in proportion to its total population, of each of the almost 200 nations in the world. Irrespective of the artificiality implied by this notion of the 'nationally constructed subject', such an 'international' or 'united nations' city would in no way get close to the tens of thousands of world ethnic and linguistic groups which made up these nation-states.

The relevance of suggesting this ideal (or perhaps absurd) model, however, is to demonstrate that, from a demographic viewpoint, no so-called world city can, or ever will, in any way approximate to it. In all world cities there is a numerically dominant population from the host society, and in each the proportion who are 'foreign-born' comes from such a diverse range of cultures, religions, and ethnicities, and as a result of such historically different circumstances, that the monolithic, even xenophobic category 'foreign-born' can, for all except legal purposes (though this is clearly a highly significant exception) be rejected. From very specific and given points of view, to assume that 'foreign birth' provides commonality amongst a vast range of peoples, in twenty cities of five continents, is as absurd as suggesting that 'domestic birth' can be used to characterize culturally those born in the host society. Similarly, to suggest that the 15 per cent of the Paris population who are 'foreign-born' (*sic*) and coming primarily from North Africa (Algeria, Morocco, Tunis), Armenia, or Mauritius (Ambroise-Rendu 1993), the 29 per cent in New York (over half of whom are from the Caribbean and Central America, with significant proportions from Europe, South America, East Asia and Africa (Bayer and Perlman 1990)), and some 20 per cent 'foreign-born' in London (from South and South-east Asia, Ireland, continental Europe, East, West and South Africa, the Caribbean, North America and Australasia (London Research Study 1994; Merriman 1993)) – to say that they have somehow more commonalities than differences seems to be a somewhat grandiose claim.

Clearly, the historical, cultural, and political status and power (or lack of it) possessed by migrants from different countries, when relocated in the cities of another society, are highly variable and differentiated. Given that a large proportion, both in Europe and North America, are from Third World, post-colonial societies, their colonial histories, with their linguistic and cultural links (as well as the residual racial stigmata attributed by the receiving societies), place different kinds of migrants in very different situations of power and lack of power, irrespective of their relation to the (economic) labour market. Their influence on the culture and politics of the dominant society, however, can be considerable. There is no better example than the very significant influence which post-colonial criticism (e.g. by Edward Said, Homi Bhaba, Stuart Hall, Gayatri Spivak) has had on the epistemology of the Western academy, at least in the humanities (Spivak 1988, 1991). In terms of cultural politics and critique, quantification is irrelevant. Salman Rushdie is, after all, only one person.

Moreover, in cities which have a significant proportion of migrants, the political, economic, administrative, or social influence which they wield varies in direct proportion to their status and weight of representation in the halls of municipal and national power; whether in regard to their control over the school curriculum, the interpretation and implementation of the law, or the shape of the built environment. The degree to which cultural diversity is permitted and visibly constituted in space, and whether in the public realm or the private, varies immensely, not simply according to social and political pressures and the existence of planning laws and building codes but also in the enthusiasm and equality with which they are enforced.

To speak specifically about space and the built environment: the public display of individual or collective cultural identities through the use of distinctive building types, shapes, forms, construction materials, methods, colours, finishes, and qualities, has, in general, less impact in a city like New York, despite its very many different nationalities and cultures, because the city has only *one* dominant spatial culture: the block by block grid system – a result of the city's historical origins and the devotion of its founders to the commodification of land and the accumulation of capital (Sennet 1990: 53). It has also a relatively short history, compared to many cities in the world. Of course, cultural difference can, and indeed is, constituted in different ways in that city, and more recently the impact of Puerto Rican community activities has begun to modify spatial use, though this is still confined within the surveillance space of the block (Sciorra 1995).

Yet in particular Third World cities, grossly different construction standards, different social, cultural, and construction practices of various regional migrant groups, and immensely different modes of production and standards of living exist side by side, without the 'benefit' of 'planning', in city space. This means that cities like Bombay or Delhi, with theoretically less human 'diversity' (if that is construed in ethnic rather than social terms), and fewer representatives from other national groups, nevertheless have a much wider variety of historically and culturally constructed physical and spatial environments. The serious issue raised by these comments, of course, is whether we are speaking of cultural diversity or social inequality, a question that can be asked about New York as well as Bombay.

Elsewhere I have suggested that the frames for understanding social and cultural phenomena in world cities can appropriately include not only the political economic frame of the world-systems perspective, the culturally oriented frame of globalization, but also the more specifically historical and political frames of post-colonialism (for cities like Singapore, Hong Kong, or Bombay) and post-imperialism (for London, Paris, or Amsterdam) (King 1993). Extrapolating these frameworks allows us to examine, for example, the very different balances of power between dominant ethnicities, cultures, and social groups in, for example, the post-colonial and post-imperial city.

These frameworks, however, hardly exhaust the possibilities. For such 'semi-peripheral' cities as Jakarta or Colombo, we would need, in addition, to position them in relation to the very specific economic and geopolitical alliances and spaces of recent years. As Keeling's chapter (in this volume) implies, national airlines and their city offices (the residue, in most cases, of old imperial relations) are major clues to the cultural origins of migrants (downtown Rotterdam sports the office of Indonesian Airlines as Manchester does that of PIA).

Displaced spaces

As I have suggested above, the research of Swedish anthropologist Ulf Hannerz on the 'world system of culture', has led him to suggest that the transnational nature of contemporary world cities in the West comes especially from four categories of people: the transnational business class, Third World migrant populations, tourists, and people he describes as those 'specializing in expressive activities' (1993).

If we adopt Sharon Zukin's (1991) two spatial categories of 'landscapes of power' and 'the vernacular of the powerless' we can begin to describe the spatial and built environmental representations of these four categories. In this context, the norms and forms of the institutional, spatial, and symbolic signs of the international business class (whether in the transnational headquarters, the banks, hotels, corporate offices) conform in most ways to the norms and forms manifest in these same institutions of the hegemonic states in the world order: the USA, Japan, and Germany. These are the 'landscapes of power'. More than anything else, these institutions reproduce transnational symbolic forms and styles, in many cases financed by international banks, and often designed by First World international architectural firms located in world cities (King 1990; Sassen 1991), even though they may gesture to the concept of national cultural identity. Here, Lawrence Vale's recent account of *Architecture, Power and National Identity* (1992) is relevant, concluding as it does that the identities of capitol complexes in post-colonial states were, in effect, those of the architects (often foreign) who had designed them, and of the political leaders who commissioned them. Equally significant in determining this landscape of power is the top end of the international tourist market.

Numerically, however, the largest category of people is that of the international migrants, a small proportion of whom are members of an international élite, though the largest proportion are the relatively poor, if rarely the destitute. Here, cultural representation in space takes place in the form of what I shall call the 'double vernacular'. In the first instance, living and working space is appropriated in what was once the working-class, vernacular housing of the city, distinguished by the date of its construction, its location, and, in terms of building and architectural form, its regional identity. Appropriated by incoming migrant groups, it is transformed into the vernacular of the newcomers, modified in accordance with kinship preferences, adapted to meet cultural requirements or, by expansion, to take in tenants and accumulate capital, and modified, by external styling, to make a statement about symbolic cultural identity. Obsolete neighbourhood buildings, whether warehouses or churches, are transformed into social and cultural spaces, mosques, temples, and social clubs. We may refer here, for instance, to the spaces of the Portuguese in Toronto, Puerto Ricans in New York, or Bangladeshis in London's East End.

The fourth group Hannerz describes as a small number of people who yet tend to maintain a rather high profile in world cities, people concerned with culture in a narrower sense, people specializing in expressive activities – cultural practitioners – internationally constituted groups of professionals in art, fashion, design, photography, writing, music, etc.

I have already indicated one small but significant category that Hannerz omits here, that of academics and scholars. Another, however, is that of practitioners of architecture and urban design. It is precisely these who, in their design work, provide the surface representations, the final suit of clothing which clads the combined interests of the institutional investors, the financial industry, real estate speculators, and the organizing élite of the corporate world. These are some of the main brokers in the economy of signs in the world city. Like each of the previous three groups, one of the principal identities of their multiple identity is 'global', providing that we understand here that 'global' is, in fact, a very local and restricted category. The professional values they subscribe to encompass both an 'international' architectural practice determined principally by the values of the market, the supposedly contestatory discourse of the post-modern, and increasingly, in Robertson's (1992: 130) terms, a particular concern with 'tradition, identity and indigenization'. Their design response depends upon the 'thematization and diffusion of "universal" ideas concerning the appropriateness of being unique *in a context*' (Robertson 1992: 130).

While Hannerz seems to suggest that these four categories (we may call them the cosmopolitans) are engaged in the transnational flow of culture by being mobile themselves, it is also implicit that they have an impact on the remainder of the population (the locals).

Elsewhere, Hannerz (1992) has proposed four typical frameworks for examining cultural process in world cities organized as 'a flow of meaningful forms between people: the market, the state, forms of life, and movements'. In the market framework people relate to each other as buyer and seller, and meaning and meaningful form have been commoditized. As all commodities carry some meaning, and are to that extent cultural commodities, informational, aesthetic, and emotional appeal is all there is to a commodity.

The second framework of cultural process Hannerz identifies as the state, not as a bounded physical area but as organizational form. The state engages in managing meaning by fostering the idea that the state is a nation, and constructs people as citizens. Some states more than others promote 'cultural welfare', that is, meanings and meaningful forms are held to certain intellectual and aesthetic standards. Third is the form of life framework, where the cultural flow occurs merely between fellow human beings in their mingling with one another, a free and reciprocal flow going on as we observe one another and listen to one another in everyday situations. The fourth framework is that of movements, more intermittently part of the cultural totality than the other three and a major influence in recent decades: women's, environmental, ecological, and peace movements (Hannerz 1993; also 1991).

Hannerz's frameworks provide scope for understanding various processes in the world city: factors affecting the constructions of identity, the opportunities provided by the market, and forms of life which take on material representations.

For ethnographer, Arjun Appadurai, the central challenge is to study the 'new cosmopolitanisms' of the world city. Here, in addition to the idea of displacement, a central concern is with the idea of deterritorialization, not only of the transnational corporations and money markets, but of ethnic groups and political forms which operate in ways that transcend specific territorial boundaries and identities (Appadurai 1991: 192).

Elsewhere, Appadurai (1990) has offered suggestive concepts for exploring different dimensions of the global cultural flows in major world cities, including the idea of the ethnoscape (the landscape of ethnically differentiated persons who constitute the shifting world); the technoscape (the global configuration of technology); the mediascape (images of the world created by media); and ideoscapes (ideologies of states and counter-ideologies of movements – the concatenation of terms and images such as 'freedom', 'welfare', or 'democracy').

The process of deterritorialization is, however, simultaneously one of reterritorialization. Where Appadurai (1991) suggests that deterritorialization creates new markets for film companies, impresarios, and travel agencies which thrive on the need of the relocated population for contact with its homeland, the reterritorialization occurs, culturally, in the world city spaces where these processes take place. In many more ways than one, the world city becomes a place where the symbolic economy of new cultural meanings and representations takes place (Zukin 1995). At one level, the juxtaposition of cultures, the contestations, the redefinitions of identity, the cultural politics, the fractured identities, become the very material from which new cultural conflict arises, yet simultaneously, these also provide the new cultural content for the movies, videos, theatre, or literature. In the ten years between 1983 and 1993, seven out of ten of the novels winning the London-based publishing industry's Booker Award in the UK have been written by immigrant authors, including Salman Rushdie. Ethnic restaurants and neighbourhoods are commodified for the overlapping interests of the international business community and tourists. What were once ethnic ghettos are cleaned up and put on show – to simulate the colonial experience but without the tropical heat (McAuley 1987).

In this context, the representation itself becomes the reality (King 1995). The image is manipulated for its message. After ten years of circulation, the world city metaphor is used by city governments, financial élites, and the cultural industries (Fox 1991; LPAC 1991) as a mirror in which to assess their own fortunes, or to mobilize their competitive image.

NOTES

1   At the symposium at which this paper was first presented, it was suggested that were a bomb to fall on the conference hall in which a large majority of

world and global city theorists were assembled, would the 'world city' disappear?

2   'As far as I understand it, the notion of textuality should be related to the notion of the worlding of a world on a supposedly uninscribed territory. When I say this, I am thinking basically about the imperialist project which had to assume that the earth that it territorialized was in fact previously uninscribed. So then a world, on a simple level of cartography inscribed what was presumed to be uninscribed. Now this worlding actually is also a texting, textualizing, a making into art, making into an object to be understood'. Gayatri Chakravorty Spivak, *The Post-Colonial Critic: Interviews, Strategies, Dialogues*, ed. S. Harasym (New York and London: Routledge and Kegan Paul, 1990), p. 1. Cited in Mahmut Mutman, 'Pictures from afar: shooting the Middle East', in *Orientalism and Cultural Differences*, ed. Mahmut Mutman and Meyda Yegenoglu (Inscriptions 6, Center for Cultural Studies, University of California, Santa Cruz, 1992), p. 35.

3   This idea was prompted by Nihal Perera.

REFERENCES

Abu-Lughod, J. 1991. 'Going beyond global babble'. In *Culture, Globalization and the World-System*, ed. A. D. King, pp. 131–8. Department of Art and Art History, SUNY, Binghamton and London: Macmillan.

Appadurai, A. 1990. 'Disjuncture and difference in the global cultural economy'. In *Global Culture. Nationalism, Globalization, and Modernity*, ed. M. Featherstone, pp. 295–310. Newbury Park CA: Sage.

   1991. 'Global ethnoscapes: notes and queries for a transnational anthropology'. In *Recapturing Anthropology: Working in the Present*, ed. R. G. Fox, pp. 191–210. Santa Fe: School of American Research Press.

Ambroise-Rendu, M. 1993. 'The migrants who turned Paris into a melting pot'. *Guardian Weekly*, 27 June 1993, p. 14.

Barnes, T. and Duncan, J. S. 1992. *Writing Worlds. Discourse, Text and Metaphor in the Representation of Landscape*. London and New York: Routledge and Kegan Paul.

Bayer, D. and Perlman, J. 1990. 'Here is New York – 1990'. Paper presented at the conference on Mega-cities of the Americas. State University of New York at Albany, 5–6 April 1990.

Bourdieu, P. 1977. *Outline of a Theory of Practice*. Trans. Richard Nice. Cambridge: Cambridge University Press.

Donald, J. 1992. 'Metropolis: the city as text'. In *Social and Cultural Forms of Modernity*, ed. R. Bocock and K. Thompson, pp. 1–54. Cambridge: Polity Press in association with the Open University.

Fox, C. 1991. *London – World City*. New Haven: Yale University Press.

Friedmann, J. and Wolff, G. 1982. 'World city formation. An agenda for research and action'. *International Journal of Urban and Regional Research*, 6(3): 309–44.

Frost, M. and Spence, N. 1993. 'Global city characteristics and Central London's employment'. *Urban Studies*, 30(3): 547–58.

Giddens, A. 1990. *The Consequences of Modernity*. Cambridge: Polity Press.

Gottman, J. 1989. 'What are cities becoming the centers of? Sorting out the possibilities'. In *Cities in a Global Society*, eds. R. V. Knight and G. Gappert, pp. 58–67. London, Newbury Park CA, New Delhi: Sage.

Hannerz, U. 1991. 'Scenarios for peripheral cultures'. In *Culture, Globalization and the World-System. Contemporary Conditions for the Representation of Identity*, ed. A. D. King, pp. 107–28. Dept. of Art and Art History, SUNY, Binghamton, and London: Macmillan.

1992. *Culture, Cities and the World*. Amsterdam: Centrum voor Grootstedeljk Onderzoek.

1993. 'The cultural role of world cities'. In *Humanizing the City: Social Contexts of Urban Life at the Turn of the Millennium*, ed. A. Cohen and K. Fukui. Edinburgh: Edinburgh University Press.

Harvey, D. 1989. *The Condition of Postmodernity*. Oxford: Basil Blackwell.

King, A. D. 1990. *Global Cities: Post-Imperialism and the Internationalization of London*. London: Routledge and Kegan Paul.

1991. 'Spaces of culture, spaces of knowledge'. In *Culture, Globalization and the World-System. Contemporary Conditions for the Representation of Identity*, ed. A. D. King, pp. 1–18. Dept. of Art and Art History, SUNY, Binghamton, and London: Macmillan.

1993. 'Identity and difference: the internationalization of capital and the globalization of culture'. In *The Restless Urban Landscape*, ed. P. L. Knox, pp. 83–110. Englewood Cliffs: Prentice Hall.

1994. 'Terminologies and types: making sense of some types of dwellings and cities'. In *Ordering Space. Types in Architecture and Design*, ed. L. Schnee Kloth and K. Franck. New York: Van Nostrand Reinhold.

1995. 'Cities, texts, and paradigms'. In *Representing the City. Ethnicity, Capital and Culture in the 21st Century Metropolis*, ed. A. D. King. London: Macmillan.

London Planning Advisory Committee (LPAC). 1991. *London. World City Moving into the 21st Century*. London: HMSO.

London Research Study. 1994. *London's Ethnic Minorities. One City, Many Communities*. London Research Study, 81 Black Prince Rd, London SE21.

Macdonald, D. 1986. *Theories of Discourse*. Oxford: Basil Blackwell.

McAuley, I. 1987. *Guide to Ethnic London. A Complete Handbook to the Many Faces of London and its Ethnic Neighborhoods. Everything from Restaurants and Shops to Historical Walks and Cultural Celebrations*. London: Michal Haag.

McGrew, A. 1992. 'A global society?' In *Modernity and Its Futures*, ed. S. Hall, D. Held, and T. McGrew, pp. 61–116. Oxford: Polity Press in association with the Open University.

Merriman, N. (ed.). 1993. *The Peopling of London. Fifteen Thousand Years of Settlement from Overseas*. London: Museum of London.

Perlman, J. 1990. 'Here is New York – 1990'. Paper presented at a conference on Mega-cities of the Americas, State University of New York, Albany, 5–6 April 1990.

Robertson, R. 1992. *Globalization: Social Theory and Global Culture*. London and Newbury Park CA: Sage.

Rosenau, J. 1980. *The Study of Global Interdependence*. London: Frances Pinter.

Sassen, Saskia. 1991. *The Global City: New York, London, Tokyo*. Princeton NJ: Princeton University Press.

Sciorra, J. 1995. 'Metaphors of home. Puerto Rican vernacular architecture in New York City'. In *Re-Presenting the City. Ethnicity, Capital and Culture in the 21st Century Metropolis*, ed. A. D. King. London: Macmillan.

Sennet, R. 1990. *The Conscience of the Eye*. New York: W. W. Norton.

Spivak, G. C. 1988. *In Other Worlds*. London and New York: Routledge and Kegan Paul.

1992. *Architecture, Power and National Identity*. New Haven: Yale University Press.

Wolff, J. 1992. 'The real city, the discursive city, the disappearing city: postmodernism and urban sociology'. *Theory and Society*, 21: 553–60.

Zukin, S. 1991. *Landscapes of Power*. Berkeley: University of California Press.

1995. 'Space and symbols in an age of decline'. In *Re-Presenting the City. Ethnicity, Capital and Culture in the 21st Century Metropolis*, ed. A. D. King. London: Macmillan.

13   Theorizing the global–local connection

Robert A. Beauregard

In their seminal article (1982) John Friedmann and Goetz Wolff encouraged us to explore how the integration of cities in the world economy is 'reflected' in the 'character of their urbanizing processes', specifically, how people live within these cities. The central issue, they maintained, was whether resident populations, transnational corporations, or the 'nation states that provide the political setting for world urbanization' would control urban life (Friedmann and Wolff 1982: 309).

This framing of theoretical tasks suggests that our attention should be turned not only outward to world-city hierarchies but also inward to the 'duality' of contemporary world cities (Castells and Mollenkopf 1991; Marcuse 1989; Schurmann and Close 1979). The issue is the extent to which social, economic, and political relations and processes *within* cities – that is, at the urban scale – are influenced by forces operating at a global scale.[1] This is a quite different concern to asking how world cities are constituted within global hierarchies and subsequently organize the world (or at least most of it) for capital accumulation (Friedmann 1986, see appendix to this volume).

Over the last two decades numerous theorists have addressed the relation between the global and the local. Their ruminations appear under various rubrics: locality studies (Cooke 1989; Lancaster Regionalism Group 1985); global cities (Alger 1990; Fainstein, Gordon, and Harloe 1992; Rodriguez and Feagin 1986; Sassen 1991); economic restructuring (Beauregard 1989a; Henderson and Castells 1987; Scott and Storper 1986; Smith and Feagin 1987); and world development (Kennedy 1993; Peet 1991). In each instance, 'thinking globally' is privileged over 'thinking locally'. Dominance is conceded to actors and forces operating internationally, and local actors resist, adapt, or acquiesce but do not *fundamentally* alter global intrusions. The thrust of this diverse literature is to nest national and subnational scales of activity within an overarching global framework.[2]

Susan Fainstein (1987: 335), for example, has argued that an 'increasingly integrated international economy and the highly decentralized character of production within the new international division of labor' have reshaped the political importance of place. Consequently, successful opposition to the deprivations and hardships imposed by capitalism must include a broadened popular base and an overarching ideology that incorporates disparate constituent groups. It is not enough to organize locally when the forces fuelling dissatisfaction come from outside the community.

Richard Peet (1987) plays out the global and the local in a somewhat different way. He explains the deindustrialization of advanced capitalist countries and the growth of manufacturing activity in peripheral countries by reference to a global restructuring of capital that simultaneously undermines the social conditions of labour and creates the resistances and struggles that exacerbate its international wanderings. Peet writes that 'opposition from labor at the center is a powerful force propelling capital towards internationalized operations, and lower levels of labor opposition pull capital towards certain parts of the periphery of the world system' (Peet 1987: 18).

In these examples (two among many that could be cited), a clear distinction is maintained between a global level of analysis and a local level. These levels are assumed to correspond, more or less, to spatial scales and to represent quite different abilities to access financial, political, cultural, and technological resources. The result is a formidable geological metaphor that significantly influences related theoretical arguments.[3]

In this chapter, I want to unpack the premises of this perspective. What does it mean to say that global actors and forces shape local activities and conditions? How is space conceptualized in this argument and how do actors with diverse capabilities give meaning to places?

Answers to such questions enhance our awareness of the premises of global–local thinking and make us more aware of its conceptual dangers. In addition, they enable us to reflect on governmental planning and collective action, activities that ultimately occur at the local level. Friedmann and Wolff note briefly that a world-city analysis implies that 'many local problems can have only global solutions' (1982: 330), and they end their essay by calling for greater attention to the ways in which international capitalist dynamics 'create the context and opportunities for planning' (1982: 336). This chapter will end in a similar fashion, drawing forth from a theoretical critique the implications for practice.

Global–local thinking

In order to analyse the global–local perspective, we need to elaborate its basic premises. Drawing from the literature cited above I have identified five general claims. First, the dominant global forces are economic. Second, these forces penetrate to the local scale in an uneven fashion and even bypass certain institutions, industries, people, and places. Third, global forces are sometimes embraced, sometimes resisted, and sometimes themselves exploited. Fourth, economic, political, and social forces operate at a variety of spatial scales: global, national, regional, urban, and neighbourhood, for example. Finally, and as a result, because each scale is relatively autonomous from the others, global forces are mediated as they penetrate downward.

Within the overall perspective only two categories of actors are deemed significant on the world stage – transnational corporations and national states – and the former are the most powerful.[4] This is held to be true for the following reasons: national states are (in part) the products of global economic relations; states depend on economic stability and growth for their persistence and well-being and this makes them structurally subordinate to transnational corporations as a whole; and national boundaries are not major impediments to global production and exchange (Cohen 1981). Lacking international political bodies of sufficient power to control international finance and production, the world is primarily integrated economically and only secondarily is it integrated politically.

In addition, the world economy is becoming increasingly globalized as information technologies and multiorganizational forms combine with ever-expanding financial networks to spread capitalism throughout the world (Castells 1991: 307–47; Thrift, 1987). The influence of global economic forces is thereby further enhanced by the hypermobility of capital that enables decisions about investment and disinvestment to be implemented rapidly in response to changing global and local conditions. Within this context, states and non-governmental entities are mainly reactive, although sometimes resistant, to transnational corporations.

The presence of a highly dynamic world economy has three important implications. First, it diminishes the influence and importance of states and national boundaries at the same time that states are organizing the legal and financial infrastructures that enable capitalism to function globally. Second, since capital can easily find other places in which to do business, it diminishes the importance of specific places.[5] Contrarily, other theorists have argued that the dominance of the global makes local particularity more valuable and engenders the defensiveness of local actors (Cooke 1990). Finally, the location of the entities that command, control, and finance the world economy is what defines a global city (Sassen 1991); that is, the top of the world-city hierarchy. Global cities are the bases from which transnational corporations launch offensives around the world. The extent to which cities do or do not achieve global status determines both their prosperity (and duality) and also their contribution to the economic and cultural organization of internationally linked places.[6]

Global forces, subsequently, penetrate to lower spatial scales and influence processes and conditions there (Fainstein, Gordon, and Harloe 1992; Feagin and Smith 1987; Sassen 1991). They do so, however, in an uneven fashion (N. Smith 1984), impacting differentially on institutions, industries, and people.[7] Some cities thus become global places and others do not, and cities exploited or ignored by global forces are peripheralized.

This uneven penetration is not simply a matter of *which* institutions, industries, people, and places are affected but also *how* they are affected (see, for example, M. P. Smith 1992). They might be overwhelmed, exploited, or enhanced. In return, local people and places might capitulate, adapt, or attempt to turn globally induced changes into opportunities. All of this is highly contingent but the consequence is to mediate global influences rather than having them materialized locally in pure form.

The general thrust of global forces is to integrate countries, regions, and localities into a global framework.[8] To the extent that global interests are not identical with interests at these other spatial scales, however, they become viewed as undesirable and are often resisted. Because actors have different geographical commitments and divergent interests, then, resistance is both possible and likely.

Resistance is the primary way in which global forces are mediated at lower spatial scales. Numerous examples are available to us. Take the many attempts by national states to protect themselves from or exert control over the actions of transnational corporations. These resistances might take the form of trade barriers, own-source requirements placed on shared production arrangements, corporate tax policies that address profits made outside the country, regulations regarding joint ownership agreements in specific industries, or currency restrictions.[9]

It is not only states that resist global forces. A good example of popular resistance are the IMF riots that began in the late 1970s and extended through the 1980s (Walton 1987). In Peru, Zaïre, Turkey, Jamaica, Argentina, the Philippines, and El Salvador (among other countries) protesters took to the streets in response to the economic austerity imposed by the International Monetary Fund. IMF actions were themselves a response to a burgeoning Third World debt crisis that threatened to undermine global financial institutions. Within numerous cities mass action ensued in an effort to preserve local conditions against further degradation by national and international bodies.

Organizations and people often resist but also frequently acquiesce and adapt to global forces. The proliferation of clothing sweatshops in Los Angeles and New York City during the 1980s appears less a struggle against transnational corporations and the dictates of global markets than a capitulation to them. US car manufacturers responded to the threat of foreign competition by adopting some of the production techniques (for example, just-in-time supply systems and quality groups) of their competitors, and American parts suppliers were forced to cut costs, increase quality, and adapt their production processes if they wished to stay in business.

Adaptation, in fact, appears in a number of different forms. During the 1980s certain immigrant communities in New York City became tied to the residential component of a globally driven financial services sector (Sassen 1991: 193–319). Rising employment in this sector coupled with high incomes and dual-earner families led to a greater demand for home help, personal services more generally, and specialized commodities (e.g. furniture) for which immigrants provided the cheap labour. School systems in a number of major cities have instituted bilingual courses and social service agencies have developed new programmes in response to immigration induced by the global economy. As a final example, many US state governments during the 1980s established export assistance programmes to enable manufacturers within their states to enter foreign markets and thus to enhance regional growth in the face of foreign competition.

Global connections have also been celebrated and even aggressively pursued, particularly when they create new opportunities for local investors. In Battle Creek, Michigan, economic development officials have attempted to attract Japanese branch plants to the community. Their success has brought new jobs and led to Japanese language training in the local school system and the establishment of Saturday school days for the children of Japanese executives. A number of cities have undertaken 'international city' initiatives, mobilizing civic boosters to explore ways to provide more and stronger linkages between their local and the global economy. Atlanta has been particularly successful and other cities (for example Pittsburgh) are exploring this path to economic development (Steinbach and Peirce 1984).

In cities such as New York, Los Angeles, Houston, and Minneapolis, where foreign investors have been active in buying real estate, downtown real estate interests – brokers, commercial banks, real estate consultants, and property owners – have welcomed international property investment. Throughout the 1980s the infusion of foreign capital into the buying and selling of existing buildings and the construction of new buildings bolstered commercial property markets by raising rents, increasing property values, and generally expanding business opportunities (Logan 1993).

Yet it is also true that global forces bypass industries, people, and places. Not all of the world economy is organized in global networks. Many small towns and rural areas of the USA and small-scale rural farmers in countries such as South Africa and China, who produce mainly for local consumption using local techniques and materials, are hardly part of a global economy in any significant way. Regions of countries and even whole countries (e.g. Afghanistan and Lesotho) are at the far reaches of the global economy, scarcely of any importance to it and relatively unaffected in return. Certain neighbourhoods of global cities, particularly where unemployment is high and poverty deep, are peripheral to the workings of the world economy, although certain poor neighbourhoods might well house the low-wage workers for transnational firms.

Even though global forces impinge upon cities, they do so in different ways, sometimes being resisted and transformed, sometimes overwhelming local conditions and actors, and sometimes being warmly embraced. Many times, institutions, industries, and people adapt as they resist. Moreover, just as there exists a hierarchy of world cities, the penetration of global forces dissipates as it spreads, being highly concentrated and influential in some places and non-existent or insignificant in others.

Cities, of course, are not influenced solely by global forces. The existence of national and regional forces both complicates the argument and also reinforces its basic premises.[10] Forces operating at multiple spatial scales suggest that the local impact of global forces might be transformed in ways other than being mediated by local relations and conditions. Take labour relations in the branch plants of multinational corporations in countries that have a strong union tradition. One would expect that the corporation bargains with an understanding of the global implications of a labour agreement, while being aware also of national labour laws and the history of labour–management relations in that industry in that country. The labour unions enter the bargaining with a local history and some commitment to a national strategy. Workers bring to the table their sense of a fair wage as seen in comparison to local living conditions, regional wage rates, and national wage packages. The actual forging of a labour agreement is neither a local affair nor a global imposition (see Jonas 1992).

The interaction of forces operating at various spatial scales can be illustrated in a variety of ways: the construction of an office building for a foreign bank using materials from around the world; the dynamics of a major research university whose faculty consult internationally, nationally, and locally; and the corporate plant location and contracting strategies of multinational corporations such as Nike and Heinz, as they balance local labour conditions, regional locational advantages, national markets, and international investment opportunities.

In any one situation it is difficult to disentangle the forces emanating from different spatial realms. We can catalogue the geographic origins of various materials from Italian marble to Indonesian teak in the corporate office building, but separating the relative influences on the corporate performance of an international bank of its business plan, national tax policies, state banking regulations, and fluctuating currency exchange rates is a more daunting task. How is the quality of a university improved or diminished by having an internationally renowned faculty, a public policy school heavily tied to national policy-making, numerous faculty working with state agencies, and a local government research centre? What is the impact in Eugene, Oregon of Nike's offshore production arrangements and world-wide marketing strategy?

The existence of multiple spatial scales poses additional empirical and theoretical problems but also reinforces the underlying conceptual thrust of the argument: (1) global forces are the starting point for any consideration of interactions across spatial scales since they are the most powerful; (2) actors and forces emanating from each spatial scale have diverse interests and resources, otherwise the mediation of forces from higher to lower levels would not occur; and (3) unless wholly isolated and insulated, the local is the mediated outcome of forces operating at all spatial scales. Forces operating at intermediate scales add complexity to the global–local argument but do not change its essential orientation.

Critique

We need to subject this particular global–local argument to a critical reading. There are theoretical pitfalls involving not only the meaning of spatial scale and its origins but also assumptions regarding the interests of actors and the correspondence between the power of actors and their geographical reach.

Consider the notion of spatial scales. One way it appears in the argument is as a geographic description of 'nested' places. Here we understand, metaphorically, the local as appearing within the regional, the regional within the national, and the national within the global. We are asked in addition not to think of this nesting in a two-dimensional space but in a three-dimensional one in which 'larger' spatial scales are also 'higher' and thus dominant. Finally, each scale is often depicted as relatively stable in the sense that, say, the boundaries of a region endure across the short-run of the theoretical argument.[11]

Another way in which spatial scale appears is as the 'geographical reach' of an actor. Although similar to the notion of a market area as the geographical extent of a commodity's price competitiveness, geographical reach is better interpreted in terms of power and control. An actor with a global reach, that is, operating at a global scale, is able to organize a global network of relations in order to produce and market a product or achieve political ends. This second meaning of spatial scale makes it into a socio-spatial process that is not independent of actors (as is implied in the first usage) but a consequence of their actions (Massey 1984; Smith and Dennis 1987).

These two quite different meanings often become conflated and substituted. When it is argued that the local mediates (that is, resists, adapts, acquiesces to) the global, are we speaking of some quality of scales that enables them to 'filter' forces emanating from other spatial scales, independently of actors operating at these different scales, or are we referring to the frictional interaction of actors with different geographic reaches? The former seems rigid and a reification of space. The latter is more acceptable theoretically, but rejects any theorization of the global and local that does not simultaneously attach scalar notions to the actors who embody these spatial qualities.[12]

Once we focus our attention on the agents who literally make scale, the partitioning of space into global–national–regional–local seems simplistic. If agents create scale and scale is the consequence of their geographic influence, then many spatial scales seem likely to exist that fragment and multiply this basic four-part division. A multitude of actors, each with different geographical interests and influence, create a multitude of spatial scales. Places become linked to each other through highly differentiated actors (Warren 1963: 242) and not in any simple way. Highly differentiated places appear when numerous actors develop a multitude of complex spatial linkages to and from these places. Less differentiated places have few such actors. In fact, it is the mix of these actors, and the distribution of influence among them, that results in such places becoming regional, national, or international nodes in the world-system.[13]

Additionally, given the constant flux of actors and conditions, spatial relations (and thus spatial 'scales') are continually being reinscribed. That is, what we understand as regional or local is itself unstable, just as the geographical scope of any specific region or locality might expand or contract with the play of actors, particularly political actors, who control territorial boundaries. Thus, for example, the Ukraine was once a region within the Soviet Union but is now a national state whose internal regions have become more prominent politically and economically.

The more challenging theoretical problem is the likelihood that actors simultaneously have interests at multiple spatial scales; that is, their activities spread out over different geographical fields. A transnational corporation involved in consumer electronics, for example, makes regional locational decisions as regards branch plants, secures capital on international financial markets, negotiates tax advantages with national bodies, and adjusts its strategic plan to institutional shareholders from various countries. Local actors concerned about the withdrawal of investment by this transnational corporation might utililize state plant closing laws, explore pension implications as governed by national legislation, work with union organizers and experts from around the country, and even hire transnational law firms to help them consider an employee buy-out. Under this scenario, to speak of a 'pure' global force or an unadulterated global actor being mediated by 'pure' local forces is empirically and theoretically indefensible. Once we recognize that major actors frequently operate at numerous spatial scales, then we must abandon a simple geographical nesting of scales and a rigid categorization of actors in terms of spatial reach.

Such criticisms undermine an even more fundamental premise of this global–local argument. That premise is the 'original' autonomy, and thus relative independence, of actors at each spatial scale that allows global actors, for example, to be distinguished from local ones. Actors are not only presumed to have different (and complex) geographical extensions but also to be wholly under the influence, with their actions strictly determined, of powerful actors with greater geographical reach. In only this sense can one talk about distinct spatial scales and precisely differentiated global–local interactions.

A historical understanding, presented somewhat schematically here, provides the grounds for this premiss. It posits a world that was once primarily local. Centuries ago people lived their lives in relatively small areas and few actors had the capacity to link one place to another. Over time traders began to connect cities, national states emerged to tie regions together, and later, transnational corporations established a world economic system encompassing various types of places from extractive regions to global cities. This happened slowly, with each 'larger' spatial scale appearing in succession as the world expanded outward and became smaller and smaller. None the less, as the spatial reach of society was extended, lower spatial scales retained some of their earlier integrity. In fact they resisted being incorporated into larger spatial scales, whether represented by medieval kingdoms, states, world religions, or the world economy.

Contrarily, one can point to instances where localities were created by actors operating at larger spatial scales (for example, regional mining and national railroad companies establishing towns), as well as to examples of places being dismantled from 'below' as, for instance, when ethnic divisions undermine nationalist accommodations, thus reversing the purported historical sequence. Moreover, the geological metaphor that characterizes this historical story is itself inappropriate. It ignores both the 'mixing' of layers, precisely the condition in which we now exist and probably did much earlier, and the fragmentation of actors' interests. Finally, the logic of the global–local argument strongly implies that 'after' mediation the local is no longer purely local but has incorporated global (and regional and national) interests and actors. To this extent, any spatial scale exists only temporarily as 'purely' local, regional, or global.

All of this makes it very difficult to write in terms of relatively distinct and autonomous spatial scales. Certainly, because social action is contingent and power is not perfectly concentrated, actors can be relatively autonomous and thus privilege certain spatial interests over others. At the same time places are highly fragmented, with their various parts (be they areas or actors) more or less linked to actors at numerous spatial scales (Warren 1963: 239). Thus to speak of a relatively autonomous local level impacted by global forces is to skirt a number of important theoretical considerations.

These criticisms are useful for reflecting upon another major premiss of the argument: the one-to-one correspondence between spatial scale and power and control. Within the global–local perspective, global forces are almost always the most powerful, and their control, by definition, is the most spatially extensive. At the other end of the continuum is the local, where forces are hypothesized to be relatively weak and geographically limited.

Such logic harbours a theoretical problem. If the local is less powerful, how is it that it mediates rather than being simply overcome? Part of the answer flows from the relative autonomy of local actors and another part of the answer appears when we disassociate lack of power from power-lessness. In addition, we need to disabuse ourselves of any notion that power is absolute and, in contrast, note the multiplicity of sources from which power and influence can emanate, the over-determination of social struggles, and the importance of 'third-party' interventions

(Castells 1983). Regardless of how we negotiate this theoretical terrain, my point remains: the importance of making explicit an implicit and simplistic equating of spatial scale and power.

There is another aspect of the parallelism of spatial scale and power and control that needs to be addressed. Admittedly, actors who operate across national boundaries have more control over resources, knowledge, and related actors, than actors operating wholly locally. Yet all global actors have local commitments, even if relatively insignificant for their ability to act globally. To this extent the spatial assignment of power and control might be misplaced. The notion of a global city is a partial confession of this. Power and control have to originate somewhere and a global city is a *local* concentration of power and control that is constantly being delocalized. Power might be exercised primarily outside the city, but this does not negate its spatial concentration.

This point leads to a possible reversal of the global–local equation. What if the global is constituted by the local? Can we theorize in this way without falling prey to a naive aggregation (Meyer et al. 1992: 257). Friedmann and Wolff (1982: 330), for example, observe that 'local actions may have global consequences'. A stronger statement is that all activity is local and that the global only comes into being through the integration of numerous locally based actors and activities. Now this assertion has some obstacles to overcome. First, it smacks of the simple historical sequence posited earlier as regards the relative autonomy of the local scale and thus can be subjected to the same criticisms. Second, it denies the existence of what social theorists call 'emergent properties'; that is, capabilities that emerge out of the organization of actors or, to put it more colloquially, the situation that ensues when the whole is greater than the sum of its parts. Theoretically, emergent properties make sense and rejecting them throws us into the clutches of methodological individualism where the whole enterprise of the 'social' and the 'structural' is called into question.

The obvious solution is to accept that local actions might have global consequences. Take, for example, any oil tanker spill, the kidnapping of Americans in Lebanon, or the pressure exerted by exiles in Miami on US foreign policy towards Cuba. The less obvious and less defensible response is to argue that the local constitutes the global. Yet we should not dismiss it summarily. It is so contrary to what most theorists currently believe that it is worth consideration (Davis 1971). One might argue that the global is the organization of many local actors on a broader geographical canvas, and that without local places the global cannot exist. Global actors hardly begin at the global scale; they are not born global. Rather, they work outwards from the local, at least initially.

Such a theoretical position would reverse the assertion that the local is mediated by the global. It would also reverse the saying that one should 'think globally and act locally'. Instead, one should 'think locally and act globally'.

In sum, the global–local argument as presented here is built upon a shaky and under-theorized conceptual foundation. In its simplistic version it has a tendency to reify spatial scales and create pure categories that distort our understanding of world-city dynamics. In its more theoretically refined version – that positing actors as the creators rather than occupants of space – it seems to have more validity, but still suffers from a number of problems related to the complex geographic extension of any single actor, the constant transformation of spatial understandings, and the unrelenting negotiation and resistance to power and control. Many questions remain unanswered: how can actors be global and local simultaneously; what do these labels for scale really mean; how is it that resistance comes into being; how is the global actor constituted?

Modest proposals

We might begin a retheorization of the global–local argument by first accepting that the notion of spatial scales is often both a heuristic and rhetorical device and a political and ideological construct profoundly influenced by territorial claims, cultural understandings, and economic linkages, all of which are constantly in flux. Thus spatial scale must be theorized rather than adopted as a constant. This means recognizing space as a social construct that plays a role in its own formulation (Duncan 1989; Shapiro and Neubauer 1989; Soja 1980). Such theoretical retooling prods us to abandon the simple notion of spatial scale and to enrich the current poverty of spatial terminology. We need more ways to represent space.[14]

Second, actors create spatial scale and without actors scale does not exist. In addition, all actors deploy their resources around multiple interests and inclinations that have various degrees of geographical extension. The consequences of those deployments are always problematic, particularly if resisted.

Third, all social processes are processes of integration and disintegration. Any activity we undertake either ties us more tightly to some other actor (or place) or diminishes existing ties, and often does both simultaneously. The world is constantly being articulated and disarticulated. This includes not only processes of incorporation and exclusion (Friedmann 1993: 10), but also processes that adjust relationships among actors even as these actors are being integrated into or marginalized from dominant systems of relationships.

Fourth, actors exist in a world where financial, political, cultural, social, and aesthetic considerations are intertwined. The pursuit of profit is not simply an economic act. The publication of a revisionist history is not simply an intellectual event. The construction of the tallest office building in a city is not only a technological feat. Some way must be found to throw off the disciplinary categories that haunt social theory (Wallerstein 1991: 7–22) so that we can theorize in a more critical fashion.

Finally, the resistance, embrace, submission, and accommodation engaged in by actors when confronted with more powerful actors and events is not captured, and in fact is misrepresented, by an argument that the local mediates the global. Places do have histories and actors are situated in and often committed to place, but this is not a licence to ignore how the interests and actions of actors create these spatial phenomena. Global–local mediation is a conceptual short-cut to bad theory.

These proposals for a theoretical reformulation of our current global–local thinking not only enable us to include in our theorization dynamics operating in various places, since actors contributing to that differentiation are likely to have interests at multiple geographical scales, but also, and more importantly, they help us turn our gaze away from ecological processes that reify space and towards the social relations among actors who make space or, more precisely, who fragment and reconstitute space. Internal differentiation thus applies both to the city itself and to the constellation of actors who engage each other in particular places. Only in this sense do local interests mediate global interests.

This line of theorizing has implications for planning. It is obvious that 'local' planners have to be empowered to be 'global' actors. This does not mean relocating them to the global scale or creating supra-planning entities that operate internationally. It does mean that planners must be able to react to influences impinging on their 'communities', regardless of where those influences originate and which actors are responsible.

In effect, planning powers need to be extended beyond political boundaries. Planners cannot be confined to defined places but must be able to roam across political boundaries as need dictates. Additionally, planners should develop organizations that extend their spatial reach through collaborative endeavours and thereby provide another mechanism for responding to the multitude of (particularly external) actors who shape their communities.

As long as planners and theorists remain trapped in a simplistic linking of spatial scales, they will be deluded by a theoretically problematic understanding and limited by a politically structured reality. We can only overcome these constraints by reconceptualizing how it is that space is differentiated and integrated by actors operating in an historically contingent geographical space.

NOTES

1 Dual cities are characterized by sharp and deep socio-economic divisions among residents that become expressed in the spatial structure of the city. Early urban sociologists subsumed similar concerns under the rubric of internal differentiation. See Katznelson (1992: 1–42).

2 Meyer et al. (1992) distinguish between 'holism', which posits regional or local forces as insignificant in comparison to global ones, and 'naive aggregation', which argues that local forces explain dynamics and conditions operating at broader spatial scales. They reject both these positions.

3 The geological metaphor essentially 'stacks' scales vertically such that any place is comprised of layers of qualitatively different and historically particular influences. See Warde (1985).

4 This is not a dismissal of para-statal, multistate and non-profit global actors such as the United Nations, International Red Cross, Greenpeace, World Court, and International Monetary Fund. Global theorists, however, rarely consider them as powerful as transnational corporations and the leading states. Neither is it a dismissal of the historical primacy of national states or the role that national states play in organizing (parts of) the world for transnational corporate activities.

5 A related argument is Castells' (1991: 6) claim that new information technologies have created a space of flows that 'dominates the historically constructed space of places'.

6 In Europe the formation of the European Community (EC) has been an impetus for city leaders to forge such linkages. Kresl (1992: 152) argues that the EC now allows us to speak of European cities as 'being liberated from a structured and confining *national* economic space and being given the opportunity to redefine [their] comparative advantage and economic role on a European or *global* economic space' (emphasis added).

7 To quote Duncan (1989: 134), 'general processes will always be constituted in particular places and at particular times' and thus 'nearly all processes and forms will be spatially differentiated'. Duncan suggests that we also pay attention to time but that concept is poorly developed in this literature (see Beauregard 1989b). A much earlier and more general formulation of this theoretical point is Roland Warren's (1963: 237–302) depiction of the interaction between a community's horizontal and vertical patterns of relationships.

8 Anthony Giddens (1990: 21) labels this disembedding 'the "lifting out" of social relations from local contexts of interaction and their restructuring across indefinite spans of time–space'.

9 Friedmann and Wolff (1982: 312) emphasize the 'inherent contradiction between the interests of transnational capital and those of particular nation-states that have their own historical trajectory'. The Marxist and critical political economy literature generally highlights the exploitative character of global forces. Reich (1989) provides an informative comparative analysis of how state policies mediated the impacts of transnational automobile corporations on national automotive industries.

10 A number of theorists, particularly geographers, view the region, the meso-level, as the key to spatial analysis of this type. See Lipietz (1993) and Meyer et al. (1992: 273–4).

11 I do not believe that I am over-simplifying or seriously distorting what theorists write; scale is frequently evoked in this way. For one example, see Friedmann (1986, see appendix to this volume).

12 The confusion of scale with actors is abetted by 'structures of parallel dualisms'. For example, the global is equated with the contextual, the general, the necessary, and the abstract and the local with the opposite: particular, specific, contingent, and concrete. Although seductive, these are not equivalents. See Sayer (1991), Massey (1991), and Meyer et al. (1992).

13 I leave aside the question of how it is that numerous agents come to operate at the 'same' spatial scale, an agglomeration problem of sorts.

14 Neil Smith (1987: 64) has written that 'as the scale of economic activity is transformed, so too is the geographical scale at which regions are constituted, but we do not yet have either a generally agreed upon language or a theory of the development of geographical scale with which to comprehend this transformation'.

REFERENCES

Alger, C. 1990. 'The world relations of cities: closing the gap between social science paradigms and everyday human experience'. *International Studies Quarterly*, 34: 493–518.

Beauregard, R. A. (ed.). 1989a. *Economic Restructuring and Political Response*. Newbury Park, CA: Sage.

     1989b. 'Space, time and economic restructuring'. In *Economic Restructuring and Political Response*, ed. R. A. Beauregard, pp. 209–40. Newbury Park, CA: Sage.

Castells, M. 1983. *The City and the Grassroots*. Berkeley: University of California Press.

     1991. *The Informational City*. Oxford: Basil Blackwell.

Castells, M. and Mollenkopf, J. H. 1991. 'Conclusion: is New York a dual city?' In *Dual City: Restructuring New York*, ed. J. H. Mollenkopf and M. Castells, pp. 399–418. New York: Russell Sage Foundation.

Cohen, R. B. 1981. 'The new international division of labour, multi-national corporations and urban hierarchy'. In *Urbanization and Urban Planning in Capitalist Society*, ed. M. Dear and A. J. Scott, pp. 287–315. London: Methuen.

Cooke, P. (ed.). 1989. *Localities*. London: Unwin Hyman.

1990. *Back to the Future*. London: Unwin Hyman.

Davis, M. S. 1971. 'That's interesting! Towards a phenomenology of sociology and a sociology of phenomenology'. *Philosophy of the Social Sciences*, 1: 309–44.

Duncan, S. S. 1989. 'Uneven development and the difference that space makes'. *GeoForum*, 20: 131–9.

Fainstein, S. S. 1987. 'Local mobilization and economic discontent'. In *The Capitalist City*, ed. M. P. Smith and J. R. Feagin, pp. 323–42. Oxford: Basil Blackwell.

Fainstein, S., Gordon, I., and Harloe, M. (eds.). 1992. *Divided Cities. New York and London in the Contemporary World*. Oxford: Basil Blackwell.

Feagin, J. R. and Smith, M. P. 1987. 'Cities and the new international division of labor'. In *The Capitalist City*, ed. M. P. Smith and J. R. Feagin, pp. 3–34. Oxford: Basil Blackwell.

Friedmann, J. 1986. 'The world city hypothesis'. *Development and Change*, 17: 69–84. (Reproduced as appendix in this volume.)

1993. 'Where we stand: a decade of world city research'. Paper presented to the World Cities in a World-System conference, 1–3 April, Sterling VA. (Reproduced as ch. 2 in this volume.)

Friedmann, J. and Wolff, G. 1982. 'World city formation. An agenda for research and action'. *International Journal of Urban and Regional Research*, 6(3): 309–44.

Giddens, A. 1990. *The Consequences of Modernity*. Cambridge: Polity Press.

Henderson, J. and Castells, M. (eds.). 1987. *Global Restructuring and Territorial Development*. London: Sage.

Jonas, A. E. G. 1992. 'Corporate takeover and the politics of community'. *Economic Geography*, 68: 348–72.

Katznelson, I. 1992. *Marxism and the City*. New York: Oxford University Press.

Kennedy, P. 1993. 'Preparing for the 21st century: winners and losers'. *New York Review of Books*, 40: 32–44.

Kresl, P. K. 1992. 'The response of European cities to EC 1992'. *Journal of European Integration*, 15: 151–72.

Lancaster Regional Group. 1985. *Localities, Class and Gender*. London: Pion.

Lipietz, A. 1993. 'The local and the global: regional individuality or interregionalism?' *Transactions of the Institute of British Geographers*, 18: 8–18.

Logan, J. 1993. 'Cycles and trends in the globalization of real estate'. In *The Restless Urban Landscape*, ed. P. Knox, pp. 33–54. Englewood Cliffs NJ: Prentice-Hall.

Marcuse, P. 1989. ' "Dual city": a muddy metaphor for a quartered city'. *International Journal of Urban and Regional Research*, 13: 697–708.

Massey, D. 1984. *Spatial Divisions of Labor*. New York: Methuen.

1991. 'The political place of locality studies'. *Environment & Planning A*, 23: 269–81.

Meyer, W. B. et al. 1992. 'The local–global continuum'. In *Geography's Inner Worlds*, ed. R. F. Marcus, M. G. Marcus, and J. M. Olson, pp. 255–79. New Brunswick NJ: Rutgers University Press.

Peet, R. 1987. 'Industrial restructuring and the crisis of international capitalism'.

248   *Robert A. Beauregard*

In *International Capitalism and Industrial Restructuring*, ed. R. Peet, pp. 9–32. Boston: Allen & Unwin.

1991. *Global Capitalism*. London: Routledge and Kegan Paul.

Reich, S. 1989. 'Roads to follow: regulating direct foreign investment'. *International Organization*, 43: 543–84.

Rodriguez, N. P. and Feagin, J. R. 1986. 'Urban specialization in the world system'. *Urban Affairs Quarterly*, 22: 187–220.

Sassen, S. 1991. *The Global City: New York, London, Tokyo*. Princeton NJ: Princeton University Press.

Sayer, A. 1991. 'Behind the locality debate: reconstructing geography's dualisms'. *Environment & Planning A*, 23: 283–308.

Schurmann, F. and Close, S. 1979. 'The emergence of global city USA'. *The Progressive*, 43: 27–9.

Scott, A. J. and Storper, M. (eds.). 1986. *Production, Work, Territory*. Boston: Allen & Unwin.

Shapiro, M. and Neubauer, D. 1989. 'Spatiality and policy discourse: reading the global city'. *Alternatives*, 14: 301–25.

Smith, M. P. 1992. *After Modernism: Global Restructuring and the Changing Boundaries of City Life*. New Brunswick NJ: Transaction Publishers.

Smith, M. P. and Feagin, J. R. (eds.). 1987. *The Capitalist City*. Oxford: Basil Blackwell.

Smith, N. 1984. *Uneven Development*. Oxford: Basil Blackwell

1987. 'Dangers of the empirical turn: the CURS initiative'. *Antipode*, 19: 59–68.

Smith, N. and Dennis, W. 1987. 'The restructuring of geographical scale: coalescence and fragmentation of the northern core region'. *Economic Geography*, 63: 160–82.

Soja, E. W. 1980. 'The socio-spatial dialectic'. *Annals of the Association of American Geographers*, 70: 207–25.

Steinbach, C. and Peirce, N. 1984. 'Cities are setting their sights on international trade and investment'. *National Journal*, 16: 818–22.

Thrift, N. 1987. 'The fixers: the urban geography of international commercial capital'. In *Global Restructuring and Territorial Development*, ed. J. Henderson and M. Castells, pp. 203–33. London: Sage.

Wallerstein, I. 1991. *Unthinking Social Science*. Cambridge: Polity Press.

Walton, J. 1987. 'Urban protest and the global political economy'. In *The Capitalist City*, ed. M. P. Smith and J. R. Feagin, pp. 364–86. Oxford: Basil Blackwell.

Warde, A. 1985. 'Spatial change, politics and the division of labour'. In *Social Relations and Spatial Structures*, ed. D. Gregory and J. Urry, pp. 190–212. New York: St Martin's Press.

Warren, R. L. 1963. *The Community in America*. Chicago: Rand McNally.

14 The disappearance of world cities and the globalization of local politics

Michael Peter Smith

Global space is a space of flows. The global cities literature differs in its analysis of the financial, informational, migratory, and cultural circuits that are necessary and sufficient to constitute a 'world city'. The various representations of 'world cities' none the less share a common strategy for conceptualizing global cities as relocalized points of intersection of these global networks, circuits, and flows within the jurisdictional boundaries of cities like New York, London, Paris, Tokyo, or Los Angeles, operating within the clearly demarcated borders of single nation-states. This relocalizing strategy, recentres highly decentred and differentially mediated global processes of capital investment, manufacturing, commodity circulation, labour migration, refugee generation, and cultural production by sharply demarcating between an 'inside' and an 'outside', and then refocusing political-economic and socio-cultural analysis on what goes on 'inside' world cities and their respective states and societies.

This chapter seeks to question the relocalizing move implicit in the world cities problematic by examining some of the ways that the networks and circuits in which transnational migrants and refugees are implicated constitute fluidly bounded transnational or globalized social spaces, in which new, transnational forms of political organization, mobilization, and practice are coming into being. These new forms of what I will term 'transnational grassroots politics', have thus far been given scant attention in discussions of political life in world cities, because they transcend both the 'urban' level of analysis and the nation-state bounded discursive practices in which citizenship, civil society, political representation, national and urban politics are ordinarily cast. Nevertheless, the spatial extension of households and ethnic communities across national borders, in the current context of uncertain labour demand and persistent state violence, is producing new patterns of cultural and political appropriation and resistance by transnational migrants and refugees, who in some ways partake of two nation-states while in other ways move beyond either. We have yet to invent the discursive terms appropriate for representing adequately the agencies and practices that currently constitute bifocal subjects, transnational social practice, and globalized political space. This chapter is a first step in that direction.

The accelerated pace, scale, and diversity of transnational migration in the past two decades to 'core' localities and regions of the global capitalist economy has been driven by several distinct yet overlapping phenomena. These include socio-cultural as well as political and economic processes: the declining capacity of peripheral political economies to absorb the labour that is created within their borders; the austerity policies imposed on developing states and societies by international banks; the production of refugees from Central America and South-east Asia by Cold War military struggles; the disintegration of state structures ushered in by the Cold War's abrupt end; and the globalization of the media of mass communications (including television, film, videos, and music) which scatter the symbolic ingredients of 'imagined lives' and modes of self-empowerment at the 'core' to even the remotest of peripheral hinterlands. Taken together, these transnational processes have reconstituted the socio-cultural landscape and eroded the boundary-setting capacities of the nation-state. They have rendered problematic representations of the interplay between the state and civil society premised on clear distinctions between inside and outside, citizens and aliens, self and other.

The spatial extension of once nationally contained households, social networks, and ethnic communities across national borders is producing new patterns of cultural appropriation and resistance by peoples whose current circumstances render them 'borderless', and in this sense, at least, 'unbound'. The boundaries of the nation-state no longer correspond to the social spaces these borderless people inhabit. The blurring of previously accepted boundaries differentiating states, ethnicities, and civil societies is producing new spaces of daily life, new sources of cultural meaning, and new forms of social and political agency that flow across national borders. The everyday practices of borderless people currently constitute transnational social spaces of survival, self-affirmation, and political practice.

This chapter is divided into three parts. The first discusses several emergent dimensions of the globalization of culture now characterizing the lived experience of transnational migrants, exiles, and refugees. The next section argues that it is time to move our political imagery beyond the confining limits of the global–local duality in social theory and its practical expression in the political slogan 'think globally, act locally'. The third part of the chapter uses narrative means to illustrate the much more complex multilayered and multiply interwoven scales of thought and action discernible in the political practices of four social movements now active in creating the emerging contours of a 'global grassroots politics'. These include: (1) indigenous Guatemalan refugees led by Rigoberta Menchu; (2) the grassroots movement opposed to US military intervention in Central America; (3) a transnational league of Mixtec associations presently being formed in Mexico, California, and Oregon; and (4) a coalition of immigrant, refugee, and women's rights groups in San Francisco and elsewhere seeking to change international human rights policies.

The globalization of culture: new social spaces of 'community research'

Several key dimensions of the internationalization of cultural production and reception are useful starting points for the still rudimentary project of mapping the changing contours of 'global culture' (see Featherstone 1990). My enumeration of these points is intended to open up the discourse on the globalization of culture by moving beyond the usual considerations of the 'global reach' of multinational corporations and the media of mass communications to launch a new point of departure for research on cultural and political practices produced 'from below'. This effort has been inspired by a close reading of several recent works in critical anthropology (Appadurai 1990, 1991; Kearney 1991; Nagengast and Kearney 1990; Rouse 1990, 1991) that have moved beyond the theoretical exhortations of post-modern anthropologists to develop a bifocal imagination (e.g. Clifford and Marcus 1986; Marcus and Fischer 1986), by investigating the actual reception and production of cultural flows and the emergence of transnational social and political practices by spatially mobile segments of the global population such as exiles, transnational migrants, and refugees. For want of a better expression I regard this chapter as an effort to theorize and illustrate the emerging contours of the 'globalization of grassroots politics'. I hope to show that, far from being an oxymoron, this expression captures precisely the networks and boundaries of socio-cultural and political space that some groups of transnational migrants, exiles, and refugees presently constitute.

As should be clear from what has been said, not only relations of economic production and exchange, but also modes of cultural production, reproduction, and exchange are more spatially fluid and territorially unbounded in the present global epoch. Nowhere is this more apparent than in the case of transnational migrants, refugees, guest-workers, and exiles, who are currently seeking to orchestrate meaningful lives under conditions in which their life-worlds are neither 'here' nor 'there' but at once both 'here' *and* 'there'. This condition of cultural bifocality, of course, can be the source of much psychic pain, as in the case of many first-wave Vietnamese refugees to the USA after the fall of Saigon, whose ability to return or to move between 'here' and 'there' was precluded by military defeat (see, for example, Freeman 1989; Smith and Tarallo 1995; Smith, Tarallo, and Kagiwada 1991). Yet for those migrants and refugees less constrained by circumstances, who remain connected to transnational networks of affiliation, symbolic and material interdependence, and mutual support (e.g. circular migrants between the USA and Mexico), the social space for cultural reproduction has become delocalized and transnationalized. They are living lives and orchestrating futures that transcend the boundaries of the nation-states they move between. Put differently, for them geographical and cultural space are profoundly disconnected.

The delocalization of cultural reproduction

Appadurai (1991: 191) has expressed cogently the conundrum this poses for ethnography, and indeed, for 'community' research of all kinds: 'As groups migrate, regroup in new locations, reconstruct their histories, and reconfigure their ethnic "projects" the *ethno* in ethnography takes on a slippery, nonlocalized quality. Groups are no longer tightly territorialized, spatially bounded, historically unselfconscious, or culturally homogeneous.' Appadurai has usefully defined the processes of delocalization and reconfiguration in terms of the spatial practices of a variety of institutional and collective actors, including, but not limited to, multinational corporations, financial markets, ethnic groups, religious and socio-cultural movements, and new political formations. The practices of all of these sectors are being reconstituted in ways that move beyond the confines of given territorial boundaries and identities.

The deterritorialization produced by transnational migration poses two special problems for community research. First, the loosening of the ties between wealth, population, and territory, 'fundamentally alters the basis for cultural reproduction' (Appadurai 1991: 193). Second (and more on this below), ethnographers of deterritorialized peoples are increasingly finding that the 'there' or 'homeland' of transnational migrants, exiles, and refugees is, in part at least, what Benedict Anderson (1983) would call an 'imagined community', invented by deterritorialized people to make concrete the felt absences in their lives.

This raises an intriguing question. Under our present globalized conditions of existence, what kinds of lives are deterritorialized people(s) able to imagine? Appadurai provides rich examples, largely drawn from his own research and personal experience with transnational migrants to the USA from the Indian subcontinent. He shows that it is possible to investigate social reproduction in the new social space he terms the 'global ethnoscape'. This global, or at least transnational, ethnography has as its goal an understanding of the impact of deterritorialization on the imaginative resources of transnational migrants and refugees. In the face of deterritorialization Appadurai (1991: 196) asks rhetorically: 'What is the nature of locality, as a lived experience, in a globalized, deterritorialized world?' To his question I would add the following: What are the boundaries that people draw and redraw for themselves in a world where old state and social structures are in the process of unravelling but in which new, coherently understood channels of action have not yet been fashioned by new configurations of power which can signal widely perceived arenas of possibility and constraint? The following points indicate some responses to these questions discernible in the economic, socio-cultural, and political practices of various deterritorialized migrants, refugees, guest-workers, and exiles.

The appropriation of the global imaginary as a delocalizing social practice

Once again, Appadurai offers both theoretical insight and useful illustration of the growing importance of film, television, and video in bringing powerful images of possible future lives into even the remotest Indian villages. His ethnographic accounts describe vividly how dreams, songs, stories, and fantasies derived from these media have become driving forces in geographical mobility and human becoming both within India and transnationally. Reflecting on this enhancement of the power of imagination in social life, Appadurai concludes that today the ordinary lives of increasing numbers of transnational migrants are powered by possibilities that the globalized mass media suggest are available to them rather than by the traditional or material givenness of things. As he succinctly puts it (1991: 198): 'In the last two decades, as the deterritorialization of persons, images, and ideas has taken on new force ... more persons throughout the world see their lives through the prisms of the possible lives offered by mass media in all their forms. That is, *fantasy is now a social practice.* It enters, in a host of ways, into the fabrication of social lives for many people in many societies.'

Appadurai's work focuses largely, though not entirely, on the more positive possibilities of human mobility becoming embodied in the acting out of these global fantasies. My own research suggests that global fantasies also have their *noire* side. In a case study I completed recently, entitled 'Who are the "good guys"?' (Smith and Tarallo 1995), the role of global fantasies in the form of images of power, wealth, and violence appropriated from Kung Fu movies were played out in the 'representations of self' and in the demands made by four young Vietnamese hostage-takers in a Good Guys electronics store in Sacramento, California, before several hostages were shot and three of the refugee youths were killed by a county sheriff's department SWAT team while acting out their global fantasies. One of the demands of these youths, who were small children when Saigon fell in 1975, was for a helicopter to allow them to fly to Vietnam to fight communists. This brings to mind the power of many exile and refugee communities world-wide, to keep alive the myth of 'return' as a driving force of meaningful socio-spatial practice.

Reterritorializing 'lost homes'

Reterritorializing is a double-edged phenomenon. The more positive side of this 'politics of return' is exemplified by the cultural and socio-spatial transformation of the Latino and Asian sections of various large US cities into various 'Little Havana' or 'Little Saigon' ethnic enclaves, as well as in my discussion later in this chapter of the globalized political vision and practices of the indigenous Guatemalan refugee movement. The *noire* side of this kind of political imagery is discernible in the practices of other deterritorialized groups, such as right-wing 'South Vietnamese' and Hmong paramilitary organizations in various US cities, and in the brutal actions of extremist Bosnian Serbs now practising 'ethnic cleansing' in what was once Yugoslavia. Vastly different in most respects, these examples represent different forms of *reterritorialization* as a collective response to displacement and deterritorialization.

Spatial extension of intensified social relations

Yet for a large portion of today's transnational migrant and refugee populations, 'reterritorialization', is far more problematic than a matter of mass recreation of or return to lost homelands by collectively displaced peoples who remain clustered in spatial enclaves outside their former national borders. Substantial numbers of today's transnational migrants actively maintain and are sustained by widely spatially dispersed social networks. While some individual members of such social networks still live in what was once unproblematically termed 'sending communities', the migrating members of the networks spend increasing amounts of time away from a (necessarily changing) 'there', that might be recaptured or returned to. These social networks are both a medium and an outcome of social practices 'from below' by which transnational migrants, individually and collectively, maintain meaningful social relations that cut across territorial boundaries, link several localities in more than one country, and extend meaningful social action across geographical space. As increasing numbers of household, kinship, and formerly village-based social networks extend across national boundaries, becoming binational, if not multinational in spatial scale, qualitative community research becomes literally *dis-placed* from the local to the global scale. In this changed context, three basic questions emerge for those conducting 'community research' in the global ethnoscape: Who do you care about and where? What reciprocal obligations are you maintaining and where? Why and how are you actively maintaining these spatially extended social relationships?

One of the best ethnographic studies oriented around these questions is Roger Rouse's (1990, 1991) research on circular migrants who move back and forth between Mexico and the USA, orchestrating lives that are truly bifocal, i.e. involved simultaneously in more than one culture while fully living in neither. Rouse's research renders problematic the very concept of 'immigrant' when dealing with the so-called 'new immigration'. Many of the Mexican transnational migrants he has studied have developed a repertoire of strategies for managing simultaneously two distinct ways of life, for example, as proletarian factory or service workers in the USA, and as small-scale owners of family-based farms or commercial operations in Mexico. These transnational migrants have neither entirely left their country of origin nor fully oriented themselves to their new circumstances. Rather, they reside in what might be termed a state of 'betweenness', orchestrating their lives transnationally and bifocally. Rouse dubs this appropriated social space the 'transnational migrant circuit'. The circuit as a whole, rather than any single locality, is the principal setting in relation to which these migrants form understandings of their individual and collective projects. Rouse's ethnographies make clear that when one's significant social relations are spread across several sites on both sides of a putative border, not only new economic arrangements but new social spaces for identity formation and the production of meaningful social action then come into being.

The growing deployment of remittances as a social force

The cash remittances sent by transnational migrants and refugees from high to low exchange rate countries is one of the principal mechanisms by which transnational social networks are actively maintained and reproduced. The scale of these remittances has increased dramatically in recent years. For example, remittances sent to El Salvador by transnational refugees now living in the USA (estimated at nearly 20 per cent of its population) constitute nearly one-third of the GNP of that 'nation's' war-devastated economy, exceeding manufacturing and rivalling agriculture as a delocalized 'pillar' (of steel or sand?) of 'economic normalization'. The network television show *60 Minutes* recently featured a story in which a Mexican factory worker in a Los Angeles sweatshop, who had been deported four times, had saved $15,000 during his four border crossings. This was enough to make him a 'middle-class' homeowner in Mexico.

Whatever else these developments mean they suggest that the deployment of remittances is no longer merely a social practice assisting household reproduction in Third World countries. Remittances are becoming a transnational social force: powerfully affecting the economic base of peripheral nations; altering class relations in sending localities; spreading global and local signs of the possibilities for radical upward mobility to increasing numbers of imagining individuals and households world-wide; channelling material means for additional transnational migration within migratory social networks; and, ultimately, providing stories fuelling the rise of perceived 'immigration problems' in receiving states now confronting the global economic crisis. The perceived 'cash drain' and 'economic lure' of remittances has become an element of the political discourse on immigration now being shaped by state actors and other powerful sectors of developed societies with large numbers of transnational migrants and refugees and relatively stagnant economies.

The globalization of personal attention

However confined and exclusionary the debate on 'immigration problems' may be among the political and economic élites of developed societies, two more pertinent questions facing those interested in the emerging contours of the global ethnoscape are: (1) To what events do today's transnational migrants and refugees pay attention? (2) How global, national, or local are the sources of information upon which the migrants and refugees base their actions? Appadurai and other contributors to the book *Global Culture* (Featherstone 1990) argue that the images and information circulated by the global mass media are becoming just as important as the stories circulated by others in one's immediate network who have renegotiated lives in new places as sources of personal attention while transnational migrants forge new life possibilities. If this is so, then a series of questions raised by Doreen Massey in her stimulating article (1991) bear consideration here, because they reinscribe the question of migration as a question of power. If, Massey asks, paraphrasing David Harvey (1989), the instantaneity of global mass communications via cable television, film and video distribution networks, faxes, and e-mail, are really 'annihilating space by time', the central question remains one of institutional power: Who is sending and receiving these informational flows? Who is producing their contents? To these questions I would add: Who consumes these flows, and to what effect? If, as Massey maintains, the differential mobility provided by these new means of communication can weaken the leverage of the already weak, how should those studying the beliefs and practices of transnational migrants, exiles, and refugees interrogate their seemingly quite mobile time–space travellers?

At this stage of my thinking the following questions come to mind: Do transnational migrants, fuelled by global images of upward social mobility, pay as close attention to global currency exchange rates of the hard currencies they are saving as to the contents of cable TV shows depicting daily life in global metropoles? What images of men, women, and gender relations are being deployed in the instantaneous flows of global mass communications? What effect do these forms of imagined lives have on the social relations of gender; in particular, upon (a) differential rates of geographical mobility between men and women in space; and (b) changing gender relations within and among households in different migratory streams? Once women, whether motivated globally or locally, leave their old 'place' in the patriarchal domestic sphere to enter the public sphere and pursue new lives as transnational migrants, what special risks do they face as border crossers who lack a 'public space' for acting on the basis of citizen rights? I will return to these gender questions below and give them more concrete resonance in my discussion of the politics of immigrant and refugee women's rights in San Francisco and internationally.

Moving beyond the global–local duality

The global–local duality in social theory rests on a false opposition that equates the *local* with a cultural space of stasis, ontological meaning, and personal identity (i.e. the 'place') and the *global* as the source of dynamic

change, the decentring of meaningfulness, and the fragmentation/
homogenization of culture (i.e. the 'space' of global capitalism). Here we
should recall the following: the basic assumptions of modernization
theory; the traditional anthropological practice of salvaging 'disappearing' exotic local cultures; Frederic Jameson's (1984) notion of the
'confusion' of late-capitalist hyperspace; and Meeghan Morris's (1992)
powerful critique of David Harvey for his conflation of difference,
locality, Heideggerian ontology, reactionary nostalgia, and fascism in
The Condition of Postmodernity (1989). This sort of binary thinking leaves
only two spaces open for practical reason (as well as for politics): 'Think
locally/act locally' or 'think globally/act globally'. In conceptualizing
transnational migration this sort of binary thinking sets cognitive limits
on the way 'immigration' is conceived – namely, as a linear process
moving from an 'old', presumably coherent, traditional culture, through
a transitional period of delocalization, followed by a period of adaptation
and relocalization to the 'new', and presumably more 'modern', culture
and way of life.

For the past two decades the slogan 'Think globally/act locally' has
been treated in both the popular media and in academic circles as a
useful antidote to these outmoded forms of binary thinking. The
slogan has the advantage of allowing the possibility that people
operating 'on the ground' have some understanding of the wider
context in which their lives are embedded, and some capacity to resist
as well as to accommodate understood global conditions, opportunities, and constraints. Nevertheless, even the kind of politics
envisaged by this slogan is one in which the main venue used by
popular forces and movements is the locality. This way of viewing
grassroots politics restricts oppositional political action to resistance of
the actions and policies of local political and economic élites, like
mayors, urban service providers, 'growth machines', business interests,
and the local press. As we shall now see, the type of 'grassroots'
political practice that is emerging among transnational migrants and
refugees does not fit well into the restrictive boundaries of local
politics conventionally used in connecting the local to the global.

The globalization of grassroots politics

We turn now to a series of narratives exemplifying three types of 'cross-
border' grassroots politics being practised by transnational migrants and
refugees. For want of established discursive terms to characterize these
dynamic political processes, and recalling Freud's insight that 'play' is
the opposite of 'work' and not of 'seriousness', I have chosen to coin

three sets of terms to designate these processes that play upon and (I hope) allow more room for the play of difference in the global–local interplay. These are: (a) thinking locally while acting globally; (b) living bifocally: i.e. thinking transnationally while acting multilocally; and (c) thinking and acting simultaneously at multiple scales.

Thinking locally and acting globally

The story of the return in early 1993 of several thousand Guatemalan refugees to their country after more than a decade in self-exile offers a pointed example of a new type of transnational grassroots politics – a form of political practice in which the group's objectives have been largely 'localized' around the politics of class and ethnicity in Guatemala, while the political arena in which they have pursued these objectives has been largely 'global'. In this instance, a self-organized group of indigenous refugees, thinking about orchestrating the terms of their 'return' (not properly speaking a 'relocalization', but rather a reconstitution of the prevailing relations of domination–subordination in their old 'locales'), acted globally to elicit the international mediation of the United Nations, and capitalized upon the global visibility and cultural status accorded to their symbolic leader, Nobel Peace prize winner, Rigoberta Menchu, to negotiate successfully their still ongoing and increasingly uncertain 'return'.

Operating largely from a string of isolated border camps in southern Mexico, the self-organized refugees were the first international refugee community ever to overcome the institutionally defined marginality of being 'spoken for' by international and refugee relief organizations to represent itself directly during two years of internationally mediated talks aimed at specifying the terms of their own return. During the course of the talks the basically repressive, military-dominated Guatemalan government made several concessions concerning the presence of international observers (e.g. representatives of the International Committee of the Red Cross and the UN High Commissioner for Refugees) to help guarantee the safety of returnees and guard against a renewal of human rights abuses, as well as to allocate land holdings for the refugees upon their return. In commenting on the return a UN diplomat privy to the talks pointed out that by organizing their own representation at the talks, the refugees had created a new political space for the Guatemalan government as well as for themselves. By negotiating with the refugees the government avoided negotiating with rebel forces, and by making the concessions they did to the refugees they reduced the play of these issues in bargaining with rebel forces, before negotiations were delayed by the suspension of civil liberties following the state's self-orchestrated *coup d'état*. Ironically, prior to the failed *coup*, the global institutional and media attention this group of refugees gained by their unprecedented 'return', produced a situation in which both the repressive Guatemalan government and the rebel National Revolutionary Unity front both embraced the refugees and claimed credit for their political return (Robbertson 1993).

Bifocal border crossers

On 7 August 1992 a multicultural coalition of transnational refugees from Central America and University of California at Berkeley students loaded a truck full of clothing, medical supplies, and used office equipment for a journey to El Salvador. This 'local' political act was co-ordinated with the efforts of a 'nationally constituted' student organization, Students Against Intervention in Central America (SAICA), which sent an automotive caravan from campus communities in the USA to that war-torn Central American 'nation'. Although 'nationally constituted', SAICA's Caravan for Peace campaign materialized entirely as a result of grassroots efforts by local, but bifocally conscious, coalitions of students, peace activists, refugees, and immigrant and refugee rights organizations in campus communities in the states of Texas and California.

The caravan was clearly intended by its organizers to have political effects in both the USA and El Salvador, as well as elsewhere in Central America. To finance the journey and educate the public in the USA to the consequences of US foreign policy in Central America, the group showed films and sponsored benefit concerts focusing on events in Nicaragua and Guatemala as well as El Salvador. In anticipation of future elections in El Salvador, in which the FMLN opposition subsequently ran as a legal political party, the Caravan's organizers planned to leave its cars, trucks, and buses behind to facilitate rural campaigning. A spokesperson for the Berkeley contingent explained: 'This is not an act of charity. It's more moral and political support for the people of El Salvador.' A former soldier for the FMLN, who won political asylum and now lives in Berkeley, added: 'The nine bikes we are sending will allow people to get around, since many of the roads leading to smaller towns were blown up' (Ruiz 1992).

What are we to make of this story? My interpretation of what was going on is as follows: the student members of this coalition are thinking transnationally and acting multilocally. The political revolutionary who joined this coalition, while constantly aware of the global context of his actions, used his local knowledge of conditions in El Salvador and his local knowledge of the workings of the sanctuary movement in Berkeley, to shape the specific content of the caravan's supplies, with an eye toward the transformation of national politics in El Salvador and the constitution of a civil society there. Contextually, the national legal system of the USA provided the institutional framework for the 'constitution' of national legitimacy by the student component of an alliance of local grassroots coalitions whose scale of operations was actually regional, a political expression of transnational grassroots politics emanating from campus communities in California and Texas. Such are the multiple border crossings characterizing one day in the life of the emergent grassroots politics of transnational migrants and refugees.

Another example of these sorts of multiple border crossings is the emergence of Mixtec ethnicity and the creation of new forms of political practice by indigenous Mixtecs from western Oaxaca who have taken up agricultural jobs in southern California and Oregon because of deteriorating economic conditions in rural Mexico. The transnationalization of consciousness and action virtually leaps from the pages of Nagengast and Kearney's (1990) description of the political practices of the pan-Mixtec transnational associations based on shared ethnicity that have been established in California and Oregon. These associations operate binationally. One of their objectives is to promote self-help and raise money and other resources for community development projects in various Mixteca villages in Mexico. Since the passage of the 1986 Immigration Reform and Control Act (IRCA) both this objective and the conditions of work in commercial agriculture in the USA have been undermined for substantial numbers of Mixtec farm workers who did not qualify for amnesty under IRCA. The plight of the Mixtec and other undocumented workers in California and neighbouring states has become a salient issue for human and civil rights organizations in both Mexico and the USA and a priority concern of the self-organized Mixteca associations.

The following passage, from Nagengast and Kearney's (1990: 84–5) description of the Mixteca Asociacion Civica Benito Juarez (ACBJ), based in Fresno and Madera, California and Salem, Oregon is worth quoting at length because it highlights the self-produced political space that has been created by these multiply marginalized 'others', who in some ways are partaking in both their old and their new civil societies, while in other ways are working to form a wider political space in which to practise a transnational grassroots politics. The passage underlines both the poly-focality of these human agents, the coalitional strategy they are pursuing, and the still emergent character of their project. It also problematizes the 'local' as a timeless site of meaningfulness and social action. Members of the ACBJ, write Nagengast and Kearney, promote village development projects in Oaxaca but also increasingly concern themselves with discrimination, exploitation, health, and human rights abuses in Mixtec enclaves in California and Oregon, *regardless of the members' village of origin*. They are now attempting to transform one aspect of their organization into a labor contracting association in which Mixtec farmworkers would sell their labor directly to growers, thereby avoiding the usually exploitative labor contractors now depended on by most workers. Concern is also focusing on gathering and publicizing testimonies of human rights abuses through indepen-dent human rights organizations. The ACBJ participated in a *transnational conference* in Mexicali on human rights violations suffered by migrants *on both sides of the border* and in a seminar on international human rights law and its applicability to them in Los Angeles. Overall, the ACBJ is working toward forming a *transnational league* of Mixtec associations that will incorporate Mixtec groups on both sides of the border. Mixtecs in the United States say that there is '*more space*' to organize north of the border than in Mexico, meaning that overt political oppression in the United States is less intense. [My emphasis.]

The Mixteca story is not without its ironies. In response to this effort by Mixtecs to create a transnational political space capable of encompassing the binational and multilocal social space in which they are orchestrating their lives, the PRI-dominated Mexican state has taken unusual steps to reincorporate the transnational migrants into the more familiar and politically quiescent rituals and routines of patron–client politics in Mexico. Yet, ironically, to do so they too have had to cross borders. In April 1989 Heladio Ramirez Lopez, the self-identified Mixtec governor of Oaxaca, concerned about declining voter support among Mixtecs in Oaxacan and national elections, travelled to Watsonville and Madera, California to meet with Mixtec migrant workers and listen to their grievances and demands *vis-à-vis* the Mexican state. These centred around extortion by government officials and police while travelling north, the appropriation of portions of remittances by corrupt telegraph officials, and poor economic conditions in the Mixteca. Without Foucaultian irony, the governor pledged more patronage in the Mixteca and offered his regime's help to ensure more effective 'policing' of authorities (Nagengast and Kearney 1990: 85).

Interestingly, in the US–Mexican case, this type of border crossing is on the verge of becoming institutionalized. In the 1988 Mexican national elections the Cardenas-led opposition to PRI began to make significant inroads on PRI political hegemony by its growing voter support in the border states of Mexico, punctuated by well attended and enthusiastic political rallies in Los Angeles, including a visit from Cardenas. In response to this threat the ever-corporatist PRI is now pursuing a regular state policy of sending PRI governors to political meetings with transna-tional migrants in various cities in California and Texas under the aegis of the Mexican state's new Office for Mexican Communities Abroad. Although the objectives of this addition to the Mexican state apparatus are political as well as economic, its creation has been justified on cultural grounds as a crossing of borders to 'rebuild culture' and 'recapture the Mexican identity' not only of Mexican-born transnational migrants but of those who currently identify themselves as 'Mexican–American' and 'Chicano' as well.

These examples of Mexican–American cross-border politics parallel the findings of other researchers working on transnational migration, suggesting that the border crossings just described may be less unusual than one might think. For example, Dominican and Puerto Rican circular migrants in New York City also receive regular visits from homeland politicians seeking political support, cultural identification, and a steady stream of remittances to bolster their domestic economies. These efforts, however, have not stemmed the tide of cultural hybridization that is producing bifocal life-worlds, as is well illustrated in Luis Guarnizo's (1994) ethnographic study of Dominican migrants to New York who accentuate their 'Dominican cultural traits' in New York as a defence against socio-economic discrimination and as a niche for exercising political influence there yet appear 'too American' to those who have remained in their homelands when they return to visit or resettle.

The politics of simultaneity

On 8 March 1993, International Women's Day, over 150 transnational migrants, refugees, and immigrant and refugee rights activists gathered to participate in a conference at Fort Mason in San Francisco. The conference, organized by a political alliance of thirty women's and immigrants' rights organizations in the Bay area, was led by the Coalition for Immigrant and Refugee Rights and Services and Mujeres Unidas y Activas, a self-organized group of Latina domestic workers. The conference was designed to gather testimony on human rights abuses suffered by transnational migrant women working in the USA. For seven hours a parade of speakers from Chile, Mexico, Guatemala, China, the Philippines, Haiti, and other countries gave witness to acts of physical and mental torture, rape, work-place servitude, domestic violence, and other denials of human rights that they had experienced while crossing the border, living in refugee camps, and working in the USA. The testimony gathered at the conference is part of the testimony presented at the June 1993 meeting in Vienna of the United Nations Human Rights Commission's World Conference on Human Rights.

The global target of the San Francisco conference was chosen as part of an effort to raise international political awareness, dispel the myth that human rights abuses do not occur in highly developed societies such as the USA, 'genderize' the universalist conception of 'human rights', and change international policies for stemming abuses. The testimony of Bay area migrant women was one of many held by women's and human rights groups world-wide in preparation for the UN World Conference.

In addition to these overall global objectives, various parts of the testimony gathered at Fort Mason simultaneously addressed political targets located at various levels within the USA. A Chilean woman, who testified to the abuse and the withholding of pay she had experienced as a legally registered au pair for a professional couple in Rohnert Park, California, pointed out that, with the assistance of a California Rural Legal Assistance office she had successfully filed a claim with the state of California to force her employer to pay back wages and overtime. Another speaker, Maria Olea, head of Mujeres Unidas y Activas, called for a separation of nation-wide immigration regulation and local policing, pointing out that many crimes in transnational migrant and refugee neighbourhoods go unreported because of widespread fear by crime victims of being reported to the Immigration and Naturalization Service (Espinoza 1993).

The sending countries are also implicated in this multilevel mode of political practice. For instance, both to improve her own lot and to focus global attention on domestic and public practices in her country of origin, an Iranian woman testifying at the hearing pointed out that she has filed an application for political asylum in the USA on the basis of the oppression of women in Iran. Testimony concerning the sexual abuse of women at the border and in refugee camps also sought to shed light upon, and thereby alter, abusive practices of institutions outside the USA that regulate the flow of migrating women and 'police' their cross-over.

Much more could be said of the multiple texts and subtexts orchestrated by even this single San Francisco Bay area component of the emergent global coalition of women's, immigrant, and refugee rights organizations that is seeking to rewrite the UN Declaration of Human Rights through genderization. Yet enough has been said in this and the previous cases to warrant the conclusion that a good deal of global grassroots politics today is a 'politics of simultaneity' – i.e. a politics in which single political acts can have multiple targets, operating at a variety of institutional and geographical scales, mediated by the appropriation of the global means of mass communication by transnational grassroots movements, and reflecting the multiple identities of the new social subjects of global grassroots movements.

Conclusion

This chapter has shown that it is easier for ordinary people to think and act simultaneously at multiple scales and to fashion a global oppositional politics by their practice, than leading commentators on the 'post-modern condition', like Jameson (1984) and Harvey (1989), who project a fear of depoliticization wrought by the supposed 'confusion' of late-capitalist 'hyperspace', are willing to imagine. Having said this, I hasten to add that the daily practices unleashed by the emergence of new social subjects discussed in this essay are double-edged. The implosion of fantasy, self-consciousness, and political awareness into the lives of even the most marginal and subaltern groups, who once saw their lives as more or less predictably constrained by the givenness of established orders, calls forth not only new individual and collective subject positions but also new efforts by established power structures to impose discipline and surveillance on these subjects, to at least 'resubjugate' their behaviour if not recommand their loyalties. The late-modernist state continues daily to reassert its eroded sovereignty by finding new means to redefine transnational migrants in terms of a 'lack': as cultural 'aliens', 'undocumented' workers, and 'illegitimate' political refugees. Less developed states like Guatemala have resorted once again to less subtle means to depoliticize grassroots politics and regulate incipient oppositional forces within their borders. The new political spaces discussed in this chapter must be actively fought for and maintained, not because they will otherwise wither away, but because existing structures of power and domination seek to erase the new spaces, and move the scope of politics back to terrains that they currently dominate.

NOTE

This chapter draws in part on my longer article, 'Can you imagine? Trans-national migration and the globalization of grassroots politics'. *Social Text*, 39 (1994): 15–33.

REFERENCES

Anderson, Benedict. 1983. *Imagined Communities: Reflectionson the Origin and Spread of Nationalism*. London and New York: Verso.
Appadurai, Arjun. 1990. 'Disjuncture and difference in the global cultural economy'. In *Global Culture. Nationalism, Globalization, and Modernity*, ed. M. Featherstone, pp. 295–310. Newbury Park CA: Sage.

1991. 'Global ethnoscapes: notes and queries for a transnational anthropology'. In *Recapturing Anthropology: Working in the Present*, ed. Richard G. Fox, pp. 191–210. Santa Fe: School of American Research Press.

Clifford, James and Marcus, George E. (eds.). 1986. *Writing Culture: The Politics and Poetics of Ethnography*. Berkeley and Los Angeles: University of California Press.

Espinosa, Suzanne. 1993. 'Remembering the pain: female immigrants tell of abuse'. *San Francisco Chronicle*, 9 March: A11.

Featherstone, Mike (ed.). 1990. *Global Culture: Nationalism, Globalization and Modernity*. Newbury Park CA: Sage.

Freeman, James M. 1989. *Hearts of Sorrow: Vietnamese–American Lives*. Stanford: Stanford University Press.

Guarnizo, Luis E. 1994. 'Los Dominicanyork: the making of a binational society'. *Annals of the American Academy of Political and Social Science* (May).

Harvey, David. 1989. *The Condition of Postmodernity*. Oxford: Basil Blackwell.

Jameson, Frederic. 1984. 'Postmodernism, or the cultural logic of late capitalism'. *New Left Review*, 46: 53–92.

Kearney, Michael. 1991. 'Borders and boundaries of state and self at the end of empire'. *Journal of Historical Sociology*, 4(1): 52–74.

Marcus, George E. and Fischer, Michael M. J. 1986. *Anthropology as Cultural Critique: An Experimental Moment in the Human Sciences*. Chicago and London: University of Chicago Press.

Massey, Doreen. 1991. 'A global sense of place'. *Marxism Today* (June): 24–8.

Morris, Meeghan. 1992. 'On the beach'. In *Cultural Studies*, ed. Lawrence Grossberg et al. New York: Routledge and Kegan Paul.

Nagengast, Carole and Kearney, Michael. 1990. 'Mixtec ethnicity: social identity, political consciousness, and political activism'. *Latin American Research Review*, 25(2): 61–91.

Robbertson, Tod. 1993. 'Thousands of Guatemala exiles return'. *San Francisco Chronicle*, 21 January: A10.

Rouse, Roger. 1990. 'Men in space: power and the appropriation of urban form among Mexican migrants in the United States'. Paper presented at the Residential College, University of Michigan, Ann Arbor, 14 March.

1991. 'Mexican migration and the social space of postmodernism'. *Diaspora*, 1(1): 8–23.

Ruiz, Alfonso. 1992. 'Peace caravan heads south'. *The Daily Californian*, 7 August: 1, 3.

Smith, Michael Peter and Tarallo, Bernadette. 1995. 'Who are the "good guys"? The social construction of the Vietnamese "other"'. In *Bubbling Cauldron: Race, Ethnicity, and the Urban Crisis*, ed. M. P. Smith and J. R. Feagin. Minneapolis: University of Minnesota Press.

Smith, Michael Peter, Tarallo, Bernadette, and Kagiwada, George. 1991. 'Colouring California: new Asian immigrant households, social networks and the local state'. *International Journal of Urban and Regional Research*, 15(2): 250–68.

15 World cities and global communities: the municipal foreign policy movement and new roles for cities

Andrew Kirby and Sallie Marston,
with Kenneth Seasholes

In March 1993, less than a month before the World Cities in a World-System conference, a full-page advertisement in the *New York Times* asked rhetorically why the Japanese transnational corporation Nissan Shatai is trying to evict eighty ethnic Korean families from the village of Utoro near Kyoto in Japan. The villagers are descendants of conscripted labourers brought from Korea during the Second World War. Despite having lived in Japan for decades, the family members cannot vote and suffer discrimination of the sort that faces immigrant workers in many countries. The land on which their homes stand was sold by Nissan to developers in 1987, and efforts have been made to clear the site since then. With its cross-national message – written in English by ethnic Koreans living in Japan, addressed to American car buyers – this advertisement constitutes a powerful metaphor for our chapter.

By taking their plight to the readers of the *New York Times*, the Koreans blur familiar concepts: global, local, foreign, and domestic. Although this is a local – even parochial – story (how many readers of the advertisement could even locate Kyoto on a map of South-east Asia?), it possesses global veracity, as the organized racism leading to brutal attacks on 'guest-workers' in Germany indicates. And what is foreign and what is domestic in this case? The Korean–Japanese clearly hope that American car buyers will think twice about purchasing Nissan products: and as the corporation now manufactures many of its vehicles in the USA, it is possible to think about Nissan as a domestic producer, as susceptible as GM or Ford to political pressure within the USA. Most crucially, they also hope that Americans will involve themselves in their affairs, by writing to Japanese politicians, sending funds and the like, such that individuals will interact directly with one another, thus sidestepping the more prosaic relations of their respective governments.

In this chapter, we develop the themes sketched out in this dramatic advertisement. We explore the ways in which residents of cities, both large and small, are willing to place themselves on the national and even the international stage in order to press for the issues that concern them. As we shall see these are examples of collective action that transcend – or simply sidestep – the more formal realities of international affairs. Moreover, as social movements these events add another dimension to the literature on world cities that has, to this point, emphasized economic linkages at the expense of other interactions.

An alternative interpretation of world cities

The concept of 'world city' is a trope that can be examined from many vantage points. While Friedmann and his followers have in the past viewed world cities as command and control nodes, here we explore some of the developments likely in the future; we assert that citizens see their cities as a means of affecting global concerns and that the popular politics of world cities is another way to explore the construction. We are suggesting a different take – the people's take, if you will – on the world city hypothesis (cf. Alger 1990). One way to do this is to try to link the concept of the city as a 'localization of social forces' with the perspective that the city is a nodal point in the world capitalist system (Zukin 1980). We will focus in particular upon the municipal foreign policy movement – or MFP, as it is typically rendered – and show that it provides an interesting standpoint on how people are interpreting the global process of political and economic restructuring.

MFP is the label that has been taken by a loose network of citizen activists throughout the USA, who have sought to involve themselves directly in international affairs. As such, the movement is seen as being relatively radical and posing serious challenges (and a proliferation of court cases) to the functional role of the nation-state system. In addition to outlining the what and the why of MFP, it is important also to emphasize the timing of the movement; we argue that it is not simply coincidental that MFP – beginning with the anti-war and anti-apartheid movement on American campuses – coincides with the beginnings of twentieth-century global economic restructuring.

Friedmann and Wolff see the world cities perspective as a heuristic (Friedmann and Wolff 1982: 310). We want to add a component to the heuristic that softens the mechanistic and economistic character of the hypothesis and reveals how people are interpreting and acting upon the reorganization of the global capitalist system. They note that 'world cities lie at the junction between the global economy and the territorial nation-state' (Friedmann and Wolff 1982: 312). In addition, we can argue that the MFP movement is a demonstration that citizens are attempting to use cities as bases from which to circumscribe the foreign-policy objectives of the nation-state. In addition to the multiple structural tendencies they cite – the changing technological bases, the differential mobility of capital and labour, and so on – we see accompanying changes in the *political* culture, both in the USA and abroad (Friedmann and Wolff 1982: 314–18).

Cities and the public sphere

In its focus upon political action within cities, this chapter addresses the extent to which our cities' residents *can* participate in the political arenas that extend beyond their literal jurisdictions, and the technological changes that make this possible and even the imperatives that make this necessary. This account has much to tell us about the development of political discourse, the relations between city residents, and the construction of local and national politics. Central to this argument is Habermas' discussion of the public sphere. In his analytical description of the public sphere Habermas is careful to identify it as a practice of critical opinion formation undertaken by members of civil society in opposition to state authority. For Habermas, civil society is the autonomous domain of individual private interests, whereas the public sphere is created by civil society out of the relations between capitalism and the state. Thus the public sphere is an arena of civil society wherein 'private people come together as a public'; their motivation is to influence the state apparatus, via 'the public use of their reason' (Habermas 1989: 27). As such, sketched in its most skeletal form, the public sphere offers historical insight into the development of a civil society that has confronted the growth of the state apparatus. It also constitutes, however, another heuristic, insofar as it offers us a way of thinking about the nature of discourse in our societies. In particular, we can conjecture about just who can employ reason for political and social ends (Calhoun 1992; Marston 1990). Habermas, writing in the 1950s, offered a particularly circumscribed vision of the public sphere. In the intervening years we have seen new conflicts 'flare up', in the attempt to protect and restore 'endangered ways of life or of establishing reformed ways of life' (Habermas 1989: xxxv). In particular, new social movements focusing on gender and sexuality, religion and spirituality, nature and place have enriched the public sphere.

Consequently, it has been widely recognized that the public sphere in which we all operate is itself differentiated. In essence, *the* public sphere has been recast as either a series of fragmented relations or a set of practices marked by 'fields of discursive connections', such that 'cities have their own public discourse within countries, and as neighborhoods within cities' (Calhoun 1992: 38). Most crucial, however, is our point that while restructuring has obviously transformed both the state and the economy, the terrain of civil society has also been reconfigured. And as important as the 'intimate involvement' of the print media was to the development of a public sphere in the seventeenth and eighteenth centuries, so too are the more recent transformations of information technologies to civil society (as well as, of course, to the state and the economy). In short, transformed 'public' information media enable private individuals to come together – as a public sphere - more quickly and in dramatically new ways which offer seemingly infinite opportunities for critical debate around state activities.

In the USA there has always been concern for international issues. Indeed, the country was forged from a colonial relation and was immediately shaped by a number of international alliances and conflicts. Yet concerns for foreign affairs are not routinely debated within the public sphere, insofar as policy development has been restricted to the deliberations of a professional foreign service class and those who staff national political institutions – 'the intellectuals of statecraft', to borrow a phrase from Agnew and O'Tuathail (1987). On one level, this is unsurprising, insofar as that generic entity, the modern territorial state, has been forged in the international arena and much of its struggle and its bureaucratic structures have been directed to securing frontiers and competing with rivals (Mann 1988). In consequence, it is the place of the territorial state within the world order that has come to be defined as the 'national interest'.

Taylor has argued that it is common for political leaders to differentiate 'high politics' – that is, the national interest – from 'low politics' (Taylor 1990: 12). He uses the example of Britain's elected Labour Party in 1946, whose leaders took the dramatic step of constructing a nuclear deterrent entirely in secret, despite the party's commitment to democratic procedures. A more recent example is offered by Dalby, who shows the way in which the discourses of national interest in the USA are generated by the intellectuals of statecraft, as he examines the creation of what he terms the 'second Cold War' during the Reagan administration (Dalby 1991). His study is particularly important because it provides insight into the ways in which élite decision-making is legitimated. He shows that the cliché of international struggle that portrays the family huddled around the radio or the television, waiting to be given news of crisis and impending warfare, is both a passive and an inherently supportive tableau. In short, the audience without independent views on international matters is an approving audience. In this context Dalby indicates the way in which politically conservative writers during the Reagan years were able partially to destabilize messages of *détente*, popularly expressed within national political forums and in localities with progressive peace movements. They were able to deflect such sentiments on the grounds that these were ideas congruent with – and thus tainted by – the Soviet propaganda machine (Dalby 1991: 79). For this reason, namely the threat to the national interest and the alleged inability of ordinary people to grasp the complexity of events, 'foreign policy cannot be made by the citizenry', as Jean Kirkpatrick once noted (quoted in Young 1990: 84).

From such a viewpoint, we can see that until relatively recently the specifics of war and peace have been isolated from public scrutiny by the legerdemain of élite policy makers. This differentiation within the public sphere – between high and low politics – has served to exclude citizens from the deliberations that surround international affairs and to restrict them to the politics of their own backyards.

Communicative changes

The manner in which collective discourse is generated is not fixed. The media of communication – television, radio, and print – have changed in recent years and continue to do so. The technological bases of interaction have become increasingly sophisticated as computers have speeded up composition, and complex information technology as a whole has become widely available. Crucially, other forms of interaction have been added to the more common forms. Video and open access cable television and electronic mail have been used for purposes that differ wildly from what was originally envisaged. For example, video was developed for surveillance purposes, and computer networking owes its development to military communications research, while cable TV has been developed as a commercial activity.

The crucial importance of the electronic media does not lie in the fact that distant viewers can witness, in real time, the democratic movement in Tiananmen Square, demonstrations against the August *coup* in Red Square, or the victory parades in Times Square following the Gulf War. Contrary to some McLuhanist assertions, such Gestalt images on television do not constitute a political discourse (cf. Adams 1992). Of more central importance, of course, is the ability of the individual to *interact* with the participants via telephone, fax, or computer. Here we see the people's take on the global networks of communication that connect economic enterprises in the world cities; just as these threads make up the global economy, so popular travelling along these routes is generating a new political web.

In this context it is fascinating to explore the technological parallels: for instance, the way in which the instantaneous transmission of information for economic or military purposes utilizes the very same fibreoptic technology as does PEACENET, a global, interactive computer network of peace activists. Yet it is a fixation with the technology – the medium – that inevitably ignores the importance of the message itself. While it would require another chapter to outline these issues, it is now well recognized that the emergence of a global consciousness has been contingent upon (and has, in turn, contributed to) a number of important processes. These include: the decline of the USA as a hegemonic power (Kennedy 1987); the concomitant collapse of the bipolar superpower system, in large measure as a result of uncontrolled military spending (Kirby 1992); the threats to the legitimacy of the nation-state system that come from both the globalization of economies and the reassertion of ethnic regionalism (Giddens 1990); and the emergence of the new social movements already noted (Kirby 1993). In the same way that cyberpunk novels are infinitely more interesting than computer magazines, so a focus upon the traffic that makes up the electronic town hall and its counterparts is of much greater significance than the hardware itself.

In summary, we can see that technology has played a facilitating role; it has allowed citizens to develop and extend their interactions with their neighbours and with those who are distant. In this way a city's residents can become actors on an interactive stage that in the past has been shared only by representatives of the nation-states. Via electronic media localities and their representatives can 'speak' directly, without the need for diplomats and missions, and in so doing they invest the public sphere with a dramatic, electronic topology.

Municipal foreign policy

The municipal foreign policy movement is one of the most coherent examples of the changes taking place within the public sphere, though it is by no means an exclusive or an exhaustive label. In the last decade urban-based American citizen groups have become increasingly active around issues of national foreign policy and international relations. These groups, acting on the belief that action at the local level can affect national and international issues, have worked in two directions: by exhorting their political leaders and fellow citizens to address policy problems that often exist outside of the locality and are the jurisdictional responsibility of higher levels of government; and by working with counterparts in other countries directly. MFP activists have been involved with a wide range of issues, from peace and security (local

Table 15.1   *The broad content of MFP local and state-level activism*

Arms and arms control	*Trade and commerce*
• Nuclear free investing	• Municipally funded world trade centres
• No first use resolutions	• Tourism promotion
• Jobs with peace	• State world trade commissions
• Bans on designer diseases	
• Nuclear free zones	*Civil defence*
• No homeporting of nuclear vessels	• GRITT initiatives
• Economic conversion	• Lawsuits against federal use of the
• Ban nuclear testing	national guard
• Opposition to military spending	• Anti-FEMA actions
• Opposition to military transport	• Anti-GWEN actions
• Establishment of peace sites	
• Endorsement of the INF treaty	*Soviet–American relations*
	• Encouraging locale to locale trade
Human rights/war and peace	• US–Soviet comprehensive test ban
• South Africa initiatives and divestment	• Armenian actions
• Central America initiatives	• Establishment of sister cities
• Consumer boycotts	• Peace actions
• Human rights in Angola	
• Establishment of a Palestinian homeland	*Environment*
• MacBride principles (Northern Ireland)	• Protecting the ozone
• Refugee sanctuary cities	• Raising corporate consciousness
• POW/MIA resolutions	• Opposition to the Third World as a
• Mideast peace	dumping ground
• Drug war–economic development	
	Municipal state departments
Cultural relations	• Creation of development commissions
• Establishment of sister cities	• Establishment of peace commissions
• Student exchanges	• Establishment of international affairs
	agencies

referenda on a Palestinian homeland or the establishment of nuclear free zones) to economic development and co-operation (creating local world trade centres or divesting from South Africa), as well as moral issues such as the sanctuary movement. A précis of these activities is offered in table 15.1. The following brief review gives a hint of the kinds of scholarly work that is being undertaken to explore the MFP phenomenon. It also makes clear how little we know about cities and settings for global actors.

Until its demise in the spring of 1991, the most consistent and comprehensive coverage of MFP issues was found in the *Bulletin of Municipal Foreign Policy: City Involvement in Global Affairs*. Published by the Center for Innovative Diplomacy (CID), the *Bulletin* combined newsletter items and short feature articles with the aim of advocating 'direct citizen participation in international affairs' and 'promoting global peace, justice, environmental protection and sustainable development'. Its strong advocacy role, and its journalistic, rather than scholarly, format, limit its analytical value. It does, however, provide an excellent snapshot of the range of issues encompassed by MFP activities: sister-city, nuclear freeze, Central American policy, anti-apartheid, human rights, economic conversion, the environment, and a host of other issues falling under the peace, justice, and development umbrella. Under the direction of CID's president, Michael Shuman, a portion of the *Bulletin*'s content has been carried over to a new publication, *Global Communities*. *Global Communities* encompasses essentially the same range of topics as the *Bulletin*, though in less detail.

Some of the strongest academic research relevant to MFP that has emerged relates to cities and global economic interactions. Promotions of trade, investment, and tourism are some of the more active ways in which residents of cities (as well as states and some regions), have tried to increase their influence and circumvent national efforts along the same lines. Sassen's examination hinges upon the dramatic polarizing changes in the global economy in the past few decades; Fry's analysis of local–global interaction is more optimistic (Fry 1989). Relying upon a pro-trade orientation, he argues that economic competitiveness requires active global participation by actors at all geographic scales. He also sees utility in 'moral stances' – such as anti-apartheid resolutions and adherence to MacBride principles – when they are explicitly tied to economic sanctions.

Another of the most fruitful areas of relevant academic investigation relates to initiatives and referenda. Within this category are several strands, one of which deals with the mechanics of these types of voting procedures. Ranney (1981) is perhaps the most visible producer of such work. Affiliated to the American Enterprise Institute, Ranney has consistently written on referenda as they have appeared in the USA, and has also edited volumes which include historical analyses and international comparisons (see also Boyer 1982). This type of material is invaluable as a source for analysing specific proposals, although it is constrained in terms of providing any theoretical framework.

The anti-nuclear movement has also been the subject of scholarly research. MacDougall (1988) analyses advertisements advocating a nuclear test ban during the Eisenhower and Kennedy administrations. Meyer's (1990) work on SANE/FREEZE makes a connection between the severe Cold War oratory of the early 1980s and the mobilization of groups opposed to official policy. He chronicles the rise, moderation, and ultimate demise of these diverse groups and argues that they have, in fact, had an impact upon US policy, both in terms of rhetoric and substantive nuclear policy.

The sanctuary movement, too, has received some scholarly attention. Nelson and Flannery, for example, concentrate on the rhetoric that was produced on both sides of the issue (Nelson and Flannery 1990; see also Kowalewski 1990). Each of these treatments can be readily supplemented with mainstream media accounts. The newspaper coverage of the SANE/FREEZE movement during the late 1970s and early 1980s is light and not very analytical. It does, however, provide a measure of the growth and later decline of the national movement. Sanctuary was also occasionally covered by the press, as are most of the other MFP topics. The primary utility of these articles is for identifying times and places where there is MFP activism, and when these issues become part of the public discourse.

The extent to which these activities have made a difference to the constitution of the public sphere is wide open to debate. Michael Shuman (1992: 158–9), for instance, points to the cumulation of initiatives and the like in the USA:

as of 1991, more than 900 localities passed resolutions supporting a 'freeze' in the arms race; 197 demanded a halt to nuclear testing; 120 refused to co-operate with the Federal Emergency Management Agency's nuclear-war exercises; 126, plus 26 states, divested more than $20 billion from firms doing business in South Africa; 86 formed linkages with Nicaragua and, along with grassroots activists, provided more humanitarian assistance to the Nicaraguan people than all the military aid Congress voted for the *contras*; 80 demanded cuts in the Pentagon's budgets; 73 formed sister city relations with Soviet cities . . and at least 10 established funded offices of international affairs – in essence municipal state departments.

As this review suggests, although there is a great deal of MFP activity taking place, very little scholarly attention is being directed toward understanding its impact or implications. Perhaps the most interesting and least understood aspect of the MFP phenomenon is the way in which cities have been constructed by citizens as global actors. In the following section we take a look at one such city and its global intentions.

Sister city movements in Tucson

Tucson, Arizona is both cosmopolitan and provincial. On the one hand it is a border town only sixty miles from Mexico, a point at which the First World meets the Third. Like many border settlements, it has long had garrison functions, and today it is a centre for immigration control and drug interdiction. On the other hand, the city is also relatively isolated: both Tucson and its larger counterpart Phoenix are over four hundred miles from any similarly sized city.

Tucson residents have attempted to establish sister city liaisons since 1949; the first occurring with Trikkala, Greece. During this period, the contacts were both cultural and culturally imperialistic: original documents speak of applying 'American ingenuity to the problem of understanding the people of another nation and of winning their friendship'. It is important to note that this was to be Christian friendship, extended to a country of strategic importance to US interests and one in which communist influence remained high after the end of the Second World War.

The most dynamic interactions occurred during the 1980s. Attempts to make peaceful contacts overseas as part of a municipal foreign policy movement were applied to the Soviet Union during the 'second Cold War' period. For instance, a video expressing anti-war sentiments in English and Russian was sent to Novokuznetska in Siberia by the Tucson Peace Center in 1985. Efforts had been made to contact Soviet citizens in 1983, when the mayor of Novokuznetska had been approached via the National Pairing Project, although this seems to have been a failure due to the blanket manner in which, 1,500 Soviet cities were approached. A subsequent approach was made in 1988, at which time the focus was Alma-Ata in Kazakhstan, a city in a semi-arid region with some landscape similarities to Tucson. The initial delegation included city officials and representatives of business, the university, cultural activities, and peace and justice organizations such as the American Friends Service.

The interactive nature of these exchanges is revealed clearly in their subsequent evolution. The focus for Tucson Sister City projects began to change in 1989, in larger part in reaction to *perestroika* and the Soviet emphasis upon economic issues: the mayor's representative noted that 'in the past, the sister cities program had a strong cultural, artistic and educational focus. We want to give it a heavier economic development focus' (Zimmerman 1991). Twenty-six joint development programmes were proposed by Soviet officials, and by the autumn of 1989 another delegation consisted of real estate and other economic representatives. This partly reflected the demise of state socialism in the USSR but also reflected the imperative of rapid capitalist development that was manifest within the Soviet Union (cf. Zelinsky 1990).

This very brief sketch is useful for pointing out some of the significance of these interactions. The initial contacts between Tucson and the Soviet Union took place during the depths of the second Cold

War – indeed, were prompted by the worsening prospects for peace between the two nations. We should not underestimate the extent to which such non-governmental interactions, coupled of course with ongoing economic interactions of the 'vodka–cola' type, added to the ultimate improvement of relations between the USA and the USSR. Indeed, municipal governments in the former Soviet Union have shown themselves to be consistently ahead of *détente*, insofar as they have pursued foreign investment and economic development opportunities with much greater effectiveness than their national counterparts. Nor should it be assumed that all interactions are now economic in nature: recent news reports show that citizen groups in the former Soviet Union are particularly concerned to learn more about the state of human rights in Europe and the USA, particularly with regard to issues like sexuality. In this way, the cycle of concern within MFP seems to have turned fully once more.

Conclusions

As we have seen, city governments were able, throughout the 1970s and 1980s, to try to generate ties with other communities throughout the world, via what has come to be known as municipal foreign policy. In some jurisdictions, of course, this was impossible, as a majority of residents rejected such strategies as 'un-American' in ballot initiatives and other propositions (although, even when such initiatives were rejected, they contributed to a broader discourse about peace and informal networks). These events, replicated in hundreds of jurisdictions, pushed hard against the monopoly of legitimacy held by nation-states in the international arena and the assumption that 'the United States, to be effective in foreign policy, must speak with but one voice ... it cannot have a cacophony of different states and municipalities seeking to speak about foreign policy issues' (Shuman 1992: 167).

Defensive posturing by the representatives of the state indicate the salience of the MFP movement; indeed, the latter is part of a broad re-examination of the efficacy and the stability of the state system. More broadly, MFP has also focused attention back on our understanding of key concepts, such as citizenship. Of course, we cannot claim that citizen-to-citizen movements have been responsible for all the visible changes, and it is part of our own research agenda to examine exactly how MFP has contributed to the changes within the public sphere.

This notwithstanding, there is little question that the way that we have conceived of world cities requires broadening. We have noted that the economistic interpretation inherent in the original heuristic requires a more human guise that allows a consideration of agency of the forms sketched here. We have shown that the public sphere is changing, as new media of communication are pressed into service and as meaningful interactions between communities become simpler and more successful. In traditional terms, many of these communities do not qualify as world cities; that would certainly be true of Tucson, for instance, if we were to apply the classic political and economic standards.

Interestingly, however, in the October 1993 issue of *World Trade*, a monthly international business magazine, Tucson was identified as one of 'USA's ten best global cities' (Tierney 1993). Tucson's distinction as a world trading partner is based on a national survey that sought to identify, through international business indicators and expert opinion, the best places for American businesses to succeed in global trade. Eliminating obviously dominant global cities like New York, Los Angeles, and Seattle, *World Trade* pointed to Tucson (as well as Cleveland, Portland, San Diego, Raleigh-Durham, Buffalo, St Louis, Salt Lake City, Oklahoma City, and San Antonio) as world trade success stories. The bottom line is that small and medium-sized cities like Tucson, Cambridge, Oakland, and Buffalo, are active players on the global stage for many different reasons, and our conception of world cities must be stretched to recognize and account for their not insignificant role.

REFERENCES

Adams, P. C. 1992. 'Television as gathering place'. *Annals of the Association of American Geographers*, 82(1): 117–35.
Agnew, J. and O'Tuathail G. 1987. 'The historiography of American geopolitics'. Paper presented to the International Studies Association.
Alger, C. 1990. 'The world relations of cities: closing the gap between social science and everyday human experience'. *International Studies Quarterly*, 34: 493–518.
Boyer, P. J. 1982. *Lawmaking by the People: Referendums and Plebiscities in Canada*. Toronto: Butterworth.
Calhoun, N. (ed.). 1992. *Habermas and the Public Sphere*. Boston: MIT Press.
Dalby, S. 1991. *Creating the Second Cold War*. London: Pinter.
Friedmann, J. and Wolff, G. 1982. 'World city formation. An agenda for research and action'. *International Journal of Urban and Regional Research*, 6(3): 309–44.
Fry, E. H. 1989. *The New International Cities Era: The Global Activities of North American Municipal Governments*. Utah: D. M. Kennedy Center of Brigham Young.
Giddens, A. 1990. *The Consequences of Modernity*. Cambridge: Polity Press.

Habermas, J. 1989. *The Structural Transformation of the Public Sphere*. Boston: MIT Press.

Kennedy, P. 1987. *The Rise and Fall of the Great Powers*. New York: Random House.

Kirby, A. (ed.). 1992. *The Pentagon and the Cities*. Newbury Park CA: Sage.

1993. *Power/Resistance*. Bloomington: Indiana University Press.

Kowalewski, D. 1990. 'The historical structuring of a dissident movement: the sanctuary case'. *Research in Social Movements, Conflicts and Change*, 12: 89–110.

MacDougall, J. 1988. 'Disarmament, citizen activism, or what?: Beliefs and values of the nuclear test ban movement of 1957–1963'. *Journal of Voluntary Action Research*, 17(2): 74–81.

Mann, M. 1988. *States, War and Capitalism*. Oxford: Basil Blackwell.

Marston, S. A. 1990. 'Who are the people: gender, citizenship and the making of the American nation'. *Environment and Planning D: Society and Space*, 8: 449–58.

Meyer, D. S. 1990. *A Winter of Discontent: The Nuclear Freeze and American Politics*. New York: Praeger.

Nelson, J. and Flannery, M. A. 1990. 'The sanctuary movement: a study in religious confrontation'. *The Southern Communication Journal*. 372–88.

Ranney, A. (ed.). 1981. *The Referendum Device*. American Enterprise Institute for Public Policy Research.

Shuman, M. H. 1992. 'Courts v. local foreign policies'. *Foreign Policy*, 86: 158–77.

Taylor, P. J. 1990. *Britain and the Cold War*. London: Pinter.

Tierney, R. 1993. 'The USA's ten best global cities'. *World Trade*, 6(9): 32–50.

Young, I. M. 1990. *Justice and the Politics of Difference*. Princeton NJ: Princeton University Press.

Zelinsky, W. 1990. 'Sister city alliances'. *American Demographics*, 30: 42–6.

Zimmerman, C. 1991. *Arizona Daily Star*, 2 October.

Zukin, S. 1980. 'A decade of the new urban sociology'. *Theory and Society*, 9: 575–601.

16   The environmental problematic in world cities

Roger Keil

In John Berger's novel *Lilac and Flag* there is a description of a fictional trip taken from the airport periphery to the centre of the city of Troy:

> It is possible you have been to Troy without recognising the city. The road from the airport is like many others in the world. It has a superhighway and is often blocked. You leave the airport buildings which are like space vessels never finished, you pass the packed carparks, the international hotels, a mile or two of barbed wire, broken fields, the last stray cattle, billboards that advertise cars and Coca-Cola, storage tanks, a cement plant, the first shanty town, several giant depots for big stores, ring-road flyovers, working class flats, a part of an ancient city wall, the old boroughs with trees, crammed shopping streets, new golden office blocks, a number of ancient domes and spires, and finally you arrive at the acropolis of wealth. (John Berger 1990: 170)

This description guides us through the archetypical landscape of today's internationalized city. The narrator/driver/passenger (like world city researchers) most likely belongs to a new group of globe-trotters called 'transnationally literate migrants' by Gayatri Spivak (1993). These not only understand the variable semiotics of various global places but also know how to act in these places and help develop counter-discourses and strategies. They are informed in their activities by the dialectics of generality and specificity that are characteristic of the Troys of this world.

First, Berger's Troy seems to bear all the features of those places that we have come to call world cities. Troy is both the generic metropolis of the late twentieth century, the fusion of both the Fordist reality, with its airport–freeways–downtown–infrastructure, and the post-Fordist 'Dickensian hell' of fragmentation, human and environmental degradation, and polarized power. Two such cities are more or less implicitly the subject and empirical base of this chapter: Frankfurt and Los Angeles. While my research on these cases informs my analysis, this chapter is largely conceptual and theoretical. My suggestions can be thought of, then, as a modest addition to the agenda for research and action first proposed by Friedmann and Wolff (1982).[1]

Second, the short passage from *Lilac and Flag* can be read as an expression of the dialectics of utopia and dystopia in the world city. Both the 'City of Light' and the 'City of Doom' are present not so much as alternatives but as synchronous, reciprocally defining realities. Friedmann and Wolff (1982: 319) have captured this relationship using the metaphors of the 'citadel' and the 'ghetto':

World cities are the control centers of the global economy. Their status, of course, is evolving in the measure that given regions are integrated in a dominant role with the world system. And like the golden cities of ancient empires, they draw upon themselves the wealth of the world that is ruled by them. They become the major points for the accumulation of capital and 'all that money can buy'. They are luxurious, splendid cities whose very splendour obscures the poverty on which their wealth is based. The juxtaposition is not merely spatial; it is a functional relation: rich and poor define each other.

The natural and human environments of these splendid cities and, more specifically, the politics of local environmental policy are the focus of this chapter.

The world city hypothesis and its blind spots: ecology and local politics

For all its conceptual sophistication and growing body of empirical work, research following the 'world city hypothesis' (Friedmann 1986, see appendix to the present volume) has done little to integrate either the ecological problematic or the local politics of policy-making in world cities.[2]

The ecological problematic

There is an abundance of literature on the social and socio-economic degradation and polarization of world cities. Hardly ever, though, is this view integrated with a more comprehensive 'socio-*ecological*' view.[3] The environmental dimension of the social polarization of world cities has rarely been explored. In calling for a 'socio-ecological' perspective, however, it is necessary at the outset to make clear that this view should not be confused with two positions often taken in discussions about urban ecology. On the one hand, we tend to find the ecological problematic expressed as a mere function of the social problematic. This subsumption of the ecological under the social, however, underrates the conceptual breadth of urban ecology and ultimately reduces world city environmental research to the rather obvious statement that the poor in world cities live where the environment is most degraded. On the other hand, it would be false to indulge in a naive conceptualization of nature as something outside of human society and human practice. Nature is not something 'green' outside the city and ecology does not just deal with wild things. More on urban ecology below.

Local politics of policy-making

Similarly, the literature on world city formation has given comparatively little attention to local political processes. In the face of powerful transnational corporations, it is believed, local policy formation becomes an appendix to global intra-firm strategies rather than an active field of struggle and negotiation in a localized context. The growing insignificance of the 'local' has been a constant trope in some of the literature. Neither local civil society nor the local state are deemed important arenas for the formation of policy (Friedmann and Wolff 1982: 325; Keil 1993: ch. 1). In this chapter I take a different view. I will argue that local politics matter and that they might just be particularly important in the regulation of a world city's environment.

Theoretical approaches

I suggest that three theoretical discourses are important and formative for the discussion of the politics of environmental policy-making in world cities. First, there is the debate on the internationalization and globalization of urbanization. The world city is a place where the global ecological crisis manifests itself concretely. This is where social and economic globalization processes shape local environments in a specific way. The local urban and the global environment can no longer be viewed as separate entities at any time (Jahn 1991; Keil and Ronneberger 1991a). Furthermore, the global ecological crisis needs to be viewed in context with the emergence of a 'new economic order' (Lipietz 1992c). Second, the literature on the shift from Fordism to post-Fordism has shown how – due to regionally differentiated, urban regimes of accumulation and local modes of regulation – specific contradictions in the restructuring of the Fordist heritage have led to place-specific expressions of the environmental problematic. These differentiations lead to important variances in landscapes and spaces for agency in the post-Fordist city depending on its position in the restructuring process (Lipietz 1992a). The ecological problematic has moved to centre-stage in the current restructuring of the Fordist order, and it might just be one of the main axes along which a 'new compromise for the post-crisis period' will be forged (Lipietz 1992b: 310).

Third, the discourse on post-modern politics and the contingency of the social has also pointed to a new conceptualization and construction of social and natural environments as well as of the politics attached to these environments. The social problematic in this literature is not reduced to socio-economic indicators but includes processes of cultural difference and differentiation: racism and sexism being the most important among them. The recognition of difference will also be reflected, I will argue, in the way environmental policy and politics in world cities are constructed. It is not that socio-spatial cleavages and fragmentation have not existed before. But now they make a political difference; they have become constitutive of the world in which we live. Fitzsimmons et al. (1991: 15) write: 'The conditions for liberation – and this would have to be discussed in terms of ecology – move from the utopian position of total transparency of the social to the acceptance of the radical contingency of the social. In this context, stripping from the state its capitalist committed and supportive role comes to be a question of hegemonic articulations within it and against it.'

Post-modern policy-making?

A new articulation of utopia and real politics has characterized the advent of an era of politics and policy formation which often is called post-modern. In the current period, solutions to global problems tend to be articulated with the local life-worlds of people in order to be recognized as solutions. The new relationship of global problems and local solutions has become particularly evident in the way we have started to deal with the environmental problematic. It has, ideally, also heightened the awareness that policy as a top-down technological approach and a cybernetic, systems-theoretical exercise had to be replaced by a more democratic policy formation process grounded in the politics and life experience of a more recognizably pluralized society. In an increasingly fragmented polity where national modes of regulation are being supplemented and substituted by both local and global regulatory mechanisms, a new question has to be asked: who has the authority to draw up policy? This question, it seems, can now only be answered in the realm of politics. Political discourse leads to constellations in which policies are formulated.

What does this mean for environmental policy in world cities? If one accepts the above assumptions that local policy formation is immediately global in significance, takes place in the general context of the crisis of Fordism, and is structured politically by the 'condition of post-modernity' (Harvey 1989b), then the exploration of a constitutive process of world city formation has begun. One can further recognize that air, water, and soil are not the same for people from different parts of the city, from different social classes, ethnic or racial background, of different gender or age. Rather we are dealing with a whole set of varying experiences of time and space which are becoming increasingly relevant in political terms. Environmental policy-making has to come to terms with the contradictions of universalism and relativity. Although the specific realm of power and spatiality in which human agents create their environments is relevant to the success of any environmental policy, these particularities will always have to be negotiated with the larger 'global' or 'universal' concerns of ecology and society. Whatever is considered an environmentally sound policy for one fragment of world city society could be, but need not be, beneficial to any other group and there is no intrinsic value in fragmentation and identity politics, as some 'ideological post-modernists' (Hall 1991) want us to believe. Yet disregarding the plurality of our experiences would be self-defeating (Keil 1990).

The social relationships with nature

Defining the ecological problematic as related to (not identical or subordinate to) the social problematic in world cities necessitates a theoretical rethinking of urban ecology. Using the concept of 'societal relationships with nature' as developed recently by some social ecologists, one can construct a meaningful set of relationships between society and nature (Becker, Jahn, and Wehling 1991: 485ff.). The notion of an ecological crisis, then, will imply the crisis of the social forms by which a connection is made between our cultural conceptions of nature and the material and social reproduction of the relationship of society and nature. One can 'distinguish between the *basic relationship* with nature, whose permanent social regulation ensures the survival of human societies, and the *specific forms and spheres* of symbolic nature (the economic, social, political, scientific, esthetical, and sexual spheres). Basic relationships with nature include, for instance, nutrition, health maintenance, reproduction, labor, mobility/locomotion, and the regulation of the relationships between the generations and the sexes' (Jahn 1993: 7). Society and nature exist only with each other.

'Relationship' in the sense of the German term *Verhältnis* has several different meanings. It connotes a constellation of references, the connection of mediations, as well as an active behavior. A relationship can be defined only if 'society' and 'nature' are not considered as strictly separate spheres. And active behavior requires that relationships with nature are discussed as forms of action, as generated historically and politically. As we deal with *societal* relationships with nature, we have to consider their material aspects; in the case of societal relationships with *nature*, we need to discuss the cultural 'symbolization' of these material aspects – as well as the respective symbolic and epistemological construction of the differences between nature and society. (Jahn 1993: 8)

This notion of 'the societal relationships with nature' has three main implications for our discussion:

1 It emphasizes the social nature of nature and the natural base of society. Being immanent to society makes nature – at least in part[4] – subject to democratic procedures which we need to strengthen in order to survive as a collective. In turn, finding a strategy to solve ecological problems leads potentially to a democratization of society, economy, and the state. This would be a possible theoretical if not ethical basis for the development of environmental policies in world cities or elsewhere.

2 The notion of societal relationships with nature entails a concept of plurality. Instead of supposing just one linear set of relationships between society and nature, we now can talk about a plurality of relationships. In the age of ubiquitous ecological crisis, of global warming, and the disappearing ozone layer, there is no equity in the distribution of disaster and catastrophe, of pollution and radiation. The differentiation in suffering takes a variety of forms. The most obvious ones are space, class, gender, and 'race'. The lines of differentiation exist in every urban community as well as on a global scale. From this perspective the ecological crisis evaporates as a global predicament and recrystallizes in a plurality of specific crisis-ridden societal relationships with nature. The world city environment is a specific place where this concretization of the global ecological crisis takes place. In this context, we must develop a plural, sophisticated, and complex, if sometimes contradictory, approach to policy formation.

3 And finally, this re-enforces the notion of thinking about policy formation as a political process.[5] The societal realm of environmental policy formation, then, has to be pictured both as 'a space of conflict and as a space of possibility' (Keil and Ronneberger 1991b). What kinds of societal relationships with nature will prevail in this space is not a question of abstract or technological solutions to ecological problems which presuppose *one* nature and *one* society respectively provided with one set of antagonistic interests that square off on a planetary scale. Rather, this approach problematizes society, nature, and the relationships between them. It leads to a political and contingent theory of policy formation that rests on 'situated knowledges' (Haraway 1988).

Urban ecology?

The city is simply the specifically human environment. (Dieter Hoffmann-Axthelm 1993: 70)

How is it possible to apply the concept of the 'societal relationships of nature' to the urban realm, to the realm of urban ecology?[6] One school of thought argues that 'urban ecology' is a contradiction in terms. Ecology deals with nature and nature has been the historical antipode of the city. In fact, the kind of nature we think of when we use the term today emerged 'with the city as its opposite' (Trepl 1991: 167). There is, of course, a natural science called urban ecology which examines the plant and animal populations of cities (nowadays often much richer and more diverse than much of what is called nature). Yet this is not what most people mean by urban ecology. Usually the term implies a political programme. When people speak of ecological or sustainable cities they mean better, more livable cities than the ones we inhabit (Stren, et al. 1992). Theorists like Trepl (1991) deny that ecology as a science can be of much help when it comes to improving the urban habitat. If we want to save the earth, he argues, there is hardly more to expect from ecology than from physics or chemistry. He hints towards theology, or perhaps politics, for such intentions. Ecology, he argues correctly, cannot replace any religion or philosophy as a doctrine of salvation.

In contrast, Dieter Hoffmann-Axthelm has called ecology 'an always specific socially necessary balancing exercise' (Hoffmann-Axthelm 1988: 34). And he goes on to explain that in today's world, regional ecologies and regional catastrophes are so intertwined with the global eco-system that they can lead to global catastrophes. The insight, he concludes, 'that ecology has to do with a desperate balancing exercise on a global scale, can only gain practical value when one can issue an exact address. This address exists: it is the city.' In a more recent publication, Hoffmann-Axthelm (1993: 69) specifies his position: 'Urban ecology – a critical word formation full of traps. Urban ecology means to speak of the city in a catastrophic horizon which is historically produced but which has natural historic dimensions. The city then enters the stage as an ecological subject, subjected to the judgment of a natural science: ecology, science of critical border relationships.' Thus, there is a connection between the fragmented balance of biological life-worlds of the kind Trepl sees as the object of ecological study and the entirely social ecologies of the fragmented living quarters of today's cities where human beings are creating a meaningful, livable environment for themselves. Urban ecology in this sense is not the transferral of biological imagination on to urban society but is the sum of our social practices in cities related to our natural environment. In this sense social ecology – or urban ecology – has something to offer: stripped of its romanticized connotations of salvation, urban ecology can then be used quite productively to understand the strategies and tactics with which we build, use, and destroy our cities. In its very semantics, urban ecology recognizes the contradiction of growth and ecology without setting them aside as antagonistic poles. Urban ecology does not establish ecology outside society:

> The 'city' as a form of life is a specific, historically developed model of the regulation of the societal relationships with nature ... The 'urban crisis' is a crisis of the urban model of the regulations of the societal relationships with nature; accordingly, the urban struggles (*Auseinandersetzungen*) are predominantly socio-ecological struggles, since they are always about the social and material regulation and socio-cultural symbolization of societal relationships with nature. (Jahn 1991: 54)

There is, then, an interesting distinction to be made between urban ecological and biological systems: the urban process is not self-regulatory, there is always human agency involved. Automatic pressure release does not happen. There is cultural capacity, memory, love, and resistance and, one might add, there is a historical geography with political structures and a conscious experience of creation and destruction. As a consequence, we do, as purposeful actors in an urban environment, have to address ourselves to a very specific historical geography which cannot be grasped by tables on air pollution and cancer rates (Hoffmann-Axthelm 1988: 35). Such an understanding of urban ecology does not lend itself to simple technological solutions. Rather, urban ecology is located where technological projects end and the realm of urban civility begins.

World city ecologies

A global capitalism requires a global approach to the environmental question. (John Friedmann 1988: 6)

Urban ecology can help to define a life-space in articulation with, yet eventually beyond, the abstract growth logic of today's globalized urban machines. I would go on to say that, paradoxically, only in this world of near complete internationalized urbanization is such a step conceivable. And, as Jahn argues, if we want to take seriously 'the demand for an ecological restructuring of industrial society and the global perils ... any strategy must first be directed at the example of the cities and the agglomerations' (1991: 54). Ecologically sustainable and livable urban environments can now, in fact, only be achieved if we create urban civil societies that live up to the challenge of globalization. That is, the societal relationships with nature shaped in today's cities will have to encompass global populations, globalized everyday practices, and internationally diversified gender relations, as well as images and uses of nature. A world city environment, then, has to be construed as an array of urban ecologies: 'environments' in the plural. An environmental master-plan will be increasingly difficult to imagine in such a context. Only if policy-makers accept these assumptions, it seems, will they be able to develop politics and policies as well as research agendas for the new urban environments constituted by world city formation.

The 'environmental problematic' of world cities refers to a specific urban ecology which emerges from a world city's relationship to the global economy and to other world cities. In this concept, I do not want to convey the impression that the natural environment is different in any strict biological sense (the grass is not greener or less green in world cities than elsewhere); yet the discourse on ecology and the construction of the relationships of the human and the natural environments in these cities reflect their formation as world cities. World cities, as understood in this chapter, are the specific type of cities described by Friedmann and Wolff (1982 and Friedmann in chapter 2 of the present volume). There are similarities and overlap between those cities grouped together as 'mega-cities' and that select group of those among them that are studied under the project by that name (Linden 1993). The environmental problematic in world cities, however, is not just 'more extensive' than elsewhere; it is specific, due to each of those cities' role in the global economy. The political process of policy-making is largely structured by the global demands on the local environment. Some of the mega-cities in the South, particularly those marginalized even in the global exploitation of southern resources by the North, are threatened to be left to themselves for urban governance. They are, in fact, located outside of the dynamics of global capital accumulation (some of them are literally left to rot). In contrast, most of the world cities are extremely sensitive to the larger world that constitutes their status in the network of global control centres and which they, in turn, help to establish.[7]

Since so little has been written on the relationship between world city formation and urban ecology, there is only scarce evidence on the specificity of the environmental problematic in such cities. Joe Feagin's (1985) analysis of Houston provides an exception. In this city the declining demand for oil in the 1980s, due – amongst other things – to the government regulated tendency of American producers to make smaller, more fuel-efficient cars, led to a significant crisis in Houston's space economy and made a dent in its development as a world city. Conversely, Houston's extreme toxic waste problem is linked to the city's 'urban specialization' in the American and world urban system as an oil producer. That is, the historical and geographical conjuncture at which Houston's economic role as a world city is being determined also provides the framework for understanding its urban ecology.

For pragmatic reasons I propose to distinguish two dimensions of the environmental problematic in the world city: pollution and land use (growth). The overall degree of pollution of air, water, and soil in a world city, I would argue, has to do with that city's role in the world economy. Similarly, how pollution's effects are distributed internally is a function of the largely racialized, gendered, and class-based divisions created by world city formation. Land use and the cost of growth are equally determined by the world city's international role. The construction of a built environment for global capital in these cities and the transnational pressures on local land use have in most cases exacerbated the stress on residential communities, green spaces, and public spaces used by the majority of citizens.

We often find similar expressions of the environmental problematic in the realms of pollution and of land use. One of those similarities, for example, is the existence of 'environmental racism' as a structural element of a world city's social fabric. In turn, policies dealing with one aspect of the problematic are also likely to affect the other aspects. The Air Quality Management Plan for southern California, for example, which is meant to deal with air pollution, has an important land use component and might actually work as the single most important piece of regional legislation with regard to the further growth of the area (SCAQMD 1989). The Frankfurt Greenbelt plan, which on one level can be understood as a 'negative zoning plan' for the city, also has an air quality component in that it discourages automobile use, encourages bicycles and other low-energy forms of transportation, aims to 'build back' roads, and subsequently to reduce the daily throughput of cars and other traffic (GrünGürtel – Projektbüro 1991).

The politics of policy-making in world cities

My initial propositions were that world city environmental politics has to be both global and local, that it should address the issue of the restructuring of Fordism, and that it needs to locate itself in a context structured by the demands of a pluralized 'post-modern' political realm of multiple contradictions (class, gender, 'race', ethnicity, etc.). We can now carefully start to assess the politics of policy-making in the world city context.

The global and the local

The local political level has begun to be recognized as a meaningful arena of environmental policy-making and policy implementation. In fact, activating the 'local' is now considered a *necessary*, though not *sufficient*, condition by environmental policy-makers. It is necessary because strategies to solve environmental problems, in order to be successful, need to be broken down to the experiential base of the local. This is the more relevant since the discourse on urban growth and economic restructuring associated with globalization (and the respective counter-discourse) tends increasingly to be articulated with environmental concerns.[8] The local, however, is also not a *sufficient* condition for environmental policy-makers because environmental action can by no means be just local; it needs to be supplemented by regional initiatives (since urban fields span many jurisdictions and traditional distinctions such as the city and the countryside have become rather meaningless) (Friedmann 1991); it needs to be backed by those general and 'universalist' environmental policies not abandoned by the national 'Schumpeterian workfare state' (Jessop 1993); and they need to be synchronized with global and transnational activities of environmental advocacy and policy-making (Altvater 1992, 1993).

World city environmental policy-making, therefore, has to be seen in a larger context of policy formation on the national or global scale. The city of Frankfurt has, in the past, been involved in a number of European initiatives on the urban environment. The policy arena is set, for example, by the European Green Paper on the Urban Environment which (while not being binding) helps organize the discourse on environmental reform in European cities (Commission of the European Communities 1990). Certain aspects of the social mechanics of the Greenbelt project have been directly drafted with an eye on the paradigm of 'sustainable development' as stated by the Brundtland Commission's report (World Commission 1987). The city's *Umweltforum*, an administrative research and outreach institution of the Department of the Environment, has actively participated in creating and discussing these supra-urban policy documents (Koenigs 1992). In Los Angeles the major national policy that has determined the discourse on the environment has been the Clean Air Act of 1970 which required local governmental institutions to meet its standards through local action (Bloch and Keil 1991).

Restructuring

Development and urban growth in the 1980s took on a variety of forms and came in mostly post-modern cultural guise (Harvey 1989a; Logan and Molotch 1987; Stone and Sanders 1988).[9] Currently it seems to be increasingly negotiated, legitimized, limited, and defined by the discourse of environmentalism. The emergence of a new hegemony after Fordism comes with a renegotiation of the societal relationships with nature in the city. In this process 'ecology' moves to centre-stage. In Los Angeles, where urban (re)development had been tantamount to building a centre for high culture and consumption and a built environment for global capital in the downtown as well as in various ex-urban growth poles during the 1980s, the environment became the key concept around which the discourse on growth was constructed towards the end of the decade (Keil 1993). The final report of the Los Angeles 2000 Committee, a citizen task-force established by Mayor Tom Bradley, identified 'environmental quality' as one of its major goals: 'A city that recognizes the interrelations of environmental and economic issues and follows specific strategies for preserving its fragile eco-system while achieving a healthful physical environment and a vibrant economy' (LA 2000 1988: 13). Equally, while rebellious home owners on the west side of the city were claiming that 'their' city was 'Not Yet New York', the ensuing struggle around the implementation of the regulations of the Air Quality Management Plan of 1989 pointed out that the future growth and development of the city was as much at stake as the quality of the region's air. In Frankfurt a conservative government had pursued the expansion of the local world city economy throughout the 1980s with a concept of high culture and globalized infrastructures, without paying much attention to enhancing the city's natural environment. The new red–green government, in contrast, fundamentally redefined the meaning of ecology and made it a centrepiece in the coalition's agreement in 1989. Social and ecological policy goals were held equally important in the reform of the world city (Ronneberger and Keil 1993: 9).

Post-modern politics

Environmental policy-making in world cities increasingly occurs with a growing commitment of local governments to negotiate their policies with the citizens. In 1990 the Environmental Affairs Commission of the City of Los Angeles, wrote in a primer on the city's state of the environment report: 'Environmental problems and their solutions are complex and interrelated. A partnership between the city and public is essential to solving these problems. The primary bond in such a partnership is a free flowing communication/information stream between the city and its residents' (City of Los Angeles 1990).

The planners of the Frankfurt Greenbelt project openly addressed the dialectic of global and local developments and decision-making structures which forms the substance of today's local environmental policy-making in world cities:

The Greenbelt-project shows that approaches towards an alternative urban development policy are possible ... In the relationship of local state and local politics, we will also have to ask about the vertical and horizontal entanglements; along the vertical axis, there are the exogenous conditions of urban development (growth, capital, globality), along the horizontal axis, there are the local contradictions that result from those. If *urban management* deals with all problems along the 'centralist' axis, the development of a really new urbanity will not succeed ... The centrally mediated local politics must produce urban grassroots infrastructures that are sufficiently open for 'endogenous' processes of negotiation by which these infrastructures are filled for each local place respectively. (Prigge and Lieser 1992)

In fact, the Greenbelt office that worked in a semi-public realm for one-and-a-half years from 1990 to 1991 can be considered an attempt to act as a mediating institution between the local state and civil society and between global demands and local needs. An analysis of Frankfurt's world city formation and of its repercussion in the local social space was considered a necessary prerequisite for drafting local environmental policy in and around the Greenbelt (Keil and Ronneberger 1991a).

This thrust of urban environmental policy in world cities towards involvement of an increasingly diverse and pluralized citizenry seems to be a universal trend. It is necessary to note with the utmost clarity, however, that this trend did not just come to pass unaided. It is happening in these cities today because social movements (urban, labour, anti-racist, anti-sexist, and environmental) have demanded to be included in the negotiations on the future of their cities. The form such demands take differ from city to city: in Frankfurt, the Green Party has, for the most part, been a transmitter of movement demands into the realm of power (Ronneberger and Keil 1993). In Los Angeles, groups like the Mothers of East Los Angeles, the Concerned Citizens of South Central Los Angeles, the citizens of the Maple Avenue neighbourhood, and the Labor/Community Strategy Center have challenged the dominant political system. Their success to in 'getting heard' can be interpreted simultaneously as evidence for the continuing relevance of local politics generally. How the ensuing structures of participation and democracy are being constructed largely depends on local power relations, political traditions, and the kind of problems addressed. While citizens of world cities have 'discovered' the environment as a valuable and promising field in which they can influence the fate of their cities, there is, primarily in the hegemonic formulations like those initiated by local governments, a tendency to make participation a partial, controlled, and co-opted experience. Yet token participation and large-scale schemes do not seem to work as effectively as they used to. Environmental groups in urban centres have become experts in more than one sense, they have often become professionalized organizations that cannot be silenced by such measures (Keil and Ronneberger 1994). In addition, while 'the environment' has traditionally been seen as a concern of the middle classes, new popular, working class, and minority groups like the Labor/Community Strategy Center in Los Angeles have made their weight felt where it was not expected (Keil 1993; Mann 1991).

In conclusion, then, it can be said that both on the conceptual and on the empirical level, we have far from exhausted the environmental problematic in world cities. Borrowing from the urgency felt in much of the environmental discourse today, I would like to end this chapter by calling for more attention to be given to urban ecologies and the policies developed around them as part of the formation of world cities. In the light of the tremendous weight of current ecological problems, and returning to Friedmann's and Wolff's original proposition, we might venture to say that *research* on world city ecologies needs to happen fast and extensively, if our *actions* are still to make sense.

ACKNOWLEDGEMENT

I wish to thank Gene Desfor for comments on an earlier draft of this chapter.

NOTES

1 These urban regions are rather diverse, their environments and expressions of the ecological problematic differ widely from one another. What makes them comparable is their common subjection to processes of global restructuring; what makes this comparison interesting are the significant variations in how these cities have been affected and how they have dealt with these global processes. Soja (1992) has shown similar relationships of the general process and the specific outcome of restructuring for the cases of Los Angeles and Amsterdam. In his study he identifies five processes common to both places: the geographical recomposition of urban form; the

internationalization of the regional metropolis; industrial restructuring (and the trend towards post-Fordism and flexible accumulation); the tendency towards increasing social and economic polarization; and finally post-modernism and post-modernization. Space does not allow me to detail these processes for the cases of Los Angeles and Frankfurt. I will therefore simply assume a similarly contradictory – oppositional and parallel – pattern of urbanization in Frankfurt and Los Angeles. For more detailed analyses of both cities see Keil 1993; Keil and Lieser 1992; Keil and Ronneberger 1994; Ronneberger and Keil 1993.

2   For a survey of world city literature and a view that argues that the local politics of world city formation matter see Keil 1993, chapter 1. There are, of course, notable exceptions to both aspects. The ones dealing with local politics are discussed in my book; among those that deal with the environmental problematic are Feagin 1985 and Friedmann 1988.

3   For all practical purposes, 'ecological' (which is used more in the European 'green' sense of the word) and 'environmental' are meant to be used interchangeably in this chapter.

4   As Kate Sandilands reminds us, there is a part of 'nature' which does not lend itself to perception through processes of language and discourse (1993).

5   This includes Friedmann's suggestion that the very definition of environmental standards 'is a political exercise' (1988: 1).

6   While there are obvious etymological and intellectual relationships, it needs to be said at the outset that 'urban ecology' in this chapter does nowhere refer to the Chicago School of Sociology's and subsequent similar uses of the term. The meaning of the term as employed here will be clarified below.

7   This is not to belittle the often heroic efforts of mega-city populations to struggle for survival in environmental and social squalor. It is, however, necessary to point out that much of this struggle happens externally to the global formation of capital accumulation.

8   I have argued this more extensively elsewhere for Los Angeles (Bloch and Keil 1991) and Frankfurt (Keil and Ronneberger 1991a). Paradoxically, in Frankfurt, this new significance of the environmental discourse for development has recently become apparent in the attempts by local social democratic politicians panicked by social problems such as housing shortages to reverse the paradigm of 'development through the environment' and to pitch 'social housing' against 'greenspace'. The stiff resistance of the Green Party in the local government to such thinking, however, marks the shift in the conceptualization of development.

9   See also a recent issue of the *Journal of Urban Affairs*, 15(1) (1993) with papers by Molotch, Stone, and Swanstrom.

REFERENCES

Altvater, E. 1992. *Der Preis des Wohlstands (oder Umweltplünderung und neue Welt(un)ordnung)*. Münster: Westfälisches Dampfboot.
    1993. *The Future of the Market*. London: Verso.

Becker, E., Jahn, T., and Wehling, U. 1991. ' "Civil Society" und die Krise der gesellschaftlichen Naturverhältnisse'. *Prokla*, 21(3), issue 84 (September): 482–92.

Berger, J. 1990. *Lilac and Flag: An Old Wife's Tale of a City*. New York: Vintage.

Bloch, R. and Keil, R. 1991. 'Planning for a fragrant future: air pollution control, restructuring and popular alternatives in Los Angeles'. *Capitalism, Nature, Socialism*, 2(1) issue 6 (February): 44–65.

City of Los Angeles. 1990. 'State of the city's environment primer. A report of the Environmental Quality Board'.

Commission of the European Communities. 1990. *Green Paper on the Urban Environment*. 2 vols. Brussels: Commission of the European Communities.

Feagin, J. R. 1985. 'The social costs of Houston's growth'. *International Journal of Urban and Regional Research*, 9: 164–85.

Fitzsimmons, M. et al. 1991. 'Environmentalism and the American liberal state'. *Capitalism, Nature, Socialism*, 2(1) issue 6 (February): 1–16.

Friedmann, J. 1986. 'The world city hypothesis'. *Development and Change*, 17(1): 69–84. (Reproduced as appendix in this volume.)

    1988. 'Planning, politics and the environment'. Paper presented at the Second International Congress of the Association of European Schools of Planning. Dortmund, 10–12 November.

    1991. 'Der GrünGürtel ist weder grün noch ein Gürtel'. In *Vision offener Grünraüme: GrünGürtel Frankfurt*, ed. T. Koenigs, pp. 189–91. Frankfurt and New York: Campus.

    1993. 'Where we stand: a decade of world city research'. Paper presented to the World Cities in a World System conference, 1–3 April, Sterling VA. (Reproduced as ch. 2 in this volume.)

Friedmann, J. and Wolff, G. 1982. 'World city formation. An agenda for research and action'. *International Journal of Urban and Regional Research*, 6(3): 309–44.

GrünGürtel – Projektbüro im Auftrag der Stadt Frankfurt am Main. 1991. *Ergebnisbericht GrünGürtel Planung 1990/01*. Frankfurt: Stadt Frankfurt am Main.

Hall, S. 1991. 'The local and the global: globalization and ethnicity'. In *Culture, Globalization and the World-System*, ed. A. King, pp. 19–40. SUNY, Binghamton: Department of Art and Art History.

Haraway, D. 1988. 'Situated knowledge'. *Feminist Studies*, 14(3): 575–99.

Harvey, D. 1989a. *The Urban Experience*. Baltimore: Johns Hopkins University Press.

    1989b. *The Condition of Postmodernity*. Oxford: Basil Blackwell.

Hoffmann-Axthelm, D. 1988. 'Untergehende Städte?' *ARCH+*, issue 94 (April): 34–9.

    1993. *Die dritte Stadt*. Frankfurt: Suhrkamp.

Jahn, T. 1991. 'Neue Grün(en)-Politik?' *Kommune*, 9(6): 54.

    1993. 'Ecological movements and environmental politics in Germany'. *Capitalism, Nature, Socialism*, 4(1) issue 13 (March): 1–9.

Jessop, B. 1993. 'Towards a Schumpeterian workfare state? Preliminary remarks on post-Fordist political economy'. *Studies in Political Economy*, 40: 7–39.

Keil, R. 1990. 'Urban future revisited: politics and restructuring in Los Angeles after Fordism'. *Strategies: A Journal of Theory, Culture and Politics*, 3 (June): 105–29.

1993. *Welt-Stadt – Stadt der Welt: Internationalisierung und lokale Politik in Los Angeles*. Münster: Westfälisches Dampfboot.

Keil, R. and Lieser, P. 1992. 'Frankfurt: global city – local politics'. In *After Modernism: Global Restructuring and the Changing Boundaries of City Life*, ed. M. P. Smith, pp. 39–69. New Brunswick NJ: Transaction Publishers.

Keil, R. and Ronneberger, K. 1991a. 'Arkadien postmodern: Der GrünGürtel zwischen Streuobst und Gewerbepark'. In *Vision offener Grünräume: GrünGürtel Frankfurt*, ed. T. Koenigs. Frankfurt and New York: Campus.

1991b. 'Konflikt- und Möglichkeitsraum'. *Kommune*, 9(6): 46.

1994. 'Going up the country: internationalization and urbanization on Frankfurt's northern fringe'. *Environment and Planning D: Society and Space*, 12(2): 137–66.

Koenigs, T. (ed.). 1991. *Vision offener Grünräume: GrünGürtel Frankfurt*. Frankfurt and New York: Campus.

1992. *Leben in Frankfurt 2010: Einladung zum Gespräch über die Zukunft der Stadt*. Frankfurt: Stadt Frankfurt am Main, Dezernat für Umwelt, Energie und Brandschutz.

Linden, E. 1993. 'Megacities'. *Time*, 11 January: 30–40.

Lipietz, A. 1992a. 'A regulationist approach to the future of urban ecology'. *Capitalism, Nature, Socialism*, 3(3) issue 11 (September): 101–10.

1992b. 'The regulation approach and capitalist crisis: an alternative compromise for the 1990s'. In *Cities and Regions in the New Europe: The Global–Local Interplay and Spatial Development Strategies*, ed. M. Dunford and G. Kafkalas, pp. 309–34. London: Belhaven.

1992c. *Towards a New Economic Order: Postfordism, Ecology and Democracy*. London: Oxford University Press.

Logan, J. and Molotch, H. 1987. *Urban Fortunes: The Political Economy of Place*. Berkeley: University of California Press.

Los Angeles 2000 Committee. 1988. *LA2000: A City for the Future. Final Report*. Los Angeles: LA2000 Committee.

Mann, E. 1991. *LA's Lethal Air: New Strategies for Policy, Organizing and Action*. Los Angeles: Labor/Community Strategy Center.

Prigge, W. and Lieser, P. 1992. 'Metropole Frankfurt: Keine Metro, aber Polarisierung. Lokale Politik zwischen Stadt und Land'. In *Politik in europäischen Städten: Fallstudien zur Bedeutung lokaler Politik*, ed. H. Heinelt and M. Meyer, pp. 49–69. Basel: Birkhaüser.

Ronneberger, K. and Keil, R. 1993. 'Riding the tiger of modernization: a preliminary analysis of red–green municipal reform politics in Frankfurt am Main'. *Capitalism, Nature, Socialism*, 4(2) issue 14 (June): 1–31.

Royal Commission on the Future of the Toronto Waterfront. 1992. *Regeneration: Toronto's Waterfront and the Sustainable City. Final Report*. Ottawa: Supply and Services Canada.

Sandilands, K. 1993. 'Ecofeminism and the nature of politics'. Paper presented at York University, Faculty of Environmental Studies, 22 April.

SCAQMD. 1989. *Air Quality Management Plan. South Coast Air Basin.* Los Angeles: South Coast Air Quality Management District.

Soja, E. W. 1992. 'The stimulus of a little confusion: a contemporary comparison of Amsterdam and Los Angeles'. In *Comparative Urban and Community Research 4: After Modernism: Global Restructuring and the Changing Boundaries of City Life*, ed. M. P. Smith, pp. 17–38. New Brunswick and London: Transaction Publishers.

Spivak, G. 1993. 'Can discourses be countered?' Paper presented at York University, English Department, 25 February.

Stone, C. N. and Sanders, H. T. 1988. *The Politics of Urban Development.* Lawrence KS: University Press of Kansas.

Stren, R., White, R., and Whitney, J. 1992. *Sustainable Cities: Urbanization and the Environment in International Perspective.* Boulder, San Francisco, Oxford: Westview Press.

Trepl, L. 1991. 'Ökologische Stadtgestaltung'. In *Vision offener Grünraüme: GrünGürtel Frankfurt*, ed. T. Koenigs, pp. 167–72. Frankfurt and New York: Campus.

World Commission on Environment and Development. 1987. *Our Common Future.* Oxford: Oxford University Press.

17 The successful management and administration of world cities: mission impossible?

Peter M. Ward

My purpose in this chapter is to go some way to redressing two imbalances in the current literature about world cities. Specifically, I want first to focus not so much on the global as upon the local. In particular, I want to focus upon how large cities – some of which may be world cities however we define them – are administered and governed. All too often structures of city governance are either taken as a 'given', or are ignored altogether. They are almost never looked at in a comparative perspective although, importantly, the 'politics of urban planning and development' is included as one of the six themes in an SSRC collaborative investigation of New York, London, Paris and Tokyo (Mollenkopf 1993). In short, I want to put politics and government back into the world cities agenda.

The second imbalance I wish to address is the failure of much contemporary work to look seriously and systematically at large cities and at world cities in less developed contexts. As I have complained elsewhere (Ward 1993), so much urban analysis ignores the experiences and processes occurring in those contexts, despite the fact that this is where urbanization is occurring most dramatically, and that these centres are frequently the production loci for the so-called new international division of labour (Morris and Lowder 1992). Many of the insights about urban social movements, informal–formal sector interactions and interdependence, the dynamics of household and female insertion into the labour market and so on, have come originally from less developed contexts. Yet that work has often been ignored, and the wheel gets rediscovered in research conducted in advanced capitalist arenas at the front end of 'flexible accumulation regimes'. We urgently need to examine urbanization processes and world city structures in less developed contexts. How else are we to begin to interrogate the counterfactual? Sadly, even the SSRC comparative study, excellent though it is, does not include cities like Mexico City, São Paulo, Hong Kong, or Seoul among its case studies.

Therefore, in order partially to redress this imbalance I propose to examine, in broad terms, some of the principal aspects relating to city administration which I believe we should consider; and in the second half of the chapter to exemplify some of the issues in the context with which I am most familiar – that of Mexico City.

Administration and government of world cities: the missing link

Thus far, scholars who have analysed world cities have usually done so through one or more of three optics. First, they have looked at the individual and interactional role of world cities within a global economy, usually from the point of view of their importance as production, control, or financing centres. Prime examples of this work are Friedmann's originating hypothesis, and Sassen's more recent (1991) work on New York, London, and Tokyo. A second optic has been to examine the restructuring that world cities are themselves undergoing, especially as they develop new control functions to replace their earlier production roles (New York and London offer good examples; see for example, O'Neill and Moss 1991; Vogel 1993). Some analysts have also begun to look at the internal consequences of this restructuring upon poverty and social organization within these cities (Fainstein, Gordon, and Harloe 1992; Mollenkopf and Castells 1991; Sassen 1991). Third has been a consideration of the extent to which these cities are subject to converging or diverging urban processes. Particularly important here is the question of whether cities like São Paulo in less developed countries are moving in similar directions physically and culturally as their advanced capitalist counterparts.[1] However, because we have focused upon their global context and role, I am concerned that we have failed to analyse world cities *qua cities*. It is almost as if we have put aside their uniqueness: their particular political and social structures; their (often) local real estate and building production investment processes; and the role of human agency etc.[2] These cities are products not just of the now, but of the past. They are an outcome of conditioning relationships with the outside, forged through an articulation and engagement with regional local élites and multiplex social and political structures (King 1990; Roberts 1978). Therefore, these cities are highly differentiated rather than homogeneous. However, in our search for the global roles and interactions that world cities articulate, we rarely, in Sassen's words, allow the 'voice' of each city to come to the fore.[3]

Most of all, we have given insufficient consideration to the political–administrative structures through which such cities are governed and managed. In our rush to examine their economic base and international role, we have failed to ask fundamental questions about their governmental structures, governability, and almost never have we examined these in a comparative perspective. How cities are governed and organized physically tells us much about the nature of power relations in that society, and about the opportunities for citizen involvement in the management of the city. Just because the world has become more compressed in terms of time and space (Harvey 1989), is now more accessible to many, and images have become increasingly international-ized, we should not forget the need to 'interplace' global with local situations (as King reminds us in this volume). It would be perverse to extoll the virtues of 'thinking globally while acting locally' or in favour of so-called 'municipal foreign policy' as do Michael Peter Smith and Andrew Kirby in this volume, if, as is often the case, citizens are effectively disenfranchised at the local level.

Specifically, several important dimensions of analysis about city governance arise. First, what is the basis of legitimacy for principal government officers to hold positions of authority? Are they appointed or elected? If elected, is this according to partisan or non-partisan criteria? The USA has a strong tradition of non-partisanship in its 'mayor-council' and 'city-manager' forms of government (Stanyer 1976).[4] Yet in the UK most voters make their choice of city councillors according to the political party each represents, and they know or care little about the person they are electing. Thus the legitimacy of the creation of governance structures varies, as does the rationality which will subsequently govern an individual's behaviour once in office. Whether a person is appointed or elected, and the type of election, may determine how prepared they are to hold public office – their training, expertise, competence, and even their honesty or 'softness' (Wade 1989). My point is that the form whereby a city administration is created, and the terms under which it is expected to operate, shapes the whole extent of democratic opportunities for citizen involvement in city management.

A second set of issues which we need to consider relates to how activities and authority might best be organized when, spatially, the city merges into the jurisdiction of another entity. This is invariably the case for the very large cities which we are discussing in this volume. Remarkably, though, these overlapping functions and responsibilities are ignored by scholars, perhaps because we tend to trivialize local space and administrative boundaries, while playing up the globalization of space and the removal of physical borders. However, most world cities encompass a number of different administrative units, each of which is vested with a different level of authority. These may include areas with special 'federal district' status (as in Washington DC or Bogotá Special District); metropolitan authorities (councils); states and counties; 'city' authorities, municipalities, and so on. Often, too, the legitimacy and rationale of each (as outlined above) will vary. Thus, careful ordering and clarification of the various tiers of authority are required if city development is to be co-ordinated in any meaningful way. The nature of inter-governmental relations between one level of authority and another also needs to be properly understood.

Related to this issue of political–administrative organization is a third consideration, namely, what are the key activities in which administration should engage (land-use planning, infrastructural development, trans-portation, social services, service provision, security, cleansing, etc.)? And at what level should these be undertaken; specifically, how might they best be 'nested' hierarchically in order to maximize efficiency, equity, access, or whatever the local goals happen to be? A final dimension of analysis is to identify the opportunities that are provided for local self-governance by the citizens of these cities, particularly their patterns of social organization and level of social mobilization, and the extent to which they have control over decision-making and are empowered with genuine responsibility. Moreover, in each context, what is the dominant ideology governing citizenship, and how has this been 'constructed'? Within cities how much autonomy do different cultures enjoy, and how dynamic is the existing popular culture?

In short, these key issues concerned with city administration and governance have been neglected because they do not offer immediate and easy 'purchase' upon global issues, and because, at best, they are only very indirect outcomes of international processes. Yet I am sure most of my colleagues will agree that these structures demand more systematic study, since they are the heart of what these cities are like as places in which to live. Indeed, John Friedmann's own research in recent years has focused precisely upon empowerment and the effective-ness of local organization strategies for development (1992). Therefore, we need to put back into the world cities study agenda a greater consideration of politics and public administration in urban governance.

Imperatives drawn from the 1980s

Of course, the original world city hypothesis was based largely upon our understanding of events up until the late 1970s. More recent research and political change during the 1980s have, in my view, heightened the imperative that we examine structures of governance and administration. These include the democratization process in Latin America and, most dramatically, in Eastern Europe. If anything, the Friedmann and Wolff (1982) article anticipated a *decline* in democratization and a rising tide of authoritarianism. Also, the rise of so-called 'locality' studies has generated a better understanding of the importance of local symbols and meanings, and have widened consensus about the importance of local empowerment.[5]

Another imperative drawn from the 1980s is the significant shift towards decentralization and devolution that many societies are under-taking, both at intra-city and inter-governmental levels. This process also appears to be emerging strongly in some less developed contexts, and has found quickening support among international agencies, such as the World Bank (Jones and Ward 1994; Silverman 1988). In Mexico, for example, austerity measures enacted during the 1980s, along with economic restructuring and political reform, have intensified the need for the local state and for city authorities to do more with less – hence their willingness to embrace decentralization and administrative reorga-nization (Rodríguez 1992; Rodríguez and Ward 1992, 1994). City and metropolitan authorities have had to confront central government-imposed cuts in public expenditure, declining subsidies, and often a growing pressure to privatize a range of what were formerly publicly provided services. Greater fiscal responsibility is being placed upon the local level, as well as upon individual citizens. Not surprisingly, people today have become more concerned about their tax bills, particularly those directed to city hall.

Many countries, too, are experiencing a technocratization of adminis-trative and governmental procedures, such that there is greater transpar-ancy in city hall affairs and finances, and increased efficiency in the delivery of urban services. This takes us back to the issues of devolution and empowerment, since city administrators today recognize the political benefits of sharing accountability with those they serve. Local groups, often poorly organized and radical in the past, now demonstrate greater realism and pragmatism. No longer are they seeking grandiose changes and a 'qualitatively new effect in power relations' (Castells 1977); rather, they want greater opportunities for self-government, for the defence of local culture, and to be able to participate (and pay for) the upgrading and servicing of their neighbourhoods (Assies 1994; Castells 1983). New social movements are better led and more adept in their strategizing. Non-government organizations, too, have demon-strated greater pragmatism and efficacy in their relations with local authorities, and in their support for social movements and local communities.

These imperatives should encourage us to reflect analytically upon past experiences and to think imaginatively about which structures of city administration and governance within a democratic system appear to work best, and how existing structures might best be modified in order to take account of the new experiences and imperatives that have emerged during the 1980s and the early 1990s.

Structures of city government

It is not necessary to my purpose in this chapter to describe the alternative structures of local government that dominate in the UK nor the more varied forms of American city administrations (strong and weak mayor-council system; commissioner system; council-manager system, etc.) which are widely described elsewhere (Pinch 1985; Stanyer 1976). Rather my aim here is to begin to explore the primary principles upon which world city and large city administrations should be predicated. I would like to propose the following six principles. First, city administration and governance should be democratic. Whatever city administrative and management structure is adopted, those serving in a policy-making and normative capacity should be elected.[6] Second, city government at all levels should be transparent and accountable. Third, there should be one authority with responsibility for the whole of the city or metropolitan area, with executive powers over certain macro-level activities such as planning and primary zoning; collective transportation planning and development; primary service networks and procurement; as well as other first-tier services such as hospitals and higher education centres, etc. Fourth, all other activities should be decentralized to a number of local level city halls (borough or municipal), which should provide lower-order services such as planning and secondary zoning; installation and maintenance of utilities and service infrastructure; licensing; health centres and general practice organization; schools, etc. Fifth, that there be maximum opportunity for local and individual participation, and that wherever possible, decision-making be transferred to the community and neighbourhood levels. Finally, that city authorities should have maximum fiscal autonomy. This is important if mandated authorities are to be able to act without manipulation or interference from central or higher orders of government.

In the remainder of this chapter I want briefly to describe Mexico City, perhaps the largest city in the world today. My purpose is to demonstrate how existing structures in world cities may be extremely undemocratic; and to show that they are oriented towards social control rather than towards development (i.e. they are 'exclusionary' rather than 'empowered' in Friedmann's terminology). I also want to suggest how these structures might be transformed and made much more responsive to citizens' needs.

Mexico City: government without democracy[7]

For the purposes of my argument several characteristics of Mexico City need to be described at the outset. Mexico City is big; exactly how big no one appears to know accurately since there is considerable uncertainty about the 1980 population census, projections from which would have placed its total population in 1990 at around nineteen million. In fact the 1900 population census found only sixteen million. Whichever is the case, the city is huge, and, as it has grown, much of the new development has occurred outside of the Federal District boundary (figure 17.1). By the year 2000 it is estimated that one-half of the city's population will live in municipalities in the surrounding state of Mexico. Population growth in the Federal District is stable, and some inner areas are losing population. Mexico City's expansion, therefore, occurs in another political–administrative entity, and much of it is in low-income, unplanned, self-help, neighbourhoods (Ward 1990).

Thus there are two political entities with principal responsibilities for managing the city.[8] Within the Federal District (which has 'special district' status) there are sixteen subunits called *delegaciones*, while in the state of Mexico the metropolitan area embraces all or part of some twenty-one municipalities. Here, at least, the principal executive officer is elected – the state governor for six years, and local municipal presidents for three years.[9] The governor appoints his executive officers to state government, and there is an elected state legislature, but this is invariably compliant to the governor's wishes. Municipal city hall – the *ayuntamiento* – comprises department heads appointed by the municipal president, and a council called a *cabildo*, of some twelve to fourteen individuals elected on the coat-tails of the municipal president.[10] The situation is even less representative in the Federal District where there is no elected council and no elected city hall officials. The mayor and the sixteen submayors (called *delegados*), one for each *delegación*, act on the delegated authority of the national president. Individually, each appoints his or her own department heads. The rationale for this structure is that the Federal District is the seat of federal powers, and, as such, belongs to the nation as a whole. Moreover, the president, in effect, is elected to govern that seat, but given his other duties he delegates the responsibility to the *Regente* or 'Regent' (acting in his stead – the title is well chosen). The *Regente* enjoys senior cabinet rank. But within the Federal District there is no elected government.

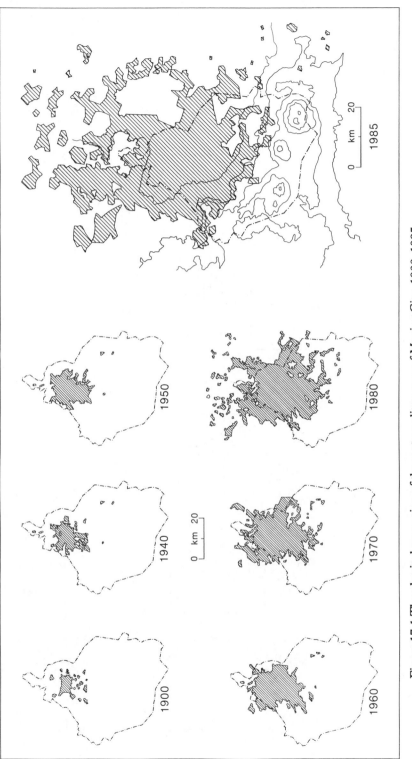

Figure 17.1 The physical expansion of the metropolitan area of Mexico City, 1900–1985

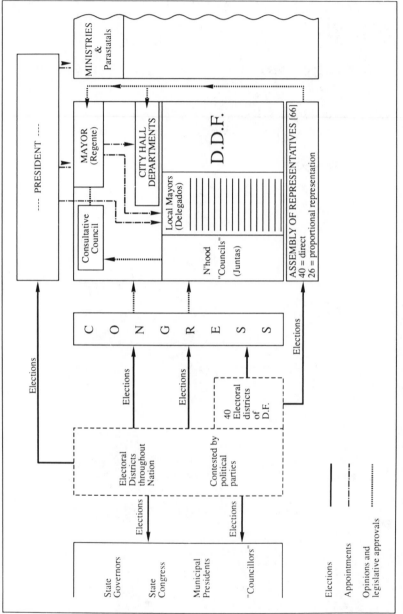

Figure 17.2 The structure of political representation and government in Mexico City

Nor is there much opportunity for citizen involvement and participation (see figure 17.2). The consultative council is precisely that – consultative – it has little influence. The neighbourhood councils or *juntas de vecinos* comprise a hierarchical arrangement of representatives, whose role is also consultative and informative, channelled through each *delegación*, the head representative of which sits on the consultative council. Since 1988 a new elected body has been created, the Representative Assembly of the Federal District. This body incorporates directly elected and proportional representation membership across all the principal parties. However, although it serves as a 'watchdog' forum and has developed an increasingly important role in monitoring the Federal District department's affairs, it falls well short of being an elected council with policy-making powers. These rather nominal representative structures have evolved more to head off demands for restoring the capital's statehood and municipal status (lost in 1928–9), and to undermine claims that the chief executive officer and the local mayors should be elected rather than imposed (Ward 1990).

Administratively, therefore, city functions and planning are split between two entities and often within each entity as well. There is no effective and ongoing collaboration between the two principal authorities (the Federal District department and the state of Mexico government). The collective transportation agency COVITUR has only very recently begun to extend its lines into the state of Mexico; previously they stopped at the Federal District boundary. Services, infrastructure provision, housing, planning, and so on are all organized independently from two centres (The DF Department and the state capital Toluca some forty miles west of the metropolitan area). Thus Mexico City's government is split, centralized in two competing political authorities and largely unaccountable.

This lack of democracy and low accountability has not passed unchallenged. Indeed it has looked increasingly anomalous, given President Salinas' (1988–94) attempts to reinforce the plurality of Mexico's democratic system nation-wide and to encourage democratization and political reform. Nor did he actually win the vote in the metropolitan area in the 1988 presidential elections, so the traditional argument that he is the 'governor' of the Federal District pales somewhat. Since the early 1980s there has been a growing public debate about the desirability of a locally elected congress (with or without a return to statehood), and about elected executive officers. In March 1993 a cross-party referendum was called on the initiative of some members of the Representative Assembly, but the government and the principal media (strongly influenced by the government) downplayed the whole event. Although the eventual vote was strongly in favour, only 6 per cent of those eligible to vote did so, and credibility in the initiative was undermined.

In addition, as I described earlier, each of the innovations designed to give some 'representation' to local citizens has, in fact, been constructed by the government determined to head off and undermine any concerted call for true representation and democratization in the Federal District. There are several reasons for this, not least of which is the fact that the governing party for the past 65 years (the PRI) would probably not carry the metropolitan area, and it would certainly lose control of some subdistricts. Another concern is the instability that might arise were there to be two political 'heavyweights' in the same entity (i.e. the president and the mayor), particularly if they came from different parties. But Mexican political leaders might look for reassurance at the innumerable experiences where two political leaders from different parties work out of the same capital without the city falling apart. My point, however, is that there has been no real move towards democratization and greater participation: quite the opposite. All experiments with 'representation' thus far, have actually had an ulterior motive which is exclusionary.

Here is not the place to evaluate the pros and cons of arguments in favour of an elected mayor. Quite literally at the time of revising this chapter for publication (late June 1993) a whole new set of reforms to Mexico City's government were being announced by the mayor. Suffice to say that, in my view, innovations and minor compromises in the past have been designed to postpone fundamental reform, and even the new proposals are strongly suggestive of the same. In the meantime, however, policy-making will intensify attempts at technical 'fixes' (palliatives) which are also designed to create a political breathing space. Management structures will be made more efficient with less leakage, yet these will continue to be undemocratic. Subsidies will be withdrawn and consumer charges for basic services will be increased, as will taxes now that an increasing proportion of the population is brought into the tax base through land legalization programmes. The city will survive, but it will not thrive. The current pattern is one of making minor changes in order to effect no fundamental change. The current project is not one of genuine democratization, greater social justice, empowerment, and the devolution of power. It is one of control, not development.

Government, democracy, and public administration in Mexico City: mission impossible?

Earlier in this chapter I presented a series of propositions about the basic principles upon which I believe that any city government should be predicated. As has become apparent, so far as Mexico City is concerned, none of my six conditions is satisfied. So in this particular context how might the city move towards creating an administrative structure that is development-oriented rather than control-based? There are, I believe, two imperatives. The first is for a single political entity for the built-up area to be created; or at least for a single 'tier' of authority to be grafted on to the structure with city-wide responsibilities. There seems little likelihood that the metropolitan area will ever become a single entity. It would be disproportionately large (one-quarter of the national population); and so powerful as to generate political imbalance nationally. Nor is it likely that the state of Mexico would fail to resist any loss or encroachment upon what is, after all, its principal source of income and fiscal revenue. But as I have suggested, Mexico City's future will be determined by what happens *outside* of the Federal District since that is where the growth and pressure points are located. An elected metropolitan council is required, with executive authority for strategic functions such as physical and economic planning, transportation, and primary service provision. In many respects this might resemble the Greater London Council which oversaw such functions for the London boroughs, each of which was responsible locally for planning, and for providing services as determined by each individual council.[11] The fact that the Thatcher government was ultimately successful in abolishing the metropolitan councils was not because they were proving ineffective, but rather, because they worked too well. The existence of an elected authority exercising autonomy and implementing policy not of its liking was anathema to Conservative central government. However, in my view it is precisely that level of vision and control that is required if Mexico City is to develop in any ordered and democratic way.

The second imperative is for the process of government to be brought under party political control. In contemporary Mexico none of the parties has a clearly enunciated urban development agenda or manifesto. The current structure resembles that of the 'strong mayor–weak council' form in the USA, except that the council is mega-weak, and, in the Federal District, neither council nor mayor are elected. However, it is probable that the non-partisan council–city manager arrangement common in the USA would not work in Mexico. Therefore, strategies and agenda for city development might best be brought *into* party politics, rather than excluded from it. These should form part of the party's election manifesto; and once elected, if their performance falls short then they will be out at the next election. Thus, I am proposing a party-based and an electorally contested basis for both the proposed new metropolitan authority, as well as for all of the local authorities below it.

Political reform 1993, 1994, 1997, and in the year 2000

The dual proposal that I have outlined above has, until now, looked like 'mission impossible'. Indeed, for the current star trekkers, the period scheduled for implementation of the reform resembles the time it takes for a space vehicle to arrive at destinations within our own solar system: hence the subtitle. The most recent proposal developed by the present *Regente* is very interesting and astute. The political reform of the Federal District proposes that first, from December 1994 (when the next president took office) the Representative Assembly will be given some legislative functions (thus giving it a policy-defining role). It will cover a wide number of areas, including electoral organization, approval of annual budget, laws of land use, employment generation, etc. Potentially it is quite comprehensive. Second, from 1997 onwards the mayor – or whatever he is then to be called – will be chosen by the president from among one of the members of the party in the Assembly with the majority (which is renewed every three years). The Assembly will vote on candidates and if it cannot ratify one of these after two votes the Senate will appoint them. Only the senate can remove the mayor. Third, from the year 2000 (i.e. the beginning of the next presidential term) both the mayor and the Assembly will operate for six-year terms. Fourth, the internal arrangements within the Federal District will be amended, but at this moment the details remain imprecise. The number of *delegaciones* will increase; citizen councils will be formed by local election, although it is not clear what powers these will have. The Metropolitan Council for the valley of Mexico will be created with responsibility for ecological and environmental issues, transportation, water, rubbish collection, and security.

Thus, it is proposed to replace the current structure with what will be in Mexico a unique parliamentary system in which the mayor will be 'first among equals'. Returning to our original models it will substitute the strong mayor–council system, eventually, for a very weak mayor–council arrangement. However, it postpones the effective starting date to 1997 and full implementation until the year 2000, and opens up the possibility for the new president to repeal or to amend the arrangement. And, by opting for the parliamentary model it avoids the emergence of a major political counterweight to the president with responsibilities for governing the Federal District and with a personal mandate from having been elected by the people. (Remember, the mayor will be selected by the president from among the majority party in the Assembly, not by the people directly.) The possibilities for divide-and-rule among a 'first-among-equals' system are enormous. Moreover, the plan fails to grasp the nettle of a metropolitan-wide tier of government that would cater for the entire city population, half of which in the year 2000 will live outside the Federal District borders. Once again we are observing an exercise in compromise designed to constrain rather than to develop fully democratic governance.

So far as other world cities are concerned, I hope that the illustrations drawn from this one particular example will convince the reader that, no matter whether our concern is for world cities, or large cities, we need to think more about the organizational structures that facilitate both the overall regulatory functions and planning, with grassroots participatory mechanisms that empower; and which give more self-management and decision-making opportunities and responsibilities to local groups. Even where 'elected' forms of representation already exist (as in most places), the challenge remains to devise structures of administration that are truly democratic and participatory. The conditioning variables to effect these changes may be helped by engagement in global economic practices, insofar as this might recast productive relations, be tied to austerity conditionalities, greater individual taxation, and individualized responsibilities for welfare needs (i.e. withdrawal of the state etc.). But above all, these changes are likely to derive from active processes already underway at the local level and which were enumerated earlier in the chapter. This articulation of levels, with decentralized and devolved responsibilities and powers (compared to centralized and top-down structures), are crucial if we are to turn world cities into cities of citizens, rather than cities of workers.

NOTES

1 Indeed, one of the main criticisms of the original hypothesis is that it has tended to overemphasize the global significance of world cities such as Mexico City and São Paulo which exist in the so-called 'semi-periphery'.

2 Belhaven Press's relatively new series on world cities (the general editors of which are Knox and Johnston) may go some way to redress this failing, although none of the texts to date has taken the Friedmann hypothesis as its point of departure.

3 As Sassen described in her presentation to the conference on World Cities in a World System. See also her chapter in this volume.

4 Interestingly, New York City is one of the very few exceptions and elects its councillors along party lines.

5 Democratization processes have intensified interest in the conditions affecting, and the nature of, the emergence of civil society. Since 1989 an important number of studies have focused upon 'regime transition' (see for example, Di Palma 1990; Graham 1993; O'Donnell 1989). On the rise of locality studies in the UK see, among others, Cooke 1989.

6 This does not mean that all executive officers should be elected, since many executive functions (i.e. the implementation of policy) are conducted by officials who are appointed by the council. But they are accountable to elected officials whose primary role is one of policy formulation.

7 A more detailed account and analysis of Mexico City's structure is contained in my book (Ward 1990).

8 In fact there is a third called the Conurbation Commission, but this extends across five states and has no executive authority. Moreover, its normative role is effectively non-existent, certainly as far as the metropolitan built-up area is concerned (Campbell and Wilk 1987; Ward 1986).

9 These terms are non-renewable since the constitution does not allow re-election.

10 In fact these aldermen or *regidores* are elected on the same slate. Once victorious, the incoming municipal president accommodates most of them in the *cabildo*, along with one or two opposition party *regidores* to ensure at least a minimal presence of parties other than his own in the *ayuntamiento*.

11 However, it should be made clear that the GLC's authority never stretched into one of the surrounding counties which would be the equivalent of a state in this case.

REFERENCES

Assies, W. 1994. 'Reconstructing the meaning of urban land in Brazil: the case of Recife'. In *Methodology for Land and Housing Market Analysis*, ed. G. Jones and P. Ward, pp. 102–19. London: University College London Press.

Campbell, T. and Wilk, D. 1986. 'Plans and plan making in the valley of Mexico'. *Third World Planning Review*, 8(4): 287–313.

Castells, M. 1977. *The Urban Question*. London: Edward Arnold.
     1983. *The City and the Grassroots*. Berkeley: University of California Press.

Cooke, P. (ed.). 1989. *Localities*. London: Unwin Hyman.

Di Palma, G. 1990. *To Craft Democracies: An Essay on Democratic Transitions*. Berkeley: University of California Press.

Fainstein, S., Gordon, I., and Harloe, M. (eds.). 1992. *Divided Cities. New York and London in the Contemporary World*. Oxford: Basil Blackwell.

Friedmann, J. 1992. *Empowerment: The Politics of Alternative Development*. Oxford: Basil Blackwell.

Friedmann, J. and Wolff, G. 1982. 'World city formation. An agenda for research and action'. *International Journal of Urban and Regional Research*, 6(3): 309–44.

Graham, L. 1993. 'Rethinking the relationship between the strength of local institutions and the consolidation of democracy'. *In Depth*, 3(1): 177–93.

Harvey, D. 1989. *The Condition of Postmodernity*. Oxford: Basil Blackwell.

Jones, G. and Ward, P. (eds.). 1994. 'Tilting at windmills: paradigm shifts in World Bank orthodoxy'. In *Methodology for Land and Housing Market Analysis*, ed. G. Jones and P. Ward, pp. 8–23. London: University College London Press.

King, J. 1990. *Global Cities: Post-Imperialism and the Internationalization of London*. London: Routledge and Kegan Paul.

1993.'Re-presenting world cities: cultural theory/social practice'. Paper presented to the World Cities in a World System conference, Sterling VA, 1–3 April. (Reproduced as ch. 12 in this volume.)

Mollenkopf, J. 1993. 'The challenge of comparative research on global cities'. Paper presented to the World Cities in a World System conference. Sterling VA, 1–3 April.

Mollenkopf, J. and Castells, M. (eds.). 1991. *Dual City: Restructuring New York*. New York: Russell Sage Foundation.

Morris, A. and Lowder, S. (eds.). 1992. *Decentralization in Latin America: An Evaluation*. New York: Praeger.

O'Donnell, G. 1989. 'Transitions to democracy: some navigation instruments'. In *Democracy in the Americas: Stopping the Pendulum*, ed. R. Pastor, pp. 62–75. New York: Holmes and Meier.

O'Neill, H. and Moss, M. 1991. *Reinventing New York: Competing in the Next Century's Global Economy*. New York: Urban Research Center.

Pinch, S. 1985. *Cities and Services: The Geography of Collective Consumption*. London: Routledge and Kegan Paul.

Roberts, B. 1978. *Cities of Peasants: The Political Economy of Urbanization*. London: Edward Arnold.

Rodríguez, V. 1992. 'Mexico's decentralization in the 1980s: promises, promises, promises...'. In *Decentralization in Latin America: An Evaluation*, ed. A. Morris and S. Lowder, pp. 127–44. New York: Praeger.

Rodríguez, V. and Ward, P. 1992. *Policymaking, Politics, and Urban Governance in Chihuahua*. LBJ School of Public Affairs: University of Texas.

1994. *Political Change in Baja California: Democracy in the Making?* UCSD, La Jolla: Center for US–Mexican Studies.

Sassen, S. 1991. *The Global City: New York, London, Tokyo*. Princeton NJ: Princeton University Press.

Silverman, J. 1988. *Public Sector Decentralization: Economic Policy and Sector Investment Programs*. Washington DC: World Bank Technical Paper no. 188.

Stanyer, J. 1976. *Understanding Local Government*. London: Fontana.

Vogel, D. 1993. 'New York, Tokyo and London as financial centers'. In *Global City: The Economic, Political and Cultural Influences of New York*, ed. M. Shefter, New York: Russell Sage Foundation.

Wade, R. 1989. 'Politics and graft: recruitment, appointment, and promotions to public office in India'. In *Corruption, Development and Inequality*, ed. P. Ward, pp. 73–109. London: Routledge and Kegan Paul.

Ward, P. 1986. 'The politics of planning in Mexico'. *Third World Planning Review*, 8(3): 219–35.

1990. *Mexico City: The Production and Reproduction of an Urban Environment.* London: Belhaven Press.

1993. 'The Latin American inner city: differences of degree or of kind?' *Environment and Planning A*, 25: 1131–60.

Appendix

The world city hypothesis

John Friedmann

Some fifteen years ago, Manuel Castells (1972) and David Harvey (1973) revolutionized the study of urbanization and initiated a period of exciting and fruitful scholarship. Their special achievement was to link city forming processes to the larger historical movement of industrial capitalism. Henceforth, the city was no longer to be interpreted as a social ecology, subject to natural forces inherent in the dynamics of population and space; it came to be viewed instead as a product of specifically social forces set in motion by capitalist relations of production. Class conflict became central to the new view of how cities evolved.

Only in recent years, however, has the study of cities been directly connected to the world economy.[1] This new approach sharpened insights into processes of urban change; it also offered a needed spatial perspective of an economy which seems increasingly oblivious to national boundaries. My purpose here is to state, as succinctly as I can, the main theses that link urbanization processes to global economic forces. The world city hypothesis, as I shall call these loosely joined statements, is primarily intended as a framework for research. It is neither a theory nor a universal generalization about cities, but a starting point for political enquiry. We would, in fact, expect to find significant differences among those cities that have become the 'basing points' for global capital. We would expect cities to differ among themselves according to not only the mode of their integration with the global economy, but also their own historical past, national policies, and cultural influences. The economic variable, however, is likely to be decisive for all attempts at explanation.

The world city hypothesis is about the spatial organization of the new international division of labour. As such, it concerns the contradictory relations between production in the era of global management and the political determination of territorial interests. It helps us to understand what happens in the major global cities of the world economy and what much political conflict in these cities is about. Although it cannot predict the outcomes of these struggles, it does suggest their common origins in the global system of market relations.

There are seven interrelated theses in all. As they are stated, I shall follow with a comment in which they are explained, or examples are given, or further questions are posed.

1   The form and extent of a city's integration with the world economy, and the functions assigned to the city in the new spatial division of labour, will be decisive for any structural changes occurring within it.

Let us examine each of the key terms in this thesis.

(a) *City.* Reference is to an economic definition. A city in these terms is a spatially integrated economic and social system at a given location or metropolitan region. For administrative or political purposes the region may be divided into smaller units which underlie, as a political or administrative space, the economic space of the region.

(b) *Integration with the world capitalist system.* Reference is to the specific forms, intensity, and duration of the relations that link the urban economy into the global system of markets for capital, labour and commodities.

(c) *Functions assigned to it in the new spatial division of labour.* The standard definition of the world capitalist system is that it corresponds to a single (spatial) division of labour (Wallerstein 1984). Within this division, different localities – national, regional, and urban subsystems – perform specialized roles. Focusing only on metropolitan economies, some carry out headquarter functions, others serve primarily as a financial centre, and still others have as their main function the articulation of regional and/or national economies with the global system. The most important cities, however, such as New York, may carry out *all* of these functions simultaneously.

(d) *Structural changes occurring within it.* Contemporary urban change is for the most part a process of adaptation to changes that are externally induced. More specifically, changes in metropolitan function, the structure of metropolitan labour markets, and the physical form of cities can be explained with reference to a world-wide process that affects: the direction and volume of transnational capital flows; the spatial division of the functions of finance, management and production or, more generally, between production and control and the employment structure of economic base activities.

These economic influences are, in turn, modified by certain endogenous conditions. Among these the most important are: first, the 'spatial patterns of historical accumulation' (King 1984); second, national policies, whose aim is to protect the national economic subsystem from outside competition through partial closure to immigration, commodity imports, and the operation of international capital; and third, certain social conditions, such as apartheid in South Africa, which exert a major influence on urban process and structure.

2 Key cities throughout the world are used by global capital as 'basing points' in the spatial organization and articulation of production and markets. The resulting linkages make it possible to arrange world cities into a complex spatial hierarchy.

Several taxonomies of world cities have been attempted, most notably by Cohen (1981). In table A.1, a different approach to world city distribution is attempted. Because the data to verify it are still lacking, the present effort is meant chiefly as a means to visualize a possible rank ordering of major cities, based on the presumed nature of their integration with the world economy.

When we look at table A.1, certain features of the classification spring immediately into view.

(a) All but two primary world cities are located in core countries. The two exceptions are São Paulo (which articulates the Brazilian economy) and the city-state of Singapore which performs the same role for a multi-country region in South-east Asia.

(b) European world cities are difficult to categorize because of their relatively small size and often specialized functions (Hall and Hay 1980). London and Paris are world cities of the first rank, but beyond that classification gets more difficult. By way of illustration, I have included as world cities of the first rank the series of closely linked urban areas in the Netherlands focused on the Europort of Rotterdam, the West German economy centred on Frankfurt, and Zurich as a leading world money market.

(c) The list of secondary cities in both core and semi-periphery is meant to be only suggestive. Within core countries, secondary cities tend on the whole to be somewhat smaller than cities of the first rank, and some are more specialized as well (Vienna, Brussels, and Milan). In semi-peripheral countries, the majority of secondary world cities are capital cities. Their relative importance for international capital depends very much on the strength and vitality of the national economy which these cities articulate.

The complete spatial distribution suggests a distinctively linear character of the word city system which connects, along an East–West axis, three distinct subsystems: an Asian subsystem centred on the

Table A.1   *The world city hierarchy*[a]

Core countries[b]		Semi-peripheral countries[b]	
Primary	Secondary	Primary	Secondary
London[*] I	Brussels[*] III		
Paris[*] II	Milan III		
Rotterdam III	Vienna[*] III		
Frankfurt III	Madrid[*] III		
Zurich III			Johannesburg III
New York I	Toronto III	São Paulo I	Buenos Aires[*] I
Chicago II	Miami III		Rio de Janeiro I
Los Angeles I	Houston III		Caracas[*] III
	San Francisco III		Mexico City[*] I
Tokyo[*] I	Sydney III	Singapore[*] III	Hong Kong II
			Taipei[*] III
			Manila[*] II
			Bangkok[*] II
			Seoul[*] II

Note: [*] National capital.
Population size categories (recent estimates, referring to metro-region):
   I   10–20 million;   II   5–10 million;   III   1–5 million.

[a] *Selection criteria include:* major financial centre; headquarters for TNCs (including regional headquarters); international institutions; rapid growth of business services sector; important manufacturing centre; major transportation node; population size. Not all criteria were used in every case, but several criteria had to be satisfied before a city could be identified as a world city of a particular rank. No city from a country of the 'peasant periphery' was included, though questions might be raised about Bombay. But India, like China, is at the present time only weakly integrated with the world market economy. Also eliminated from consideration were all centrally planned economies which are integrated into the Soviet block and are not part of the capitalist world system.

In principle, it would have been possible to add third- and even fourth-order cities to our global hierarchy. This was not done, however, since our primary interest is in the identification of only the most important centres of capitalist accumulation.

[b] *Core countries* are here identified according to World Bank criteria. They include nineteen so-called industrial market economies. *Semi-peripheral countries* include for the most part upper-middle income countries having a significant measure of industrliaization and an economic system based on market exchange.

Tokyo–Singapore axis, with Singapore playing a subsidiary role as regional metropolis in South-east Asia; an American subsystem based on the three primary core cities of New York, Chicago, and Los Angeles, linked to Toronto in the North and to Mexico City and Caracas in the South, thus bringing Canada, Central America, and the

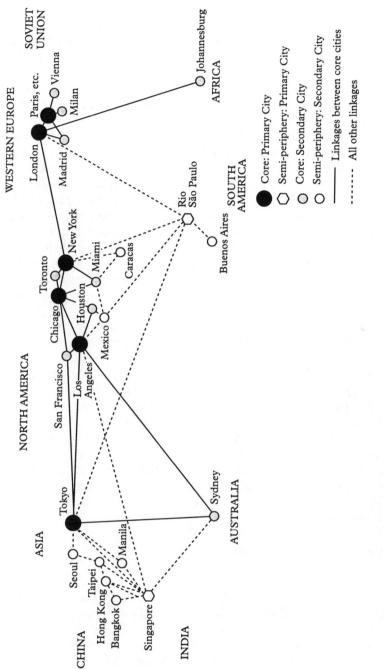

Figure A.1 The hierarchy of world cities

small Caribbean nations into the American orbit; and a West European subsystem focused on London, Paris, and the Rhine valley axis from Randstad and Holland to Zurich. The southern hemisphere is linked into this subsystem via Johannesburg and São Paulo (see figure A.1).

3 The global control functions of world cities are directly reflected in the structure and dynamics of their production sectors and employment.

The driving force of world city growth is found in a small number of rapidly expanding sectors. Major importance attaches to corporate headquarters (Cohen 1981; United Nations 1982), international finance (Jao 1979; Kindelberger 1974; Meyer 1984), global transport and communications (Jacobson 1984; Port Authority of New York and New Jersey 1982; Rimmer 1986); and high level business services, such as advertising, accounting, insurance, and legal (Noyelle and Stanback 1984).[2] An important ancillary function of world cities is ideological penetration and control. New York and Los Angeles, London and Paris, and to a lesser degree Tokyo, are centres for the production and dissemination of information, news, entertainment and other cultural artefacts.

In terms of occupations, world cities are characterized by a dichotomized labour force: on the one hand, a high percentage of professionals specialized in control functions and, on the other, a vast army of low-skilled workers engaged in manufacturing, personal services, and the hotel, tourist, and entertainment industries that cater to the privileged classes for whose sake the world city primarily exists (Sassen-Koob 1984).

In the semi-periphery, with its rapidly multiplying rural population, large numbers of unskilled workers migrate to world city locations in their respective countries in search of livelihood. Because the 'modern' sector is incapable of absorbing more than a small fraction of this human mass, a large 'informal' sector of microscopic survival activities has evolved (Kannappan 1983).

4 World cities are major sites for the concentration and accumulation of international capital.

Although this statement would seem to be axiomatic (for empirical evidence see Thrift 1984), there are significant exceptions. In core countries, the major atypical case is Tokyo. Although a major control centre for Japanese multinational capital, Japanese business practices and government policy have so far been successful in preventing foreign capital from making major investments in the city (see the article by Rimmer 1986).

In the semi-periphery, the economic crisis since 1973 has led to massive international indebtedness, originally incurred in the hope of staving off economic disaster in the teeth of a world-wide recession of unprecedented depth and duration. A combination of declining per capita incomes, slow growth in the core of the world economy, IMF-imposed policies, the high cost of capital, capital repatriation, capital flight, and obligatory loan repayments in some cases amounting to more than 35 per cent of export earnings have contributed in a number of Latin American countries to a *net export* of capital (Iglesias 1984). If this trend, extraordinary for the post-war period, should persist, the semi-periphery is bound to backslide into peasant–peripheral status. Although strenuous attempts are being made to reverse this tidal drift into economic insolvency, declining living standards for the middle classes, immiseration for the poor, and the collapse of the world economic system as it presently exists, mean that the outcome is not at all certain.

5   World cities are points of destination for large numbers of both domestic and/or international migrants.

Two kinds of migrants can be distinguished: international and inter-regional. Both contribute to the growth of primary core cities, but in the semi-periphery world cities grow chiefly from inter-regional migration.[3]

In one form or another, all countries of the capitalist core attempted to curb immigration from abroad. Japan and Singapore have the most restrictive legislation and, for all practical purposes, prohibit permanent immigration. Western European countries have experimented with tightly controlled 'guest-worker' programmes. They, too, are jealous of their boundaries. And traditional immigrant countries, such as Canada and Australia, are attempting to limit the influx of migrants to workers possessing professional and other skills who are in high demand. Few if any countries have been as open to immigration from abroad as the USA, where both legal and illegal immigrants abound.

In semi-peripheral countries periodic attempts to slow down the flow of rural migrants to large cities have been notably unsuccessful (Vining 1985). Typically, therefore, urban growth has been from 1.5 to 2.5 times greater than the overall rate of population increase, and principal (world) cities have grown to very large sizes. Of the thirty cities in table A.1, eight have a population of 15 ± 5 million and another six a population of 7.5 ± 2.5 million. Absolute size, however, is not a criterion of world city status, and there are many large cities even in the peasant periphery whose size clearly does not entitle them to world city status.

6   World city formation brings into focus the major contradictions of industrial capitalism – among them spatial and class polarization.

Spatial polarization occurs at three scales. The first is global and is expressed by the widening gulf in wealth, income, and power between peripheral economies as a whole and a handful of rich countries at the heart of the capitalist world. The second scale is regional and is especially pertinent in the semi-periphery. In core countries regional income gradients are relatively smooth, and the difference between high and low income regions is rarely greater than 1:3. The corresponding ratio in the semi-periphery, however, is more likely to be 1:10. Meanwhile, the income gradient between peripheral world cities and the rest of the national economies which they articulate remains very steep. The third scale of spatial polarization is metropolitan. It is the familar story of spatially segregating poor inner-city ghettos, suburban squatter housing, and ethnic working-class enclaves. Spatial polarization arises from class polarization. And in world cities class polarization has three principal facets: huge income gaps between transnational élites and low-skilled workers, large-scale immigration from rural areas or from abroad, and structural trends in the evolution of jobs.

In the income distribution of semi-peripheral countries, the bottom 40 per cent of households typically receive less than 15 per cent of all income and control virtually none of the wealth (World Bank 1984: table 28). These data refer to countries that, overall, have low incomes when measured on the scale of Western Europe or the USA. In many of the primary cities of the core, however, the situation is not significantly better. In Los Angeles and New York, for example, huge immigrant populations are seriously disadvantaged.

In the semi-periphery, the massive poverty of world cities is underscored by the relative absence of middle-income sectors. The failure of semi-peripheral world cities to develop a substantial 'middle class' has often been noted. Although there are important salaried sectors in cities such as Buenos Aires, their economic situation is subject to erosion by an inflationary process that is almost always double-digit and in some years rises to more than 200 per cent! Middle sectors have also become increasingly vulnerable to unemployment.

The basic structural reason for social polarization in world cities must be looked for in the evolution of jobs, which is itself a result of the increasing capital intensity of production. In the semi-periphery most

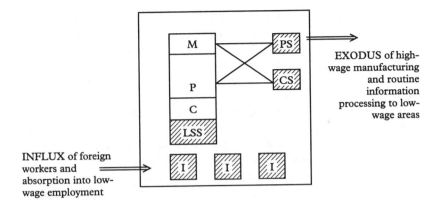

EXODUS of high-wage manufacturing and routine information processing to low-wage areas

INFLUX of foreign workers and absorption into low-wage employment

Low-wage and often informal labour markets

Production of Global Control Capacity:

M Management élites

P Professional business services*
   (predominantly male)

C Clerical (predominantly female)

LSS Low-skilled, blue collar services
     (predominantly male and/or foreign/ethnic)

PS Producer services (low-wage)

primarily catering to management élites and upper echelons of professional business services (employment predominantly female and/or foreign)

CS Consumer services (low-wage)

I Low-wage occupations in manufacturing industry (predominantly foreign and/or female)

*Many professional business services engage increasingly in international trade serving their clients, the transnational corporations, both at home and abroad. They include accounting, advertising, banking, communications, computer services, health services, insurance, leasing, legal services, shipping and air transport, and tourism. In 1981, US service exports equalled 50 per cent of merchandise exports and were still rising (see Sassen-Koob 1986).

Figure A.2 World city restructuring in core countries

rural immigrants find accommodation in low-level service jobs, small industry, and the 'informal' sector. In core countries the process is more complex. Given the downward pressure on wages resulting from large-scale immigration of foreign (including undocumented) workers, the number of low-paid, chiefly non-unionized jobs rises rapidly in three sectors: personal and consumer services (domestics, boutiques, restaurants, and entertainment); low-wage manufacturing (electronics, garments, and prepared foods); and the dynamic sectors of finance and business services which comprise from one-quarter to one-third of all world city jobs and also give employment in many low-wage categories (Ross and Trachte 1983: see also Sassen-Koob 1986).

The whole comprises an *ecology* of jobs. As shown in figure A.2, the restructuring process in cities such as New York and Los Angeles involves the *destruction* of jobs in the high-wage, unionized sectors (EXODUS) and job *creation* in what Sassen-Koob calls the production of global control capability. Linked to these dynamic sectors are certain personal and consumer services (employing primarily female and/or foreign workers), while the slack in manufacturing is taken up by sweatshops and small industries employing non-union labour at near the minimum wage. It is this structural shift which accounts for the rapid decline of the middle-income sectors during the 1970s.

7 World city growth generates social costs at rates that tend to exceed the fiscal capacity of the state.

The rapid influx of poor workers into world cities – be it from abroad or from within the country – generates massive needs for social reproduction, among them housing, education, health, transportation, and welfare. These needs are increasingly arrayed against other needs that arise from transnational capital for economic infrastructure and from the dominant élites for their own social reproduction.

In this competitive struggle the poor, and especially the new immigrant populations, tend to lose out. State budgets reflect the general balance of political power. Not only are corporations exempt from taxes; they are generously subsidized in a variety of other ways as well. At the same time the social classes that feed at the trough of the transnational economy insist, and usually insist successfully, on the priority of their own substantial claims for urban amenities and services. The overall result is a steady state of fiscal and social crisis in which the burden of capitalist accumulation is systematically shifted to the politically weakest, most disorganized sectors of the population. Their capacity for pressing their rightful claims against the corporations and the state is further contained by the ubiquitous forces of police repression.

The following essays [in *Development and Change*, 17(1), 1986], illustrate several facets of world city analysis. Sassen-Koob studies the relation between employment restructuring in New York City, local labour markets, and foreign immigration. Inquiring into the impact of 'the production of global control capacity' on New York City's labour force, she first reviews the dramatic economic restructuring taking place throughout the world and traces its specific effects on the city's economy. With this portrayal as a background, she describes the recent changes in New York's job supply and labour markets, giving particular attention to how these transformations have affected patterns of immigration from abroad and growing internationalism of the city's labour force. She concludes that (1) the rise of high-level control functions typical of current economic restructuring is accompanied by a massive expansion of low-wage jobs across a wide spectrum of employment sectors; and (2) the new spatial and socio-economic arrangements lead to a growing polarization of interests and the potential for heightened conflict, as middle-income occupations decline and the upward mobility of immigrant labour is effectively blocked.

Rimmer finds that Tokyo may indeed be regarded as a link in a system of world cities, though its internal structure corresponds as much to influences of history and national policy as it does to influences that result from its dominant global position. Thus, his investigation of Tokyo's world city status results in the confirmation that Japan's urban development and its economic landscape is significantly affected by its role in the global economic system, despite Japan's selective insulation from the 'outside world'. Rimmer confronts and assesses the problematic of delineating world city boundaries when dealing with the powerful 'Tokaido' megalopolis image. After careful data analysis, he concludes that only Tokyo itself fulfils world city criteria, particularly with reference to its role as a world-wide financial and distribution centre. Rimmer not only provides us with the immediate spatial and social consequences of world city status, but also identifies the resulting implications for planning in Tokyo.

Kowarick and Campanario, finally, show in their analysis of São Paulo how the city's economy disintegrates under the multiple impacts of dependent development and global crisis. São Paulo is perhaps the best example of a primary, semi-peripheral world city, an enormous urban complex of production and economic control and an integral part of the international economy. Kowarick and Companario's special contribution, beyond providing important details concerning the role of how multinationals have integrated São Paulo into the international economy, is their documentation of the contradictions between the 'success' of being a world city and the human price that so many of its inhabitants must endure. Here we have a vivid revelation of the cost of internationalism. The authors remind us that, despite the seeming inevitability of global economic forces, 'fate is not traced beforehand'. The struggles of people, caught in the trap of relative territorial immobility and the mobility of international capital, are a part of the dynamic which will shape both the world cities and the capitalist world economic system.

ACKNOWLEDGEMENTS

I wish to thank Edward Soja and Goetz Wolff for the close reading they have given the earlier version of this paper and for their many helpful suggestions. [The article first appeared in *Development and Change*, 17(1): 69–83, published by Sage (London, Beverly Hills, and New Delhi). Their permission to reprint it here is gratefully acknowledged.]

NOTES

1 See Browning and Roberts (1980), Cohen (1981), Portes and Walton (1981), Friedmann and Wolff (1982), Walton (1982), Soja, Morales and Wolff (1983), Ross and Trachte (1983), Thrift (1984), Hill and Feagin (1984), Glickman (1984), and Sassen-Koob (1986).
2 The sectoral theory of economic growth, such as that of Colin Clark which culminates in the growth of the 'secondary' sector of manufacturing, must therefore be at least partially revised. So far as metropolitan economies are concerned, manufacturing has become less important than in the past, and the so-called quaternary sector of advanced business services now accounts for most of the observed differential growth in income and employment (Gershuny 1983).
3 This is not to claim that international labour migrations do not occur elsewhere as well. Most significant are labour flows to the oil-rich countries of the Arabian peninsula and the migrations from the countries of the Sahel to the coastal states of West Africa.
  Capital cities of the peasant periphery frequently display social, economic, and physical characteristics that are structurally similar to those of world cities in the semi-periphery. What they often do *not* have in common is the latter's economic power.

REFERENCES

Apter, David and Sawa, Nagayo. 1984. *Against the State: Politics and Social Protest in Japan*. Cambridge MA: Harvard University Press.

Browning, Harley L. and Roberts, Bryan R. 1980. 'Urbanisation, sectoral transformation and the utilisation of labour in Latin America'. *Comparative Urban Research*, 8(1): 86–104.

Castells, Manuel. 1972. *La question urbanine*. Paris: Maspero.

1983. *The City and the Grassroots*. Berkeley: University of California Press.

Cohen, R. B. 1981. 'The new international division of labour, multi-national corporations and urban hierarchy'. In *Urbanization and Urban Planning in Capitalist Society*, ed. Michael Dear and Allen J. Scott. New York: Methuen.

Development and Dialogue. 1981. Special issue on 'Towards a new information and communication order'.

Ecodevelopment News. 1984. Special issue on 'The informal economy and beyond', 31: 25–37.

Friedmann, John and Wolff, Goetz. 1982. 'World city formation. An agenda for research and action'. *International Journal of Urban and Regional Research*, 6(3): 309–44.

Gershuny, Jonathan. 1983. *Social Innovation and the Division of Labour*. New York: Oxford University Press.

Glickman, Norman J. 1984. 'Cities and the international division of labor'. Paper presented at the Second World Congress of the Regional Science Association, Rotterdam. The Netherlands, 10 June 1984.

Hall, Peter and Hay, Dennis (eds.). 1980. *Growth Centers in The European Urban System*. Berkeley: University of California Press.

Harvey, David. 1973. *Social Justice and the City*. London: Edward Arnold.

Hill, Richard Child and Feagin, Joe R. 1984. 'Detroit and Houston: two cities in global perspective'. Paper presented at the 79th Meeting of the American Sociological Association, San Antonio, Texas, 29 August.

Iglesias, Enrique V. 1984. 'Balance preliminar de la economia latinamericana durante 1983'. *Revista de la CEPAL* (April): 7–38.

Jacobson, Robert. 1984. 'Global information technology networks and the world-city world'. Unpublished paper.

Jao, Y. C. 1979. 'The rise of Hong Kong as a financial center'. *Asian Survey*, 19: 674–94.

Kannappan, S. 1983. *Employment Problems and the Urban Labor Market in Developing Nations*. Ann Arbor: University of Michigan, Graduate School of Business Administration.

Kindleberger, Charles P. 1974. *The Formation of Financial Centers: A Study in Comparative Economic History*. Department of Economics, Princeton University: Princeton Studies in International Finance, no. 36.

King, A. D. 1984. 'Capital city: physical and spatial aspects of London's role in the world economy'. Unpublished paper.

Kowarick, Lucio and Companario, Milton. 1986. 'São Paulo: the price of world city status'. *Development and Change*, 17(1): 159–74.

Linn, Johannes. 1983. *Cities in the Developing World: Policies for their Equitable and Efficient Growth*. New York: Oxford University Press.

Meyer, David R. 1984. 'The world system of cities: relations between international financial metropolises and South American cities', (manuscript). Providence, RI: Department of Sociology, Brown University.

Noyelle, Thierry J. and Stanback, Jr. Thomas M. 1984. *The Economic Transformation of American Cities*. Totawa NJ: Rowman and Allanheld.

Port Authority of New York and New Jersey. 1982. *The Teleport: A Satellite Communication Center*. New York: Port Authority.

Portes, Alejandro and Walton, John. 1981. *Labor, Class, and the International System*. New York: Academic Press.

Rimmer, Peter J. 1984. 'Japanese seaports, economic intervention and state intervention'. In *Seaports, Systems and Spatial Change*, ed. B. S. Hoyle and D. Hilling. London: Wiley.

1986. 'Japan's world cities: Tokyo, Osaka, Nagoya or Tokaido megalopolis?' *Development and Change*, 17(1) (January): 121–58.

Ross, Robert and Trache, Kent. 1983. 'Global cities and global classes: the peripheralization of Labor in New York City'. *Review*, 6(3): 393–431, Binghampton, NY: SUNY-Binghampton.

Sassen-Koob, Saskia. 1982. 'Recomposition and peripheralization at the core'. *Contemporary Marxism*, 5: 88–100.

1984. 'Capital mobility and labor migration: their expression in core cities'. In *Urbanization in the World System*, ed. M. Timberlake. New York: Academic Press.

1986. 'New York City: economic restructuring and immigration'. *Development and Change*, 17(1): 85–119.

Schiller, Herbert. 1981. *Who Knows? Information in the Age of the Fortune 500*. Norwood, NJ: Ablex Publishing Co.

Soja, Edward. 1985. 'Regions in context: spatiality, periodicity, and the historical geography of the regional question' (unpublished manuscript). University of California, Graduate School of Architecture and Urban Planning.

Soja, Edward, Morales, Rebecca, and Wolff, Goetz. 1983. 'Urban restructuring: an analysis of social and spatial change in Los Angeles'. *Economic Geography*, 59(2): 195–230.

Thrift, Nigel. 1984. 'The internationalisation of producer services and the genesis of a world city property market'. Conference paper for the Symposium on Regional Development Processes/Policies and the Changing International Division of Labour, Vienna, August.

Todado, Michael P. 1976. *International Migration in Developing Countries: A Review of Theory, Evidence, Methodology, and Research Priorities*. Geneva: International Labour Organization.

United Nations Centre on Transnational Corporations. 1982. *Transnational Corporations and Transborder Data Flows: A Technical Paper*. New York: United Nations, ST/CTC/23.

Vining, Daniel R. Jr. 1985. 'The growth of core regions in the Third World'. *Scientific American*, 252(4): 42–9.

Wallerstein, Immanuel. 1984. *The Politics of the World Economy*. Cambridge: Cambridge University Press.

Walton, John. 1982. 'The international economy and peripheral urbanization'.

In *Urban Policy Under Capitalism*, ed. I. Norman and S. Fainstein, pp. 119–35. Beverly Hills CA: Sage.

World Bank. 1984. *World Development Report, 1984*. New York: Oxford University Press.

Zukin, Sharon. 1980. 'A decade of the new urban sociology'. *Theory and Society*, 9: 575–601.

Index